ENGLISH
WOMEN'S VOICES
1540–1700

Edited by

CHARLOTTE F. OTTEN

FLORIDA INTERNATIONAL UNIVERSITY PRESS
Miami

Library of Congress Cataloging-in-Publication Data

English women's voices, 1540–1700 / edited by Charlotte F. Otten.
p. cm.   Includes bibliographical references and index.
ISBN 0–8130–1083–7. — ISBN 0–8130–1099–3 (pbk.)
1. English literature—Women authors. 2. Women—England—History—
Renaissance, 1450–1600—Sources. 3. Women—England—History—17th century—
Sources. 4. English literature—Early modern, 1500-1700. 5. Women—England—
Literary collections. 6. Autobiography—Women authors. I. Otten, Charlotte F.
PR1110.W6E54   1991
820.8'09287'09031—dc20   91–16313

Material from the following works has been quoted in this volume with the
permission of the publishers and owners: Antonia Fraser, *The Weaker Vessel,*
copyright 1984 by Antonia Fraser, pp. 76, 238–39, reprinted by permission of
Alfred A. Knopf, Inc.; Michael MacDonald, *Mystical Bedlam* (Cambridge:
Cambridge University Press, 1981), pp. 82, 87, 89, 100; Elizabeth Richardson,
excerpts from *A Ladies Legacie to Her Daughters,* by permission of the
Houghton Library, Harvard University; *The Meditations of Lady Elizabeth Delaval,*
ed. Douglas Greene (Durham, England: Surtees Society, 1978), pp. 77–79,
161–79 (copies may be purchased from the Society at The Prior's Kitchen,
The College, Durham, United Kingdom DH1 3EQ).

The University of South Florida Press is a member of University Presses of Florida,
the scholarly publishing agency of the State University System of Florida. Books are
selected for publication by faculty editorial committees at each of Florida's nine
public universities: Florida A&M University (Tallahassee), Florida Atlantic
University (Boca Raton), Florida International University (Miami), Florida State
University (Tallahassee), University of Central Florida (Orlando), University of
Florida (Gainesville), University of North Florida (Jacksonville), University of South
Florida (Tampa), University of West Florida (Pensacola).

Orders for books published by all member presses should be addressed to
University Presses of Florida, 15 NW 15th Street, Gainesville, FL 32611.

for STEPHANIE AND CHELSEA

CONTENTS

Part Seven   Women Meditating and Praying

Part Eight   Women Defending Their Right to Preach

ILLUSTRATIONS

PREFACE

A new anthology of women writers of the sixteenth and seventeenth centuries owes much to its predecessors. Within the last fifteen years women scholars have attempted to enlarge the canon of the male-only anthologies. Finding resistance on the part of male anthologists to including women writers in the standard collections of English literature, women scholars have compiled female-only anthologies. Women anthologists have generally followed the genre-chronology formatting of the standard anthologies and have included poetry, drama, biography, autobiography, letters, and polemical writing in their chronologically arranged collections. Some of the anthologies contain most of the genres; others are exclusively one-genre anthologies and contain only poetry, say, or polemical writing.

This collection is a departure from the traditional pattern of anthology organization. Breaking away from genre and chronology, it retrieves the lives of women as they are revealed in a number of genres. The focus of this anthology is not on females writing "literature" but on the actual lives of women, as women described them and lived them. This approach to female writing cuts across genres and rearranges chronology. Because the emphasis in this collection is on the recovery of lost female lives, it contains no fictional writing. Even the two poems included are factual accounts of incidents in a life by a woman who found poetry as nonfictive a medium as prose.

Eight subjects that are important in the lives of women give the anthology its direction. The anthology begins with women writing about abuse, a subject as important in the lives of sixteenth- and seventeenth-century women as it is in the lives of women today. The anthology ends with women voicing their ideas and airing their theological and political views in a medium forbidden them for centuries: preaching, a subject still relevant for women today who continue to struggle for the right to be heard in the pulpit. Between abuse and preaching, women reveal their lives in prison; through political statements and petitioning; in writings on love and marriage; on health care; on childbirth, sickness, and death; and through meditation and prayer. Whether recorded in diaries, letters, sermons, formal petitions, health manuals, biographies, autobiographies, or poems, the voices of women that were unheard for several centuries, that have been buried in research libraries and on microfilm, can now be heard again.

Almost all the writers in this collection are new to anthologies. Prominent women who appear regularly in the anthologies of female writers (Queen Elizabeth, Aemilia Lanier, Margaret Cavendish, Katherine Philips, Aphra Behn, Anne Killigrew, and others) do not appear in this collection. Their voices, largely fictive, have been heard for a decade or more and now appear even in the standard anthologies of English literature. The women who appear in this anthology are those who were published in their own day but whose works, after the sixteenth and seventeenth centuries, were buried under a heap of male writing. A few of the writers were not published until the nineteenth century, when their writing was discovered by their families or by friends of their families.

The voices speaking in the anthology are vibrant with personal concerns and with religious, political, and social issues. These voices pierce the consciousness of the twentieth-century reader, who will undoubtedly recognize affinities and shared concerns. The passing of several centuries has not obliterated the significance of female contributions to understanding life in the sixteenth and seventeenth centuries. Women's insights into psychology, medicine, philosophy, and religion throw new light on the literature of those centuries. Without these female voices, the age retains its exclusively male—and partial—representation of its characteristics.

The anthology is intended for a multiple audience. The introductions to each part, which contextualize the writings that follow, have been written for both students and scholars working in a number of areas: women's studies, literature, history, religion, sociology, psychology, and medicine. It is hoped that although the introductions undoubtedly contain information familiar to scholars, the information and interpretations will nevertheless serve as useful summaries and as bases for discussion. The *Short Title Catalogue* (STC), *Wing Catalogue*, and film reel numbers that appear in source notes and in the general bibliography will benefit those who wish to consult the original documents in their entirety on microfilm. Although I have modernized and Americanized spelling in the writings to provide easy access for the modern reader,

I have retained the irregular and erratic spellings of names of people and places. Each part contains a list of suggested readings designed to stimulate exploration and further reading.

It would have been impossible, of course, to include all the women writers and the complete body of their writing from sixteenth- and seventeenth-century England. The comprehensive bibliography at the end of the anthology shows how extensive their writing was, even though the number of women writing compared to the number of men writing was small. Each woman writer in this anthology was chosen on the basis of her experiences; her insights into her experiences; her forthrightness and reliability in chronicling those experiences; her contribution to, and reflection of, the society in which she lived; her lively writing style; and her appeal to a twentieth-century audience.

Acknowledgments

An anthology of primary sources from the sixteenth and seventeenth centuries could not have been compiled without the use of research libraries. I wish to express my thanks to the British Library, the Houghton Library (Harvard University), and the libraries of the University of Chicago, the University of Michigan, and Michigan State University for extending me courtesies over the years. Thanks are due especially to Emily Walhout of Houghton Library and Susan Iversen of Michigan State University Library (microfilm).

A book that has been long in the making accumulates debts. It is a pleasant task to thank Calvin College for a sabbatical leave and a faculty research grant; Conrad Bult and Jo Duyst, Calvin College librarians, for assistance in tracing bibliographic entries; Kathleen Struck for obtaining interlibrary loans; and the staff of the English department—Alma Walhout and her student assistants Rachel Berens, Keri Bruggink, and Sandra Hoeks—for typing the manuscript in various stages.

My debt to my husband grows with the years. I thank him for sharing my excitement in uncovering the lives of women whose voices were buried for centuries under a heap of male writing.

Figure 1. Illustration from the Dutch edition of *The Mothers Legacie to Her Unborne Childe*, by Elizabeth Joceline (Amsterdam, 1748). Courtesy of the Newberry Library, Chicago.

GENERAL INTRODUCTION

Theoretical Barriers against Women Writers

The climate for women writers in sixteenth- and seventeenth-century England was not congenial. Commanded for centuries to be "chaste, obedient, and silent," women who violated the prohibition of silence risked disapproval, even castigation, by a society dominated by males. Moreover, a woman going into print was a challenge to the theological and medical grounds that supported the inferiority of women—an inferiority that demanded silence.

Theological Grounds

The passage from the scriptures that was invoked to support the inferiority of women is Genesis 2:21, where woman is described as being created out of the rib of Adam. The prevailing view of the sixteenth and seventeenth centuries was that woman was metaphysically an inferior creature, created only to alleviate the loneliness of man and to be his helpmeet.

In addition, woman was considered morally inferior to man. When Eve succumbed to the temptation of Satan in the Garden of Eden (Genesis 3), she doomed the rest of womankind to moral deficiency and moral inferiority. It was woman who caused Adam to fall; it was woman who was responsible for subsequent evil in the world and for the human predicament. Moral theology asserted that the treachery of Eve was passed down to all her female descendants, and hence woman could only be viewed as deceptive, unreliable, seductive. The fall of their Grandmother Eve in Paradise (Eve was commonly referred to in this way, even in the horticultural manuals) placed all women in a morally inferior, subservient position.

On the basis of Eve's decision, woman would always be subject to the morally superior male. Chastity, obedience, and silence were not externally imposed commands but enjoinders that sprang from what was regarded as the essential nature of woman: chastity, because of Eve's seductive act in tempting Adam to sin and the sexual consequences of that act; obedience, because of her failure to obey the divine command not to eat of the fruit of the Tree of Knowledge of Good and Evil; silence, because Eve's words to Adam were untrustworthy and perfidious.

Silence was the most oppressive demand. It required negation of the identity of a woman. Considered an inherently dependent being whose independence might again lead mankind astray, woman could not be encouraged to use the written word. For a woman to have the self-possession necessary to write required that she reassess her place in the reigning theological order established by male interpretation of the scriptures. A quiet state that suppressed acknowledgment of the existence of the self had to be replaced by a new state that placed woman in the redemptive order of the New Testament.

Medical Grounds

In *The Renaissance Notion of Woman*, Ian Maclean observes: "The subject of woman as seen by physiologists, anatomists and physicians is complex and multifaceted, because of its contiguity (a coincidence) with spermatology, hysterology, the science of the humours and theories of physical change" (28). The traditional Aristotelian and Galenic view of woman was that "woman is less fully developed than man. Because of lack of heat in generation, her sexual organs have remained internal, she is incomplete, colder and moister in dominant humours, and unable to 'concoct' perfect semen from blood. Two axioms are implied here: that the hottest created thing is the most perfect, and that a direct comparison can be made between the genitalia of man and woman in function, number and form" (Maclean, 31).

The Aristotelian and Galenic view of woman had not died in the medical theory of the sixteenth and seventeenth centuries. Physicians continued to regard heat as male, and cold as female. If heat is male, male is equated with intellectual acumen. If cold is female, cold is equated with inferior intellectual powers. Dominated by cold humors, subject to the malignity of menstrual periods, swayed by an unstable uterus (which in turn could ignite the passions—hate, anger, fear), woman was not the kind of human being who had the intellectual and psychological equipment necessary to produce writing of any consequence or credibility. If a woman—granted her metaphysical, moral, and medical limitations—did take to writing and publishing, men feared that her writing would be misleading, even threatening to the equanimity of the anatomically and intellectually superior male.

The Aristotelian and Galenic perspective was not the only medical view current in the sixteenth and seventeenth centuries, although it was the dominant one. There were competing outlooks, and the Aristotelian and Galenic view itself underwent modifications and clarifications. Few women, however, were in a position to reexamine the medical theory that imposed such limitations on female intellectual capacity. Anatomy was destiny for males and females of those centuries.

The implications for female writing are obvious. First, women hesitated to write at all; second, they felt the need to apologize for everything they wrote, even meditations and prayers for their daughters.

Education for Domesticity

That education of the sex deemed morally deficient and metaphysically and intellectually inferior was markedly different from that of the other sex is not surprising. Even though there was a brief golden period of classical education for a limited number of women between 1520 and 1560, a liberal arts education was generally regarded as unsuitable for the sex that was born to serve. As Lawrence Stone observes in *Family, Sex and Marriage in England, 1500–1800*: "Access both to the sacred truth and to new learning was monopolized by men, thus increasing their prestige and influence and reducing that of women. In Elizabethan England this discrepancy between the sexes in terms of education was true at all levels of society, from the male artisans who could sign their names to the male elite who could write letters and read the Bible, and often also Cicero. Most of their wives were unable to emulate their husbands in these respects, which significantly reinforced their sense of inferiority" (158).

Even women themselves believed that education of females should have a different focus and content than that of males. Elizabeth Joceline, for example, in her frequently reissued *The Mothers Legacie to Her Unborne Childe,* asks her husband to bring up the child, if it is a daughter, in "learning the Bible, as my sisters do, good housewifery, writing, and good works: other learning a woman needs not: though I admire it in those whom God hath blest with discretion, yet I desired not much in my own having seen that sometimes women have greater portions of learning than wisdom, which is of no better use to them than a mainsail to a flyboat, which runs it under water. But where learning and wisdom meet in a virtuously disposed woman, she is the fittest closet for all goodness. She is like a well-balanced ship that may bear all her sail" (*Mothers Legacie,* *"Letter to My . . . Husband"*). Joceline herself had been educated by her grandfather, Dr. Chaderton, bishop of Chester and Lincoln and professor of divinity, Queen's College, Cambridge. She was taught languages, history, some arts, and studies in religion. Even so, she expresses the era's typical female hesitancy about writing a book, in her case a manual of instruction and a guide for the education of her unborn child.

Women in the sixteenth and seventeenth centuries were educated in the home and, in some cases, in boarding schools. Men were educated at home, in grammar schools, and at the universities. The universities were closed to female students. For women, "learning the Bible," as Elizabeth Joceline puts it, was an impetus to learning to read. To be able to read the Bible in the vernacular was a liberating experience that freed the reader from hearing only the set passages read in the church and interpreted by the church. A Protestant woman was expected to read the scriptures daily, to meditate on them, and to memorize portions of them. In addition, a woman was expected to instruct her entire household in "learning the Bible" by holding instructional and devotional times each day for all household members, including the servants.

The private reading of the Bible by women inevitably affected the way they wrote. Much of the writing in this anthology gives evidence of absorption of the scriptures by women writers. Interwoven into the fabric of their prose are the cadences, rhythms, vocabulary, phrases, and substance of the English Bible.

Later in the seventeenth century women began to plead for education beyond domesticity. Bathsua Makin, onetime tutor to the daughter of King Charles I and founder of a school for girls at Tottenham-High-Cross, wrote a tract recommending expansion of female education. "I do not deny," she argues in *An Essay to Revive the Antient Education of Gentlewomen,*

but women ought to be brought up to a comely and decent carriage, to their needle, to neatness, to understand all those things that do particularly belong to their sex. But when these things are competently cared

AN ESSAY

To Revive the

Antient Education

OF

Gentlewomen,

IN

Religion, Manners, Arts & Tongues.

WITH

An Anſwer to the Objections againſt this Way of Education.

LONDON,

Printed by *J. D.* to be ſold by *Tho. Parkhurſt,* at the Bible and Crown at the lower end of *Cheapſide.* 1 6 7 3.

Figure 2. Title page from *An Essay to Revive the Antient Education of Gentlewomen,* by Bathsua Makin.

for, and where there are endowment of nature and leisure, the higher things ought to be endeavored after. Merely to teach gentlewomen to frisk and dance, to paint their faces, to curl their hair, to put on a whisk [neckerchief], to wear gay clothes, is not truly to adorn, but to adulterate their bodies; yes (what is worse) to defile their souls. This (like Circe's cup) turns them to beasts; whilst their belly is their god, they become swine; whilst lust, they become goats; and whilst pride is their god, they become very devils. Doubtless this underbreeding of woman began amongst heathen and barbarous people. . . . It is practiced amongst degenerate and apostate Christians, upon the same score, and now is a part of their religion; it would therefore be a piece of reformation to correct it; and it would notably countermine them who fight against us, as Satan against Adam, by secluding our women, who then easily seduce their husbands. Had God intended women only as a finer sort of cattle, he would not have made them reasonable. (22–23)

Outlining the curriculum at her own school, Makin insists that women learn languages, since "the tongue is the only weapon women have to defend themselves with, and they had need to use it dextrously" (11). The curriculum would begin with learning Latin and French and, where desired, would include Greek and Hebrew, Italian and Spanish. (Makin herself was fluent in many languages.) In addition, women would be taught astronomy, geography, arithmetic, history, experimental philosophy (science), painting, and poetry. She did not omit, however, what was required of women of the day: they were also taught dancing, singing, writing, and keeping accounts.

The women writers who appear in this anthology were educated in the home. Many of them continued their private education by self-instruction: in the midst of their domestic life they read and they wrote. Writing became for them, and for their female readers, a path of knowledge that ran parallel to the road of education for males. Writing became an education in itself.

Suggested Readings

Astell, Mary. *A Serious Proposal to the Ladies.* London, 1694.
Brink, J. R. "Bathsua Makin: Educator and Linguist." In *Female Scholars*, ed. J. R. Brink. Montreal: Eden Press, 1980.

Crawford, Patricia. "Women's Published Writings 1600–1700." In *Women in English Society 1500–1800*, ed. Mary Prior. London: Methuen, 1985.

Goreau, Angeline. *The Whole Duty of a Woman*. New York: Dial, 1985.

Hageman, Elizabeth H. "Recent Studies in Women Writers of the English Seventeenth Century." ELR 18 (Winter 1988): 138–67.

———. "Women Writers of Tudor England." ELR 14 (Winter 1984): 409–25.

Hannay, Margaret Patterson, ed. *Silent But for the Word*. Kent, Ohio: Kent State University Press, 1985.

Hogrefe, Pearl. *Tudor Women: Commoners and Queens*. Ames, Iowa: Iowa State University Press, 1975.

Joceline, Elizabeth. *The Mothers Legacie to Her Unborne Childe*. London, 1624.

Kamm, Josephine. *Hope Deferred: Girls' Education in English History*. London: Methuen, 1965.

Maclean, Ian. *The Renaissance Notion of Woman*. Cambridge: Cambridge University Press, 1980.

Makin, Bathsua. *An Essay to Revive the Antient Education of Gentlewomen*. London, 1673.

Reynolds, Myra. *The Learned Lady in England, 1650–1760*. Gloucester, Mass.: Peter Smith, rpt. 1964.

Schurman, Anna Maria van. *The Learned Maid; or Whether a Maid May Be a Scholar?* London, 1659.

Stone, Lawrence. *Family, Sex and Marriage in England, 1500–1800*. New York: Harper and Row, 1977.

Wolley, Hannah. *The Gentlewomans Companion*. London, 1675.

PART ONE

WOMEN TESTIFYING TO ABUSE

જ

Introduction

"to keep that hid . . ."

Abuse can take many forms. It may be physical, psychological, religious, economic. Abuse can occur in almost any area of human life and to any age or sex, but the female is more frequently the victim of abuse than is the male. Wherever, whenever, and however abuse occurs, the instinct of an abused person is to keep that abuse hidden. To admit orally to being abused takes courage and may even be precarious. To write about it takes not only moral strength but a sense of self-worth.

Today women who are victims of abuse may confide in a counselor precisely because the counseling room is a safeguard of privacy. To tell the world in writing that one is a victim of abuse is a risk: it may arouse contempt in the reader (why did she permit it?), prurience (what did he do to her?), or negative judgment (she must have contributed to it). Even today, when some of the more abhorrent forms of abuse appear in print (particularly sexual abuse such as incest), the writer-victim often chooses to remain anonymous.

In the sixteenth and seventeenth centuries, when society was structured rigidly along patriarchal lines, some forms of abuse were tolerated (wife beating), some were brought to trial (rape), but most accounts of abuse did not appear in published form. Since males ruled over females in domestic, ecclesiastical, and civil life, the only appropriate response of the female to such pervasive, all-encompassing authority was obedience. To write about beating or rape or any other form of abuse would have exposed the female to ignominy and ostracism. Any assertion of independence on the part of the female could have resulted in further punishment. Since punishment slips rather easily into abuse, it is not surprising to discover that women who were perceived as disobedient could be victimized and their victimization rationalized by both the abuser and the abused.

A notorious case of abuse was revealed in a London pamphlet published in 1688. Addressed to "All Married Men and Women" by an anonymous pamphleteer, the details of the abuse and consequent murder are described in a series of couplets. Titled *Being the Full Confession of Mary, the French Midwife, Who Murdered Her Husband on the 27th of January 1688 (As also the Cause Thereof) for Which She Receiv'd Sentence to be Burnt Alive*, the pamphlet describes a typical pattern of abuse. After persistent physical abuse by her husband, Mary Hobry escaped from him for several months. When "he swore he never would abuse her as before," she returned to him. One night, however, he came home drunk and attacked her first with a blow to the stomach, next with a blow to the breast, and then

> . . . he took her in his Arms with all
> His force, till he did stop her Vital Breath,
> So that she wished for a sudden Death . . .
> Forcing much Blood from her, she cried out . . .
> Wherewith he threw her on the Bed again,
> And bit her like a Dog kept in a yard.

Exhausted, he fell into a drunken stupor. She pulled off his garter, doubled it about his neck, and strangled him. Her next problem was disposal of his body. Enlisting the aid of her son, she dismembered the corpse. Together they threw most of the parts of the body on a dunghill; they threw the head into the privy of a friend living in the Savoy. The head was discovered, the face recognized, and Mary Hobry was sentenced to death for the murder of her husband. On Friday, March 22, 1688, she was burned to ashes in Leicester-Fields.

Only rarely did physical abuse lead a wife to murder her husband. In many instances, if the wife was disobedient or ungovernable, beating was condoned as a legitimate punishment and the wife did not protest officially. There were pastors, for example, who argued for the legitimacy of wife beating and who urged wives to accept beating as an appropriate punishment for the crime of challenging a husband's authority. A few pastors, however, such as Robert Snawsell, asked men to refrain from beating their wives (*A Looking Glasse for Maried Folkes*, 1610). Gratuitous wife beating was prosecuted in the church courts and at quarter sessions. Michael MacDonald in *Mystical Bedlam*, a study of the medical practice of the clergyman-physician Richard Napier, cites the case of an Essex official who charged William Staine in 1587 with "misusing his wife with stripes contrary to all order and reason" (102).

Rape was another matter. Servant girls, dependent unmarried females, and widows who were raped had few options. The threats of loss of employment, of protection in a household, or of food for a family kept them from resisting sexual assault. The psychological consequences of rape, however, were difficult to suppress. Napier's case histories reveal the distress of those who had been raped: "For three years, Agnys Burton confessed, she had been anxious and guilty: 'Did dwell with my cousin March (that dead is) and he did overcome her and abused her; yet had no child. Ever since ill . . . and can take no rest nor sleep.' Agnys Fenkes's master fell in love with her, and when he found out that she was already in love he 'turned [her] out of doors two days and cried "he cometh, he cometh" ' " (MacDonald, 87).

There were random rapes. *Chronicle from Aldgate* reports: "A little girl of six and another of thirteen were murdered by rapists (12 May 1587; 13 July 1594). The men responsible were identified, but there is no mention in the parish records of inquest or prosecution" (Forbes, 159). *An Account of the Tryal, Condemnation, and Execution of Mary Goodenough* shows the plight of a penniless widow:

Mary Goodenough, Widow, aged about forty years, lived at Bradwell in the County of Oxford. Being in great poverty and straits, even to the want of bread for her and hers, she was seduced by a neighboring baker (reported infamous for like practices with others) through his promise of some allowance towards her necessary maintenance, to the commission of adultery with him, who was a married man: She becoming with child by him, concealed it to her time of travail, which, when she fell into, she also concealed under pretense of sickness, till on the third day, two or three neighbors suspecting the matter, came to her, and upon search presently discovered by her breasts, etc., that she had had a child. Upon their charging it, she immediately owned and directed them to the infant, which lay wrapped up in a blanket at her feet in the bed dead. She had a son about seven years old, and a daughter about eleven, whom she shut out of the room in the time of her labor. . . . About ten days after her travail, she was brought to Oxford, committed prisoner to the castle, and toward the end of February, being about a month after her commitment, she was brought forth and tried before Judge Ayres, at the Assizes there. The witnesses (who were the neighbors above mentioned) deposed the matter of fact, as above declared; and she acknowledged the purport of it and particularly . . . with relation to the child afterwards, that it perished for want of suitable help and due attendance; so that upon the whole matter, she was justly convicted of murder and received sentence of death. . . . (1)

In a letter to her children, she wrote
My Dear and Loving Children,

It is no small addition to my troubles that I cannot see and speak to you before I go hence and be no more in the Land of the Living. . . . I am now forced to take this way of writing and to beg the help of another hand, my own hand being as my heart is, trembling. . . . (4)

As for soldiers and suitors, although accounts of rapes by soldiers were frequently exaggerated by the enemy, there is evidence that soldiers garrisoned in homes and marching through a territory raped unprotected women. Rape by a suitor was also a possibility that a woman had to guard against. Once deflowered, she was regarded as "spoiled goods"; she was robbed not only of her virginity but of her status and her choice of a husband.

There is no doubt that the misogynistic literature which these centuries inherited contributed to the abuse of women. This literature promoted the stereotype of woman as deceitful, destructive, disruptive, deficient, and hence in need of punishment. In the Western world the poet Hesiod regarded Pandora, the first female, as the punishment Prometheus received from Zeus for stealing fire from the gods. Pandora the female became the symbol of evil; it was she who, by opening the box, released all the ills of human life on humankind. Running parallel to the Pandora myth was the Eve tradition. The wife of the first man, Adam, ate the forbidden fruit of the Tree of the Knowledge of Good and Evil and by eating it caused all the subsequent woe in human life. The Church Fathers Tertullian and Jerome, in urging celibacy for the male, attacked the female element in life as seductive and as a potentially pernicious influence on males.

Verbal attacks on woman continued to be virulent throughout the Middle Ages and into the Renaissance. The pamphlet wars of the sixteenth and seventeenth centuries debated vehemently the nature of woman, perpetuating the notion that woman was the source and propagator of evil. Some women entered into the fray and defended females. But traducing the female was a way of life, even an obsession, as the pamphlet wars indicated. Because women were regarded in the misogynistic literature as seducers and destroyers, inflicting punishment on them seemed a necessity.

Abuse was not limited, however, to physical attacks on women. Women were also abused economically, sometimes by desertion, sometimes by exploitation. It was assumed by the patriarchy that strategies had to be devised to suppress women and to keep them powerless. Physical attack was a limited way of doing that. In order to stabilize the status of woman as "the weaker vessel," male oppressors abused women economically and hence psychologically. A husband could, for example, design a prolonged absence from his wife and family without making provision for their economic support. Or a husband could abuse his wife and family while remaining with them by squandering the wife's money, property, and possessions, leaving her and their family destitute and with no means of support. His control of her property and income was an undisputed right; by common law a married woman could not own property.

Women who were financially abused by their husbands often experienced mental stress and breakdown. Dr. Napier, who left case histories of the women he treated for stress and anxiety, provides evidence of the suffering of women:

> Nineteen wives reported that their husbands failed in their duty to support their families. Some, like Mistress Dorothy Abrahall, were vexed because their husbands were "unthrifts" and squandered their small resources carousing. Stephan Rawlins was one of these. His distraught wife told Napier that he "thinketh little to gad a-drinking. Careth not to return until his wife fetch him home when he fondly spendeth his money amongst ill company." She had also to endure beatings and abuse each time he went on a drinking spree. Elizabeth Easton's husband was joined by his family in mistreating her. She owed her despair to "her husband's friends, as mother and brother, that would rate her and slap [her] as a dog—and a husband ready to beat her. She brought some money and her husband's friends, as father, mother, brother, helped to spend it; now they live poorly." (Mac-Donald, 100)

In the ecclesiastical world, the male hierarchy regulated the most intimate space in a woman's life—her soul. Her mode of worship was predetermined and her silence reinforced. In the Anglican and Roman Catholic communions, the husband was regarded as the authority and spokesman for his family. In the Presbyterian and Puritan communions, women might be allowed to hold minor offices and to instruct their households in the faith, but they remained subject to male authority.

Emancipation was offered to women by certain dissenting groups and sects. A woman might defy both the church establishment and her husband by joining a sect such as the Quakers or the Fifth Monarchists. In those communions women were encouraged to speak and to contribute to worship as well as to participate in the governance of the fellowship. Female presence there was more than silence.

To defy ecclesiastical and domestic authority, however, was to invite punishment and abuse. A religious assembly of over five persons meeting outside the established church was contrary to civil and ecclesiastical law; those who gathered in such meetings were punished and their worship services disrupted. Violence was a regular means employed by the civil authorities to break up religious meetings. Since women were frequently in the majority in these sects, even playing a "disproportionate role" (Thomas, 45), it follows that women experienced firsthand the abuse inflicted on them by the criminal justice system. There are recorded instances of women who died as a direct result of this kind of excessive force and brutality.

A woman who escaped from spiritual oppression by stepping out of the religious establishment might meet her downfall in domestic, social, and economic life. If her husband wished her to remain in the established church, she would have to leave him in order to exercise her right of conscience. Women could find themselves alone, unsupported by family, their writings confiscated and destroyed. When Elizabeth Avery published her book of prophecy in 1647, her brother, Thomas Parker, abused her in print in 1648. He attacked her on various fronts:

> Who would have thought or dreamed, that such expressions should have ever come out of the mouth of Sister Avery? What will you make yourself to be? What, higher than Moses and any of the Prophets, above the holy Apostles and Primitive Saints, which all were under Ordinances? . . . O Sister! you seem to be lifted up, as if you were a goddess, and as if all should bow upon you, as singularly beloved above others, yea, as Christ himself, and as one with God. . . . Your affectation and writing of Assurance did not formerly so well savor, and your printing of a Book, beyond the custom of your Sex, doth rankly smell. . . . But Sister, (alas, alas) by reason of your Book, you are (as I am credibly informed) printed by Name in the Catalog of Heretics of this time, as one of the infamous Apostates: Redeem your name and credit amongst Saints, which now is lost, by protesting against that horrid Book, and by humbling yourself for an attempt above your gifts and Sex. (Parker, 5–17)

By going into print, Elizabeth Avery embarrassed her brother. Offi
cially she was castigated and relegated to the realm of the apostates by
the established church. Her offense in their judgment was that she had
written a religious book and thereby attempted to elevate herself above
her "gifts and Sex."

Abuse came to public attention in various ways: when women testified to it in court, when they wrote books or pamphlets vindicating
themselves, when the sects printed abuses perpetrated against them. It
remained private in the diaries of women and in the case histories kept
by physicians.

Elizabeth Freke's marriage was marred by abuse, as evidenced by
the excerpts from her diary that appear in this section. Soon after her
wedding, her husband abandoned her temporarily, and throughout
their marriage he deserted her for long periods of time. As head of the
house, he confiscated her property, appropriated her money, and attempted to coerce her into selling her Norfolk estate so that he could
purchase property in Ireland. When she refused to sell this property,
which was her only remaining security, he left her in great anger. For
most of her married life her husband consigned her to live in poverty; he
was guilty of nonsupport. Elizabeth was forced to rely for financial
support on her father, who frequently came to her rescue. Once, she
records in her diary, her father gave her £200, charging her to keep it
"private from [her] husband's knowledge and buy needles and pins with
it." After investing it, she had £800, "which Mr. Freke took from [her]
the year after" (30).

Her diary (which was not published until 1913) gives detailed information on desertion, financial disaster, coercion, and verbal abuse on
the part of her husband. Many entries in the diary record recurring
financial helplessness: "My dear father sent me over to Ireland a hundred pounds for a New Year's gift, it being my unhappy birthday, and
ordered me that if Mr. Freke meddled with it, it should be lost, or he to
answer it with the Irish interest to my son. But Mr. Freke took it from
me" (31).

A poignant entry describes a reunion between wife and husband,
with the husband admonishing her for unspecified wrongs: "I hearing
Mr. Freke was like to die at the Bath, though not well able, left my house
and servants at Billney and came to London, and so, as fast as I could,
to the Bath, where I came the 21 of June, above two hundred miles in
four days. Where, though I found him very ill, yet I humbly thank my

good God, he was well enough to chide me, though he had not seen me in near three years before; this, though it was not kind, I expected it" (50). After twenty-six years of marriage, with often "no place to rest [her] wearied carcass in," and having been shuttled back and forth to Ireland where she was mistreated by her husband and his family, she escaped her husband's tyranny by settling into her own estate at West Billney, where she successfully managed a small farm for the rest of her life. (See part 6 for her description of childbirth, sickness, and death.)

Lady Margaret Cuninghame, third daughter of Lord Glencairn, wrote "the just and true account" of her unhappy marriage to Sir James Hamilton of Crawfoord-John, a mean-spirited, irascible, abusive, and violent man. Not only did he openly consort with women, getting Jennat Campbell pregnant, but he frequently deserted Lady Margaret, refused to support her, subjected her to financial distress, and ejected her naked from their home, threatening to kill her and her gentlewoman if they did not leave immediately. Although Lady Margaret may have written her diary for therapeutic reasons and probably intended to keep the record of abuse hidden from all but her own eyes, the diary circulated apparently both in original and copied form. The nineteenth-century editor found two copies (not the autograph), one of which was in the possession of a family related to Lady Margaret; the other was the property of Sir Walter Scott. First appearing in printed form in 1827, the diary is an all-too-familiar chronicle of abuse.

An eleven-year-old girl, Joan Seager, was raped by Dr. John Lamb, a physician. She had brought a basket of herbs to his office—herbs that her mother gathered and sold to him for his medicinal preparations. It was the testimony of a woman named Mabel Swinnerton that brought him to trial. He was charged with sexual assault, that he "feloniously and violently did ravish, deflower, and carnally know" Joan Seager. Mrs. Seager, Joan's mother, had asked Mabel Swinnerton to talk to Joan and to examine her. Both mother and daughter were distraught, and they summoned another woman to help them. Upon examination of Joan, Mabel discovered that Joan's vaginal area was so badly infected that the entire area was "smoking" and festering. Not only had Dr. Lamb raped Joan but he had also transmitted a venereal disease to her.

The court, accepting Mabel Swinnerton's evidence, sentenced Dr. Lamb to death. The king, however, pardoned him. So heinous was the crime that all who heard about it regarded the pardon as justice aborted. More than a year later a crowd attacked Dr. Lamb as he was leaving the Fortune Theatre and broke his skull.

The printed record of his trial and death considers it just that one who had violently attacked a young defenseless girl should die a violent death. The publication of the testimony was an important step in alerting women to their role in and access to justice.

The charges brought by the countess of Castle-Haven and her daughter against their husband and father, the earl of Castle-Haven, were shocking: "abetting a rape upon his countess, committing sodomy with his servants, and commanding and countenancing the debauching his daughter." The defendant's attorney questioned whether a wife could testify against her husband. The lord chief justice ruled that in criminal cases a wife would be permitted to testify against him. Because of the nature of the alleged sexual perversions—forcing his wife and daughter to have sexual relations with servants while he watched—the countess requested that she be permitted to give written testimony rather than oral. This request was denied; the trial transcript contains descriptions of the earl's sexual proclivities and his abusive activities over a period of years.

The earl defended himself by charging his wife with extramarital affairs (he called her a whore) and with plotting with his son to take over his estate at his death. The earl attacked his wife's character, stating that "if a wife of such a character may be allowed to be a witness against her husband, no man is safe when his wife dislikes him, and would have a younger husband."

The earl's defense was discredited, his wife's and daughter's testimonies credited, and he was sentenced to death by hanging. On appeal, the sentence was changed to death by beheading. Given several days to repent, compose himself, and prepare for death, he was executed on May 14, 1631.

It took courage for the countess and her daughter to bring the earl to trial for sexual abuse. Their own reputations were besmirched; their privacy was invaded. The trial transcript was published in 1699, although the trial had taken place in 1631.

When a woman challenged the religious establishment by publishing spiritual prophecies, she was subject to virulent attack by the established church and, in the case of Anne Wentworth, also by her husband. In her *Vindication* Wentworth describes herself as a reluctant writer of prophecies; in fact, she argues, it took eighteen years for God to convince her that it was appropriate for a woman to publish her insights into spiritual matters. Her husband responded to her writings by confiscating them. Unable to dissuade her from writing prophecies, he threatened her life. Unable to remain safely in her home and denied financial support, she fought back and revealed the opprobrium hurled at her by males: "I am reproached as a proud, wicked, deceived, deluded, lying woman, a mad, melancholy, crack-brained, self-willed, conceited fool, and black sinner, led by whimsies, notions and knick-knacks of my own head; one that speaks blasphemy, nor fit to take the name of God in her mouth; an heathen and publican, a fortune-teller, and enthusiast, and the like much more" (*The Revelation of Jesus Christ* [1679], 19).

Anne Wentworth was a Baptist and a millenarian who predicted that at the return of Christ her husband and her male persecutors would be punished. She saw herself as one recruited by God—the God who considered a woman a fit instrument for his grace and his message. She was, consequently, unwilling to accept abuse from the patriarchy; by publishing her prophecies and her vindication, she declared herself an equal with men.

While the males of the household were in military service during the English Civil War, Alice Thornton's mother was defending herself, her home, and her daughter from soldiers who wished to be quartered in her home. To permit soldiers to live in her home was to relinquish the safety of the household. Her daughter Alice was young and unmarried and hence particularly vulnerable to sexual abuse. When Captain Innis, a Scotsman, threatened to burn down the house and to destroy the cattle if Alice would not be made available to him in marriage, Alice's mother thwarted his plans by hiding Alice and paying others to house him. The captain continued his threats, however. Alice escaped sexual abuse when a soldier whose hand she had healed alerted her to the captain's intentions to kidnap her when she was on a walk. After that, Alice never left the house; she describes herself as self-imprisoned.

In the three small volumes that Alice Thornton wrote (1629–1669), she chronicles her deliverances from measles, smallpox, drowning, fire, falling, shipwreck, hemorrhaging, wounds, childbirth, and from sexual abuse by soldiers and suitors. The strength of women to defend themselves during wartime shows their ability to grapple with abuses during an interrupted life. (See part 6 for Thornton's description of childbirth, sickness, and death.)

Suggested Readings

An Account of the Tryal, Condemnation, and Execution of Mary Goodenough, at the Assizes Held in Oxon, in February, 1692.

Ashley, Maurice. *England in the Seventeenth Century.* New York: Harper and Row, 1980.

Avery, Elizabeth. *Scripture-Prophecies Opened.* London, 1647.

Being the Full Confession of Mary, the French Midwife, Who Murdered Her Husband. . . . London, 1688.

Brundage, James A. *Law, Sex, and Christian Society in Medieval Europe.* Chicago: University of Chicago Press, 1987.

Bullough, Vern. *The Subordinate Sex: A History of Attitudes toward Women.* Urbana: University of Illinois Press, 1973.

Forbes, Thomas Rogers, ed. *Chronicle from Aldgate.* New Haven: Yale University Press, 1971.

Henderson, Katherine Usher, and Barbara F. McManus. *Half Humankind.* Urbana: University of Illinois Press, 1985.

Hobby, Elaine. *Virtue of Necessity: English Women's Writing 1649–88.* Ann Arbor: University of Michigan Press, 1989.

MacDonald, Michael. *Mystical Bedlam.* Cambridge: Cambridge University Press, 1981.

Masek, Rosemary. "Women in an Age of Transition 1485–1714." In *The Women of England,* ed. Barbara Kanner. Hamden, Conn.: Archon Books, 1979.

Parker, Thomas. *Letter from Her Brother.* London, 1648.

Pearson, Lu Emily. *Elizabethans at Home.* Stanford, Calif.: Stanford University Press, 1957.

Rogers, Katharine. *The Troublesome Helpmate: A History of Misogyny in Literature.* Seattle: University of Washington Press, 1966.

Ruggiero, Guido. *The Boundaries of Eros.* New York: Oxford University Press, 1985.

Snawsell, Robert. *A Looking Glasse for Maried Folkes.* London, 1610.

Thomas, Keith. "Women and the Civil War Sects." *Past and Present* 13 (April 1958): 42–62.

Weiner, Carol. "Sex-Roles and Crime in Elizabethan Hertfordshire." *Journal of Social History* 8 (1975): 38–60.

Williams, Penry. *Life in Tudor England.* London: B. T. Batsford, 1964.

Woodbridge, Linda. *Women and the English Renaissance: Literature and the Nature of Womankind, 1540–1620.* Urbana: University of Illinois Press, 1984.

1

DIARY (1671-1714)[*]

Mrs. Elizabeth Freke

1671

Thursday, November 14, 1671, and Childermas or Cross day, and dreadfully rainy, I was in London privily married to Mr. Percy Freke by Doctor Johnson. . . .

After about six or seven years being engaged to my dear cousin, Mr. Percy Freke, and all my three surviving sisters married . . . without my dear father's consent or knowledge, in a most dreadful rainy day, a presager of all my sorrows and misfortunes to me.

1672

Being Thursday, the 26 of July, 1672, I was again remarried by my dear father, who then gave me himself to Mr. Freke, by Doctor Uttran, at St. Margaret's Church in Westminster in London; in a dreadful windy day, as my other was rainy (by a license kept in Mr. Freke's pocket 4 or 5 years).

Mr. Freke, August 26, coming over St. James Park about 12 o'clock at night, challenged my Lord of Roscommon, either to fight him in St. James Park presently, or to pay him down a thousand pounds my Lord had long owed Mr. Freke, but the King Charles being in the Park prevented the present quarrel. And the next morning by three o'clock, ten men of the Life Guard came and fetched Mr. Freke out of his bed from me; and immediately hurried him to Whitehall before Secretary Coventry; I not knowing what it was for more than words spoken. This was the beginning of my troubles for my disobedience in marrying as I did, without my dear father's knowledge.

*Ed. Mary Carbery (Cork, Ireland: Guy and Company, 1913), pp. 21-22, 30-35, 47.

1673

In or about February 14, my dear father, Mr. Ralph Freke, was pleased to bestow on me for a portion a mortgage on Sir Robert Brook's estate of 500£ a year, near the Green Man in Epping Forest, five miles from London, for 5,664£ or thereabouts, which neither my dear father or myself or any of my five trustees knew anything of till about July the 7— so off it was sold. This was not kind done, for by it I were turned out of doors, and not a place to put my unfortunate head in, and my money in a banker's hand, viz.—Alderman Forth's,— was in danger to be spent by us or lost by him, which a little after, great part was, to the value of fifteen hundred pounds.

About the middle of September, Mr. Freke, endeavoring to place the remaining part of my fortune on an estate in Hampshire of one Mr. Cooper's, and trusting to one Mr. Worldlige as his agent in the purchase, we were cheated by them on a composition for about fifteen hundred pounds, as the least loss, or else Cooper's cheat was above two thousand pounds in false mortgages, he not being worth anything. . . .

Thus was three of my unhappy years spent in a married life's comforts in London, where I twice miscarried, and where I lost two thousand and five hundred and sixty pounds out of my six thousand seven hundred sixty-four pounds, and I never had to my remembrance five pounds of it and very little of my husband's company, which was no small grief to me, I being governed in this my marriage wholly by my affections, without the consent or knowledge of any of my friends.

And now being apprehensive all my fortune would be thus spent, I resolved to go for Ireland and try my fortune there while something was left, which I did attempt. . . .

1683

About the middle of February Mr. Freke came to my father's to Hanington, unknown to me, to fetch me and my son over for Ireland: but on the ill usage I had there suffered from them, I positively refused ever to stay with him for his life, and their unkindness to me whenever I were in their power of command; besides, his last parting wish at Kingsaile, which was that he might never see my face more, etc. This stuck deep in my stomach, though to this day I never let my father, or any friend I had, know of the least difference between us, or any unkind usage from the family I received in that home or elsewhere, for fear of grieving of my dear father. . . .

1684

Being thus left by my dear husband to shift for myself and family, and not a place to put my unhappy head in England or Ireland, and but fifteen pounds in the world, all which I laid out next day . . . I were forced to try my fortune amongst my friends, and hearing my dear sister Austin was very ill after her being brought to bed of a dead child, I went down to Tenterden to my dear sister and brother about the 15 of October, I making a virtue of necessity by being thrown off by my unkind husband, who never in his life took any care for me, or what I did.

1685

24 *December.* Mr. Freke came over by Dublin from Ireland by post, I having hardly heard of him or from him in three quarters of a year by reason of the embargo of King James; and while Mr. Freke was in this kingdom, he was daily importuning of me to sell my Billney to Sir Standish Harts Tongue for the like in Ireland.

As he came unlooked for by me, so he was very angry with me for being on this side of the country, though in all his times of his being from me, he never took care for a penny for my subsistence or his sons, for which God forgive him. My husband's errand for England was to make me join with him in the sale of West Billney, but I being the only trustee for myself and my son, God gave me the resolution and courage to keep what I had, rather than by parting with it, be kept by the charity of my friends, or trust to his or anyone's kindness; so in a great anger Mr. Freke left me alone again and went for Ireland, where he stayed from me almost two years.

1698

February 16. I left my dear sister Austin's house, being just recovered of my malignant fever, though hardly able to stand; and I came a Saturday the 19th to my own Billney, to take, in Mr. Freke's name, possession of my house, the Lady Richerson's dowry, who was in her closet burned to death the Christmas before, and concealed it from me.

I took, by God's leave, possession of West Billney Hall, and with it a house to put my unfortunate head in, I having been married above six and twenty years, and have had no place to rest my wearied carcass in, but tossed from place to place and troubling my friends. . . .

2

A PART OF THE LIFE OF LADY MARGARET CUNINGHAME, DAUGHTER OF THE EARL OF GLENCAIRN, THAT SHE HAD WITH HER FIRST HUSBAND, THE MASTER OF EVANDALE

The just and true account thereof,
as it was at first written with her own hand*

I was married upon the 24th of January 1598, and I remained with my Lord my father three years, without receiving anything of my husband's living, but was furnished by my Lord my father in . . . all things needful.

In February 1601, I rode home to Evandale, and was boarded in a hostler house, while the next May following, and then I rode again to my Lord my father, being great with bairn: and I bore with his Lordship my eldest son James, on the 4th of July, and I remained with his Lordship till the next February.[1] Then I rode home to Evandale again, and was boarded in a hostler house six weeks, and then they would furnish me no longer, because they got evil payment. So then I was destitute, and I requested my goodfather and my goodmother to deal with my husband to give me some reasonable money to live upon. . . .

In May 1602, my husband conceived a great anger against me (he being in fancy with Jean Boyd), and he would not come into the house I was in. I took sickness, and lay bed fast six weeks. I requested my Lady his mother to deal with him in my favors, but he would neither speak to me nor give whereupon to sustain myself; so being altogether destitute,

---

*Edinburgh: James Ballantyne, 1827; pp. I–II.

1. October, in Sir Walter Scott's MS.

I was forced to advertise my parents, and my Lady my mother sent my sister Mrs. Sussana to Evandale to me, and desired me to come with her to Finlaystone.[2]

My sister dealt earnestly with my husband in my favors. He gave her fair words and made her many fair promises, but performed none of them. So in July 1602, I was compelled to ride with her in a very disordered estate, as my Lord my father, and my Lady my mother, can bear record; for my gown had never been renewed since my coming from them. So they furnished me with clothes, and I remained with them till the next harvest, when my Lord Marquess of Hamilton caused my husband come to Finlaystone with his Lordship, which he did at his Lordship's request, and remained two or three nights, and was reconciled with me, and promised that he should send for me, and bring me home again to him; but that day that he was to ride away with my Lord Marquess, my Lord and my Lady, my parents, accused him before my Lord Marquess (who was then his young chief, my Lord, his Lordship's father being yet alive) why he had used me so rigorously without cause; and because they spoke sharply to him before my Lord his chief, his anger was renewed again toward me, and so he . . . would not let me come home to him at that time; so I remained still with my Lord my father till the next Mertimesse [Martinmas]: and then, after many fair letters of request that I wrote to him, he suffered me to come home at the Mertimesse, and I was boarded in a hostler house fifteen weeks.

In March 1603, my husband caused me ride up to Crawfoord-John, to save his mains there, . . . and remained there twenty days, boarded in a hostler house. Then I came to Evandale again, and ate in my Lady my goodmother's house eight weeks. Then my husband caused me to ride again to Crawfoord-John, where I remained eight weeks, very ill furnished by a hostler, who was unable to furnish me without good payment; and he was informed by the parson of Crawfoord-John, that he would never get payment. Therefore he would furnish me no longer, which I wrote ofttimes to Evandale to my husband, but I received no answer; so having nothing there to live upon, I was forced to come to Evandale again, being great with bairn. . . .

2. Finlaystone, in Renfrewshire, was the seat of the Glencairn family. In the year 1470, Thomas Kyrkpatrick, dominie of Closburn, dates a procuratorial resignation "apud *Newwerk* de Finlawstoun." Probably about that period the castle had been re-edified; when the Cuninghames disposed of their property in Glencairn, a small knoll near the church was reserved as a relic of their former possessions.

In April 1604, my husband came home out of France; at his coming, he came to Finlaystone to me and promised to behave himself more lovingly to me nor he had done in time past, which, indeed, he did for the space of a quarter of a year, for within a month after he came home, he took me home to Evandale, where I remained with him, very lovingly used by him, for he was reformed and behaved himself both holily and civilly, so that he and I dwelt together very contentedly; howbeit, in the meantime, he had little of living to the fore, for all he took with him to France was spent, except a little quantity thereof, wherewith he caused John Stodhart, his servant, buy provision to his house, and contained himself very modestly and quietly the space of eight weeks; but alas, he continued no longer in that estate, for then he boarded himself and me, and all his family, in his servant John Hamilton's house, in which time he made filthy defection from God, and turned to all his wonted iniquities, so that he was in a worse estate nor ever I knew him before; and . . . he neglected his duty towards God, he kept no duty to me, but became altogether unkind, cruel, and malicious, as appeared plainly by his carriage towards me, which was openly seen in all the country, to his great shame. He would not suffer my gentlewoman to remain with me, who was known to be a very godly and discreet woman, one of his own name, Abigail Hamilton, father's sister to the Laird of Stenhouse; he gave credit to misreports of her and me both, and cruelly, in the night, put both her and me forth of his house naked, and would not suffer us to put on our clothes, but said he would strike both our backs in two with a sword. . . .

Then, on the first of November 1606, I was delivered of his second daughter, Christian, at which time I sent to him to come to speak with me, which he refused, and came not till fifteen days after my delivery, when he came to me, and told me that he would baptize his daughter within three days after, which he desired the minister to do; but he would not come into the church himself. Within two days thereafter, he rode to Edinburgh and said he would bring home his father's corpse to bury and wrote to his honorable friends to meet him in Edinburgh; but he came not to them, but rode to the Ley, and received the money for Carstairs, and rode to Edinburgh, but entered not into the town, but rode straight way to Berwick. His friends, getting knowledge thereof, caused his uncle Robert, and Mr. Robert Boyd, [to] follow him to Berwick, where they found and desired him to put some order to his ados. He left his mother's brother, the Laird of Benhaith, and the parson of Crawfoord-John to be commissioners and intrometers, with his living during his absence. So he left no provision to me and his bairns, but committed us to the discretion of his two uncles. . . .

In April 1608, I was delivered of his third son Thomas. I sent to Evandale to him, showing my weak estate and earnestly desiring him to come to me, but he would not. I sent to him again, desiring him to come and baptize his son and to give me some silver to buy necessaries to the house in the time of my lying, for I was then evil provided, in respect the flesher in Lanark would furnish none, because he was not paid; but he cared for nothing that I mistered [required], neither came he to me till five weeks after I was delivered, and then he came to me and would have accompanied with me for his filthy pleasure, which I refused for divers respects, especially for his wicked life, at the present being ex-communicate for slaughter; and, also, Jennat Campbell being with bairn to him, with many other heinous sins that he daily committed without any appearance or amendment, which terrified me that I durst not accompany with him.

Then I caused baptize his son quietly. . . . I remained, thereafter, in Libertoun half a year, he never but once visiting me nor his bairns, nor caring for us. Then in August 1608, he being in a great anger against me, wrote a letter to me, commanding me to remove out of his house within four days, which, if I did not, he would come and force me to remove. . . . I being visited by the hand of God with sickness, sent to him the minister of Libertoun to show him my estate, desiring him to stay his rigor till his meeting with my father and friends, which was appointed in Hamiltone within eight days; but he would not grant to the minister to stay. Then I requested the Laird of Symington to deal with him, and he stayed his fury till the tryst, at which meeting there was little done, but a new tryst appointed that same day month. In the meantime, he promised to my Lord my father, and my Lady Marquess my sister, that he should write to his bailzie [bailiff] in Libertoun, to . . . answer me in all things needful till the next tryst; but he kept not his promise. . . . The next tryst not being come, I remain destitute at the present of any money to sustain me, my bairns and family, remaining in Libertoun the 29 of September, 1608.

3

A BRIEF DESCRIPTION OF
THE NOTORIOUS LIFE OF J. LAMB

Testimony of Mabel Swinnerton
before the King's Bench*

Here followeth the effect of an indictment preferred against Doctor Lamb at the King's Bench Bar, for a rape by him committed, upon the body of Joan Seager, of the age of eleven years.

The jury for our Sovereign Lord the King, upon the Holy Evangelist, do present: That John Lamb, late of St. George in the borough of Southwarke in the county aforesaid, gentleman, not having the fear of God before his eyes, but by a diabolical instigation being moved and seduced, the tenth day of June, in the year of the reign of our Sovereign Lord James by the grace of God, of England, France, and Ireland, King, defender of the faith, etc. the 21 and of Scotland the 56 with force and arms, etc. at the parish of St. George aforesaid, in the borough of Southwarke aforesaid, in the county aforesaid, upon one Joan Seager, a virgin, of the age of eleven years, in the peace of God, and our said Sovereign Lord the King then and there being, an assault made, and her the said Joan against her will, then and there feloniously and violently did ravish, deflower, and carnally know, against the peace of our said Sovereign Lord the King, his crown and dignity: and also against the form of the statute in this case made and provided, etc.

Upon which indictment he was arraigned before the King's Majesty's Justices of his Highness' Court, called the King's Bench, and was there found guilty of the said rape, and had judgment to die, but by his Majesty's especial grace he was pardoned.

*Amsterdam (London), 1628. STC 15177, Reel 803, pp. 15–21.

Here followeth the effect of the proofs produced against him concerning this rape.

Concerning the ravishment of Joan Seager, of the age of eleven years,
done by John Lamb, prisoner in the King's Bench.
The examination of Mabel Swinnerton, wife to William Swinnerton,
bricklayer, dwelling in St. Martin's parish, near unto the new exchange.

Who saith, that Elizabeth Seager, the mother of Joan Seager, came to her house, she then dwelling in Southwarke on the Friday in Whitsun week, and in a pitiful manner wringing her hands like a woman overwhelmed with extreme grief, crying out and saying, I am undone, I am undone:

"I then asked her how her husband did, for at that time he was a prisoner in the Counter upon an execution, and at that time lay very sick to all such as saw him there, thinking him no man for this world: she answered me and said, her husband was very ill and lay very hardly; but that was not that matter of her grief as then, for it was a worse sorrow than that! O Lord said I, what more sorrows than these you have already; yet whatsoever they be, desire God to give you patience, for nothing can happen to you, but by God's foreknowledge: but I pray said I, tell me what sorrows these are that thus distract you, she still continued as before wringing her hands, and said she was not able to tell me, for she was undone, at last with my importance she said Joan was undone, and she said she could tell me no more she was not able, but prayed me to come home: so forthwith I shut my door and went with her, and by the way I demanded the cause of her, she told me it was that villain Doctor Lamb had undone her child, and said she could say no more, her grief was so great, but ask the girl, said she, and she will tell you: so coming to the child, I questioned with her, but she being much abashed and ashamed, was long before she would tell me: but at the last she told me, that on Whitsun-even, Lamb's women being all very busy at her mother's house, there was nobody to carry a basket of herbs over to the bench: but she, who when she came to Doctor Lamb, his man was in the chamber with him scraping of trenchers, and Doctor Lamb took her herbs of her and set her to play on the virginals, and then he sent out his man on a message and locked the door, and then took her and led her into his closet and made fast that door, and took her upon a joint-stool, and put his tongue in her mouth to kiss her, but she was wondrous fearful of him, and strived with him as much as she could, but he would not let her alone, but strove with her."

There are certain passages which are upon the records which for modesty's sake are here omitted.

"I asked her why she told it not at the first, she said she was afraid her mother would have beaten her: but then at her mother's entreaty, I took her home and dressed her, but when I opened her to dress her: the place did smoke like a pot that had seething liquor in it that were newly uncovered, and I found her to be very sore, and could not abide to be touched: but I perceived that somebody had dressed her, and I asked her if anybody had meddled to dress her, she told me Lamb's maid Becke had brought her a thing in a dish, and had dressed her, but there was a little speck of the venomous substance of it, that stuck upon the inside of her thigh, and when I pulled it away, it had festered the place where it stuck, as if one had touched it with an end of iron, so vile and venomous was that base substance. So by the entreaty of goodwife Seager, I went over to Doctor Lamb to show him what indeed he knew before, which was on the morrow after we knew of it: which when I came, I saw the chamber well fraught with women, and not past three men in all, and I saw the Doctor (not indeed knowing what he was) very busy folding of linen, shaking of them betwixt him and another, and a white cloth pinned about him and white sleeves up to his elbows, and as nimble as a vintner's boy setting every one in order. I demanded of his woman to speak with the Doctor, they told me, that was he in the white apron: so at last he went into his closet and called to me, and asked me if I would speak with him, I asked if his name were Doctor Lamb? That is it said he. Marry said I, I am come to do a message unto you, that I am both sorry and ashamed to do, sorry said I in respect of the child, and sorry for you, that you should offer to do such a thing, for you have undone an honest man's child, for well she may recover her health of body again, but never her credit, for it will be a stain to her reputation whilst she lives: so many strumpets in the town and to seek the ruin of a poor child, I would to God said I, you had not done it: With that he railed upon my Lord of Windsor grievously, with many base words, and said, he did more good deeds in a week, than my Lord of Windsor did in a year. . . . But I made answer, I did not know my Lord of Windsor, he was an honorable gentleman for aught I know: but this concerns not him at all, but you, for you have undone her: then said he: let her come to me, that I may see how she is, Nay said I, she hath been too late with you already, she will come no more here. He said he would have her searched with twelve women, you may do as you please said I for that matter: I will have her searched to see if she be torn, nay said I, she is not so much torn, for I will wrong nobody for a thousand pound: but in plain terms you have burnt her, either you have a foul body, or you have dealt with some unclean person, besides I told him he had sent his maid to dress her, for the dish was at home still, and so I left him."

And this is the truth, concerning this business with many appurtenances besides pertinent to the matter.

After his reprieve upon the rape, he hired a house near the parliament house, where he lived about the space of a year and a quarter, in such a course of life, as differed not at all from his former practices. Upon Friday being the thirteenth of June, in the year of our Lord 1628, he went to see a play at the Fortune, where the boys of the town, and other unruly people having observed him present, after the play was ended, flocked about him, and (after the manner of the common people, who follow a hubbub, when it is once afoot) began in a confused manner to assault him, and offer violence. He in affright made toward the city as fast as he could out of the fields, and hired a company of sailors, who were there present to be his guard. But so great was the fury of the people, who pelted him with stones, and other things which came next to hand, that the sailors (although they did their endeavor for him) had much ado to bring him in safety as far as Moorgate. The rage of the people about that place increased so much, that the sailors for their own safety, were forced to leave the protection of him; and then the multitude pursued him through Coleman Street to the old Jury, no house being able, nor daring to give him protection, though he had attempted many. Four constables were there raised to appease the tumult; who all too late for his safety brought him to the Counter in the Poultrey, where he was bestowed upon the command of the Lord Mayor. For before he was brought thither, the people had had him down, and with stones and cudgels, and other weapons had so beaten him, that his skull was broken, one of his eyes hung out of his head, and all parts of his body bruised and wounded so much, that no part was left to receive a wound. Whereupon (although surgeons in vain were sent for) he never spoke a word, but lay languishing until eight o'clock the next morning and then died. This lamentable end of life had Doctor John Lamb, who before prophesied (although he were confident he should escape hanging), that at last he should die a violent death. On Sunday following, he was buried in the new churchyard near Bishops-gate.

Finis.

4

THE TRIAL AND CONDEMNATION
OF MERVIN LORD AUDLEY
EARL OF CASTLE-HAVEN AT WESTMINSTER,
APRIL THE 5TH, 1631

For abetting a rape upon his countess,
committing sodomy with his servants,
and commanding and countenancing
the debauching his daughter *

Clerk of the Crown. Mervin Lord Audley, thou art here indicted, etc. for that thou and Gyles Broadway, Gen. both of Fountain Gifford, in the County of Wilts, not having the fear of God before your eyes, but being moved and seduced by the instigation of the devil, did on the twentieth day of June in the sixth year of the reign of our Sovereign Lord Charles, by the grace of God, of England, Scotland, France, and Ireland, King, Defender of the Faith, etc. at Fountain Gifford aforesaid, in the County aforesaid, did by force and arms, etc. in and upon Ann Lady Audley, then being in the peace of God and our Sovereign Lord the King, make an assault; and the aforesaid Gyles Broadway, the aforesaid Ann Lady Audley, by force and arms against the will of the said Ann, then and there did violently, and feloniously ravish, and the said Ann then and there against her will did carnally know against the peace of our Sovereign Lord the King, his crown and dignity, and against the statute in that case made and provided; what sayest thou Mervin Lord Audley, art thou guilty of the rape of which thou standest indicted, or not guilty?
　Lord Audley. Not guilty.

*London, 1699.

Clerk of the Crown. How will you be tried?
Lord Audley. By God and my peers. . . .

* * *

Lord High Steward. May it please your Grace my Lord High Steward; here are two indictments against Mervin Lord Audley, the first is for rape, and the second is for sodomy; the prisoner is honorable, the crimes of which he stands indicted are foul and dishonorable, and if they should be proved true, I dare be bold to say, that never poet invented, nor historian related anything so odious, inhuman, and abominable. Suetonius has with horror displayed the vices of some heathen emperors, that having ingrossed an absolute power, were fearless of punishment, and shameless in committing abominable enormities; yet no author has produced a man that ever equaled or came near the crimes that this Lord is accused of. This is a crime, to the honor of our nation be it spoken, that is scarcely heard of in an age, and whenever it happens calls aloud for timely punishment, that the infection spread no farther, nor provoke divine vengeance to pour down the vials of his wrath upon the whole kingdom. I can speak it with great satisfaction, that in all King James's reign, and from his Majesty's first accession to the crown, till now, I never heard the like occasion to speak against a Peer of the realm; and as God knows I do it now with abundance of regret, so I hope I shall never have the like occasion to do it any more. His Majesty, who is your pattern of virtue, not only as a king, but in his personal capacity, and of whom it is hard to say, whether he excels most in justice, or mercy (though I am inclined to believe 'tis in his mercy) would have my Lord Audley, the prisoner at the bar, heard with as much favor as a crime of that horrid nature will allow. When the notice of this crime came first to His Majesty's knowledge, he was amazed, and gave strict command that the truth might appear, and his throne and people might be cleared from the guilt of such abominable impieties; therefore the prisoner was indicted according to law in his own country, and by gentlemen of known worth and integrity; Billa Vera being found against him, he is brought to this bar to be tried by these honorable Lords, his Peers; of whose wisdom and justice there can be no question, and therefore we may expect the event accordingly. First I shall begin with the rape.

Now rape is defined to be an unlawful carnal knowledge, and abuse of a woman by force against her will. This was felony by the Common

Law, and though the Statute of Westminster, 1. Cap. 13. lessened it into a misdemeanor, yet it was soon after 13. Ed. l.C.34. made a capital offense without clergy, agreeable to the law of the Almighty Legislator, Deut. 22 and Gen. 34. and was accounted by our forefathers so detestable and abominable a crime, Bracton, l.3, p. 147, that those who were guilty of it were punished with the loss of their eyes, and their privy members, that they might at once be deprived of the wicked inlets, and instruments of their base and unlawful lusts; but I shall not try your Lordships' patience with citing authorities, nor enlarging upon the heinousness of an offense that admits of no aggravation, and therefore shall only mention three or four rules in law, relating to the present case; the truth of which I submit to the opinions of my Lords the Judges.

First, when any offense is felony, either by the Statute, or Common Law, all accessories before and after, are incidentally included, so that if any be aiding, assisting, or abetting any to do the act, though the offense be personal, and done by one only, as it is in this case, not only he that doth the act is principal, but also they that are present, abetting and aiding the misdoer, are principals also.

Secondly, if the party on whom the crimes was committed be notoriously unchaste, and a known whore, yet there may be a ravishment.

Thirdly, in an indictment of rape, there is no limitation of time for the prosecution; for *Nullum tempus occurrit Regi,* no time occurs against, or prevents the King's suit; but in case of an appeal of rape, if the woman do not prosecute in convenient times, it will bar her.

Fourthly, if a man take away a maid and ravish her by force, and afterward she gives her consent and marries him that did the act, yet it is a rape.

* * *

Then the Lady Audley appearing as an evidence, she was sworn, and the Attorney General said to her:

Attorney General. Will your Ladyship be pleased to inform the Peers with the real truth concerning my Lord's vile and unheard-of actions to your Ladyship?

Countess. My noble Lords, I should be glad if a way might be found out, that I might deliver my testimony in a written affidavit, and not by word of mouth in this public audience.

Lord High Steward. I will propound it to the Judges, and if the law will allow it, you shall be at your own election. My Lords the Judges, you have heard what the Countess desires of us; will you give your opinions, and satisfy her Ladyship about it?

Lord Chief Justice Hyde. By the law, the testimony relating to matter of fact, that is what relates to the charge in the indictment, must be made *viva voce* and not otherwise; and the reason is, because persons may take a greater liberty of inserting in an affidavit what is not really true; which the awe of the court, or asking apt questions, may probably prevent, or discover the falsehood.

Lord High Steward. Your Ladyship I hope is satisfied with the Judge's opinion and the reasons on which it is grounded.

Countess. Why then my Lords, the first or second night after we were married, Antill came to our bed, and the Lord Audley talked lasciviously to me, and told me my body was his, and if I lay with any man with his consent, 'twas not my fault, but his. He made Skipwith come naked into our chamber and bed; and took delight in calling up his servants to show their nudities, and forced me to look upon them, and to commend those that had the longest. Broadway, a servant of my Lord's, by his Lordship's command, lay with me, and I making resistance, my Lord Audley held my hands, and one of my feet, and I would have killed myself with a knife afterwards, but he took it from me; before that act of Broadway's, I had never done it. He delighted to see the act done, and made Antill come into the bed to us, and lie with me in such a manner, as he might see it, and though I cried out, he never regarded the complaint I made, but encouraged the ravisher.

Attorney General. Pray young Lady Audley, will you give my Lord High Steward and these Lords an account of your father's barbarous usage of you?

Young Lady Audley. I was married to my husband by a Romish priest in the morning, and at night by a prebend of Kilkenny. I was first compelled to lie with Skipwith, by the Earl's persuasions and threatenings, saying, I should have nothing but what Skipwith gave me. He saw Skipwith and I lie together several times, and so did many servants of the house besides. He tempted me to lie with others also, telling me my husband did not love me, and if I would not, he would tell my husband I did lie with them. He used oil to enter my body first, for I was then but twelve years of age, and usually lay with me by the Earl's privity and command.

The next evidence that appeared was sworn, was Broadway, to whom the Solicitor General said, Broadway, give a true account of what you know of my Lord Audley's unnatural doings.

Broadway. I lay at his Lordship's bed's feet, and in the night he called for some tobacco, which, when I brought to him, he caught hold of me, and bid me come to bed, which I at first denied, but at last consented, and went into the bed on the Lord's side, but he turned me upon my Lady, and bid me lie with her; my Lord Audley held both her hands, and one of her legs, and at last I lay with her, notwithstanding her resistance. The Lord Audley also used my body as a woman, but never pierced it, only spent his seed betwixt my thighs. I have seen Skipwith lie with the young lady in bed, and when he got upon her, the Lord Audley stood by and encouraged him to get her with child. He also made Skipwith lie with his own Lady, telling him he could not live long, and it might be the making of him, and the like he said to me!

Lord High Steward. Pray Mr. Attorney, let Skipwith be called, that we may hear what he can say?

Skipwith. For the most part I lay in bed with the Earl. He gave me his house in Salisbury, and a manor of two hundred and sixty pounds a year. I lay with the young lady very commonly, there being love between us before and after. My Lord said he had rather have a boy of my getting than of any other. She was but twelve years of age when first I lay with her, and I could not enter her body but by art, and my Lord gave me things to open her body.

Sir John Finch. Pray let Fitz-Patrick be called. Is your name Fitz-Patrick?

Fitz-Patrick. Yes, Sir.

Sir John Finch. Well, be sure you speak the truth, and give these Lords the true, and whole account, of what you know concerning the charge against my Lord Audley.

Fitz-Patrick. Henry Skipwith was the great favorite of my Lord Audley, he usually lay in bed with him, and the Lord would make him lie with his own Lady, and with the young Lady his daughter, and these things I saw several times, it being done in my Lord's sight also. My Lord made me lie with him at Fount-hill and Salisbury, and once spent his seed, but did not penetrate my body, and I understood he had often done the like with others. He kept a woman in his house called Blandina, who was a common whore to his Lordship and his servants. His house was a common brothel-house, and the Earl himself took delight not only in being an actor but a spectator while other men did it. Blandina was once abused by himself and his servants, for the space of seven hours together, until she got the French pox.

Lord High Steward. You Gentlemen of the King's Counsel, have you any more witnesses to produce, if you have pray be expeditious.

Mr. Sergeant Crew. My Lord, we have several more, and desire that Frere may be examined.

Lord High Steward. Where is he, call him.

Frere. Here, my Lord.

Lord High Steward. Pray speak what you know about my Lord Audley; but be sure it be the truth.

Frere. I only know that Skipwith and the young Lady Audley lay several times together while my Lord was present, and that he said he would fain have her have a boy by him.

Attorney General. May it please your Grace, my Lord High Steward, we have several witnesses more to produce, but their testimonies being the same your Lordships have already heard, and what I humbly conceive is sufficient to prove the charge in the indictment against the prisoner at the bar, I shall give your Lordships no further trouble; but shall leave it to the clearness of the proofs which your Lordships have heard, for I know your wisdoms to be such, that you know in so dark a business, a clearer proof can't be made; for men though ne're so wicked, do not use to call witnesses to see it; I shall say no more but commit the whole to your Lordships' considerations.

Lord High Steward. My Lord Audley, when I came first thither, I could not have believed there would have been such manifest proofs as you find has been produced of horrible crimes against a person of your honor. I shall give you all the liberty you can desire in making your defense, and therefore desire to know what you have to say for yourself in reference to what has been sworn against you.

Lord Audley. I humbly thank your Grace for the favor you are pleased to grant me, though being no scholar, nor learned in the law, I have nothing to depend upon in my defense but my own innocence and your Lordships' good construction of my weakness. My Lords, I must acknowledge that Skipwith was but poor when he came to me, that he lay with me several times when I was straightened for room in my house, and being a good servant I gave him good rewards. Antill I thought deserved my favor also, and therefore had my consent to marry my daughter, and I gave him a good fortune with her.

Lord High Steward. I advise you, my Lord, not to deny what is plainly proved against you, lest you give the Lords cause to suspect the truth of the rest.

Lord Audley. My wife has been a whore, and has had a child, which I concealed to save her honor. She and my son and one Mr. William Wroughton have plotted against my life, and all that's alleged against me is only their inventions, and gives a dangerous example in the kingdom; for no Peer, or any other person, can be secure of his life, that has (as I have) a wife who desires a younger husband, and a son that is gaping after my estate, and has the devil and wicked servants to assist their malice, in endeavoring to take away my life wrongfully. This, my Lords, is my condition, and I hope your Lordships will take care that you don't involve the Peers, the Gentry, and Commons, under a dangerous precedent in my condemnation; for, if a wife of such a character, may be allowed to be a witness against her husband, no man is safe when his wife dislikes him, and would have a younger husband.

Lord High Steward. If your Lordship had proved a conspiracy to take away your life, you had urged what had been material; but for want of proof it signifies nothing: However, I will propound your objections to the Judges.

My Lords, the Judges, can a rape be committed against a whore? And can a wife be a legal witness against her husband?

Lord Chief Justice. If the woman on whom the crime is committed be a whore, yet it may be a ravishment: And in civil causes a wife can't be a witness against her husband, but in criminal causes she may.

But, my Lord, what do you say to what these fellows your servants have sworn against you?

Lord Audley. They are persons of mean and base extraction, and suborned by my wife and son to take away my life, and witnesses, according to law, should be honest men, and of untainted reputation, which these are not. Fitz-Patrick is a recusant and therefore cannot be a witness; besides, I have often beat him for his knavery, and turned him away, and now he is hired by my son to swear against me.

To which the Judges answered, it did not appear he was convicted of recusancy; that all are held legal evidences for the King till they are convicted of crimes that may disable them; and as to their reputation, no men of unstained credit could be witnesses of such monstrous inhumanities; besides, what the witnesses have sworn has put their own lives into the same danger with his Lordship's.

* * *

The SENTENCE. For as much as thou, Mervin Lord Audley, hast been indicted of divers felonies, and by thy Peers hast been found guilty of them, thy SENTENCE therefore is, That thou return to the place from whence thou camest, and from thence to the place of execution, and there be hanged by the neck, till thy body be dead. And the Lord have mercy on thee.

The Lord Audley hearing his sentence fell upon his knees, denied the fact, and desired the Lords to intercede with His Majesty, to grant him a little time to reconcile himself to God; which their Lordships promised they would, and then the court was dissolved.

At the intercession of the Lords, he had time given him by the King till Saturday the fourteenth of May, and the SENTENCE was changed into that of beheading. His coffin was sent to him about a week before his death, and he was daily visited by Dr. Wickham, Dean of S. Paul's, to prepare himself for his dissolution. The day of his execution being come, he ascended a scaffold on Tower Hill, in a plain black grogram suit, a falling band, and a black hat without a band; accompanied by Dr. Winners and Dr. Wickham and several noblemen and gentlemen.

* * *

After this, his Lordship betook himself to his private prayers, and then undressed and prepared himself to receive the fatal stroke: Then taking leave again of the Lords and Doctors, he prayed a while by himself, pulled his handkerchief over his face, laid his neck upon the block, and having given the sign, the executioner at one blow, divided his head from his body.

5

A VINDICATION OF
ANNE WENTWORTH*

. . . He [her husband] has in his barbarous actions toward me, a many times overdone such things, as not only in the spirit of them will be one day judged a murdering of, but had long since really proved so, if God had not wonderfully supported and preserved me . . . it was necessary to the peace of my soul to absent myself from my earthly husband, in obedience to my Heavenly Bridegroom, who called and commanded me (in a way too terrible, too powerful to be denied) to undertake and finish a work, which my earthly husband in a most cruel manner hindered me from performing, seizing and running away with my writings. . . . And I do further declare, That in the true reason of the case, I have not left my husband, but he me. . . . And that I always stand ready to return to my husband, or to welcome him to me. . . .

And I do further declare that the things I have published and written, and which are such an offense to my husband, and indeed the cause of all the persecutions I have suffered from others, were written sorely against my own natural mind and will; that I often begged of God I might rather die than do it. That I was commanded of God to record them. That my own natural temper was so greatly averse to it, that for eleven months together I withstood the Lord, till by an angel from heaven he threatened to kill me, and took away my sleep from me. . . . I only wrote the way he led me in a wilderness of affliction for eighteen years, to do me good, and declared my experiences, my great and wonderful deliverances, my many answers to prayers in difficult cases from time to time: but most true it is, I did not speak of these things, nor set pen to paper (for several reasons) till the Lord commanded and by his word and Spirit constrained me so to do at eighteen

*London, 1677. Wing W1356 (pamphlet), pp. 4–9.

years' end, after I was consumed with grief, sorrow, oppression of heart, and long travail in the wilderness, and brought even to the gates of death, and when past the cure of all men, was raised up by the immediate and mighty hand of God. And being thus healed, I was commanded to write and give glory to him who had so miraculously raised me up from the grave. And yet I must declare, it would have been much more agreeable to my spirit to have concealed the miscarriages of my husband than to have exposed them. . . . And whereas my enemies have presented me as one distracted, and beside myself . . . I also judge it the mistaken and rotten interest of my adversaries, not only to report, but to believe me a person beside myself. . . . And lastly, I am well assured that it will speedily, very speedily, be known that I am not mad, as my enemies have reported. . . .

6

THE AUTOBIOGRAPHY OF
MRS. ALICE THORNTON
(1643–1644)*

In this time, after the battle of Hessom Moore, when the blessed King
Charles had by treachery lost the field, and his two generals, Prince
Rupert and Lord of Newcastle, exposed all the brave whitecoats' foot
[foot soldiers wearing white coats] that stood the last man till they were
murdered and destroyed, and that my poor brother George Wandesforde was forced to fly to hide himself at Kirklington, and brought my
brother Christopher behind him; after which time we got to Hipswell,
and lived as quietly as we could, for the madness of the Scots who
quartered all the country over, and insulted over the poor country and
English. My dear mother was much grieved to be abused by them in
quartering them at her own house, yet could not possibly excuse herself
totally from the men and horses, though she paid double pay, and was at
1s. 6d. a pt. [apiece] when others at ninepence only in a month. She kept
off the quartering captains and commanders, and would never yield to
have them. At length there came one Capt. Innis, which was over that
troop we had in town, and he coming on a surprise into the house, I
could not hide myself from them as I used to do; but coming boldly into
my mother's chamber, where I was with her, he began to be much more
earnest and violent to have stayed in the house, and said he would stay
in his quarters, but we so ordered the matter that we got him out by all
the fair means could be to get quit of him, who was so wild a bloody
looked man, that I trembled all the time he was in the house; I calling to
mind with dread that he was so infinite like in person my Lord Mac-
guire, the great rebel in Ireland, was in a great consternation for fear of

*Published for the Surtees Society, Durham, London, Edinburgh, 1875; pp. 44–47.

him. After which time this man impudently told my Aunt Norton that he would give all he was worth if she could procure me to be his wife, and offered three or four thousand pounds, and Lord Adair should come and speak for him. She said it was all in vain; he must not presume to look that way, for I was not to be obtained. And she was sure he might not have any encouragement, for I was resolved not to marry, and put him off the best she could; but wrote me private word that my Lord of Adair and he would come to speak to me and my mother about it, and wished me to get out of his way. It was not to further that desire in me, who did perfectly hate him and them all like a todd [fox] in such a kind; and immediately acquainted my dear mother, which was surprised and troubled, for she feared they would burn her house and destroy all; wished me to go whither I would to secure myself; and I did so forthwith, ran into the town, and hid myself privately in great fear and a fright with a good old woman of her tenants, where, I bless God, I continued safely till the visit was over, and at night came home. We were all joyful to escape so, for my dear mother was forced to give them the best treat she could and said, indeed, she did not know where I was, and sent out [servants?] a little to seek me, but I was safe from them. After which time this villain captain did study to be revenged of my dear mother, and threatened cruelly what he would do to her because she hid me, though that was not true, for I hid myself; and about the time that the Scots were to march into Scotland, being too long here on us, when my mother paid often £25 and £30 a month to them, this Scot in a boasting manner sent for his pay, and she sent all she ought to him, which he would not take from her, but demanded double money, which she would nor could not do; so on Sunday morning he brought the company, and threatened to break the house and doors, and was most vile and cruel in his oaths and swearing against her and me; and went to drive all her goods in her ground, having this delicate cattle of her own breed. I went up to the leads to see whether he did drive them away, and he looked up and thought it had been my dear mother, cursed me bitterly, and wished the deal blow [to deliver blows] me blind and into the air, and I had been a thorn in his heel, but he would be a thorn in my side, and drove the cattle away to Richmond, where General Leceley [Leslie] was. So my dear mother was forced to take the pay he was to have, and carried it to the general that laid at my Aunt Norton's, and acquainted him how that captain had abused her and wronged her; which, by mercy of God to her, this General Lecely did take notice of, and took her money, and bid her not trouble herself, for he would make him take it, or punish him for his rudeness. He said more, did Innis, that if ever any of his countrymen came into England, they would burn her and me and all she had; but yet she served that God which did deliver us out of the Irish rebellion, and all this bloodshed in England till this time, and did now deliver her and myself and all we had from him. This was a great deliverance at last, and joined with my own single deliverance from this beast, from being destroyed and deflowered by him, for which I have reason to praise the great and mighty God of mercy to me. There was one of his men that I had cured of his hand, being cut of it, and lame; so that fellow did me a signal return of gratitude for it. Thus it was sometimes a refreshment to me after I had set up much with my dear weak mother in her illness, or writing of letters for her, that she did bid me walk out to Lowes with her maids to rest myself, so I used this sometimes. But this captain man who I cured, came to me one day, saying, "Dear mistress, I pray do not think much if I desire you, for God's sake, not to go out with the maids to Lowes." I said, "Why?" He said again, he was bound to tell me that his captain did curse and swear that he would watch for me, and that very night he had designed with a great many of his comrades to catch me at Lowes, and force me on horseback away with them, and God knows what end he would make of me. I said, I hoped God would deliver me from all such wickedness. And so I gave the man many thanks, who was so honest to preserve me from these plots, rewarding him for his pains, and did never go abroad out of the house again, but forced to keep like a prisoner while they were here. Blessing the great God of heaven, who did not suffer me to fall into the hands of those wicked men, nor into the hand of Sir Jeremy Smithson, who could never prevail by any means to obtain me for his wife, and I was then delivered also from such a force by the discovery of Tom Binkes. Lord make me truly thankful for preservation of me, thy poor handmaid, and make me live to Thy glory. Amen.

PART TWO

WOMEN DESCRIBING
PERSECUTION AND
LIFE IN PRISON

૨ઓ

Introduction

"I do not suffer as an evildoer . . ."

Women protesters were not restricted to one class in society. They came from various classes and from different social and economic backgrounds. They espoused diverse religious and political views. Sometimes they banded together and marched in protest in front of the buildings of Parliament; sometimes they presented petitions to Parliament; and sometimes they were lone protesters. (For more about the petitioners, see part 3.) Their voices were clearly heard in the sixteenth and seventeenth centuries, and although they were separated by chronology, by region, and by belief, they had one thing in common: as women they overcame the stereotypical "weaker vessel" myth by showing courage and endurance in the face of persecution, imprisonment, and death. The four women whose writings are presented in this section acted alone, but even so they were considered politically disruptive. Their causes were regarded as erroneous, their public statements seen as inflammatory. The fact that they were persecuted and sent to prison shows how unsettling was a woman's articulation of her beliefs in a society that sentenced women to silence.

In publicly declaring their affiliation with "God's cause," they redefined that cause to the detriment of the dominant church and the existing government. Whether these women lived in pre–English Civil War days or in post–English Civil War days, whether they were subject to a king, queen, or a protector, they were denounced as destabilizers of both church and state. Although threats against them materialized into action against them (some were racked for their persistence in their beliefs; others suffered lengthy imprisonment or death), they refused to be intimidated or silenced. When they were in prison, they spoke through their writings.

Women were especially prominent in the religious sects, since the separatists emphasized spiritual equality of the sexes. According to

Keith Thomas, "there were said to be more women than men in the very first large body of English separatists, in London in 1568. . . . It was of course among the Quakers that the spiritual rights of women attained their apogee. All the Friends were allowed to speak and prophesy on a basis of complete equality, for the Inner Light knew no barriers of sex. . . . Women were the first Quaker preachers in London, in the Universities, in Dublin and in the American colonies" (44–45, 47).

The sexual equality granted by the sects meant that women as well as men could be formally accused of errors, heresies, blasphemies—all punishable offenses. The Quaker woman Anne Audland, for example, was indicted for blasphemy. Although the jury declared her not guilty of blasphemy but of a misdemeanor in calling the minister a false prophet, she was sent back to prison where she had been nine months earlier. She was not silenced, however. For fifty-two years her voice was heard in England; she remained active and visible in the Quaker movement in spite of imprisonment (Audland and Waugh, *A True Declaration,* 3). Jane Waugh, who came to visit her imprisoned friend, asked to appear before the mayor and the justice of the peace to plead for Audland's release. In response to her plea, Waugh was sentenced to five weeks' imprisonment. When Waugh returned to Banbury, the magistrates there asked her to take the oath of abjuration. Refusing to take any oath, she was again sentenced to prison, this time for twelve months in winter, where she was often over her shoes in cold water (Townsend, 7–9).

Sarah Tims was imprisoned in Banbury for eleven weeks because she had said in the graveyard to the priest, "Man, fear the Lord." The people there "hurried her, and struck her with their hands, others kicked her, and stoned her with stones . . . after she was beaten and abused, she was sent to prison." Not only was she persecuted and imprisoned, but she was chided by Mayor John Austine and informed that "sweeping the house, and washing the dishes was the first point of law to her" (*A True Declaration,* 8).

Although women protesters were charged with engaging in subversive activities, with attempting to undermine the established order in home, church, and state, they continued to assert the right of women to be heard in defense of a cause worth dying for. Even women who were nursing a baby did not exclude themselves from witnessing to the truth. Jane Whitehead was brought to Ilchester Prison with a "young child sucking at her breast, through the envy and wickedness of the priest of North-Cadbury, one John Atwood." He accused her of coming into his congregation with force and arms and disturbing his whole congregation. She denied this charge, was sentenced to a term at Ilchester Prison, and appeared at the sessions at Wells to defend herself against the "fallacious actions of the priest." Sentenced to return to prison, she remained there all winter with her baby (Townsend, 16).

In spite of the fact that persecution in the 1650s "exceeds the persecutions that were in former ages, either by the Jews, or from those in Queen Mary's days . . . men and women are beaten, buffeted, haled, stoned, and stocked, and after that thrown into prison, holes and dungeons . . . and not so much freedom afforded them in prison, as to thieves and murderers, whose friends are not kept from visiting them," many women refused to bow to what they deemed to be unjust authority. They defended themselves in the courtrooms and in their narrative accounts of trials, persecution, and imprisonment (*A True Declaration,* 10).

Their defense, however, extended beyond their personal, individual beliefs. They pressed for political and ecclesiastical reforms, the two being inseparable in most instances. Puritan women, in denouncing certain doctrines and practices of the established church (whether Anglican or Roman Catholic), urged the hierarchy to reconsider and to change or purify beliefs and practices. Nonconformist women (Quaker, Brownist, Fifth Monarchist, Independent, Anabaptist, or any other of the more than fifteen sects or groups that arose in this period) preached equality of the sexes, prophesied change, and disrupted Anglican church services, and some openly predicted the coming of King Jesus to the throne of England, at which time he would usher in the millennium and abolish gender roles. Women's verbal activities not only threatened the stability of the hierarchy (both political and religious) but also had the effect of elevating women to verbal and spiritual equality with men. Theirs was a dangerous two-pronged thrust.

Obviously these women had remarkable personal and religious resources. They proclaimed the truth as they believed Christ and his spirit revealed it to them. When their speaking and writing turned prophetic and they were denounced by males as babbling, irrational, typical females, they refused to be deflected from their purpose. By sprinkling their speaking and writing with passages from both the Old and New Testaments, women validated their claims to having received the prophetic voice from outside themselves, from the same spirit revealed to males. Their air of transcendence only infuriated their persecutors, who recognized themselves symbolically in the pronouncements, prophecies, and denunciations of these women.

Dressed in the guise of Old Testament prophets, two Quaker women, for example, disturbed the worship service at St. Paul's Cathedral: "One of them being moved to go at that very time into that place with her face made black, and her hair down with blood poured in it, which ran down upon her sackcloth which she had on, and she poured also some blood down upon the Altar, and spoke some words, and another Woman being moved to go along with her, they were both taken away to Bridewell, where they remain to this day, and were not yet tried for any fact, nor any evil yet justly laid to their charge" (*A Brief Relation,* 5). Coming as prophets, they were not proclaiming women's rights but the right of prophets to be heard. The authorities understood, however, that women were proclaiming the right of *women* prophets to be heard, and therein lay the offense.

In the days of Henry VIII, Anne Askew, a Protestant woman, was burned at the stake at age twenty-five. She was married young to a staunch Roman Catholic, who considered her a heretic and "cruelly drove her out of his house" (Askew, *Lattre Examinacyon* II, 15v). Brought to trial by the civil and ecclesiastical authorities because she openly opposed the doctrines and practices of the established church (at that time Roman Catholic), she showed herself a skillful combatant with her male interrogators. Her knowledge of the scriptures and of Reformed doctrine baffled and enraged her accusers. Among the charges bishops brought against her was her alleged violation of St. Paul's injunction against women preaching in public. She replied that she knew the scriptures as well as they and that she had never preached from a pulpit, and hence had violated no scriptural prohibitions.

In prison Anne Askew wrote two *Examinations,* which are her personal accounts of the events leading up to her death. She openly disputed the views of ecclesiastical authorities (as Christ did before her in the temple), but by winning the argument she lost her own life. The hierarchy convicted her of heresy (her position on the nature of the sacraments was pivotal) and pressed her on the rack to renounce her heretical beliefs. The authorities also insisted that she reveal the names of women who were her coconspirators and coheretics:

Then they did put me on the rack, because I confessed no ladies nor gentlewomen to be of my opinion, and thereon they kept me a long time. And because I lay still and did not cry, my lord Chancellor and master Rich took pains to rack me [with] their own hands, till I was nigh dead.

Figure 3. The Burning of Anne Askew, John Lacels, John Adams, and Nicholas Belenian. From The Actes and Monuments of John Foxe (1838).

Then the lieutenant caused me to be loosed from the rack. Inconti-
nently [immediately] I swooned, and then they recovered me again.
After that I sat two long hours reasoning with my lord Chancellor upon
the bare floor, whereas he with many flattering words persuaded me to
leave my opinion. But my Lord God (I thank his everlasting goodness)
gave me grace to persevere, and will do (I hope) to the very end. (*Lattre
Examinacyon* II, 44v–47)

It would be a mistake to accuse women like Anne Askew of having a
"martyr complex," of exhibiting an obsessive need to suffer. They did
not regard themselves as paradigms of suffering or models of martyrdom. They resisted fame and claimed no heroics, although after Askew's
death John Bale and John Foxe publicly acknowledged her heroism.
Indeed, until recently Anne Askew's fame came through the writings of
Bale and Foxe rather than through her own *Examinations*.

Women like Anne Askew believed firmly that their cause was not
gender specific. Truth, they knew, makes no gender distinctions. Suffering, then, was not defeat but victory. An eyewitness to Anne Askew's
death, Mr. Loud of Lincoln's Inn, recorded that she had "an angel's
countenance and a smiling face; though when the hour of darkness
came, she was so racked, that she could not stand, but was holden
up between two sergeants" (Rowton, 30). While confined in Newgate
Prison, Askew wrote a ballad that reaffirmed her faith; the scriptural
borrowings in the ballad were obviously a source of sustenance for her:

> Like as the armëd knight
>   Appointed to the field,
> With this world will I fight,
>   And faith shall be my shield.
>
> Faith is that weapon strong
>   Which will not fail at need:
> My foes therefore among
>   Therewith will I proceed.
>
>   * * *
>
> More enemies now I have
>   Than hairs upon my head.
> Let them not me deprave,
>   But fight those in my stead.
>   (stanzas 1–2, 7)

When she perceived that church and state were not only denying a woman the right to articulate her faith publicly but were contradicting divine authority, she took a stance. Knighthood, although traditionally a male activity, became in her ballad a mode of combat no longer closed to women. She clearly placed herself in the context of Ephesians 6:11–17, where the shield of faith is wielded against "the fiery darts of the wicked." Consequent persecution, imprisonment, and death were gender equalizers.

Lady Eleanor Audeley, known as Eleanor Davies after her first marriage, to Sir John Davies, and as Eleanor Douglas after her second marriage, to Sir Archibald Douglas, prophesied prolifically—predicting personal deaths, royal births, and even the execution of King Charles I. Viewed as more than a disruptive influence, she was regarded as a subversive who was attempting to bring chaos into the patriarchy. When brought to trial for her copious writings and dire predictions, she was fined £3,000 and sentenced to the Gatehouse Prison. Her books were burned publicly. Later, after still more predictions, she was sentenced to another prison. She describes her experience upon entering the prison: "Not long after . . . between two of them carried down thence, instantly shut and bolted was [thrown] into the Dungeon-Hole, Hell's Epitome, in the dark out of call or cry, searching first her coat's pockets: Frustrate that way, with the key took away the candle, there left in their pest-house on the wet floor to take up her lodging" ("Dougle Fooleries," 97). Released from prison and also having spent a brief time in Bedlam, a hospital for the insane, she continued to prophesy, this time favorably for Cromwell. In 1648 she went to his army headquarters and presented Cromwell with a book of her prophecies. After her death in 1652, her family rescued her reputation (many men considered her mad) in an epitaph which reads, "a woman's body, a man's spirit" (Ballard, 280).

In 1623 London had eighteen prisons. Among the eighteen that John Taylor describes, the Tower and the Bridewell were unique, with the Tower serving also as a royal residence and as a prison particularly for those "that do their Sovereign or his laws oppose," and the Bridewell "for Vagabonds and Renegades/for Whores . . ." (*The Praise and Vertue of a Jayle and Jaylers*, b3v–b5r). Conditions varied from prison to prison, but much depended on the economic resources of the prisoner. Prisoners had to pay for bed, bedding, food, and any amenities. In many cases prisoners were assessed additional fees, including entry and discharge fees. Even the room assignment depended not so much on the nature of the offense but on the ability of the prisoner to pay. Extortion by the keeper and by the underkeepers and stewards was common. "Close" prisoners were often denied visitors and writing materials, although concessions could be made if the appropriate bribe was forthcoming.

Torture and extreme discomfort were common in the prisons. A rat-infested dungeon without windows, a room so small that the prisoner could not move or stand in it, a room near dunghills and seeping water—it is not surprising that sections of the Tower were called Little Ease and Little Hell.

The standard instruments of torture were the rack, the "scavenger's daughter" (which compressed the body so severely that blood gushed from the mouth and nostrils), manacles and gauntlets (which suspended the body by the wrists from a wall), bilboes (which prevented movement), thumbscrews, leg and wrist shackles, and the iron collar (which was filled with lead). Death could be inflicted by beheading (ax or sword), hanging (which could include drawing and quartering), pressing, or burning.

Lady Jane Grey, the granddaughter of Henry VIII's younger sister Mary, was queen of England for only nine chaotic days. She was named by Edward VI as his successor to the throne and was removed from the throne when her supporters were defeated. Mary, the daughter of Henry VIII, was then crowned queen in her stead. Sentenced to imprisonment in the Tower by the new queen and later found guilty of treason, Lady Jane Grey was beheaded at age sixteen.

In the tangled politico-religious affairs of the time, she was probably executed because her father had joined the rebellion of Sir Thomas Wyatt, although she was also an aggressive and outspoken defender of Protestantism in the reign of the Roman Catholic Mary. Others were sentenced to death for their views on the nature of the Lord's Supper.

Lady Jane Grey was the intellectual equal of university-trained men. She was educated as a person of royal blood should be educated, whether male or female. Proficient in Latin, Greek, Spanish, Italian, and French, her education in biblical studies from the Reformed perspective was rigorous. During the last six months of her life in the Tower, Lady Jane Grey wrote eloquent defenses of the Reformed faith. She left expositions of the central doctrines of the Reformation, including the basic tenet of justification by faith. Her polemic on the nature of authority and of the Lord's Supper was incisive. Her writings from prison included her narrative account of vigorous theological debates with ecclesiastical representatives of the government of Queen Mary. Lady Jane Grey fought on equal ground with the male establishment, and with well-honed intellectual weapons she deftly frustrated and thwarted her opponents.

In his *Actes and Monuments,* a history of persecutions in England, John Foxe memorialized Lady Jane Grey by reproducing the documents she had written in prison and by giving an account of her life and death, part of which is reproduced as the first document in this section. The judge "who gave the sentence of condemnation against her, shortly after he had condemned her, fell mad, and in his raving cried out continually to have the lady Jane taken away from him; and so ended his life" (Foxe, VI.425). Foxe implies that the judge's madness and death were swift, appropriate punishments for his participation in the execution of Lady Jane Grey.

Anna Trapnel was not of aristocratic birth, yet she was as fearless as one born to command. Her father was a shipwright who lived in Stepney Parish. Her mother, a devout woman, died praying that the Lord would give to Anna a double portion of his spirit. This prayer, which echoed the request of the Hebrew prophet Elisha when he asked Elijah to give him a double portion of his spirit (2 Kings 2:9), reflected a mother's belief that the spirit of God could fall on the female as well as on the male.

The day after her mother's death, while listening to a sermon, Anna was enraptured by the spirit of the Lord. From then on she frequently broke into prophecy. Her prophecies, based on mystical visions and on her reading of the scriptures, had a strong political cast: she joined the Fifth Monarchists, who predicted the imminent downfall of Cromwell and the triumph of King Jesus and the rule of Jehovah Protector in a Fifth Monarchy (the four preceding monarchies being those of Assyria, Persia, Greece, and Rome). Her audience was large—her ecstatic utterings attracted hundreds.

Anna Trapnel's pronouncements were perceived as threats by an already unstable government in the interregnum of 1649–1660. Her outpourings (visions, trances, songs, poetry) were considered so radical as to cause her to be labeled in scurrilous pamphlets as a witch, an imposter, a vagabond, a whore, and a "dangerous seditious person . . . to move, stir up, and raise discord, rebellion, and insurrection among the

good people of England" (Trapnel, *Report and Plea,* 49–52). On the basis
of these charges, the civil and religious authorities sentenced her to
prison. She spent fifteen weeks in a "man's prison" and eight weeks in
Bridewell. The authorities brought her to court and demanded that she
cease and desist from prophesying, but she refused to be silent and
continued to speak and write. Proclaiming truth as God revealed it to
her (and as he had commanded the male prophets before her) was her
vocation, she insisted. No persecution or imprisonment could divert her
from her calling.

Anna Trapnel broke the rules. Without using a male intermediary,
she dialogued with God, she as questioner, he as respondent. God's
replies to her questions were in the words he had used to the great
figures of the Old and New Testaments—David, Moses, Hannah,
Isaiah, Paul. When denounced by clergy and court, Anna argued,
"Though I am a poor inferior, unworthy to be compared with any of the
holy men or women reported of in the Scripture; yet I can say with Paul,
Through grace I am what I am" (*Report and Plea,* "To the Reader"). She
never doubted that she stood in the long tradition of the saints who
proclaimed God's word to the world. God's continuing revelations to
her assured her of the validity of her vocation. Her oral defenses in court
and her published writings show her as logical and eloquent; in these
defenses she used nonmystical, combative prose.

Anna Trapnel's vivid account of her life in prison serves as a docu-
mentary of prison life of the time. What emerges with particular clarity
is the role women played in supporting and sustaining her. Women
accompanied her to prison, provided for her, helped her in sickness, and
prayed all night with her. Ursula Adman stayed with Anna for seven of
the eight weeks that Anna was confined in Bridewell.

In "Women as Prophets during the English Civil War," Phyllis Mack
calculates that there were over 300 "women visionaries, of whom about
220 were Quakers" (24). Dorcas Dole was one of the 220. Seeing herself
as prophet, she castigated the citizens of Bristol and all of England and
urged them to repent of their sins. For her outspoken condemnations,
she was dragged into prison, cast into a dark hole, and forbidden to
pray and to preach.

Like the women of strength who surrounded and supported her,
Dorcas Dole drew on the example of other women. Her prime example
was Mary Magdalene, whom Christ "indued with wisdom and power
and sent her to preach the resurrection to His disciples; for if Christ

send us a message, whether the words be few or many, it is preaching the everlasting gospel, whether it be male or female, they are all one in Christ; for as the woman fell first into transgression, so in the restoration Christ first appeared unto her and sent her to declare unto the men that he was risen" (*Once More*, 14).

Not deflected by the threats and actions of the sheriff, the constable, and a turnkey at the prison, Dorcas Dole reminded them of their own mortality, chided them for their brutality, and endured the suffering inflicted on her in the dark hole. She was denied bread and water and was imprisoned with "felons and debtors," where water was thrown on her as she prayed. Her life in prison was bleaker than Anna Trapnel's.

Barbara Blaugdone, a Quaker, believed that God called women to prophesy and preach. She challenged authority wherever she spoke. Traveling widely with her message, she was arrested everywhere she went. She spent time in prisons in Marlborough, Devonshire, and Ireland. The punishment she describes exceeded that of Anna Trapnel and Dorcas Dole. She was whipped until the blood ran down; she was forced to speak in public and then was threatened by a butcher with a cleaver; she was accused of being a witch and dragged over stones; she was forced to live in "wet and filth."

All four of the women whose writings appear in this section were able to endure extreme bodily harm. All four believed that although males made gender distinctions in religious callings, forbade women to speak in public, and discouraged publication of their writings, God had commissioned them. No amount of punishment could cause these women to renounce this belief.

Suggested Readings

Askew, Anne. *The First Examinacyon of Anne Askewe . . . with the Elucydacyon of Johan Bale*. Wesel, 1546.

————. *The Lattre Examinacyon . . . .* Wesel, 1547.

Audland, Anne, et al. *The Saints Testimony . . . or, The Proceedings of the Court Against the Servants of Jesus*. London, 1655.

————, and Jane Waugh. *A True Declaration of the Suffering of the Innocent*. London, 1655.

Ballard, George. *Memoirs of Several Ladies of Great Britain Who Have Been Celebrated for Their Writings or Skill in the Learned Languages Arts and Sciences*. Oxford, 1752.

Beilin, Elaine V. *Redeeming Eve.* Princeton, N.J.: Princeton University Press, 1987.

Brailsford, M. R. *Quaker Women, 1650–1690.* London: Duckworth, 1915.

A Brief Relation of the Persecutions and Cruelties . . . upon the People Called Quakers. London, 1662.

Dobb, Clifford. "London's Prisons." *Shakespeare Survey* 17. Cambridge: Cambridge University Press, 1964.

Douglas, Eleanor. *The Blasphemous Charge Against Her.* London, 1649.

———. *The Gatehouse Salutation.* . . . London, 1647.

———. *The Lady Eleanor Her Appeal.* London, 1646.

"Dougle Fooleries." *Bodleian Quarterly Record* 8, 1932.

Foxe, John. *Actes and Monuments of These Latter and Perillous Dayes.* London, 1563.

Fraser, Antonia. *The Weaker Vessel.* New York: Knopf, 1984.

Grey, Lady Jane. *The Life, Death, and Actions of.* London, 1615.

Haselkorn, Anne M., and Betty S. Travitsky, eds. *The Renaissance Englishwoman in Print.* Amherst: University of Massachusetts Press, 1990.

Hill, Christopher. *The World Turned Upside Down.* New York: Viking, 1972.

Hobby, Elaine. *Virtue of Necessity: English Women's Writing 1649–88.* Ann Arbor: University of Michigan Press, 1989.

Levin, Carole. "Lady Jane Grey: Protestant Queen and Martyr." In *Silent But for the Word,* ed. Margaret Patterson Hannay. Kent, Ohio: Kent State University Press, 1985.

Mack, Phyllis. "Women as Prophets during the English Civil War." *Feminist Studies* 8 (Spring 1982): 19–45.

Masek, Rosemary. "Women in an Age of Transition 1485–1714." In *The Women of England,* ed. Barbara Kanner. Hamden, Conn.: Archon Books, 1979.

Rowton, Frederic. *Cyclopaedia of Female Poets.* Philadelphia: Lippincott, n.d.

Taylor, John. *The Praise and Vertue of a Jayle and Jaylers.* London, 1623.

Thomas, Keith. "Women and the Civil War Sects." *Past and Present* 13 (April 1958): 42–62.

Townsend, Theophila. *A Testimony Concerning the Life and Death of Jane Whitehead.* London, 1676.

Trapnel, Anna. *The Cry of a Stone.* London, 1654.

———. *Strange and Wonderful Newes from White-Hall.* London, 1654.

Wails, Isabel. *A Warning to the Inhabitants of Leeds.* London, 1685.

7

THE LIFE, DEATH, AND ACTIONS OF THE MOST CHASTE, LEARNED, AND RELIGIOUS LADY, THE LADY JANE GREY, DAUGHTER TO THE DUKE OF SUFFOLK*

After the Lady Jane had finished this exhortation to her sister and sent it away by her servant, there came unto her two bishops and other learned doctors, who likewise held with her more than two hours conference, striving with all their powers to have drawn her to have died in the obedience of their church and fellowship, but found themselves infinitely deceived: for her faith being built upon the rock of Christ, was by no worldly persuasion or comfort to be either moved or shaken, so that after the expense of time and the loss of much speech, they left her (as they said) a lost and forsaken member, but she, as before, prayed for them, and with a most charitable patience endured their worst censures.

The next day she was called down to go to the place of execution, to which she had prepared herself with more diligence than either the malice of her adversaries could desire or the vigilance of any officer for the discharge of his duty expect, and being come down and delivered into the hands of the Sheriffs, they might behold in her a countenance so gravely settled with all modest and comely resolution, that not the least hair or mote either of fear or grief could be perceived to proceed either out of her speech or motions, but like a demure body, going to be united to her heart's best and longest beloved: so showed forth all the beams of a well mixed and tempered alacrity, rather instructing patience how it should suffer, than being by patience any way able to endure the travel of so grievous a journey. With this blessed and modest boldness of spirit undaunted and unaltered, she went towards the scaf-

*London, 1615. STC 7281, Reel 955.

Figure 4. Lady Jane Grey. Attributed to Master John. By permission of the National Portrait Gallery, London.

fold, till, whether through the malice of some great adversary or the indiscretion of the officers (but the latter is more credible), she encountered upon the way (as she went) the headless trunk of her new dead Lord and husband, the Lord Guilford Dudley, at that instant returning from the scaffold to the Tower to be buried. This spectacle a little startled her, and many tears were seen to descend and fall upon her cheeks, which her silence and great heart soon dried, and being now come upon the scaffold, after reverence done to the Lords and others in commission (turning herself round about to the people), she spake these words as followeth.

The Lady Jane Dudley's Words
upon the Scaffold before Her Death

My Lords, and you good Christian people, which come to see me die, I am under a law, and by that law (as a never-erring judge) I am condemned to die, not for anything I have offended the Queen's Majesty, for I will wash my hands guiltless thereof, and deliver to my God a soul as pure from such trespass as innocence from injustice, but only for that I consented to the thing which I was enforced unto, constraint making the law believe I did that which I never understood. Notwithstanding, I have offended almighty God in that I have followed overmuch the lust of mine own flesh and the pleasures of this wretched world, neither have I lived according to the knowledge that God hath given me, for which cause God hath appointed unto me this kind of death, and that most worthily, according to my deserts, howbeit I thank him heartily that he hath given me time to repent my sins here in this world, and to reconcile myself to my Redeemer, whom my former vanities have in a great measure displeased. Wherefore (my Lords, and all you good Christian people), I must earnestly desire you all to pray with me and for me whilst I am yet alive, that God of his infinite goodness and mercy will forgive me my sins, how numberless and grievous soever against him: And I beseech you all to bear me witness that I here die a true Christian woman, professing and avouching from my soul, and trust to be saved by the blood, passion, and merits of Jesus Christ, my saviour only, and by none other means . . . and at those words she repeated the Psalm of *Miserere mei:* which done, she said, Lord save my soul which now I commend into thy hands, and so with all meekness of spirit, and a saint-like patience, she prepared herself to the block.

8

ANNA TRAPNEL'S
REPORT AND PLEA

*OR, A narrative of her journey from London into
Cornwall, the occasion of it, the Lord's encouragements
to it, and signal presence with her in it.* *

I was through Divine Power brought safe in the coach to Fox Hall,
where we lighted, and the coachman and Lieutenant told me, I must
bear all my charges, both by the way and the coach hire, so I did, and I
was brought from Fox Hall by water to Westminster, and stayed awhile
at the George in Kings-street, and then one of the messengers came,
and carried me in a coach to Titon's, but my friends paid the coach hire;
and at Titon's house in Covent Garden, there that messenger left me,
which brought me thither; it was that messenger that took hold of
Vavasor Powel and carried him before the Council; I told him it was no
good office to be so employed to lay hold of the saints in that kind, but I
said, though I was troubled at him for his taking Mr. Powel, yet for
taking me, and conducting me into custody, I was no whit troubled at
him, but I told him his office was not good; this I said, as I was riding to
Titon's; and there I was had to my chamber, which was Mr. Feak's
prison first, so that I was quickly raised in my joy, in thinking of that
prayer, which had been put up in that room, for the coming of King
Jesus to reign on the earth, and to throw down Babylon, for this did that
dear servant of Christ cry earnestly, and the Lord made an unworthy
handmaid to second those cryings, and to ring a peal to Whitehall
ward, but they had not a mind to hearken, though the cry of a stone was
brought near them again, occasioned by their own doings, thinking to
silence alleluia's triumphing over the beast, and the false prophet, but

*London, 1654. Wing T2033, pp. 36–53.

they could not do it. The secret voice of thunder hath a louder report than men's great cannons. The Lord renewed my joy much at the sight of my friends, and in the thoughts that I was brought near Whitehall to be a witness against their black doings, the which I hope I shall witness against unto the death: that time at Titon's was spent much in prayer, and singing forth Babylon's fall, and the ruin of those which endeavored to be nurses and rockers to Babylon's brats; the Lord will cut off those breasts that give Babylon milk; for the whore of Rome, the Lord will not have nourished by any, high or low, rich or poor, much was sung to this purpose at Titon's; and I often told of a present from heaven, which was much better than the present of partridge eggs; yea, it was costlier than the gold of Ophir, or rubies and pearls from a far country. I would fain have had the great Council, and their Protector, to have received a present sent from the great Protector, which is indeed, a Protector of the faithful, who makes use of silly handmaids to carry his present some-times; and I said this, O great ones of the earth, is the present from the great Jehovah to you? even his son Christ; in that you profess yourselves to be builders, the great God hath presented to you a cornerstone elect and precious, a sure foundation, an excellent platform for those that are willing to build to purpose; now therefore said I unto you, that love rarities for presents, here are rarities indeed, not like those things that will fade in their beauty, nor like that which soon loseth its scent, though never so well perfumed, nor like that which in time will be wafted and gone, nor like eggs that are subject to rot or to break before they come to be large partridges, or any at all; but it was said, oh that Protector, and his Council and clergy, would all agree to receive such a present that fades not, nor cannot wait, nor be broken, nor rot, nor is not subject to any casualty; and for presenting them with the Lord's present, they sent their messengers with a Bridewell reward to me, for all my pains and good will, and love to their welfare.

I was eight days at Titon's house, expecting to be sent for before the Council every day, according to their orders, declaring that I was to come before them; but they had no time to hear the truth from such a silly nothing creature; and they sent an order honored with President Laurence's hand to it, which was brought by two messengers late at night . . . the hour they came for me, and of their loathness to show me the order for my removal, but they did show it me before my departure from thence.

And now I am further to tell you how I fared at my last prison, which was in Bridewell, unto which I was brought at 11 of the clock in the night, the Matron received me off the messengers; and, being brought by the messengers of the Council, she thought I was some exceeding guilty person; and her words declared as much, for she said, "I warrant you are one of the plotters." "It's my portion," said I, "to be dealt so with, as if I were one of them, but I am sure that I am none"; then she said, "I don't think but I have had in my keeping such as you are before now"; then she looked steadfastly in my face and asked me, whether I did not know one Mistress Cook. I said, I had heard of such a one, but I had no knowledge of her. "I warrant you are one of that crew," she said; "there is a company of ranting sluts of which I have had some in my house, who have spoken a great many good words like you; but they had base actions." This discourse passed from her, and much more that night. And I said to her, "It's no hurt to me to be ranked among such vile ones," which she likened me to; "but I bless the Lord," said I, "that I am no such, but do abhor such evil practices"; much was spoke while we waited for my friends coming, whom I had sent for to take care for the maid that came out of Cornwall with me. The Matron was loath to have sit up till my friends came, for it was almost twelve o'clock at night; but at last my friends came, who said, "This our sister is no vagabond; it's well known by many in the City, her civil manner of life from a child, though the Council is pleased to deal thus with her, to send her to such a place, among harlots and thieves." Much to this purpose they spoke that night, and they desired to see my lodging; so she had me upstairs into a large room, but it was very close, there being but a little window at one corner of the room, and the common shore running under the window-place, which sink smelt grievously, and there was such a filthy smell with the rats that abode much in that room, so that at the first coming in, these scents entered much into my nice stomach; and having been newly fetched out of the country too, and my friends that lived there hard by were not able to endure the scent of the room, without stopping their nostrils; but they said nothing to me that night of what offended them because they would not discourage me. So the bed was made for me, which was a hard flock-bed, and my friends saw it, and were much grieved to see my hard usage, but they saw it was in vain to find fault that night. So they departed, and I was left alone. The Matron would not admit of the maid's being with me who came from Cornwall with me, but said she would tend me, I should not have a maid to wait on me there. So my friends departed from me, leaving me in the Lord's protection, and the Matron bid me make haste to bed, for she must fetch away the candle, for she said, she did not trust her prisoners to put it out.

And when she was gone down, as I was making myself unready, I was much assaulted by Satan and my own heart, who said, "To be so forward for God, see what thou hast got by it; thy mother little thought this would have befallen thee, when she prayed that God would double his spirit on thee. Now thou mayest see what her prayer is come to." I then was tempted to murmur at that prayer, and the Tempter bid me speak against that prayer, and the Tempter said to me, that I should be a byword and a laughingstock while I lived, and that everyone would point at me as I went up and down the streets; when I came out, they would say, "There goes a Bridewell bird," and then many will gather about thee, to mock and deride thee; and as for thy kindred, they will be ashamed of thee, and will not care to hear thy name mentioned in their ears, because of Bridewell reproach; "and therefore," said Satan, "wilt thou still retain thy faith concerning Christ as King and Governor in the Earth?" And I was tempted to let go my confidence as to this, but my Father kept me, and gave me a discovery of my Savior, as he was hung between two thieves, and also brought those scriptures to my thoughts which makes a report of Christ, as he was ranked among transgressors; and how he that knew no sin was dealt with, so as to endure the contradiction of sinners.

And now the Lord talked with me about my Savior's suffering much for me, "and therefore do not hearken to Satan," said the Lord, "but look unto him that suffered the contradiction of sinners for thy sake," and then was my heart cheered, and I went unto the unlovely lodging, and the Matron locked me in, or bolted me in, I know not well which, but there I was shut in alone, and yet not alone, for Christ was with me; and when I had lain a while, I grew very sick, for the hard damp bed struck much into my stomach, and the cold sheets; so that all this set me into an ague, and I shook much, and my limbs smarted with cold, and I smelt such a strong scent about the bed, that my heart panted, and lay beating, and my stomach working, and my head aching exceeding much, most part of my being in that lodge this first night; and at the break of the day, I threw off the clothes from my stomach, for I was almost spent, being very sick, and in much pain some hours: and I said, "Dear Father, hast thou brought me to Bridewell to die?" The Lord and my Father answered me presently, and said, "No; thou shalt not die but

live, and declare the works of the Lord"; and he further told me, that
though my heart and my strength failed me, the Lord was the strength
of my heart, and my portion forever, and he would never leave me nor
forsake me; the Lord said, he would be my safety from the horn of men
and devils; and I then recovered a little strength, and I sang forth
hallelujahs song of thanksgiving, and I out of that fell in a little slumber;
and my friends came, and waked me presently, against their will they
did it, for they were very tender of me, and it grieved them greatly,
when they heard what a night I had. They then spake awhile to me, and
soon after I rose, and made me ready, and then went to prayer with
some of my sisters that came that morning, and after prayer I received
much reviving in my outward man, but was not well, yet I walked
about the house all that day, and was in the lower room with my friends,
who came that day many of them, whom I walk in fellowship with, and
many others; for they thought I was put in a place that would daunt me,
if the Lord did not much appear to me; and they came to express their
tender love and care that they had of my welfare, and they pleaded very
much with the Matron, and fetched out the order that brought me
there, and procured a copy of it, which cost them fifteen pence, a
few words copying out; and this copy of the order was showed to the
Matron, how that nothing was laid to my charge, and that I was only to
be kept there, till further order; and my friends prayed her to let me
have another bed, and other sheets, the which they offered me of theirs,
but that she would not grant, but they prevailed at length with her after
much persuasion, to lay me on one of her beds, and to let me have other
sheets, the which I had the second night; and they procured one to be
with me, for they said, I was not fit to be alone, for that I was ofttimes
weak in body, and required help: so they also obtained that, some
engaging to the Matron, that they would bear her harmless in her
giving way to this: many that day so sweetened my chamber with several perfumes, and strewed it with herbs and flowers, that it much
altered the smell, yet it smelled very offensive all the time of my being
there, though I every day sometimes was burning many several things
in the room for the first week, and several times while I was there, and
after this day, I was very sick; yet the Matron urged me with the first
day of the week to go hear their Minister at Bridewell, but I told her, I
was very ill; she said, she thought I dissembled at the first, but afterward she thought it was a judgment from the Lord, my sickness, because I was unwilling, she said, to hear their Minister: and she said, she

saw by my high color, that I was not well, and indeed I was much in a
fever that day only. I had the ague a little while in a cold fit, and I lay,
not desiring to be spoke to, because it was painful for me to speak, or to
turn myself in my bed: and the next day the ague and fever was much
upon me, so that my heart even sunk within me, I being so burning and
in so close a room, and friends had a great ado to get to see me, the
Matron was so strict, and would hardly let them in, but some friends
came, who made me plasters to lay to my wrists, and posset drink, to
drink the next fit.

But that second day in the night, I was pleading with the Lord, and
asked of the Lord a removal of that sickness, and saying, "Lord, it's very
grievous to lie sick in this place." The Lord answered me, and said, "I
have taken away thy sickness, thou shalt be sick no more, while thou art
here in Bridewell, for I will fill thee with more triumph here, than ever
thou hadst in thy life," so the Lord did I am sure; and it was further said
to me, "Thy friends have provided means to take away thy ague, but
the Lord hath been thy physician aforehand"; and he further said, he
would take me into the mount that day, for the perfect cure of my
sickness, and so the Lord did, and I spake by way of prayer and singing
from morning till night, and felt no sickness nor pain, nor faintness, not
all that day, nor at night when I came to myself, to be capable of a body;
for truly, all that day I was wrapped up, so that I could not tell, whether
I was in the body or out: and yet I sung with understanding, as to the
things the Lord was doing among the sons and daughters of men; and at
night, I had sweet rest all night, and in the morning, it being the fourth
day, the Matron came and told me, that it was a Court day, and I must
rise and go to the Court. "I have been sick," I said, and I prayed her to
tell them so; she came the second time, and bid me rise to go before the
Court; I told her I was weak, and had lain in my bed three days, only I
rose the second day, and could hardly endure up while my bed was
made, and I thought it not safe to rise up, being I was in a sweat, and go
presently into the air; she came the third time, and said, "If you will not
rise, I must send the man to call you up," that was an old man, that
called up the harlots and thieves, every morning betimes to beat hemp,
he was to slap them up to work; and she threatened to send him to fetch
me up, but I said, "Tell the Court I have been sick, and am not fit to rise
out of the bed"; but many of my friends came who persuaded me to
strive to rise and go to the Court, so I did, my sister Ursula Adman
helping me, and other of my sisters, and they led me up to the Court, for

I was very weak, so that the Court gave me leave to sit down before them. They were very courteous to me, and they spoke not much to me, only said, it was the custom they had to see all their prisoners at their first coming in; I told them, "Truly, Gentlemen, I would have waited on you sooner, but I have been sick and therefore I stayed so long before I came before you." There was through some words spoken an opportunity given me to tell them of my sickness, the Matron finding fault with so many people coming to see me. I told them that if I had not been put into such a place, it was probable so many would not have come; but further I said to them, I being put into such a close room, coming out of the fresh air it was very offensive to me, the room and the bed had such a strong scent and damp that it set me into an ague and a fever; one of them said, "They did not use to have their beds smell where their prisoners lay, for they were looked well to." I said, "But the scent was grievous to me, and the bed was damp having not been laid upon, not lately it may be"; I said, "Truly Sir, if you had been there, you might have smelled it, the scent was very grievous to me and others who smelled it as well as I; I am sure." I told them it was a cause of my sickness; for I was well when I came there: Then the Matron said, I spoke to wrong her, but I did not: only I would have it known what was the reason of my sickness. I am certain I had no revenge any way towards her; then she told them that I would have men come to me, and that word went to my heart, I knowing my bashful nature, and my civil life was known to many; and I said to them, "Truly, Gentlemen, my delight is not nor never was in men's company": And I said, that the Officers of the Church was to look after the members of the Church. They said it was reason they should, and they were not against it: They asked me how many was of them Officers, I said about ten I thought: they asked me how many I would have come to see me of my sisters at a time, I said six, so it was granted; but some would have had their names penned down, that so only those half a dozen might have come; but it was procured other ways by friends. And after this the Lord gave health and strength and stomach to my food, and a better digestion than ever I had since I can remember.

The Lord also filled me with joy unspeakable, and full of glory in believing, and many visions and Hallelujah songs I had there; and more frequent they were than they ever had been: I was at Bridewell Court, once more only to be gazed on; for little was said to me, only they asked me, why I lay there still; and I said, I waited upon the pleasure of the Council: and they asked me, why my friends did not seek to get my liberty? I said, "I know not, they know what they have best to do themselves." One said, "But they come every day to see you, do not they tell you what they will do?" I said, "I do not ask them, I leave it to them." Something more was said, and I came away, and retired to my chamber, wherein I kept most of those eight weeks, paying five shillings a week for it; it cost forty shillings, and I bless the Lord that I had friends and some means of my own, else I must have lain in the jail upon straw: The Matron told me so the first night, and when some said, If I must beat Hemp, they would beat for me, she said, I should beat it myself: and for ought she knew I was to beat hemp, but she did not know me; and so spoke as she used to speak to those that deserve harshness; for after she had knowledge of me, she was very loving, and respectful both to me and to my Sister Ursula Adman, who kept me company seven weeks of my being there: She was a friend born for the day of adversity, as Solomon speaks; and indeed she, night and day, showed her tenderness to me and helped to bear my burden. And therein she fulfilled the law of Christ, and she did this as a freewill offering, love constraining her thereunto, so that it was thereby made easy to her to bear and endure that which few would, especially so freely without reward; yet I am confident the Lord will reward her double for that prison kindness, she let out to me without any fainting, or being troubled that the time was long or the noises burdensome; there was many difficulties to undergo night and day; but little quiet sleep to be had, there was such scolding among the prisoners near our lodging: and they were brought in often a nights, which made a great noise, and the rats ran about our bed and made a great noise, like dogs and cats in the room; and this was no pleasant prison sure to such that were brought up tenderly, and never knew any hardship as to the outward man: And truly the Lord made this and many more annoyances received in Bridewell prison to be very pleasantly embraced by divine love appearing in the midst of all trials; my God made this smarting scourge (as from man it was so) but God I say made it easy; for his tenderness was much, he made foes become friends, and the harsh to be kind, and overcame the rough and hasty spirits; the Lord is worthy of all praise. I had but a little while affliction in my spirits, which was occasioned by a friend, and that made it grievous, but the Lord made that little storm, to work abundance of good to me many ways: and all things that were afflictive, the Lord quickly broke such fetters. I said not, O when will there be an end of this or the other affliction, but I often said, and desired a purging out of my corruptions, before a removal of sufferings, that so I might come out more holy and more humble, and more self-denying and self-debasing, and abhorring them when I went into prison: That so I might all my days be willing to take up the Cross of Christ and follow him, whithersoever he would have me, either to do or suffer: I shall begin to shorten my relation, lest I should be too tedious to the reader, and leave the visions and opening of Scriptures, that the Lord brought to my soul, while I was in Bridewell for my own benefit, and for others that are his little flock, with whom he hath made an everlasting covenant, well ordered in all things and sure.

At the time near my coming out, some came and desired me to petition, I told them I had not offended man, whereby to seek to him; and they knew that I was in prison by their order; but some said they may forget: I said, that they could not, for many of their friends still told them: The Protector said, he did not know that I was put in Bridewell, till I had been there above a week, that one went and informed him: but it was a strange thing that servants should do such an act without their master, and great Governor's knowledge; surely, if he had not like of it, he would have reproved them: but said I, "Now he knows it, and yet he doth not send for me out." Again, some others came and said, they knew they could quickly procure my liberty: I told them, I would not come out upon base terms: said one to me, "What are your terms, let us hear them?" I said, "They shall acknowledge the reproach and odium they have brought upon me through this their prison": said one, "Is that your terms? then you may lie long enough; but surely all rational men will say, this was but equity." Then after this, some spoke great matters, what they would do for my liberty: and they went to the Council and spoke to them, and President Laurence said, if that I would or any for me engage, I might come out; but said Captain Kettlebeator, none can engage, for she herself cannot engage as to a dispensation, that she is so taken up in, that she knows not what is done about her at that time, nor capable of any being with her in the room: And he told him, that he had known me many years: And my whole deportment of life had been and was very civil and religious; he spake more to that purpose: And the President said, so he had understood; some more speech they had, and they came to tell me that, nay what they had spoken in my behalf: I said, "I will never engage to that which lies not in me to perform, for what the Lord utters in me, I must speak": so one said, he would go again to the Council; I told him I desired no favor of them but justice and equity: and if he could procure my coming before them to hear what they have against me, that's all I desire of you I said; and what he said or did, it was of his own offering: so he said, he would not leave them so, but he would go again and try what they would do; but I heard no more concerning him, he was forgetful it may be, like his master. After this some others undertook this business and came to hear what I would say to it. And one asked me upon what account I suffered imprisonment, whether it was for Christ, and if so then I had a great deal of comfort in my sufferings, for he said, he had found it so, having been imprisoned for the testimony of Jesus; I told him the Council never sent for me, to tell me upon what account they imprison me here for; and I said, the recognizances are taken off concerning Cornwall business, so that I was merely upon the pleasure and wills of the Council and of Lord Laurence; for indeed I will call him my Bridewell Lord, for that his hand was in chief to the order: but I told them, I was sure I suffered for Christ. And I enjoyed his presence abundantly; and I gave them some account of my sufferings, and of the Lord's comforts therein. Then after some further discourse, they asked me whether I would be willing to go out, if an order should come for my liberty? I told them, I would never engage: they said, that was not desired; I said, yes but it was, for my Lord Laurence told some if I would engage, I might come out: then they said, but if the order come, and give you liberty freely, will you accept of it? I was silent, only my sister said, if we can have liberty, we will choose it rather than bonds: so after a little while these departed.

And the next week after, upon the sixth day of the week, I rose early in the morning and walked about my chamber, putting up requests to the Lord secretly for purging grace, that I might go out of prison much more purified from the dross of corruptions than when I went into prison fire; that so others might see it had been a purifying furnace to me: And after I had been up some hours, I said to my sister that abode with me, "I think," said I to her, "everyone that I hear coming to the door, comes from the Council with an order for my liberty; come let us pray before it comes, and ask counsel of God concerning it," and the Lord indeed counseled me, and took me into the mount of heavenly rapture that day, so that my friends were fain to take me off my knees and lay me upon my bed, where I lay praying and singing more than ever I did in my life unto many public concernments, the which I am sure will be accomplished in due time: and I often desired that they in high places had some of the dainties with me at Bridewell; and that day the order was brought, and I lay silent when they came with it; but I was talking with the Lord who showed me many things, which I know shall come to pass, and the Lord told me that my freedom out of that place was near, the which I saw three weeks before, and sang it forth, so I did now; one of them tarried that brought the order, I was told so afterwards; but I knew not that any was by me, when I thus lay, either silent or speaking. That day I spake to some that said, he would choose imprisonment for gain, he spoke of an outward gain, but if he got by his imprisonment formerly; I am sure I cannot say, nor those that are imprisoned upon this account for the Fifth Monarchy, cannot say so: we would not gain for our outward man, if we might, by robbing others, to enrich ourselves; I can say, I have refused what hath been tendered me freely: I took nothing save for my necessity, unto which I had enough supply, had not the rulers put me to such charges through their imprisonment, and bringing me from place to place, and making me pay for it. So that I have been robbed, but I have robbed none: I had rather go in a canvas coat, or any mean garb, than so do. . . .

I shall further relate in the close of this relation, how the next day I came forth, for I came not into a capable frame to speak to anybody, till late at night, on the sixth day; and when I spoke that night, my friends said, "Do you know you are set at liberty? You sang as if you had known"; I said, "The Lord hath given it me, I will thank him for it"; "so you told us today in your singing," said my friends: And the next morning the Keeper of Bridewell came, and said I was free by order from the Council, and I might go out when I pleased: I told him they should fetch me out that put me in; had they put me among thieves and whores, and now did they send for me out without acknowledging the reproach they had brought upon me? He said, the same order with the same hands that puts you in fetches you out: I desired to see my order; so I should, he said, if I would pay sixteen pence for a copy of it: so I sent for it and read it. And seeing I might go out upon no dishonorable terms, and the Lord having instructed me beforehand, he being my guide and counselor in my imprisonment and in my coming out. And I said to a friend, go tell your masters, though they will not see me they shall be sure to hear from me, and so they have: for I sent letters to them, that so they might not say, they had not heard of the injustice acted under their dominion: Now I have given a declaration, through the assistance of the Lord, and not to set up myself and throw down others; but to throw down lies, and exalt truth; the Lord would not have cities nor countries, nor Whitehall Council, a refuge for lies: For his people are recorded in the 63 of Isaiah v. 8 to be children that will not lie, so he became their Savior: I desire that truth may be written in buff and sent through Europe; I would have the whole world taste the sweetness of truth, that all people may know, and see, and consider, and understand together, the hand of the Lord, and what he is doing, and will do for his that trust in him; And sure wisdom is justified to her children: Come, O you children of wisdom, observe that you may understand, and seek after Christ's reign, and say with me: "Come Lord Jesus come quickly, according to thy saying; Even so come Lord Jesus." Let those that wait on the Lord's coming say, "Amen, even so be it."

A Defiance to all reproachful, scandalous, base, horrid, dreaming speeches, which have been vented by rulers, clergy, and their auditors, and published in scurrilous pamphlets up and down in cities and countries, against Anna Trapnel, late prisoner in Bridewell for the testimony of Jesus the Lord.

I am forced out of my close retired spirit by rulers and clergy, who have brought me upon the world's stage of reports and rumors. . . .

Further, they call me imposter; pray which of the ways and ordinances or statutes of the Lord have I perverted through deceit? Canst thou, Oh man, or woman, lay anything of this nature to my charge? Do then; but through grace you cannot: Therefore I can defy this saying also.

Again, you call me vagabond; but how will you make that good? All the art, skill or policy that any politician hath among you, cannot make this saying true, not in the least: I lived with my mother till she died, which was about twenty years, then I kept house with the means my mother left me, and paid taxes towards maintaining of the Army then in the field; and this I did not grudgingly, but freely and willingly; I sold my plate and rings, and gave the money to the public use; you did not call me vagabond then. . . . The sum of money my mother left me, I freely gave for the Army's use, and I wrought many nights hard to get money, the which I cheerfully bestowed, not on my own back nor belly cheer, but fared hard, that so I might minister towards the relief of the

nation; and if that little means which I have left had been in money, I
could not have kept it from you; Oh army and rulers, that then would
not have defamed me; I pray why are you so unchristianlike in your
carriages to me now? you have taxes from me still; and am I a vagabond
for this? Ask your lawyers, will they not say you were much to blame
herein? Let all that knew me, speak, when they saw or knew me a
vagabond: After the time was over of my keeping house, I was desired
by Mrs. Spenser, a minister's widow, to abide with her and her daughters, who were sober, holy, humble walkers with God, and not of a
frothy, wanton, light, giddy carriage and deportment. . . . I lived among
these, taking up my abode with Mrs. Harlow, daughter to the aforementioned Mrs. Spenser, who lived near her mother in the Minneries;
she, her maid, and I lived together awhile, and they are my witnesses,
whether I was then idle, and others beside them can witness for me; I
kept close to the Word and fasting and prayer, and so observing times
for civil employment; was I a vagabond then? Then I was desired by
Mrs. Wythe, my kinswoman, a merchant's wife in Fan-Church-Street
to live with her, with whom I lived six years; could I be a vagabond
there? They shall be my judges in this, I lived with them in city and
country till rulers were displeased at a dispensation above their understanding, and therefore gave out threatening speeches, that my relation
and friend where I lived was afraid to receive me for losing his place:
And now I have related my places of abode from my childhood until the
11. month 1653, all which time I suppose no rational man will say I was a
vagabond: And as for the time since, as soon as I was rejected of my
kinsman for the rulers' sake, many friends would have let me into their
houses, which are very grave, godly, conscientious, wise, sober, persons, that are unwilling to entertain vagabonds; but to this day I have
a settled habitation, and pay assessments; therefore stand convinced
from this day, and hereafter, all you rulers, clergy, and people in all
places and countries, that I Anna Trapnel am no vagabond, nor rene-
gade person, though I have and may sometimes live in the city, and
sometimes in the country, as yourselves do, and why should I be accounted a vagabond more then you?

Let me yet further, bid defiance to those that have called me whore,
which language hath proceeded from Court, I hear so; and will any that
have said so, stand to their words without blushing? Truly, I would try
them, were there any law up, save the wills of men; you may peradven-
ture say, this savors of revenge; I answer, it doth not, for Solomon saith,

"The name of the righteous is as a precious ointment," and therefore dead flies are to be cast out, which would putrify it, and it's to be carefully preserved because costly and precious for use, so that if it be putrified it's not of use; so Christ's flock are for his use, and he keepeth them, that nothing can putrify them in that newborn state they are in; yet as to that usefulness for the benefit of saints and sinners, herein they may be hindered, through the dead flies' stinking-scent brought on their names. And as to this charge, being I do not suffer as an evildoer, I will triumph and give glory to the Lord my God, who hath kept me from open profaneness and from secret sins, and in a great measure hath freed me from my iniquity, which is the sin of my disposition, which doth not run out, nor incline to lustfulness, neither of the flesh nor eye, nor pride of life. . . . Yet I bless the Lord, and my Father, as unto men's reports I am not guilty, nor a transgressor in their sense, for the which I praise Jehovah, and still I will advance him who is my All in All.

I have a further word with the Cornwall jurors, who say they are for the Lord Protector of the Commonwealth of England, Scotland, and Ireland, etc. and upon their oaths present Anna Trapnel to be a dangerous seditious person, not only, say they, imagining, but devising and maliciously intending the peace, tranquillity and felicity of the good people of this Commonwealth of England to disturb, but, say they, to move, stir up, and raise discord, rebellion and insurrection among the good people of England, as aforesaid; this they affirmed upon oath, in their indictment; all which I bid defiance to as false. . . . Oh jurors, when you say you are for the Lord Protector, I am sure you do not mean the great Lord Protector of heaven and earth, sea, and dryland, who hath indeed all dominions belonging unto him: And as for him you call your Protector, you do not give him that tithe in love to him more than to another, nor so much as to old King Charles and to his son, who is in your hearts, you love a King dearly. Oh that you did love King Jesus, he would never fail you, he would teach you to make your indictments truer, and not upon persons undeserving, he would teach you not to use his children as witches, and vagabonds when they come into your parts: I pity you, oh you envious jurors. You have not injured me, not indicted me, but yourselves, and though I could say, when before you examined, Not guilty, I could say so with a clear conscience, yet I am sure you cannot say so, at the Lord's judgment seat; when he shall read the Bill of Indictment against you, can you say to him, you are not of a devilish mind, nor of a wicked imagination, nor seditious, nor maliciously bent against the great Lord Protector and his subjects, against whom you imagine, devise, stir up, and raise discord, rebellion and insurrection against the great Lord Protector, and his good People aforesaid, endeavoring to bring his righteous and just actions into contempt, disgrace, and hatred amongst all sorts of people, good and bad. And be it known unto you, that the Jehovah Protector is my King, Priest, and Prophet whose Kingly power I obey, and all government consonant to it. . . .

9

ONCE MORE A WARNING TO THEE O ENGLAND: BUT MORE PARTICULARLY TO THE INHABITANTS OF THE CITY OF BRISTOL*

Dorcas Dole

From Newgate Prison in Bristol, 1683

. . . and in the meantime came in Sheriff Arnold with others in his company, who took me off my knees from prayer and sent me away by his man to Newgate, and he and the rest followed after to disturb Friends [Quakers] here; and when they came in the outward rooms, that they might come to the innermost room in the prison, to see if they could find any preaching or praying, but Friends being sitting in silence, they could hear no words till after they came in; a Friend spake to them to fear the Lord, because his name is great, and for these words, or such like, was he commanded to be taken away out of his lodging room (from the rest of Friends) and put him down into a dark room, called the West-house; and they commanded that I should be put from the rest of Friends also and not be suffered to meet with them; and so I told them, they were but mortal men and that the sword of mortality hanged over their heads, which was near ready to cut them down, and therefore my desire to them was to repent.

So the turnkey took me down into a dark hole; and Thomas Lugg, an informer and now a constable, one of the company that came along with the Sheriff, followed after, and spoke of chaining of me, and that I should have neither bread nor water. And the next meeting day, being

*Wing D1834, Reel 814, pp. 11–12.

locked and kept one from another in several rooms, I being at prayer, the jailor and his man came where I was and took me off my knees, and would not suffer me to stay with the rest of my Friends that lodged in the same dark room, it being a place where felons use to lodge, and would not suffer one Friend to go along with me, but put me among the felons and debtors, where I was derided and shamefully treated, and water thrown on me for no other cause but praying to the living God; and ever since I am not suffered to stay in the room with my Friends on our meeting days, but in a little time taken forth and put from the rest of my Friends, though drunkards and swearers are suffered frequently to meet and make themselves drunk, without being used after the manner that we are used. . . .

10

AN ACCOUNT OF THE TRAVELS,
SUFFERINGS, AND PERSECUTIONS
OF BARBARA BLAUGDONE*

And as Mary Prince and I was coming arm in arm from a Meeting, that was at George Bishop's house, there was a rude man came and abused us, and struck off Mary Prince her hat, and run some sharp knife or instrument through all my clothes, into the side of my belly, which, if it had gone but a little farther, it might have killed me; but my soul was so in love with the truth that I could have given up my life for it at that day.

And then I was moved to go to Marlborough, to the Marketplace and Steeple-house, where I had pretty much service, where they put me in prison for six weeks, where I fasted six days and six nights, and neither eat bread nor drank water, nor no earthly thing. . . .

And a while after I was made to go into Devonshire, to Molton and Bastable and Bediford, where I had a prison in all those places: and I went to the Earl of Bathes, where I had formerly spent much time in vanity . . . and I asked to speak with the Countess, but they refused to let me in, but one of the servants that knew me bid me go to the back door, and their Lady would come forth that way to go into the garden; and they sent forth a great wolf-dog upon me, which came fiercely at me to devour me, and just as he came unto me, the Power of the Lord smote the dog, so that he whined and ran in crying, and very lame. . . .

And then the Lady came forth, and stood still and heard me . . . and when I had done, she gave me thanks, but never asked me to go into her house, although I had eat and drank at her table and lodged there many a time. [Blaugdone then went to Great Torrington in Devon-

*London, 1691. Wing A410, pp. 10-16, 26-28, 30-31, 36, 38.

shire and from there was sent to Exeter Prison on charges of being a vagabond.]

. . . and the next day the sheriff came with a beadle, and had me into a room, and whipped me till the blood ran down my back, and I never startled at a blow . . . and I sung aloud; and the beadle said, "Do ye sing; I shall make ye cry by and by," and with that he laid more stripes, and laid them on very hard. I shall never forget the large experience of the love and power of God. . . . Ann Speed was an eyewitness of it, and she stood and looked in at the window and wept bitterly. And then the sheriff . . . bid him forbear, for he had gone beyond his orders already. So when he had left me, Ann Speed came in and dressed my wounds; and the next day they turned me out with all the gypsies, and the beadle followed us two miles out of the city. . . .

This my service for God was great, and he made it to prosper. And then I went to Cork, where my motion was at first, and great were my sufferings there, for I had a prison almost wherever I came. . . . And I was made to speak in a marketplace, and there was a butcher swore he could cleave my head in twain; and had his cleaver up ready to do it, but there came a woman behind him and caught back his arms and stayed them till the soldiers came and rescued me. . . . and some said I was a witch . . . they would drag me along upon the stones and hale me out and shut the doors. . . .

So then I went to Dublin, where I spoke in the High Court of Justice amongst the judges; and then they put me in prison, where I lay upon straw, on the ground, and when it rained, the wet and filth of the House-of-Office ran in under my back: and they arraigned me at the bar and bid me plead guilty, or not guilty. . . .

I took shipping for England again . . . and coming towards Mineyard, we met a pirate, which had abundance of men on board . . . so they came on board us and took away all that I had, and one of my coats from off my back. . . .

But in all my travels, I traveled still on my own purse, and was never chargeable to any, but paid for what I had.

And I have written these things that Friends may be encouraged, and go on in the faith, in the work of the Lord. For many have been the trials, tribulations, and afflictions, the which I have passed through, but the Lord hath delivered me out of them all; glory be given to him, and blessed be his name forever and evermore.

PART THREE

WOMEN MAKING POLITICAL STATEMENTS AND PETITIONING

Introduction

"A proportionable share in the Freedoms of this Commonwealth . . ."

Powerless in politics, legally and politically subordinate to males, women discovered that there was power in petitioning. In collaboration women demanded that their voices be heard in Parliament. When they gathered first in small groups, then in large numbers at the doors of Parliament, they began to realize that powerlessness need not remain a permanent and frustrating condition of their sex. On February 4, 1642, women assembled at the doors of the Houses of Parliament, refusing to be ignored by that political-legislative body. Parliament members saw and heard them clamoring outside and delegated Sergeant-Major Skippon to address them. He reported back to Parliament: "there being great multitudes of women at the Houses, pressing a petition to the Parliament: and their language is that where there is one woman now here, there would be five hundred tomorrow; and that it was as good for them to die here as at home." (McArthur, 698).

These particular women assembling at that moment in 1642 were wives and widows of tradesmen who feared the loss of trade if the queen should leave England and go into exile in Holland. The loss of trade for these women meant the loss of the ability to earn a living. Threatened with economic hardship through the loss of employment and income, they did what males had done so often before them: they demanded direct access to Parliament.

Their carefully worded petition, employing proper legal diction and form (some said the petition was written by men), outlined the theoretical foundation for women to make demands through the process of petitioning. The petition included a request for an immediate and practical response to what they regarded as a life-threatening situation. This petition, bolstered by the women's mass protest, sprang from a need to survive economically. Undoubtedly an acute sense of political deprivation lurked underneath the surface of the petition and formed the theoretical basis and subtext of the document, but the right to vote and the right of a female to stand for Parliament were not a part of their concern at this time. Their primary aim was to have their petition accepted, read, taken seriously, and acted upon—up to this time formal petitioning was largely a male prerogative and strategy.

Women protested other issues and petitioned other causes. In 1643, during the English Civil War, a number of women became peace protesters. Wearing white silk ribbons in their hats, they were known as Women for Peace. In "The Reactions of Women, with Special Reference to Women Petitioners," Patricia Higgins quotes from original documents to sketch in the features of these petitions and the sequence of events in the protests. The women had

> "a petition for peace, which they presented to the House of Commons by the hands of one of the members of that House." . . . *Mercurius Civicus* reproduced the petition *in extenso* and this is almost identical with an undated petition in the Tanner MSS., the only important difference being that the latter bears the additional information that the petition was presented "To the Honorable the Knights, Citizens and Burgesses of the House of Commons." The women addressed the Commons as "the physicians that can restore this languishing nation, And that our bleeding Sister Kingdom of Ireland," and they asked that "the just Prerogatives and Privileges of King and Parliament" be maintained, "the true liberties and properties of the Subject" be restored, "all honorable ways and means for a speedy peace" be endeavoured, and "some speedy course may be taken for the settlement of the true Reformed Protestant Religion . . . and the renovation of trade. . . ." The House of Commons "received and read" the petition. . . . It is noted in the Commons' Journals that six members . . . were appointed to acquaint the women with the House's desire for peace, that they would have the "greatest care of the public as may be" and would consider their petition further "very speedily." (193–94)

The women felt, however, that they were only being mollifed and that their demands for peace were not being met. The violence that followed Parliament's response is corroborated by eyewitness accounts. The women (now numbering more than 5,000) kept beating on the outer doors of the house and threatening to have the blood of the prowar members of Parliament. The women advanced to the doors at the upper stairs, from which position they were pushed down for two hours. Then, after being subdued and ejected into the courtyard, they were shot at by trained guards. The women retaliated with brickbats found in the courtyard and threw them at the guards, several of whom were disarmed by the women. As they struggled the women cried, "Give us these traitors that are against peace that we may tear them in pieces." Finally, the women were dispersed by the use of swords and then by mounted troops who struck them with canes. Afterward many women were sent to prison. The *Parliament Scout* concluded: "Thus we see, to permit absurdities is the way to increase them; tumults are dangerous, swords in women's hands do desperate things; this is begotten in the distractions of Civil War" (Higgins, 194–98). It is apparent that in crisis situations (although they still accepted the patriarchal designation of them as "the weaker vessel") women raised their voices in petition, even using physical force to be heard. No male physical force, no political coercion, could dissuade them.

Women involved themselves in other issues besides economic survival and the desire for peace in the country. They petitioned against bishops, stating that they feared sedition and persecution. They petitioned for return of the king. They petitioned against harsh bankruptcy and insolvency laws (McArthur, passim). On the strength of the evidence, however, the conclusion cannot be drawn that the majority of women in England in the sixteenth and seventeenth centuries petitioned Parliament. The women who petitioned were definitely in the minority.

What must have been infuriating for these women were the typical responses to their petitions:

> . . . the House could not take cognizance of their petition, they being women, and many of them wives, so that the Law took no notice of them. (Higgins, 211)

> That the matter you petition about is of an higher concernment than you understand, that the House gave an answer to your husband; and therefore that you are desired to go home, and look after your own business, and meddle with your housewifery. (Higgins, 212)

> It is fitter for you to be washing your dishes, and meddle with wheel and distaff; we shall have things brought to a fine pass if women come to teach the Parliament how to make laws. It can never be a good world when women meddle in State matters . . . their husbands are to blame that they have no fitter employment for them. (Higgins, 213)

A member of Parliament said that "it was not for women to petition, they might stay at home and wash the dishes." A woman responded, "Sir, we have scarce any dishes left us to wash." Another member of Parliament said that it was strange for women to petition. A woman replied, "It was strange that you cut off the King's head, yet I suppose you will justify it." (Fraser, 238–39)

The harshness that characterizes all-male responses shows male repugnance for women petitioning. The legislative body obviously recognized the implications of such activity. In the act of petitioning women claimed equal rights to the freedoms guaranteed to men, whose derisive and contemptuous responses to the women were an attempt to crush even the impulse to petition, and to ridicule women into silent submission.

Not all women petitioners directed their petitions to the legislative body. There were those women who made a direct appeal to the king; others, in the interregnum, appealed to Oliver Cromwell, the Lord Protector, and his Privy Council; other women petitioned the mayor and aldermen. Not all women petitioners pleaded for economic, political, and religious liberty. Some took an active part in petitioning for the just distribution of property to those under their guardianship; some, seeing economic hardship and inequity for the elderly, petitioned for restitution to solvency. And some petitioned for the life of a husband sentenced to execution for treason. Dame Mary Hewytt, for example, charged Oliver Cromwell with "thirsting after blood" and the president of his High Court of Justice with murder, and she demanded reparations for damages.

The first petition in this section, delivered to Parliament by Mrs. Anne Stagg, a gentlewoman and brewer's wife, with many others of her "like rank and quality" on February 4, 1642, made essentially one demand: that purity of religion be guaranteed. The women cite the reprehensible conditions that exist in the kingdom because papists and prelates are violently suppressing true religion. There are rapes of women by soldiers in Ireland; husbands and children are murdered; mothers' milk is mingled with infants' blood in the streets; houses are set on fire; souls and consciences are in thralldom. Using Queen Esther as their paradigm (she risked her life to petition King Ahasuerus for the safety of her people), the petitioners argued for equal rights of women:

1. Women, sharing with men in the salvation offered by Christ, must have an equal share in obedience to Christ; obedience implies sharing the mandate to maintain pure religion in Britain and taking action against repression.

2. Freedom in church and commonwealth is as important to the happiness of women as to that of men.

3. Women are not exempt from persecution by prelates; women, along with men, are sentenced to prison and denied liberty of body, mind, and conscience.

The reply of Mr. Pym to this petition accorded the women dignity and showed that Parliament took their petition seriously. He promised "all the satisfaction which we can possibly give to your just and lawful desires." He urged them to return home and to pray for Parliament in its efforts to "perform the trust committed" to them by God, king, country, and loyal subjects.

Mary Cary, a millenarian, was a fervent member of a radical sect. She petitioned two members of Parliament to read her interpretation of events occurring in the Revelation of St. John and her application of those mystical events to current political events in England. She wished to provide Parliament with a radical woman's justification of the parliamentary war against the king. It is dubious whether her petition actually fortified the parliamentary cause and gave Parliament a prophetic basis for its war, since the prophecies of women were generally not held in high regard. In her later writings, Mary Cary petitioned for the abolition of lawyers and tithes, for reform of the universities, and for relief of the poor. After the Restoration in 1660, her voice was no longer heard.

Elizabeth Lilburne's life is a history of petitioning on behalf of her husband. John Lilburne was a Leveler who was frequently imprisoned for publishing unlicensed materials. His books were incendiary: he demanded that kingship be abolished, that the present Parliament be dissolved, and that a new Parliament be established—one that distributed authority equally among all citizens. One of his treatises, *The Freemans Freedome Vindicated* (1646), was a major source of concern for the existing government.

Elizabeth Dewell first met John Lilburne when he was in Fleet Prison. After his release, they were married. For Elizabeth, the years of her marriage were marked by separation, homelessness, poverty, and sickness (five of her ten children died; she herself barely escaped death from smallpox). John Lilburne died at age forty-three, leaving his wife destitute and with a large fine that he owed the government. The Cromwellian government (both Oliver and Richard) did finally agree to cancel the fine and to settle on her a small income (after she agreed to surrender her husband's papers to Richard Cromwell).

During the stormy seventeen years that she petitioned for her husband and the Levelers' cause, she was joined by a great many Leveler women. Antonia Fraser describes 1649 as the banner year for the Leveler cause—and for women's political involvement in that era:

> The presentation of *The Humble Petition of divers well-affected Women inhabiting the City of London, Westminster, the Borough of Southwark, Hamblets and places adjacent to the House of Commons* in April 1649, and the events surrounding it, represented the high point of political female activity at this period; just as the ardent demonstration at the funeral of the executed Leveller soldier Robert Lockyer was the most overt instance of public Leveller sympathies. The coffin was decorated with sprigs of rosemary dipped in blood. The long column of mourners adorned with black and sea-green ribbons—sea-green was the adopted colour of the Leveller cause—was brought up by a body of women at the rear, sea-green and black ribbons mingled at their breast.
>
> The women petitioners for the release of Lilburne, Overton and others, first tackled the House of Commons on 23 April, when they were simply told that the House was too busy to receive them. . . .
>
> On 25 April twenty women were at last admitted to the lobby of the House of Commons bearing a petition, although the attendant soldiers threw squibs at them, and cocked their pistols. The women, with equal determination if not equal violence, grabbed Cromwell's cloak and began to lecture him on their grievances. "What will you have?" cried Cromwell in answer to their tirade. "Those rights and freedoms of the Nation, that you promised us. . ." was the ominous reply. (238–39)

By the Restoration the Levelers had almost disappeared from the politico-religious scene.

The language of Elizabeth Lilburne's petition in the brief excerpt that appears in this section shows how fearlessly she attacked the injustices perpetrated on her husband by the High Court of Parliament. Words and phrases like *tyrannical, barbarous,* and *Spanish Inquisition-like Interrogatories* indicate the risks that she was willing to take.

The tone of Mary Love's petition is altogether different from that of Elizabeth Lilburne's petition, although both women were concerned with the fate of their husbands. The outcome of the petitions was altogether different also. John Lilburne was pardoned; Christopher Love was executed.

As an individual petitioner, Mary Love pleaded for her husband's release from prison and a stay of execution. Christopher Love, a Presbyterian minister, preached against what he regarded as errors in the *Book of Common Prayer;* more seriously, however, he was later charged with corresponding with the exiled royal family and plotting against the Commonwealth. Sentenced to the Tower for high treason, he was scheduled to be executed in July 1651.

What is revealed in Mary Love's petitions is the plight of a pregnant woman facing widowhood with two small children and a third about to be born. In her first petition, she pleads her status as a "poor handmaid" and asks for compassion. She guarantees the acquiescence of her husband in the new government and asks for a stay of execution and a release from prison. In her second petition, she asks for his banishment, since she senses that a pardon is not forthcoming. In her third petition, she thanks Parliament for postponing the execution for a month and expresses the wish that she and her unborn child could be considered ransom for the life of her husband. Parliament, as was to be expected, rejected her offer. Her husband was executed on August 22, 1651.

In 1663, after the Restoration, Mary Love's petitions and the exchange of letters between her and her husband just before his death were published under the name *Love's Name Lives.* The letter that appears in this section shows the deep feeling she had for her husband but also reveals the composure of a woman who can urge her husband, when he puts his head on the block, to think that he is simply putting his head into his Heavenly Father's bosom.

Mary Love was not a petitioner for the rights of women. Hers was the voice of desperation. A desperate situation called for desperate language. She pleaded her weakness, not strength. She asked for compassion, not justice. Compassion, however, was hardly an option for a government that feared the return of monarchy.

Although Elizabeth Hooton petitioned for herself and directly to the king, hers was the voice of all suffering Quakers, both in England and New England, both male and female. Converted to Quakerism when she was nearly fifty years old by the great Quaker preacher George Fox, she spent the rest of her life preaching and petitioning against "laws to persecute the conscience."

When she heard about persecutions of the Quakers in New England, she and Joan Brocksoppe traveled to Boston to protest hangings and imprisonments. Mary Dyer, for example, had been hanged in Boston in 1659; Elizabeth Hooton and Joan Brocksoppe spoke openly in Boston against such practices and were themselves imprisoned there.

In the petition included in this section, Elizabeth Hooton touches on a number of issues, such as restoration of her confiscated goods; tithes, taxes, assessments, and rents and their impact on farming and farmers; and imprisonment of Quakers. Ultimately, she argues in her petition, these issues transcend the personal: they are matters of justice and equity in the Commonwealth. She insists that every citizen, no matter of what religious persuasion, deserves equal consideration under the law.

Her importunity to the king left her vulnerable to ejection, punishment, and ridicule by the king's attendant soldiers, since she pursued the king when he was at tennis, in the court at Whitehall, in the palace yard, riding in the park. Her feelings of psychological disenfranchisement and her belief in the rights of Quakers to equal treatment and respect led her to appeal to the highest source of power that she knew—the king.

Margaret Beck's petition is the petition of a mother. Her appeal was to Oliver Cromwell, Lord Protector of England, on behalf of her fatherless son, who, she claimed, deserved to have the title to the lands of the duchy of Lancaster. Her plea, although it uses emotional terms to describe her son's poverty-stricken state, is a strictly legal appeal that deftly provides legal documentation. She cites precedents and case histories; she supplies the lineage of her son in order to justify his claim to the lands.

Her son Samuel's claims to the Lancaster lands can be traced back to John of Gaunt, the fourteenth-century duke of Lancaster (father of Henry IV, grandfather of Henry V). She takes Cromwell and his Privy Council through the convoluted history of the land and its owners. She then focuses on recent history: on her husband's claims to King Charles, who resolutely denied Nevil Beck the lands and even a maintenance, since Charles feared that he would use the maintenance fee to bring the case to court. After the death of Charles and of her husband, Margaret claims that she is the only person left to fight for the rights of her family and her son to inherit the lands. To prevent the sale of the lands (which was ordered by the self-declared Parliament after the death of Charles) she pleaded her case to the Lord Protector of England, hoping there to receive fair treatment through a legal hearing.

The Privy Council was not easily convinced, however. They replied to Margaret Beck with a refutation of the lineage of her son by tracing the house of Lancaster down a different line. Undeterred, she responded with additional evidence and supplied counterevidence that seems irrefutable.

The title of Margaret Beck's petition is subtle. It attributes oppression, tyranny, and injustice to the kings and queens of England and implies that the new antimonarchical government will, by awarding to Samuel Beck the land to which he is the rightful heir, combat these monarchical vices. The voice of Margaret Beck may be the voice of "the widow and fatherless," but its strength derives from clear, distinct, and self-confident claims that are made with legal precision and political discernment.

In one of her many pamphlets, Elinor James writes: "O that I were but a man, I would study night and day, and I do not doubt but I should be more than a conqueror, and so I hope to be nevertheless" (*Mrs. James's Vindication*, 2). In the petition included in this section she attempts to be a spiritual conqueror over the forces of darkness.

The petition is to the mayor and aldermen on behalf of an old man whose children not only denied him financial assistance but prevented him from selling property in order to support himself. When, in severe distress, he suggested to his children that he had legal rights to sell his property, they threatened to take him to court. Elinor James pleads on his behalf and calls herself the spokesperson for parental rights. She excuses the children by attributing their filial cruelty to the machinations of Satan. Since her own efforts to achieve unity between the father and his children proved futile, she petitioned the mayor and the aldermen, expressing faith in the local government to stand in the place of Christ to achieve reconciliation within the family.

Elinor James's petition is evidence of a woman's concern for a male neighbor; it is also a sign that a woman could assume the role of petitioner without apology.

Suggested Readings

Cary, Mary. *Twelve Humble Proposals to the Supreme Governours of the Three Nations.* London, 1653.

Crawford, Patricia. "Women's Published Writings 1600–1700." In *Women in English Society 1500–1800,* ed. Mary Prior. London: Methuen, 1985.

Fraser, Antonia. *The Weaker Vessel.* New York: Knopf, 1984.

Gregg, Pauline. *Free-Born John: A Biography of John Lilburne.* London: Harrap, 1961.

Hewytt, Mary. *To the honorable knights, citizens, and burgesses of the Commons House. . . .* London, 1660.

Higgins, Patricia. "The Reactions of Women, with Special Reference to Women Petitioners." In *Politics, Religion and the English Civil War,* ed. Brian Manning. New York: St. Martin's Press, 1973.

Hill, Christopher. *The World Turned Upside Down.* New York: Viking, 1972.

Hobby, Elaine. *Virtue of Necessity: English Women's Writing 1649–88.* Ann Arbor: University of Michigan Press, 1989.

James, Elinor. *Mrs. James's Vindication of the Church of England.* London, 1687.

Lilburne, John. *The Freemans Freedome Vindicated.* London, 1646.

McArthur, Ellen A. "Women Petitioners and the Long Parliament." *English Historical Review* 24 (1909): 698–709.

Reay, Barry. "The Quakers, 1659, and the Restoration of the Monarchy." *History* 63 (June 1978): 193–213.

Severall petitions presented to the Honourable Houses of Parliament . . . concerning . . . the Queenes intended voyage. 1641.

To the right honourable the house of Peers . . . the humble petition of many thousand of courtiers, citizens, gentlemens and tradesmens wives. 1641.

To the supreme authority of England the Commons . . . the humble petition of divers well-affected women. April 24, 1649.

Unto every individual member of Parliament, the humble representation. July 29, 1653.

The womens petition to . . . General Cromwell. October 30, 1651.

A TRUE COPY OF THE
PETITION OF THE GENTLEWOMEN
AND TRADESMENS WIVES,
IN AND ABOUT THE CITY OF LONDON

Delivered, to the Honorable, the Knights, Citizens, and Burgesses,
of the House of Commons in Parliament, the 4th of February, 1642

Together, with their several reasons why their sex
ought thus to petition, as well as the men;
and the manner how both their petition and reasons was delivered.
Likewise the answer which the Honorable Assembly sent
to them by Mr. Pym, as they stood at the house door. *

To the Honorable Knights, Citizens and Burgesses,
of the House of Commons assembled in Parliament.
The most humble Petition of the Gentlewomen, Tradesmen's Wives,
and many others of the female sex, all inhabitants of the
city of London, and the suburbs thereto.

With lowest submission showing,

That we also with all thankful humility acknowledging the unwearied pains, care and great charge, besides hazard of health and life, which you the noble worthies of this honorable and renowned assembly have undergone, for the safety both of church and commonwealth, for a long time already past; for which not only we your humble petitioners, and all well affected in this kingdom, but also all other good Christians are

*London, 1642. Wing T2656, Reel 249.

bound now and at all times acknowledge; yet notwithstanding that many worthy deeds have been done by you, great danger and fear do still attend us, and will, as long as Popish Lords and superstitious bishops are suffered to have their voice in the House of Peers, and that accursed and abominable idol of the Mass suffered in the kingdom, and that archenemy of our prosperity and reformation lieth in the Tower [Archbishop Laud], yet not receiving his deserved punishment.

All these under correction, gives us great cause to suspect that God is angry with us, and to be the chief causes why your pious endeavors for a further reformation proceedeth not with that success as you desire, and is most earnestly prayed for of all that wish well to true religion, and the flourishing estate both of king and kingdom; the insolencies of the papists and their abettors, raiseth a just fear and suspicion of sowing sedition, and breaking out into bloody persecution in this kingdom, as they have done in Ireland, the thoughts of which sad and barbarous events maketh our tender hearts to melt within us, forcing us humbly to petition to this honorable assembly, to make safe provision for yourselves and us, before it be too late.

And whereas we, whose hearts have joined cheerfully with all those petitions which have been exhibited unto you in the behalf of the purity of religion, and the liberty of our husbands' persons and estates, recounting ourselves to have an interest in the common privileges with them, do with the same confidence assure ourselves to find the same gracious acceptance with you, for easing of those grievances, which in regard of our frail condition, do more nearly concern us, and do deeply terrify our souls: our domestical dangers with which this kingdom is so much distressed, especially growing on us from those treacherous and wicked attempts already are such as we find ourselves to have as deep a share as any other.

We cannot but tremble at the very thoughts of the horrid and hideous facts which modesty forbids us now to name, occasioned by the bloody wars in Germany, his Majesty's late Northern Army, how often did it affright our hearts, whilst their violence began to break out so furiously upon the persons of those whose husbands or parents were not able to rescue: we wish we had no cause to speak of those insolencies, and savage usage and unheard-of rapes, exercised upon our sex in Ireland, and have we not just cause to fear they will prove the forerunners of our ruin, except Almighty God by the wisdom and care of this Parliament be pleased to succor us, our husbands and children, which are as dear and tender unto us as the lives and blood of our hearts, to see them murdered and mangled and cut in pieces before our eyes, to see our children dashed against the stones, and the mothers' milk mingled with the infants' blood, running down the streets, to see our houses on flaming fire over our heads: oh how dreadful would this be? We thought it misery enough (though nothing to that we have just cause to fear) but few years since for some of our sex, by unjust divisions from their bosom comforts, to be rendered in a manner widows, and the children fatherless, husbands were imprisoned from the society of their wives, even against the laws of God and nature, and little infants suffered in their fathers' banishments: thousands of our dearest friends have been compelled to fly from Episcopal persecutions into desert places amongst wild beasts, there finding more favor than in their native soil, and in the midst of all their sorrows such hath the pity of the Prelates been, that our cries could never enter into their ears or hearts, not yet through multitudes of obstructions could never have access or come nigh to those royal mercies of our most gracious sovereign, which we confidently hope would have relieved us: but after all these pressures ended, we humbly signify that our present fears are, that unless the bloodthirsty faction of the Papists and Prelates be hindered in their designs, ourselves here in England as well as they in Ireland, shall be exposed to the misery which is more intolerable than that which is already past, as namely to the rage not of men alone, but of devils incarnate (as we may so say), besides the thralldom of our souls and consciences in matters concerning God, which of all things are most dear unto us.

Now the remembrance of all these fearful accidents aforementioned do strongly move us from the example of the woman of Tekoa (II Samuel 14.2–20) to fall submissively at the feet of his Majesty, our dread sovereign, and cry Help, oh King, help oh ye the noble Worthies now sitting in Parliament: And we humbly beseech you, that you will be a means to his Majesty and the House of Peers, that they will be pleased to take our heartbreaking grievances into timely consideration, and to add strength and encouragement to your noble endeavors, and further that you would move his Majesty with our humble requests, that he would be graciously pleased according to the example of the good King Asa, to purge both the court and kingdom of that great idolatrous service of the Mass, which is tolerated in the Queen's court, this sin (as we conceive) is able to draw down a greater curse upon the whole kingdom than all your noble and pious endeavors can prevent, which was the cause that the good and pious King Asa would not suffer idolatry in his own mother, whose example if it shall please his Majesty's gracious goodness to follow, in putting down Popery and idolatry both in great and small, in court and in the kingdom throughout, to subdue the Papists and their abettors, and by taking away the power of the Prelates, whose government by long and woeful experience we have found to be against the liberty of our conscience and the freedom of the Gospel, and the sincere profession and practice thereof, then shall our fears be removed, and we may expect that God will pour down his blessings in abundance both upon his Majesty, and upon this Honorable Assembly, and upon the whole land.

For which your new petitioners shall pray affectionately.

The reasons follow.

It may be thought strange and unbeseeming our sex to show ourselves by way of petition to this Honorable Assembly: but the matter being rightly considered, of the right and interest we have in the common and public cause of the church, it will, as we conceive (under correction) be found a duty commanded and required.

First, because Christ hath purchased us at as dear a rate as he hath done men, and therefore requireth the like obedience for the same mercy as of men.

Secondly, because in the free enjoying of Christ in his own laws, and a flourishing estate of the church and commonwealth, consisteth the happiness of women as well as men.

Thirdly, because women are sharers in the common calamities that accompany both church and commonwealth, when oppression is exercised over the church or kingdom wherein they live; and an unlimited power have been given to Prelates to exercise authority over the consciences of women, as well as men, witness Newgate, Smithfield, and other places of persecution, wherein women as well as men have felt the smart of their fury.

Neither are we left without example in scripture, for when the state of the church, in the time of King Ahasuerus, was by the bloody enemies thereof sought to be utterly destroyed, we find that Esther the Queen and her maids fasted and prayed, and that Esther petitioned to the King in the behalf of the church: and though she enterprised this duty with the hazard of her own life, being contrary to the law to appear before the King before she were sent for, yet her love to the church carried her through all difficulties, to the performance of that duty.

On which grounds we are emboldened to present our humble petition unto this Honorable Assembly, not weighing the reproaches which may and are by many cast upon us, who (not well weighing the premises) scoff and deride our good intent. We do it not out of any self-conceit, or pride of heart, as seeking to equal ourselves with men, either in authority or wisdom: But according to our places to discharge that duty we owe to God, and the cause of the church, as far as lieth in us, following herein the example of the men which have gone in this duty before us.

A relation of the manner how it was delivered, with their answer, sent by Mr. Pym.

This petition, with their reasons, was delivered the 4th of Feb. 1641/2, by Mrs. Anne Stagg, a gentlewoman and brewer's wife, and many others with her of like rank and quality, which when they had delivered it, after some time spent in reading of it, the Honorable Assembly sent them an answer by Mr. Pym, which was performed in this manner.

Mr. Pym came to the Commons door, and called for the women, and spake unto them in these words: Good women, your petition and the reasons have been read in the house; and is very thankfully accepted of, and is come in a seasonable time: You shall (God willing) receive from us all the satisfaction which we can possibly give to your just and lawful desires. We entreat you to repair to your houses, and turn your petition which you have delivered here into prayers at home for us; for we have been, are and shall be (to our utmost power) ready to relieve you, your husbands, and children, and to perform the trust committed unto us towards God, our King and country, as becometh faithful Christians and loyal subjects.

12

THE RESURRECTION OF
THE WITNESSES AND
ENGLAND'S FALL FROM
(THE MYSTICAL BABYLON) ROME*

Mary Cary

To the Honored Francis Rouse and Thomas Boon, Esquires,
Members of the Honorable House of Commons in Parliament

Honored Sirs,

It being the great design of God the Father to set up his Son our Lord
Jesus Christ, as his King upon the holy hill of Zion, and (though the
heathen rage, and the people imagine vain things, saying, come let us
break their bonds in sunder, and cast away their cords from us) to give
him the heathen for his inheritance, and the uttermost parts of the earth
for his possession. I say, this being God's design, he hath for the effect-
ing of it, given all power and authority in heaven and in earth into his
hand, and accordingly Jesus Christ hath undertaken to execute all
God's decrees, which are mentioned in the prophecy of the Book of the
Revelation, where we find that God had decreed, that for an appointed
term of time, his church, his temple, his saints should be in an afflicted,
persecuted, depressed, low condition, and that the beast, and the Baby-
lonian enemies of his church should have power to grow great, and to
flourish, and to make war against the saints, and to blaspheme God,
and his name, and his saints, for an appointed time, also and that after
that time was expired, that then Jesus Christ should improve that power
that was for that end given to him, in giving a glorious deliverance to his

*London, 1648. Wing C737A, Reel 1546, The Epistle Dedicatory, pp. 97–102.

church, and ruining totally the beast, great Babylon, and all his enemies, that so the kingdoms of this world may become his kingdoms, and that in such a manner, as they were not before, even so as all that are in authority, that will not cast their crowns at his feet, shall be broken in pieces, for he the Lord must be exalted in that day; there must be one Lord, and his name one in all the earth. Now as it most clearly appears to me from the divine oracles of the Scripture, having compared the works of God, and his Word together, I have in the ensuing discourse held it forth (for the encouragement of all that wait for the appearing of the Lord Jesus Christ for the overthrowing of his enemies, and the deliverance of his people from their persecutions) that the time is already come, wherein the appointed time of the prevailing power of the beast over the saints, is come to a period; and accordingly Jesus Christ hath begun to bring down the power of the beast, and to lift up his saints out of that low, afflicted, persecuted condition in which they have been, and that in order to the perfecting of these things England is already fallen from the mystical Babylon, Rome.

Now, honored sirs, you having been glorious stars, shining with a great deal of splendor in your country both in the publicness of your spirits, and the holiness of your conversations, wherein you have been eminent examples, and special encouragements unto others, and knowing that it is the desire of your souls to see the Lord Jesus alone advanced, whoever be thrown down. I have presumed to present this little treatise unto you, not doubting of your ingenuous and favorable acceptance of it. But though I publish it under your name and favor, yet do I not thereby desire you to patronize anything in it (if there should be anything) that is not truth, and for the truth that is in it, I need desire no patron; for great is the truth, and it will prevail. Yet notwithstanding the sons of truth, as far as the truth appears to them in truth will own it, and contend for it, and doubtless so will you. I am

Sirs

A Petitioner to heaven for Zion's, this Kingdom's and your prosperity, M.C.

Revelation, 11:11

And after three days and a half, the Spirit of life from God entered into them.

As the late war made by the beast against the witnesses, doth fully agree with all the circumstances of it, laid down in the former verses; so it agrees exactly with what is laid down in this verse also: for after the witnesses had been in so low a condition, as they were (as Paul was when he was stoned) supposed to be dead, for three years and a half: they did not lie as dead a day longer, but at the very day, when the three years and a half were expired; then the Spirit of life from God entered into them, and they began to stand upon their feet.

For on the 23rd day of October, 1641, did the beast begin the war in Ireland; and he continued overcoming the witnesses, the saints of Jesus Christ, in Ireland, and in England, until the 5th day of April, 1645, and from the 23rd of October, 1641, unto the 5th of April, 1645, there is just a thousand two hundred, and sixty days; which according to the Scripture account (though not according to the heathen account) is three years and a half complete. And when this three years and a half were expired; which was, I say, on the 5th of April, 1645, then was the resurrection of the witnesses: for they having lain dead for three years and a half before, then the Spirit of life from God entered into them. And the year 1645 as it is the year wherein the witnesses were raised from the dead; so it is the year, wherein the term of time in which they were to prophesy in sackcloth, and to be trodden underfoot, was to expire, and the year also wherein the prevailing power of the beast over the saints was to expire, as is made evident in the opening of the 2nd verse, page 60 etc. Now that on the 5th day of April, 1645, the saints, witnesses, and servants of Jesus Christ, were raised up, and that then a Spirit of life from God entered into them, appears thus:

On the 5th day of April, 1645, the Parliament's Army, who had stood for the defense of the saints against the beast; and had been before that time exceedingly overcome, and were brought into a very low condition at that time, being new modeled, and having a great many precious saints in it, both eminent commanders, inferior officers, and common soldiers; and being then put under the conduct of Sir Thomas Fairfax; they then began to march against the enemy, and then had a Spirit of life from God, that entered into them, as did appear in all their actings afterward; for they went on with such vigor, courage, life, and fortitude, as they effected every work they took in hand; defeated all the enemies with whom they did encounter; had the victory in every battle they fought; never sat down before any city, town, or castle, but they took it in, before they raised their siege. Thus they acted like men raised from that dead, low condition they were in before. And why? Because now a

Spirit of life from God was entered into them: and unto God did they give all the praise, and so let them do still: for they had as surely fled before their enemies, and been beat down as the mire in the streets then, as ever they had been before, if the Spirit of life from God had not been put upon them.

Thus the 5th day of April, 1645, did the witnesses, the saints (of whom the beast thought to make an utter end) stand upon their feet having a Spirit of life from God put upon them; when the army that fought their battles, and defended their righteous cause, began to march against the army of the beast, to the overthrowing of it.

And they stood upon their feet, and great fear fell upon them that saw them.

The saints being raised from the dead, from that dejected, low condition in which they were, for three years and a half; a Spirit of life from God being put upon them: they then stood upon their feet, to the fear, and amazement of their enemies. Before indeed the saints did lie dead in the street, and were as the street to them that went over them: but since the Spirit of life from God entered into them, they have stood upon their feet; and as men that stand upon their feet, so long as they do stand upon their feet, are not in a capacity of being trod underfoot of men: So the witnesses, and saints of Jesus Christ, since they stood upon their feet, could not be trodden underfoot of men. Though they have been trodden underfoot a thousand two hundred, and threescore years, and the beast hath had power so long to trample them underfoot; yet since the Spirit of life from God entered into them, and they stood upon their feet, it was not possible for the beast, nor any of his adherents, so to trample them underfoot anymore.

And they stood upon their feet, and great fear fell upon them which saw them.

The witnesses standing upon their feet, as men risen from the dead, did cast a great fear and terror upon their enemies: for now they begin to fear what will become of themselves, and their great idol, the beast; they seeing the witnesses of Jesus to stand upon their feet, fearfulness doth surprise them because now they conceive that their kingdom is going down; as indeed it is going down wonderfully, as they did rejoice, and make merry, when they saw the saints, or Puritans, as they termed them, brought into a low condition, when they lay dead; so now on the contrary, they seeing these Puritans, the precious sons of Zion to stand upon their feet, now a fear, a great fear is fallen upon them.

13

THE HUMBLE PETITION OF
ELIZABETH LILBURNE,
WIFE TO LEUT. COLL. JOHN LILBURNE

Who hath been for above eleven weeks by past, most unjustly divorced from him, by the House of Lords, and their tyrannical officers, against the law of God, and (as she conceives) the law of the land*

To the chosen and betrusted knights, citizens, and burgesses, assembled in the High and Supreme Court of Parliament

. . . For the lords in a most tyrannical and barbarous manner . . . have since committed her husband, for about three weeks close prisoner to Newgate, locked him up in a little room, without the use of pen, ink, or paper. . . . [She cites the law in many instances, including Edward Coke, an eminent jurist.] For though they summoned him up to their bar, June 10, 1646, to answer a charge, yet they refused to show it him, or give him a copy of it, but committed him to Newgate June 11, 1646 . . . merely for refusing to answer to their Spanish Inquisition-like Interrogatories, and for delivering his legal protestation. . . . All which, she the rather earnestly desireth, because his imprisonment in the Tower is extraordinarily chargeable and insupportable . . . and also lost divers hundreds of pounds, the year he was a prisoner in Oxford Castle for you . . . do render the condition of your petitioner, her husband, and children, to be very nigh ruin and destruction.

*London, 1646. Wing L2077.

14

LOVE'S NAME LIVES

*OR A publication of divers petitions presented by Mistress Love
to the Parliament in behalf of her husband
with several letters that interchangeably passed between them
a little before his death**

Mary Love

*To the supreme authority, the Parliament of the
Commonwealth of England, the humble petition of Mary,
the distressed wife of Christopher Love*

Sheweth,

That whereas the High Court of Justice hath lately sentenced to death
her dear and tender husband, in whose life the life of your petitioner is
bound up; in the execution of which sentence your poor handmaid
should become an unhappy widow and the miserable mother of two
young, fatherless children: And she being so near to her appointed
hour, having sorrow upon sorrow, be forced through unexpressible
grief, to bow down in travail and give up the ghost; and so with one
blow there be destroyed both father and mother and babe in one day.

Yet her spirit is somewhat revived with the thought that there is hope
in Israel concerning this thing, when she considers that her humble
petition in this day presented before so many professing godliness, who
have tasted abundantly how gracious the Lord is, and who through
mercy are called of God to inherit a blessing and to be a blessing to the
afflicted in the midst of the land.

Therefore your distressed handmaid throwing herself in all humility

*London, 1663. Wing L3142, Reel 1234, pp. 1–2, 10–11.

To the Supreme Authority, the PARLIAMENT
of the Common-Wealth of ENGLAND.

The humble Petition of MARY, the distressed Wife of CHRISTOPHER LOVE.

Sheweth,

That whereas the High Court of Justice hath lately sentenced to death her dear and tender Husband, in whose life, the life of your Petitioner is bound up; in the execution of which sentence, your poor hand-maid should become an unhappy widow, and the miserable mother of two young fatherless children: And she being so near to her appointed hour, having sorrow upon sorrow, be forced, through unexpressable grief, to bow down in travell, and give up the ghost; and so with one blow, there be destroyed, both Father, and Mother, and Babe in one day.

Yet her spirit is somewhat revived with the thought that there is hope in *Israel* concerning this thing, when she considers, that her humble Petition is this day presented before so many professing godliness, who have tasted abundantly how gracious the Lord is, and who through mercy are called of God to inherit a blessing, and to be a blessing to the afflicted in the midst of the Land.

Therefore your distressed hand-maid, throwing her self in all humility at your feet, beseecheth you by the womb that bare you, and brests that gave you suck, in the bowels of the Lord Jesus Christ, mercifully to interpose, that this fatall blow may be prevented: which act of compassion in you, will be to your poor hand-maid as resurrection from the dead; and not only all the tender-hearted Mothers in *England*, but even the Babe yet unborn shall rise up and call you blessed; and this will be to you a glory, and crown of rejoycing in the sight of the Nation, when the blessing of them that are ready to perish shall come upon you. And your poor hand-maid humbly conceives, That your mercy herein will be no danger to the State, for that your poor Petitioners Friends are willing to give all sufficient security, that her Husband shall live peaceably and quietly for the time to come, and never act any thing to the prejudice of this Common-wealth, and present Government.

Now the God of heaven bow your hearts to shew mercy:
And your Petitioner shall pray, &c.
MARY LOVE.

To the Supreme Authority, the PARLIAMENT of the Commonwealth of ENGLAND.

The humble Petition of Mary, the Wife of Christopher Love, Condemned to dye.

Sheweth.

That whereas your distressed hand-maid hath in all humility, in the exceeding great bitterness of her spirit, poured out her very soul to this Honourable House, for the life of her condemned Husband: which Petition was mercifully received and read in Parliament (as your Petitioner is informed.) For which high favour she desireth to bless God, and be thankfull to your Honours. And although she hath great cause to be very sensible of your high displeasure against her Husband, for which she is heartily sorry; Nevertheless she hoping that your bowels yearn towards her in this her sad condition, adventures once more to make her humble supplication, and doth pray,

That if your poor Petitioners Husband hath provoked you so far, as to render him utterly uncapable of your full pardon; yet you would graciously be pleased to let your hand-maid find so
much

Figure 5. Page from *Love's Name Lives,* by Mary Love. Courtesy of University of Chicago Library, Department of Special Collections.

at your feet, beseecheth you by the womb that bore you and breasts that gave you suck, in the bowels of the Lord Jesus Christ, mercifully to interpose that this fatal blow may be prevented, which act of compassion in you will be to your poor handmaid as resurrection from the dead; and not only all the tenderhearted mothers in England, but even the babe yet unborn shall rise up and call you blessed; and this will be to you a glory and crown of rejoicing in the sight of the nation, when the blessing of them that are ready to perish shall come upon you. And your poor handmaid humbly conceives that your mercy herein will be no danger to the state, for that your poor petitioner's friends are willing to give all sufficient security that her husband shall live peaceably and quietly for the time to come, and never act anything to the prejudice of this commonwealth and present government.

> Now the God of heaven bow your hearts
> to show mercy: and your petitioner shall pray, etc.

> Mary Love

To the supreme authority, the Parliament of the Commonwealth of England, the humble petition of Mary, the wife of Christopher Love, condemned to die

Sheweth,

That whereas your distressed handmaid hath in all humility, in the exceeding great bitterness of her spirit poured out her very soul to this Honorable House, for the life of her condemned husband: which petition was mercifully received and read in Parliament (as your petitioner is informed). . . . And although she hath great cause to be very sensible of your high displeasure against her husband, for which she is heartily sorry; nevertheless, she hoping that your bowels yearn towards her in this her sad condition, adventures once more to make her humble supplication, and doth pray,

That if your petitioner's husband hath provoked you so far as to render him utterly incapable of your full pardon; yet you would graciously be pleased to let your handmaid find so much favor in your eyes as that you will say of your petitioner's dear husband, as Solomon said of Abiathar, though thou art worthy of death, we will not at this time put thee to death. Oh pardon your perplexed handmaid if she again beseech you by the wombs that bore you, and the breasts that gave you suck, in the bowels of the Lord Jesus Christ, reprieve him for a time, till she may recover her strength, before he depart hence and be seen no more, lest at one terrible stroke in his execution the lives of him, her, and the tender babe in her womb be cut off, and two poor innocent orphans be left behind to begin and end their days in misery. And though he may not be thought worthy to breathe in English air (which God forbid), yet give him, Oh give him leave to sigh out his sorrows under your displeasure in the utmost parts of the earth, wheresoever you shall think fit to banish him, which, although it be a very great punishment in itself, yet your handmaid and her dying husband shall acknowledge even this to be a great mercy, and shall thankfully receive it at your hands.

And shall pray, etc.

Mary Love

To the supreme authority, the Parliament of the Commonwealth of England, the humble petition of Mary, the wife of Christopher Love

Sheweth,

That your poor petitioner hath great cause to say, blessed be God, and blessed be you, for your merciful vote the 15th of July (a day never to be forgotten) in adding a month to the life of her dear husband, which hath opened a door of hope to her in the midst of the valley of Achor, and made her glad, though she be a woman of a sorrowful spirit: yet your distressed handmaid is overwhelmed with grief and anguish of soul and cannot be comforted, when she remembers the doleful day, the 15th of August, so near approaching, her heart doth almost die within her, and she is as one giving up the ghost before she is delivered of the fruit of her womb.

Wherefore your greatly distressed handmaid doth again pour out her soul with renewed and importunate requests, beseeching your Honors to commiserate her deplorable condition by putting on bowels of pity and compassion to her dear and condemned husband, that she may not grapple with the intolerable pains of travail and the unsupportable thoughts of her husband's death in one day. Oh that the life of your handmaid and her babe might be a ransom for the life of her condemned husband; she had rather choose out of love to die for him than for sorrow of heart to die with him. Now the good Lord incline your hearts to give him his life for a prey, wheresoever it shall please your Honors to cast him.

And your petitioner shall ever pray, etc.

Mary Love

Another of Mistress Love's to Master Love

My heavenly Dear,

I call thee so because God hath put heaven in thee, before he hath taken thee to heaven. Thou now beholdest God, Christ, and glory as in a glass; but tomorrow heaven-gates will be opened, and thou shalt be in the full enjoyment of all those glories which eye hath not seen, nor ear heard, neither can the heart of man understand. God hath now swallowed up thy heart in the thoughts of heaven; but erelong thou shalt be swallowed up in the enjoyment of heaven: And no marvel there should be such quietness and calmness in thy spirit, whilst thou art sailing in this tempestuous sea; because thou perceivest by the eye of faith a haven of rest, where thou shalt be richly laden with all the glories of heaven. O lift up thy heart with joy, when thou layest thy dear head on the block, in the thought of this, that thou art laying thy head to rest in thy father's bosom; which, when thou dost awake, shall be crowned, not with an earthly fading crown, but with an heavenly eternal crown of glory. . . . O let not one troubled thought for thy wife and babes arise within thee; thy God will be our God and our portion; he will be a husband to thy dear widow and father to thy children. . . . O let me hear how God bears up the heart, and let me taste of those comforts that support thee, that they may be pillars of marble to bear up my sinking spirit. I can write no more, Farewell, farewell my dear, till we meet there where we shall never bid farewell more; till which time I leave thee in the bosom of a loving, tenderhearted Father; and so I rest,

Till I shall forever rest in Heaven,

August 21, 1651   Mary Love

[Christopher Love was executed on August 22, 1651.]

15

IN PURSUIT OF THE KING[*]

Elizabeth Hooton

Friends,

My going to London hath not been for my own ends, but in obedience to the will of God, for it was laid before me, when I were on the sea, and in great danger of my life, that I should go before the King to witness for God, whether he would hear or no, and to lay down my life as I did at Boston, if it be required. And the Lord hath given me peace in my journey, and God hath so ordered that the taking away of my cattle hath been very serviceable, for by that means have I had great privilege to speak to the faces of the great men. They had no ways to cover their deceits nor send me to prison whatsoever, I said, because the oppression was laid before them, and there waited I for justice and judgment and equity, from day to day. So did this oppression ring over all the Court, and among the soldiers, and many of the citizens and countrymen and watermen that were at the Whitehall, and I labored among them both from morning till night, both great men and priests and all sorts of people that there were.

I followed the King with this cry, "I wait for justice of thee, O King, for in the country I have had no justice among the magistrates, nor sheriffs, nor bailiffs, for they have taken away my goods, contrary to the law." So did I open the grievances of our Friends all over the nation; the cry of the innocent is great, for they have made laws to persecute conscience; and I followed the King wheresoever he went with this cry, the cry of the innocent regard. I followed him twice to the tennis court, and spoke to him when he went up into his coach, after he had been at his sport; and some of them read my letters openly amongst the rest; the

[*]*Elizabeth Hooton, First Quaker Woman Preacher (1600-1672)*, ed. Emily Manners (London: Headley Brothers, 1914), pp. 36-37, 47-49.

King's coachman read one of my letters aloud and in some the witness of God was raised, to bear witness against the scoffers with boldness and courage, and confounded one of the guards that did laugh, and stop the mouths of the gainsayers, and they cry they were my disciples, and so great service there were for the Lord in these things.

I waited upon the King which way soever he went. I met him in the park and gave him two letters, which he took at my hand, but the people murmured because I did not kneel; but I went along by the King, and spoke as I went, but I could get no answer of my letters, so I waited for an answer many days, and watched for his going up into the coach in the Court. And some soldiers began to be favorable to me, and so let me speak to the King, and so the power of the Lord was raised in me, for I spoke freely to the King and Council that I waited for justice, and looked for an answer of what I have given into his hand. And the power of the Lord was risen in me, and the witness of God rose in many that did answer me; and some wicked ones said that it was of the devil, and some present made answer and said they were my disciples, because they answered on truth's behalf, and the power of the Lord was over them, and I had pretty time to speak what the Lord gave me to speak, till a soldier came and took me away and said it was the King's Court, and I might not preach there. But I declared through both courts as I went along, and they put me forth at the gates, and it came upon me to get a coat of sackcloth, and it was plain to me how I should have it; so we made that coat, and the next morning I were moved to go amongst them again at Whitehall in sackcloth and ashes. And the people was much strucken, both great men and women was strucken into silence. The witness of God was raised in many, and a fine time I had amongst them, till a soldier pulled me away and said I should not preach there; but I was moved to speak all the way I went up to Westminster Hall, and through the palace yard, a great way of it, declaring against the lawyers that were unjust in their places, and warning all people to repent; so are they left without excuse, if they had never more spoken to them, but the Lord is fitting others for the same purpose, but he made me an instrument to make way, that some others may follow in the same exercise. . . .

Elizabeth Hooton

London, the 17th of the 8th Month, 1662.

To the King and Council

This is to let you understand how I have been in service to God and to the King and his Commission in New England: My message for the Lord was to bear witness to his truth against those persecuting people who fled from the bishops because they would not suffer. And now in New England are become greater persecuters than the bishops were, both in fining, imprisoning, banishing, whipping, and hanging some of those that came out of England, for vagabond Quakers, who called their own country people vagabonds. And when the King sent his Commissioners amongst them, I was in that country, and oft had been imprisoned, oft whipped, oft driven into the wilderness among the wild beasts in the night; yet did God preserve me, though I had many miles in it to go amongst the wild beasts and many great waters. Now the King's Commission coming thither, they would not receive them so freely as our Friends did; and therefore they durst not trust their lives with them as they did with our Friends. And moreover they made a decree against them, to rise in four and twenty hours against them, to fight with them. And when I heard that, I went among several of their church members and warned them to take heed what they did, for if they did fight against them, they would destroy themselves, for there were enough that would take the King's Commissioners' parts; and I said to them, "You had better (as we have such an example) to suffer rather than fight, or else conform as some of your brethren in old England do; but if you do fight, you will destroy your country."

* * *

And many more things I would declare, but it would be too much answering the King's behalf. And now I am come hither for some justice and to have my goods restored again, which were taken away in my absence, or else my Friends restored out of prison, which never did the King nor the Council any harm. And so in love to all your souls, I have written this paper to let you know that by my going to New England, I was made serviceable to the King and his Commission. Therefore, reward not me evil for good, as some do threaten me; and let not our Friends be put into the hands of wicked and unreasonable men; nor into the hands of the priests who would destroy all that we have for tithes; that take tithes and make a spoil of their corn and keep their bodies in prison many over England. If they will have their tithes, let our Friends have their bodies at liberty to work for more; for husbandmen are impoverished much, and ready to throw up their farms by reason of tithes, taxes, and assessments, and great rents. And if husbandmen cast up their farms what will ye all do, for there is great oppression in the country and little money to be had for anything. The cattle and corn will not pay their rents and taxes and assessments; chimney money and excise is a great oppression. For the King I believe hath not the tenth part of what is taken, for when they are not able to pay their chimney money, they take away their bedding in the country. And so consider this, all ye that sit in authority, and let justice and equity be done in the country: for the Lord he will arise and he will plead the cause of the innocent.

I am a lover of your souls who came not hither in my own will.

Elizabeth Hooton

16

THE REWARD OF OPPRESSION, TYRANNY, AND INJUSTICE COMMITTED BY THE LATE KINGS AND QUEENS OF ENGLAND, AND OTHERS, BY THE UNLAWFUL ENTRY AND UNLAWFUL DETAINER OF THE DUTCHIE LANDS OF LANCASTER

Declared in the case of Samuel Beck, an infant, and directed to His Highness, Oliver, Lord Protector of England, and to the Honorable His Privy Council *

Margaret Beck, Widow, Late Wife of Nevil Beck, Mother and Guardian of the Infant

**To His Highness Oliver,
Lord Protector of England, etc.**

May it please your Highness

To look upon the case of the poor child concerning his title to the lands of the Duchy of Lancaster.

It hath pleased God, that the power of justice is now devolved on your Highness, and the most honorable Privy Council. And you are now the fountain thereof.

King Ed. 4 and his Council, heard the cause of the masters and poor brethren of the hospital of St. Leonard's in York, complaining that Sir Hugh Hastings, John Wombel, and others, withdrew from them a great

*London, 1656. Wing B1649, Reel 1195.

part of their living, which consisted chiefly upon the having of a thrave of corn of each plowland in the counties of York, Westmoreland, Cumberland, and Lancashire, and for which they, being very poor men, were not able to sue for at the Common Law: Rotulo pat. de An. 8. E. 4. Part 3. memb. 14, and yet they had for that hospital a special Act of Parliament made for them, to give them action in that very case: 2 Hen. Cap. 2.

That there are many precedents in the like case, where the single person and his Privy Council heard and determined causes for the poor against oppression, she makes bold to offer this to your Highness with confidence, because heretofore you knew her poor husband, and have pitied his case, and have been a friend to him out of your bounty and goodness.

May it please your Highness, she is so poor, that she is fain by her needle to maintain herself and poor child, hardly.

Therefore her humble petition is, that your Highness will be pleased to order her a hearing in the behalf of her child, before your Highness, and your Privy Council, in this case; and to assign her Counsel, and in the meantime out of your bounty and goodness to allow her for the present maintenance for her child, a petition as it hath pleased your Highness graciously to afford to others; and the prayers of the widow and fatherless will be for your Highness's happiness, etc.

To the Right Honorable the Lords of His Highness's Most Honorable Privy Council

The humble petition of Margaret Beck, widow, humbly showeth,

That in all ages extraordinary causes were heard and determined before the single person and his Privy Council, as in the case of Bogo de Clare, notwithstanding he was dismissed out of Parliament for error in the complaint; yet the King commanded him by Writ ad faciendum recipiendum quod per Regem concilium fuerit faciendum: and so proceed to a reexamination of the whole cause 18. E. 1.

And in the case of Elizabeth, the widow of Nicolas Audley, against James Audley concerning her dowry, 4. E. 3. . . . .

Henry the 4. after his coronation created Thomas Beaufort Earl of Dorset, and gave him 20£. per An. out of the exchequer, for maintaining the King's Title to the Crown, both at home and abroad, and also made a Charter of the Dukedom of Lancaster, to the second House of Lancaster in expectancy, which then was the Earl of Dorset, who after the decease of H. 4 by virtue of the Charter did enter into the Dukedom, and did enjoy the same nine years in the reign of H. 5 and six years in the reign of H. 6 and being lawfully thereof seized, died without issue, after whose decease the said Dukedom descended to the next heir at the common Law, which was Joan Countess of Westmoreland, his sister, who had issue George Nevil Lord Latimer, who had Sir Henry Nevil, who had issue Richard Lord Latimer, and Thomas Nevil twins, Richard died without issue; Thomas had issue Elizabeth his only daughter and heir, who intermarried with Wil. Beck, Esq. who had issue Sam. Beck, who had issue Nevil Beck, who had issue Sam. Beck, an Infant now living.

H. 6 contrary to the Charter made by H. 4 entered by intrusion, for which the quarrel began between the Houses of York and Lancaster.

E. 4 conquered H. 6 and entered upon all his lands as escheated, because he found the lands of the Dukedom of Lancaster in his possession, he kept that also for his better strength and security, and died; who had issue Edward and Richard, infants, murdered in their infancy by Richard 3 who usurped both the Crown and the Lands of the Dukedom of Lancaster.

H. 7, who had been banished, came into England with forces only to claim the Earldom of Richmond, and fought with, and killed R.3 and took upon him the Crown, and also entered upon the Dukedom of Lancaster, taking his precedent from R. 3, E. 4, and H. 6 and kept it all his time, and left it to H. 8.

In the first year of Mary an office was found, after the death of Elizabeth, daughter of the Lord Latimer and wife of William Beck, whereby Samuel Beck, grandfather to this infant, was found heir to the Dukedom of Lancaster, as heirs to his mother who had been lamentably persecuted, and constrained to flee from place to place, for fear of being burnt for heresy (as they called it) by that cruel woman Queen Mary.

This office was prosecuted and bound by one Heath, father-in-law to Samuel Beck, the grandfather, he being an infant, and at school at Westminster, and in the third year of Philip and Mary, Samuel Beck being under nine years of age, was seized by warrant, and delivered to Rixam, a Romish Priest, to be bred up in the Romish religion (the Queen then pretending love to him being her kinsman) and he must be carried away from all his honorable kindred, and there must be called

Heath after his father-in-law's name, hoping by this cheat to defraud the Office, and that he was not that party found heir in the Office.

When that Queen died, Heath found out the child, and bred him at Oxford, and matriculated him by the right name of Beck: and when he came to be capable of the ministry, Queen Elizabeth gave him two great benefices in Devonshire and Cornwall, with which preferment he contented himself until much importuned by many of his noble kindred, and especially the then Earl of Worcester, to challenge his right to the Dukedom of Lancaster; where upon he made his application to Queen Elizabeth by petition, who answered that the Dukedom was cast upon her without her means or procurement, and that she desired to have him advanced to his right and dignity, he being so near allied to her, and ordered that no more grant of the Duchy lands should pass until it was tried in Parliament, and also offered him great honor and dignity in the Church of England; but before it was determined in Parliament, the Queen died.

Then he petitioned King James for a hearing in Parliament, and to assign him Counsel, who did (viz.) Sergeant Harris, Sergeant Jones, Mr. Dyett, and Mr. George Crook, and then contrary to law committed him close prisoner, without ink or paper, and so kept him in prison until a little before his death, that the King intended to call a Parliament, and being fearful that the horrible piece of tyranny would be questioned, he released him, and promised him fair (as he knew well enough how to dissemble, and called it nothing but King-craft) but performed nothing during his life. And after his death, it being told King James that the Duke of Lancaster was dead, he answered, "God have mercy on Charles and his issue, for he had done the Duke of Lancaster mickle [much] wrong, and that he (meaning Mr. Beck) had left a heavy curse behind him"; which were King James his own words; for it was Mr. Beck's custom when he spake with the King to desire God to deal by the King and his, as the King had dealt with him. Shortly after King James died.

Then Nevil Beck being in his travels beyond the seas came back to claim his right to the Dukedom of Lancaster of King Charles, who delayed him, and would not consent to a hearing, whereupon Nevil Beck desired 400£ per Annum for his maintenance for the present; but the King answered that if he gave him that, it would enable Nevil Beck to make a case of it, and so go to Law with him; whereupon some high words of discontent passed from Nevil Beck in relation to this wrong, that the King in fury caused him to be put out of the Court Gates, and gave order that porters should not suffer him to come in at any time after, which caused Nevil Beck to use these words to the King's servants, "I do believe I shall live to see him turned out, and that neither he nor his shall have anything to do with this house," meaning Whitehall.

Then Nevil Beck petitioned the Lords and Commons of the late long Parliament to hear his case, who deferred the hearing of it, telling him that he must first get an allowance from the King, who was then at Oxford in open hostility against the Parliament; and unless that were first done they could not give allowance to his Bill, which how impossible that was to be done let the world judge; and after the King's execution they answered him, that they had pulled down the house of York, and abolished Kingship, and therefore it would be dangerous to set up the house of Lancaster; but issued out to him some small sums at several times, which kept him only from starving, and also forbade the sale of the Duchy Lands, and after his death issued out 20£ to the use of his Son Samuel Beck, the Infant, by way of acknowledgment.

The Duchy Lands were unsold until the assembly after at Westminster (who voted themselves a Parliament) ordained the sale of the Duchy Lands.

The answer of His Highness Most Honorable Privy Council,
to the case of Samuel Beck, as followeth.

John of Gaunt had the Dukedom of Lancaster by his first wife, heir of Henry, Duke of Lancaster, pag. 326.

By that first wife he had H. 4 and Philip [Philippa] married to John King of Portugal, and Elizabeth married to John Holland Duke of Exeter, and afterwards to Sir John Cornwall.

But Thomas Earl of Dorset came from Katharine Swinford the third wife, so did Joan Beufort married to the Earl of Westmoreland, from whom Beck claims pag. 327.

And pag. 328 it is said that H. 4 united the Dutchie to the Crown which himself held, and H. 5 and H. 6 which are true heirs to it.

Neither is it likely that H. 4 would pass it to a female descended from Katharine Swinford, who had divers sons himself pag. 992. Joan Beufort, sister of Thomas Beufort of Dorset, was second wife of Ralph Nevil Earl of Westmoreland, and this Earl had a son called Richard Nevil Earl of Salisbury, in right of his wife, and he had issue first Richard Nevil the King-maker, and six daughters, from whom came the Earl of

Derby, Earl of Arundel, the Lord Beuchamp, the Earl of Huntingdon, the Earl of Pembrook and Montgomery, he had also a ninth son called William Nevil, Lord Falconberg after Earl of Kent, whose three daughters married Coyners Strange waies, and Bedbaring, and a twelfth was George Nevil, Lord Latimer (whom the printed paper cites) which Barony his father purchased with the Lands of Latimer, and bestowed them on his son George, Lord Latimer from whom Beck claims in the papers.

But how can anything descend on the daughter of this Lord Latimer from Joan Beufort, when all the families before mentioned, Derby, Arundel, etc. descend from the elder son of Joan Beufort by marriage with his daughters, and George Latimer was the twelfth son of that eldest son.

The reply of Margaret Beck widow, Mother and Guardian to the Infant

It is true, that John of Gaunt had the Dukedom of Lancaster by his first wife, and that he had H. 4 and two daughters by the first wife as is expressed in the paper.

And that Thomas Earl of Dorset, and Joan de Beufort came of the body of Katharine Swinford his third wife.

As to pag. 328 the paper saith, it is said that H. 4 united the Dukedom of Lancaster to the Crown, which proves nothing, but it will be proved that H. 4 was so far from uniting of it to the Crown, that he made a Charter of the Dukedom, and confirmed it by act of Parliament to Thomas de Beufort in expectancy after his death, and that after his death Thomas did enter, and did enjoy it all the time of H. 5 and six years in the time of H. 6 and in all that time let Lease, and granted Estates.

And for that it was unlikely that H. 4 would pass it to a female, which is no proof; for Beck's case is not that H. 4 passed it to a female, but that Thomas dying without issue, Joan was his next heir at the common Law.

And it doth appear by the grants made by H. 4 to Thomas de Beufort that he esteemed him above all others of his family, for in the grants it is for maintaining his Title to the Crown both at home and abroad, and so might very well trust him to keep up his children's title to the Crown after his decease.

Also, it appears by record that H. 4 created him Earl of Dorset, and afterwards Duke of Exeter, and after that this grant of the Reversion of the Dukedom of Lancaster thereby the more to enable him to maintain his children's title to the Crown.

It doth not appear that Ralph Nevil had any more children by Joan de Beufort, his second wife, than George Nevil Lord Latimer, and Cicilia, afterwards married to Richard Plantagenet Duke of York, from whom the Stuarts family descended, but it must needs be that the children of Ralph Nevil were of his first wife, otherwise how could it be found in the office after the death of Latimer, and wife of Beck, that her child was heir to Joan Countess of Westmoreland, and so to Thomas Earl of Dorset, and Duke of Lancaster. All this appeared by the copies of the records allowed by King James taken out of the Tower, Court of wards, and Herald's office, when King James assigned the child's grandfather counsel.

Notwithstanding all this the mother and guardian of the child do submit to the Lord Protector and his Privy Council, to deal with her and her poor child as they shall please, whereupon the child was sent to Eton College to be bred there at school, to eat the bread given by H. 6 who first intruded on the Duchy Lands; but the Privy Council would not hear any further in the case.

Observations

Henry 6 entered first by intrusion of the Duchy Lands of Lancaster after the death of Thomas de Beufort Earl of Dorset, and Duke of Lancaster and Exeter, and was afterwards conquered by E. 4, taken prisoner, and murdered in prison, and so lost the Duchy Lands, Crown and Life. Also, E. 4 kept it by wrong all his life, who was wicked in murders, and adultery. He caused his brother George Duke of Clarence to be drowned in a Butt of Malmsey, his adultery with Jane Shore and others, and had wars all his time, with those who took part with the house of Lancaster, his two sons after his death murdered in the Tower by R. 3. The children are paid for the sins of the father.

R. 3 would not part with it until H. 7 killed him at Bosworth field where his body was disgracefully drawn to Lecester, and there buried basely.

H. 7 entered upon the Duchy Lands and sold much of it, and made abundance of money by that and unlawful taxes upon the people, as a most wicked tyrant, and left it to his son H. 8 who as wickedly spent it as his father got it, and left E. 6 his son, who died an infant, and Mary his eldest daughter, who wickedly persecuted her sister Elizabeth. She reigned all her time in a bloody persecution, and died; all three children of H. 8 reigning successively one after the other, and dying childless, a curse upon that line.

King James entered upon the Lands of the Dukedom left unsold and kept it by oppression, died unnaturally by poison, as hath been apparently proved, and left King Charles, who refused to restore the lands or give any satisfaction: His end most miserable, arraigned, condemned, and executed at his own door, his wife and children constrained to live on alms, in strange countries: And for the members of the late long Parliament, they were disgracefully turned out of that power: And lastly, for the Assembly who called themselves a Parliament, break up themselves in confusion, oppression, and injustice, visibly punished in this very case.

It is observed by good historians that from the body of John of Gaunt Duke of Lancaster have descended lineally one Empress, 32 Christian Kings and Queens, 2 Cardinals, 10 Princes and Princesses, and 49 Dukes and Duchesses, etc., as from another Abraham, whereof this infant Samuel Beck is the last only heir of that line left in England. The Stuarts family is also descended from the second house of Lancaster, in expectancy from Joan Countess of Westmoreland, the daughter of John of Gaunt, but their descent is by her youngest daughter the Lady Cecilia, who intermarried with Richard Plantagenet Duke of York, who had E. 4 and R. 3, but Samuel Beck is lineally descended from George the son of Joan Countess of Westmoreland, who was brother of the whole blood to Cecilia, Duchess of York, and the issue of the son, in right of his mother, is to be answered before the issue of the daughter; which clears the case for Samuel Beck the infant.

17

THE CASE BETWEEN
A FATHER AND HIS CHILDREN*

Elinor James

Humbly Represented to the Honorable Lord Mayor
and Court of Aldermen

My Lord,

Since God's providence hath so highly advanced you to that honor and dignity as to be in some measure a father to this city, that hath been famous for loyalty, justice, and equity; and I, knowing your Lordship to be so good, that you hate to do anything that should lessen the grandeur, or to encourage rebellion or disobedience, and I question not but your Brethren the Aldermen are of the same mind: Therefore I thought I could not apply myself to any fitter persons than your Worships, neither can I expect that any should consider my case so well as your Honor. I beseech your Lordship to pardon me in giving you this trouble, it is the great love I bear to unity, and the consideration that I am a mother of children, and in some part am sensible of the excellency of obedience, and how it prevails over the hearts of parents; so that thereby they are instrumental to obtain the blessing of God spiritual and temporal; but what a lamentable case it is when children are disobedient and rebellious, it provokes the wrath of God and man, and makes them miserable in this world and the world to come, without repentance. The serious consideration of this hath caused me to present to your Lordship, and the Aldermen your Brethren, a case between a father and his children.

There is a certain friend of mine that lives near me, whose virtue and

*London, 1682. Wing J416, Reel 498.

patience is known to all the neighborhood, and that he is the most
indulgent father, and loveth his children extraordinary; therefore he
thought himself happy and did not question their assistance when he
stood in need thereof, but the children taking no notice of his necessity,
he was compelled to crave their assistance; but the children finding
their father in necessity, they dealt subtly, and said amongst themselves,
we will deal by him as we please, and he shall condescend to our proposals, for who knows whether our father hath walked according to the
rules of law or no, and if not, we will get advantage thereby, and so we
will not allow any succor to our father, nay not so much as respect them
that love him, neither shall they succor him, but we'll hate them with a
mortal hatred that shall either lend him, or give him anything; nay
moreover, our father shall not sell anything, for we will count them our
great enemies that shall buy anything; so we are resolved to humble our
father, to comply with our desires, or to make of him miserable, in not
ministering to his necessities: But God, that overrules all things, took
pity of this good father, and indued him with patience to bear it, and the
Lord helped him, and when his children were a little peaceable and
quiet, he thought with himself, I will try whether my children walk by
the law or no; if they do, certainly I shall have justice done me, for the
law of God and man is on my side; for they both exhort to love and
obedience: But when the father proposed this question, though it was
with mildness and sweetness, they were so far from acknowledging their
faults, that they would right themselves by the law; and though they
would not assist their father in his necessity, yet they could find cash
to encourage the lawyers. But I'll appeal to your Lordship and your
Brethren, whether these children are not unkind and ungrateful?
Should not they rather humble themselves, and acknowledge their
faults, and amend it for the time to come? For they may very well think
that their father is wise, and would not take any notice of anything,
before he had good ground. Therefore I beseech you for the Lord's sake
to favor me so much as not to despise my poor weak endeavors, who
longs for a unity between the father and his children, but cannot be so
happy without your Lordship and the Aldermen your Brethren's assistance; and through you and by you I do not question but to obtain it.
Therefore I beseech you for the Lord's sake, to use all pious endeavors to
make up this breach and to decide this controversy, for blessed are the
peacemakers; undoubtedly my Lord, thrice blessed will you be to be
instrumental in his peace, for this end Christ took humanity upon him,

to make reconciliation between God and man, so that they might be able to cry, Abba Father. These children hath been naturally good, but only too much inclined to hearken to the whisperings of Satan and his instruments, to incense them against their father, as he did in the beginning with our first parents, to make themselves miserable by their disobedience. So Satan envies these their happiness, and therefore persuades them to disobedience; thinking thereby to make them miserable and wretched: for it is seldom known that an unkind child to a temporal father was ever counted an obedient servant to God, if not obedient then rebellious. What against heaven? Then God's hand will be against them, which the Lord of his mercy prevent, shall be always the prayers of

Your humble servant and soul's well-wisher,

Elinor James

PART FOUR

WOMEN WRITING ABOUT LOVE AND MARRIAGE

Introduction

"but one mind throughout our lives . . ."

Although there were conflicting theological views on the nature of love and marriage in the sixteenth and seventeenth centuries (Roman Catholics considered marriage a sacrament, the sect of Antinomian Ranters advocated free love, and Anglicans, Puritans, and various sects positioned themselves somewhere in between), males regarded marriage as the only vocation for a woman, and females seemed to agree, or at least they acquiesced. A woman's life was societally defined: it consisted of three stages—virginity, marriage, and widowhood. *The Lawes Resolutions of Womens Rights* (1632) summarizes the legal, social, and theological implications of the place in society assigned to women:

> . . . in this consolidation which we call wedlock is a locking together. It is true, that man and wife are one person, but understand in what manner.
>
> When a small brook or little river incorporateth with Rhodanus, Humber or the Thames, the poor rivulet loseth her name; it is carried and recarried with the new associate; it beareth no sway; it possesseth nothing during coverture. A woman as soon as she is married is called "covert"; in Latin "nupta," that is "veiled"; as it were clouded and overshadowed; she hath lost her stream. I may more truly, far away, say to a married woman, her new self is her superior, her companion, her master. . . .
>
> All [women] are understood either married, or to be married, and their desires are subject to their husbands. . . . the common law here shaketh hand with divinity. (124–25, 126)

Since marriage was what every woman was preparing for—or being prepared for—it is not surprising to discover that courtship could in certain instances be traumatic. Generally seen as a period of delight and anticipation, courtship could turn into a time of anxiety and frustration, even despair. A female could find herself tormented by love or by lovers. If she resisted marriage to a person she did not love, she suffered psychological stress and parental displeasure. On the other hand, she might discover that courtship was a process of growth that found its deepest fulfillment in marriage.

The complicating factor in courtship, of course, is the nature of love itself. Love between the sexes was expected to create harmony in the body and soul of the lovers, but sometimes it destroyed physical, psychological, and spiritual equanimity. Although love between the sexes is difficult to define, Edward Reynolds in *Treatise of the Passions* (1650) describes it as "the inmost and most visceral affection" (109). A physical affection, by its definition, can cause both harmony and disequilibrium in the body and soul of the lover. The ancient physician Aretaeus the Cappadocian defined love as "an unrestrainable impulse to connection" (*Extant Works,* 288). This definition admits stress and turbulence into the life of the person affected by love.

According to medical theorists of the sixteenth and seventeenth centuries, the "unrestrainable impulse to connection" had its source in the physical nature of the lover. Liver, brain, and heart were affected by and involved in this type of love, according to the French physician Jacques Ferrand, who wrote a holistic treatise on the disturbing effects of love. Since love between the sexes could endanger the vital organs and the life processes, a human being had to exercise caution in love. It was understood by theorists, as well as by those who experienced love firsthand, that love could be disorienting; that body, mind, soul, and volition were coconspirators in love, inflicting both physical and spiritual disorder on the lovers. The irony is that lovers conspired in their own distress and delight.

The poetry, prose fiction, and drama of these centuries abound with descriptions of love, lovers, and the ecstasy, disquietude, and pain of being in love. Convulsions of the heart, the violence of desire, the immense power of beauty—these are common themes in fictive literature. It is difficult, however, to uncover similar accounts in the nonfictive writing of the era. The diaries, letters, and autobiographies of women do discuss, as might be expected, love and its polarity: the effects of love and occasionally this polarity appear in individual female accounts of courtship days. But it is in the medical case histories that the stresses of courtship are diagnosed and charted. The seventeenth-century physician Richard Napier, for example, treated both men and

STRESS, ANXIETY, AND FAMILY LIFE

Nature of Complaint	Males	Females	Totals
All courtship	63	118	181
Lovers' problems	51	90	141
Patients in love	35	37	72
Lovers' quarrels	15	44	59
Jilted lovers	3	20	23
Seduced and betrayed	0	4	4
Other premarital sex	8	5	13
Marriage broken off	17	42	59
No culprit/lovers blamed	7	12	19
Parents object	6	15	21
"Friends" object	3	14	17
Master/Mistress objects	1	2	3

Note: Because some cases included more than one stress, they have been counted only once in the totals (MacDonald, 89).

women who suffered agony during courtship, agony of such emotional and physical intensity as to cause the sufferers to go to a physician for diagnosis, treatment, and cure. According to Michael MacDonald in *Mystical Bedlam,* "Lovers' quarrels, unrequited love, and double-dealing accounted for the emotional turmoil of 141 persons [in Napier's practice], about two-thirds of whom were young women (see table); another 40 patients mentioned that they had been in love before they were married. These young people suffered the unmistakable pangs of romantic love" (89).

Dorothy Osborne, a Royalist, and William Temple, a Puritan, were in love at a time when Royalists and Puritans were at war with one another. This love was a combination that inevitably produced stress. Osborne's correspondence with Temple reveals much about her love, but it also admits to struggles with despair over their ever marrying. Faced with opposition from both families, they persevered and remained constant in their love for each other. Finally they were permitted to marry in 1655.

In her letters Osborne captures the various emotional states that she experienced in her lengthy courtship:

Dear! shall we ever be so happy, think you? Ah! I dare not hope it. Yet 'tis not want of love gives me these fears. No, in earnest, I think (nay, I am sure) I love you more than ever, and 'tis that only gives me these despairing thoughts; when I consider how small a proportion of happiness is allowed in this world, and how great mine would be in a person for whom I have a passionate kindness, and who has the same for me. (221)

My heart has failed me twenty times since you went, and, had you been within my call, I had brought you back as often, though I know thirty miles' distance and three hundred are the same thing. (223)

Good God! what an unhappy person am I. . . . . If your father would but in some measure satisfy my friends that I might but do it in any justifiable manner, you should dispose me as you pleased, carry me whither you would, all places of the world would be alike to me where you were, and I should not despair of carrying myself so towards him as might deserve a better opinion from him. (266)

Theirs was a long marriage with undiminished love. Dorothy died in 1695, William in 1699.

Although Frances Coke left no diary or letters, historical records reveal much about the trauma that she experienced in courtship and marriage. Forced by her father, Sir Edward Coke, to marry Sir John Villiers, who was twelve years her senior, she was the prisoner of her father's attempts to regain favor with King James I. The fact that she could not love Sir John Villiers (he was a most unsuitable partner because he suffered from frequent bouts of insanity) was regarded as irrelevant by her father. His daughter, he asserted, owed him submission in these affairs, as in all others, and Frances was whipped into submission to marriage in 1617 at age fourteen. Her life then became a history of love for Sir Robert Howard, a love (labeled adulterous) that brought her into political, religious, and legal entanglements. She spent most of her tumultuous life escaping from her husband and living with Sir Robert Howard. Their life together was marred by public humiliation, imprisonment, and banishment. Frances died at Oxford in 1645, still in love with someone to whom she was never legally married.

As for marriage, Sara Mendelson tabulates the records of marriages that are described in diaries and memoirs of women in the Stuart period:

Of the twenty-three women [diarists], two remained spinsters. (Incidentally, to all appearances, both were perfectly happy in their maiden state.) Of the twenty-one women who married, four of them married twice, making a total of twenty-five unions. Four of these marriages do not offer sufficient information for our purposes. Among the twenty-one remaining ones, there were fifteen loving and companionable marriages, and six unsatisfactory marriages. Although it might appear that the numbers are biased in favour of happy unions because loving husbands would have preserved their wives' manuscripts, this tendency is sufficiently balanced by those disgruntled wives who wrote their memoirs in order to vilify their husbands. There does not seem to be an obvious explanation for the high proportion of happy unions. In thirteen of the twenty-one marriages, however, there is some information about the circumstances in which these unions were contracted. Eight happy marriages included the following patterns: two love matches in which parents were displeased but finally gave consent; three cases of free choice (two were second marriages); two arranged marriages with a clear veto allowed to the bride; one arranged marriage in which the bride was only 13. Five unhappy unions included the following circumstances: one elopement; two forced marriages; the two marriages of Lady Anne Clifford, of which the first was arranged, and the second her own choice. (193)

A well-known "loving and companionable" marriage was that of Lady Ann Fanshawe, who married Sir Richard Fanshawe in 1644(5?). Her *Memoirs* show that she shared a lifelong happiness with her husband, and her love for Sir Richard helped her to face with poise the life of a married woman. She had fourteen pregnancies and miscarried with triplets; she frequently moved with her husband on his diplomatic missions for the king; she visited her husband in prison and petitioned for his release; she was forced to sell possessions in order to return to England after her husband's death in Madrid. Writing to her only surviving son about the depth of her love for her husband, she speaks with the sincerity that characterizes her *Memoirs:* "Glory be to God we never had but one mind throughout our lives, our souls were wrapped up in each other, our aims and designs one, our loves one, and our resentments one. We so studied one the other that we knew each other's mind by our looks; whatever was real happiness, God gave it me in him. But to commend my better half (which I want sufficient expression for) methinks is to commend myself, and so may bear a censure; but might it be permitted, I could dwell eternally in his praise most justly" (5–6).

On the other hand, there is Lady Anne Clifford, whose diary records her two unhappy marriages. Married first in 1609 to Richard Sackville, earl of Dorset, she describes her new life in candid entries:

All this time my lord [her husband] was in London, where he had all and infinite great resort coming to him. He went much abroad to cocking, to bowling alleys, to plays and horse races, and commended by all the world. I stayed in the country, having many times a sorrowful and heavy heart, and being condemned by most folks because I would not consent to the agreements. So as I may truly say, I am like an owl in the desert. (April 12, 1616)

The 20th, being Easter Day, my lord and I . . . received the communion by Mr. Ran. Yet in the afternoon my lord and I had a great falling out. . . . (April 20, 1617)

This night my lord should have lain with me, but he and I fell out about matters. (April 23, 1617)

After Dorset's death in 1624, Lady Anne remained a widow for six years, remarrying in 1630. Her second marriage, to Philip Herbert, earl of Pembroke and Montgomery, was no happier than her first. Most of her life with her two husbands was spent in legal wrangling and harassment over her property. Upon Herbert's death in 1649, she finally regained her property and achieved happiness in her second widowhood. The remainder of her life was spent apart from the oppression of patriarchy and in the presence of poets, architects, sculptors, and with poor widows, to whom she gave a residence and with whom she dined once a week.

The Holy Life of Mrs Elizabeth Walker was published posthumously by her husband in 1690. Throughout her marriage Elizabeth Walker kept a diary, which she made her husband promise not to read while she was alive. *The Holy Life* is a collaboration of husband and dead wife: in it he indicates Elizabeth's words by putting them in quotation marks. Her diary entries (which include descriptions of the plague of 1665, the great fire of 1666, and her eleven pregnancies and miscarriages) are interrupted by her husband when he reflects on the love they felt for each other. In an account reminiscent of Shakespeare's *Henry IV, Part I,* where Kate asks Hotspur, "Do you not love me? Do you not, indeed? / Well, do not then; for since you love me not, / I will not love myself. Do you not love me?" (II.iii.96–98), Elizabeth Walker's husband writes: "She would often come into my study to me, and when I have asked her what she would have, she would reply, 'Nothing, My Dear, but to ask thee how thou dost, and see if thou wantest anything?' and then with an endearing smile would say, 'Dost thou love me?' to which I replied,

Figure 6. Lady Anne Clifford, wife of Richard Sackville, Third Earl of Dorset. From the portrait at Knole by Mytens. Reproduced from *The Diary of the Lady Anne Clifford* (1923).

'Most dearly'; 'I know it abundantly,' would she answer, 'to my comfort, but I love to hear thee tell me so' " (54). This account, although it gives a male perspective on marriage, does indicate that for Elizabeth Walker love was the linking structure of a happy marriage.

The first letter that appears in this section is anonymous. It seems to be a genre piece, much in vogue at the time, and is probably not an actual account by a "debauched" lady. The publisher, however, in his preface to Volume I, says that these letters were sent to him by the Penny Post after he had published *The Adventures of Olinda*. He insists that he has made no alterations or additions.

The second volume, from which this letter is taken, includes the *Memoirs of Eloisa and Abelard,* with one long letter purportedly written by Eloisa (and, obviously, not received by the Penny Post). There is a letter from Phryne to Eugenia against marriage; a letter from a "Sylvia"; a letter signed "Artemisia." The women were either disguising themselves by taking on pseudonyms or writing letters designed for publication in these volumes, or perhaps the letters were written by the publisher and a collaborator.

This particular letter, written by a jilted woman whose love remained constant in spite of abandonment by her lover, is a plea that her lover spare other women the ruin he has inflicted on her. Her concern for other women reveals the fears that invaded female lives in courtship. Although poets like John Donne wrote about the inconstancy of women in the male fashion of the time, this letter gives a woman an opportunity to speak for all young women. She portrays the devastating power of male inconstancy with more accuracy than males portrayed female inconstancy in their poetic fictions.

Lady Anne Halkett left a detailed account of her courtships and marriage. She describes her years of courtship as erratic and prolonged. Her first love, for Thomas Howard, created an upheaval in her family and consequently in her own life. Although Thomas Howard was from a distinguished family, he was without financial resources. A marriage to him would have been economically disastrous for both families and both parties.

Anne writes the story of her life (which is alternately titled *Autobiography* or *Memoirs,* depending on the editor) with narrative suspense, clearly regarding herself as an active participant in an exciting drama. Never self-deprecating, although she was deceived by two lovers, she describes her first love affair with the freshness of one who has just experienced it. Using dialogue, she attempts to capture both her own emotions and his in their encounters. She reports Thomas Howard's confessions of love for her, his emotional states in approaching her, and his promises of undying love. These states were marked by medically recognizable symptoms: he was "much disordered," "pale as death"; he had shortness of breath and trembling hands; and on one occasion his declaration and pleading were accompanied by his fainting for love (she responded with kisses).

Her own emotions were caught between adamant material opposition to the match and the suffering and credibility of her lover. Her mother, however, recognizing the vulnerability of a young woman, took precautions to prevent her daughter from an imprudent decision. Anne was guarded at night by another person sleeping in her room; she was forbidden to see Thomas Howard ever again. Anne used equivocation as a strategy in this courtship; rather than disobey her mother, she said good-bye to him blindfolded.

Anne's love for Thomas Howard caused a rift in mother-daughter relations, with the mother refusing to speak to the daughter (except to scold her) for fourteen months. When Thomas Howard returned to England, he abandoned his vow never to marry anyone other than Anne and was wed to another woman. Anne does not fail to report that his marriage was known to be an unhappy one.

Anne was unfortunate in another love affair, this time with Colonel Joseph Bamfield. She met him during wartime and collaborated with him in several daring maneuvers on behalf of the Royalist cause, even helping the duke of York to escape to the Continent. Although she seems to have lived with Colonel Bamfield under the promise of marriage (he alleged that his wife was dead) during these ambiguous times, she did not marry him, for, as she discovered later to her great dismay, he already had a wife who was very much alive.

After the war she became a governess in the household of Sir James Halkett, a widower. In 1656, at the age of thirty-four, she married him, attesting to the clear direction of God in this important choice. They lived together happily for twenty years. When her husband died, leaving her with insufficient funds to support the family, she brought upper-class children into her home and taught them. Later her financial crisis was eased when James II provided her with an income for helping him in the English Civil War.

Anne Halkett's voice throughout the *Autobiography* rises above the

exigencies of female life. She was able to chronicle her life with a remarkable absence of vindictiveness because she did not allow herself,
even though she was a woman, to be maligned, humiliated, or defeated.
(For an account of her medical work during the war, see part 5.)

Mary Boyle Rich, countess of Warwick, remembers the anguish it
cost her to disobey her father when he arranged for her to marry James
Hambletone. No matter how much she wished to please her father and
how much he wished to secure her financial future, she could not marry
a man for whom she had so extraordinary an aversion. She remarks
that she was only thirteen or fourteen years old at the time.

Her life after this refusal was difficult. She was moved to London by
her father, where she was courted by many men. Again her candor
surfaces in her diary: she admits to "an aversion to marriage." After
a desperate courtship, she gained her father's permission to marry
Charles Rich, although his fortune was inadequate and his future as a
younger son uncertain. Mary's father relented so much as to give her a
dowry of £7,000 a year. Later, and quite unexpectedly, Charles Rich
became the earl of Warwick and inherited the large Warwick estate.
(Upon his death, he left the estate to Mary.)

Her diary entries for the early years of her life give insight into the
marriage patterns of the day. Her brother and Thomas Howard fought
a duel over a woman; Thomas Howard won and married the woman.
Another brother was married to a girl too young for the marriage to be
consummated. The bride came to live in the Boyle household while her
husband lived abroad. This young bride was active at court and intro-
duced Mary to court life. Mary's father-in-law was married three times,
the second time to a citizen (who was discriminated against in aristocratic society) and the third time to the countess of Sussex. Mary lived
comfortably and peaceably with her two mothers-in-law, in whose presence and company she delighted.

Her husband's twenty-year illness and death were distressful to her.
She describes his illness: "He had for many years quite lost the use of his
limbs, and never put his feet to the ground, nor was able to feed himself, nor turn in his bed but by the help of his servants; and by those
constant pains he was so weakened and wasted that he was like a mere
skeleton, and at last fell into most dangerous convulsion fits and died of
the fourth. . . . I had this comfort that nothing I could think was good
for either his soul or body was neglected; and I had much inward peace,
to consider that I had been a constant nurse to him, and had never

neglected night or day my attendance upon him when he needed it, which he was so kind as to reward in his will, giving me his whole estate for my life and a year after, and making me his sole executrix" (34).

Since her husband was so frequently indisposed, marriage provided for the countess of Warwick outlets for her many talents. Her involvement in charitable causes extended to supporting scholars, to assisting in the education of children, and to providing more than amply for the poor. Among her neighbors she was known for her skill in arbitration. During her husband's life and after his death, she managed a large estate with integrity and competence.

The countess of Warwick died at age fifty-three, much admired and loved. In an extravagant sermon preached at her funeral, Dr. Anthony Walker described her as "thou great, heroic, noble, blessed soul" (22). He gave a long catalog of her virtues and accomplishments.

Dorothy Leigh, a Puritan mother, wrote *The Mother's Blessing* for her three sons. Although she uses the familiar female apologies for writing a book for publication, she deliberately took on the father's role and assumed its authority in speaking to three males. The mother's insights and the father's authority are here blended into one compelling book of instructions by a woman whose writing exudes confidence.

In the excerpt that appears in this section, Dorothy Leigh gives advice to her sons on the selection and treatment of a wife. The basic requirement, she insists, is that the son choose a wife who is godly. Once having selected a godly woman for marriage, however, the son must continue to love her throughout their married life. Any failure to continue to love a wife is regarded by Dorothy Leigh as childish and unacceptable. She insists that a continuing and stable love on the part of the male is not only fundamental to a happy marriage but is also a primary obligation to the wife. So vital is undying love for a wife that she, as mother, gives her sons an ultimatum: if they continue to love their wives, she, their mother, will continue to love her sons; if they cease to love their wives, she, their mother, will cease to love her sons.

Emerging in her book is a theory of companionate marriage. The wife, as Dorothy Leigh sees it, is not a servant or drudge but a companion and friend. This theory appears to defuse the patriarchy, for she employs gender-equal diction: "The wife is worthy to be thy fellow."

Dorothy Leigh's book was unusually popular and had an audience far beyond her three sons. It went into seventeen editions between 1616 and 1640.

Suggested Readings

Aretaeus. *The Extant Works of Aretaeus, the Cappadocian.* Tr. and ed. Francis Adams. London, 1856.

Clifford, Lady Anne. *The Diary of the Lady Anne Clifford.* Ed. Vita Sackville-West. London: Heinemann, 1923.

Fanshawe, Lady Ann. *The Memoirs. . . .* Ed. John Loftis. Oxford: Oxford University Press, 1979.

Ferrand, Jacques. *Erotomania. . . .* Tr. Edmund Chilmead. Oxford, 1640.

———. *A Treatise on Lovesickness.* Tr. and ed. Donald A. Beecher and Massimo Ciavolella. Syracuse, N.Y.: Syracuse University Press, 1990.

Fraser, Antonia. *The Weaker Vessel.* New York: Knopf, 1984.

Hill, Christopher. *The World Turned Upside Down.* New York: Viking, 1972.

The Lawes Resolutions of Womens Rights. London, 1632.

MacDonald, Michael. *Mystical Bedlam.* Cambridge: Cambridge University Press, 1981.

Mendelson, Sara Heller. "Stuart Women's Diaries and Occasional Memoirs." In *Women in English Society,* ed. Mary Prior, 181–210. London: Methuen, 1985.

Osborne, Dorothy. *Letters from Dorothy Osborne to Sir William Temple.* Ed. Edward Abbott Parry. London: Dent, 1914(?).

Reynolds, Edward. *Treatise of the Passions.* London, 1650.

Walker, Anthony. Sermon preached at Felsted in Essex, April 30, 1678. In *Memoir of Lady Warwick.* London: Religious Tract Society, 1847.

Walker, Elizabeth. *The Holy Life of Mrs Elizabeth Walker.* Ed. Anthony Walker. London, 1690.

18

LETTERS OF LOVE AND GALLANTRY
WRITTEN BY LADIES
(VOLUME II)*

Letter XVIII

*From a Lady to a Gentleman, who promising her marriage, debauched her,
and then left her, taking a journey beyond the sea.*

Cruelest of all your Sex.

I write not now that I'd remind you of your forsaken vows, for sure
you need not these as a reproach to your past crimes, which always will
remain in you as an opprobrious object to your future reflections, that
you have brought an unhappy wretch to ruin; one, who unskilled in
mankind's falsehood, had this in her fate, that she was too loving; whence
comes the cause of all my misfortunes. My tender heart unwarily ran
out and lodged itself with you, which, rifled of all its treasure, you have
sent home bleeding, and full of wounds, which your unkindness made,
and left it nothing but the experiment. How wretched have you made
me. Ah! Could you have returned me all, how many sighs and tears
would you have saved me? But Oh! 'tis out of Nature's reach, and as I
was then forsaken by my good angels, I am likewise left by you forever.

Yet as you are going, I will not trouble you with my sorrows, nor any
farther make known to you how miserable love has made me. Let my
_____ go, and with him go all the kind stars, no matter what becomes of
me; of whom you have no farther use then only to remember as an
example how you may ruin more. Go then, and if in all your travels you

*London, 1694. Wing L1785, Reel 605.

meet a wretch so frail and so unfortunate as I, think with a relenting thought of me again, and save the fond believer from the ruin I am in, who, though undone by you, yet cannot help, subscribing myself,

Yours forever.

19

THE AUTOBIOGRAPHY OF
LADY ANNE HALKETT*

In the year 1644 I confess I was guilty of an act of disobedience, for I gave way to the address of a person [Thomas Howard] whom my mother, at the first time that ever he had occasion to be conversant with me, had absolutely discharged me ever to allow of: And though before ever I saw him several did tell me that there would be something more than ordinary betwixt him and me (which I believe they fudged [concluded falsely] from the great friendship betwixt his sister and me, for we were seldom asunder at London, and she and I were bedfellows when she came to my sister's house at Charleton, where for the most part she stayed while we continued in the country) yet he was half a year in my company before I discovered anything of a particular inclination for me more than another; and, as I was civil to him both for his own merit and his sister's sake, so any particular civility I received from him I looked upon it as flowing from the affection he had to his sister, and her kindness to me. After that time, it seems he was not so much master of himself as to conceal it any longer. And having never any opportunity of being alone with me to speak himself, he employed a young gentleman (whose confidant he was in an amour betwixt him and my Lady Anne his cousin-german) to tell me how much he had endeavored all this time to smother his passion, which he said began the first time that ever he saw me, and now was come to that height that if I did not give him some hopes of favor he was resolved to go back again into France (from whence he had come when I first saw him) and turn Capuchin. Though this discourse disturbed me, yet I was a week or ten days before I would be persuaded so much as to hear him speak of this subject, and desired his friend to represent several disadvantages that it would be to

*Printed for the Camden Society, London, 1875; pp. 3-19, 90-94, 101-3.

him to pursue such a design. And, knowing that his father had sent for him out of France with an intention to marry him to some rich match that might improve his fortune, it would be high ingratitude in me to do anything to hinder such a design, since his father had been so obliging to my mother and sister as to use his Lord's interest with the Parliament to prevent the ruin of my brother's house and k[in?]; but when all I could say to him by his friend could not prevail, but that he grew so ill and discontented that all the house took notice, I did yield so far to comply with his desire as to give him liberty one day when I was walking in the gallery to come there and speak to me. What he said was handsome and short, but much disordered, for he looked pale as death, and his hand trembled when he took mine to lead me, and with a great sigh said, "If I loved you less I could say more." I told him I could not but think myself much obliged to him for his good opinion of me, but it would be a higher obligation to confirm his esteem of me by following my advice, which I should now give him myself, since he would not receive it by his friend. I used many arguments to dissuade him from pursuing what he proposed. And, in conclusion, told him I was two or three years older than he, and were there no other objection, yet that was of such weight with me as would never let me allow his further address. "Madam (said he), what I love in you may well increase, but I am sure it can never decay." I left arguing, and told him I would advise him to consult with his own reason, and that would let him see I had more respect to him in denying than in granting what with so much passion he desired.

After that he sought, and I shunned, all opportunities of private discourse with him; but one day, in the garden, his friend took his sister by the hand and led her into another walk, and left him and I together: and he, with very much seriousness, began to tell me that he had observed ever since he had discovered his affection to me that I was more reserved and avoided all converse with him, and therefore, since he had no hopes of my favor, he was resolved to leave England, since he could not be happy in it. And that whatever became of him that might make him displease either his father or his friends, I was the occasion of it, for, if I would not give him hopes of marrying him, he was resolved to put himself out of a capacity of marrying any other, and go immediately into a convent. And that he had taken order to have post horses ready against the next day.

I confess this discourse disturbed me, for though I had had no respect for him, his sister, or his family, yet religion was a tie upon me to endeavor the prevention of the hazard of his soul. I looked on this as a violent passion which would not last long, and perhaps might grow the more by being resisted, where as a seeming complacence might lessen it. I told him I was sorry to have him entertain such thoughts as could not but be a ruin to him and a great affliction to all his relations, which I would willingly prevent if it were in my power. He said it was absolutely in my power, for, if I would promise to marry him, he should esteem himself the most happy man living, and he would wait whatever time I thought most convenient for it. I replied, I thought it was unreasonable to urge me to promise that which ere long he might repent the asking; but this I would promise to satisfy him, that I would not marry till I saw him first married. He kissed my hand upon that with as much joy as if I had confirmed to him his greatest happiness, and said he could desire no more, for he was secure I should never see nor hear of that till it was to myself.

Upon this we parted both well pleased, for he thought he had gained much in what I promised, and I looked upon my promise as a cure to him, but no inconvenience to myself, since I had no inclination to marry any. And though I had, a delay in it was the least return I could make to so deserving a person. But I deceived myself by thinking this was the way to moderate his passion, for now he gave way to it without any restraint, and thought himself so sure of me as if there had been nothing to oppose it, though he managed it with that discretion that it was scarce visible to any within the house; not so much as either his sister or mine had the least suspicion of it, for I had enjoined him not to let them or any other know what his designs were, because I would not have them accessory, whatever fault might be in the prosecution of it. Thus it continued till towards winter that his sister was to go home to her father again, and then, knowing he would want much of the opportunity he had to converse with me, he was then very importunate to have me consent to marry him privately, which it seems he pleased himself so with the hopes of prevailing with me that he had provided a wedding ring and a minister to marry us. I was much unsatisfied with his going that length, and, in short, told him he need never expect I would marry him without his father and my mother's consent; if that could be obtained, I should willingly give him the satisfaction he desired, but without that I could not expect God's blessing neither upon him nor me, and I would do nothing that was so certain a way to bring ruin upon us both. He used many arguments from the examples of others who had practiced the same, and was happy both in their parents' favor and in one another, but finding me fixed beyond any persuasion, he resolved to acquaint my sister with it, and to employ her to speak of it to his father and my mother. She very unwillingly undertook it, because she knew it would be a surprise to them, and very unwelcome. But his importunity prevailed, and she first acquainted my mother with it; who was so passionately offended with the proposal that, whereas his father might have been brought to have given his consent (having ever had a good opinion of me and very civil), she did so exasperate him against it, that nothing could satisfy her but presently to put it to Mr. H.'s choice either presently to marry a rich citizen's daughter that his father had designed for him, or else to leave England.

The reason I believe that made my mother the more incensed was, first that it was what in the beginning of our acquaintance she had absolutely discharged my having a thought of allowing such an address; and though in some respect his quality was above mine, and therefore better than any she could expect for me, yet my Lord H.'s fortune was such as had need of a more considerable portion than my mother could give me, or else it must ruin his younger children, and therefore my mother would not consent to it, though my Lord H. did offer to do the utmost his condition would allow him if she would let me take my hazard with his son. But my mother would not be persuaded to it upon no consideration, lest any should have thought it was begun with her allowance; and to take away the suspicion of that did, I believe, make her the more violent in opposing it, and the more severe to me. My sister made choice of Sunday to speak to it. First, because she thought that day might put them both in a calmer frame to hear her, and confine their passion, since it would be the next day before they would determine anything. But finding both by my mother and my L. H. that they intended nothing but to part us, so as never to meet again, except it was as strangers, Mr. H. was very importunate to have an opportunity to speak with me that night, which I gave.

My sister being only with me, we came down together to the room I appointed to meet with him. I confess I never saw those two passions of love and regret more truly represented, nor could any person express greater affection and resolution of constancy, which with many solemn oaths he sealed of never loving or marrying any but myself. I was not

satisfied with his swearing to future performances, since I said both he
and I might find it most convenient to retract; but this I did assure him,
as long as he was constant he should never find a change in me, for
though duty did oblige me not to marry any without my mother's consent, yet it would not tie me to marry without my own. My sister at this
rises, and said, "I did not think you would have engaged me to be a
witness of both your resolutions to continue what I expected you would
rather have laid aside, and therefore I will leave you."

"Oh, madam (said he), can you imagine I love at that rate as to have
it shaken with any storm? No; were I secure, your sister would not
suffer in my absence by her mother's severity, I would not care what
misery I were exposed to; but to think I should be the occasion of
trouble to the person in the earth that I love most is unsupportable";
and with that he fell down in a chair that was behind him, but as one
without all sense, which I must confess did so much move me, that
laying aside all former distance I had kept him at, I sat down upon his
knee, and laying my head near his I suffered him to kiss me, which was
a liberty I never gave before, nor had not then, had I not seen him
so overcome with grief, which I endeavored to suppress with all the
encouragement I could, but still pressing him to be obedient to his
father, either in going abroad or staying at home, as he thought most
convenient. "No (says he), since they will not allow me to converse with
you, France will be more agreeable to me than England, nor will I go
there except I have liberty to come here again and take my leave of
you." To that I could not disagree if they thought fit to allow it; and so
my sister and I left him, but she durst not own to my mother where she
had been.

The next morning early my Lord H. went away, and took with him
his son and daughter, and left me to the severities of my offended
mother, whom nothing could pacify. After she had called for me, and
said as many bitter things as passion could dictate upon such a subject,
she discharged me to see him, and did solemnly vow that if she should
hear I did see Mr. H. she would turn me out of her doors, and never
own me again. All I said to that part was that it should be against my
will if ever she heard of it. Upon Tuesday my Lord H. writ to my
mother that he had determined to send his son to France, and that upon
Thursday after he was to begin his journey; but all he desired before he
went was to have liberty to see me, which he thought was a satisfaction
could not be denied him, and therefore desired my mother's consent to

it; which she gave upon the condition that he should only come in and take his leave of me, but not to have any converse but what she should be a witness of herself. This would not at all please Mr. H., and therefore seemed to lay the desire of it aside. In the meantime my chamber and liberty of lying alone was taken from me, and my sister's woman was to be my guardian, who watched sufficiently so that I had not the least opportunity either day or night to be without her.

Upon Thursday morning early my mother sent a man of my sister's (whose name I must mention with the rest that at that [time] was in the family, for there was Moses, Aaron, and Miriam all at one time in it, and none either related or acquainted together till they met there)—this Moses was sent to my Lord H. with a letter to inquire if his son were gone. I must here relate a little odd encounter which aggravated my misfortune. There came no return till night, and, having got liberty to walk in the hall, my mother sent a child of my sister's and bid him walk with me, and keep me company. I had not been there a quarter of an hour but my maid Miriam came to me and told me she was walking at the back gate and Mr. H. came to her and sent her to desire me to come there and speak but two or three words with him, for he had sworn not to go away without seeing me, nor would he come in to see my mother, for he had left London that morning very early and had rode up and down that part of the country only till it was the gloom of the evening to have the more privacy in coming to see me. I bid her go back and tell him I durst not see him because of my mother's oath and her discharge. While she was pressing me to run to the gate, and I was near to take the start, the child cried out, "O, my aunt is going"; which stopped me, and I sent her away to tell the reason why I could not come. I still stayed walking in the hall till she returned, wondering she stayed so long.

When she came, she was hardly able to speak, and with great disorder said, "I believe you are the most unfortunate person living, for I think Mr. H. is killed." Anyone that hath ever known what gratitude was, may imagine how these words disordered me; but impatient to know how (I was resolved to hazard my mother's displeasure rather than not see him), she told me that while she was telling him my answer there came a fellow with a great club behind him and struck him down dead, and others had seized upon Mr. T. (who formerly had been his governor, and was now entrusted to see him safe on shipboard) and his man. The reason of this was from what there was too many sad examples of at that time when the division was betwixt the king and Parliament, for to betray a master or a friend was looked upon as doing God good service. My brother-in-law Sir Henry Newton had been long from home in attendance on the king, for whose service he had raised a troop of horses upon his own expense, and had upon all occasions testified his loyalty, for which all his estate was sequestered, and with much difficulty my sister got liberty to live in her own house, and had the fifth part to live upon, which was obtained with importunity. There was one of my brother's tenants called Musgrove, who was a very great rogue, who farmed my brother's land of the Parliament, and was employed by them as a spy to discover any of the Cavaliers that should come within his knowledge: he, observing three gentlemen upon good horses scouting about all day and keeping at a distance from the high way, apprehends it was my brother who had come privately home to see my sister, and resolves to watch when he came near the house, and had followed so close as to come behind and give Mr. H. that stroke, thinking it had been my brother Newton, and ceased upon his governor and servant (the post boy being left at some distance with the horses).

In the midst of this disorder Moses came there, and Miriam having told what the occasion of it was, he told Musgrove it was my Lord H.'s son he had used so; upon which he and his complices went immediately away, and Moses and Mr. H.'s man carried him into an alehouse hard by and laid him on a bed, where he lay some time before he came to himself.

So, hearing all was quiet again, and that he had no hurt, only stonished [stunned] with the blow, I went into the room where I had left my mother and sister, which being at a good distance from the back gate they had heard nothing of the tumult that had been there. A little after Moses came in and delivered a letter from my Lord Howard, which after my mother had read, she asked what news at London. He answered, the greatest he could tell was that Mr. H. went away that morning early post to Deepe, and was going to France, but he could not learn the reason of it. My mother and sister seemed to wonder at it, for none in the family except my maid knew anything that had fallen out, or had any suspicion I was concerned in it, but my mother and sister. After Moses went out, my mother asked me if I was not ashamed to think that it would be said my Lord H. was forced to send away his son to secure him from me. I said I could not but regret whatever had occasioned her displeasure or his punishment, but I was guilty of no unhandsome action to make me ashamed, and therefore, whatever were my present misfortune, I was confident to evidence before I died that no child she had had greater love and respect to her or more obedience; to which she replied, it seems you have a good opinion of yourself.

My mother now believing Mr. H. gone, I was not as former nights sent to my bed and the guard upon me that was usual, but I stayed in my mother's chamber till she and my sister (who lay together) was abed. In the meantime Mr. H. had sent for Moses and told him whatever misfortune he might suffer by his stay there, he was fully determined not to go away without seeing me, and desired I would come to the banqueting house in the garden and he would come to the window and speak to me; which he told me, and with all that Mr. T. (who was a very serious good man) did earnestly entreat me to condescend to his desire to prevent what might be more inconvenient to us both. I sent him word when my mother was abed I would contrive some way to satisfy him, but not where he proposed, because it was within the view of my mother's chamber window.

After I had left my mother and sister in their bed, I went alone in the dark through my brother's closet to the chamber where I lay, and as I entered the room I laid my hand upon my eyes, and with a sad sigh said, Was ever creature so unfortunate and put to such a sad difficulty, either to make Mr. H. forsworn if he see me not, or if I do see him my mother will be forsworn if she doth not expose me to the utmost rigor her anger can invent! In the midst of this dispute with myself, what I should do, my hand being still upon my eyes, it presently came in my mind that if I blindfolded my eyes that would secure me from seeing him, and so I did not transgress against my mother, and he might that way satisfy himself by speaking with me. I had as much joy in finding out this means to yield to him without disquiet to myself as if it had been of more considerable consequence. Immediately I sent Moses to tell him upon what conditions I would speak with him; first, that he must allow me to have my eyes covered, and that he should bring Mr. R. with him, and if thus he were satisfied, I ordered him to bring them in the back way into the cellar, where I with Miriam would meet them the other way; which they did.

As soon as Mr. H. saw me, he much importuned the taking away the covert from my eyes; which I not suffering, he left disputing that, to employ the little time he had in regretting my not yielding to his importunity to marry him before his affection was discovered to his father and my mother, for had it been once past their power to undo, they would

[have] been sooner satisfied, and we might have been happy together and not endured this sad separation. I told him I was sorry for being the occasion of his discontent, but I could not repent the doing my duty whatever ill success it had, for I ever looked upon marrying without consent of parents as the highest act of ingratitude and disobedience that children could commit, and I resolved never to be guilty of it.

I found his greatest trouble was the fear he had that my mother in his absence would force me to marry M. L. (who was a gentleman of good fortune who some people thought had a respect for me). To this I gave him as much assurance as I could that neither he nor any other person living should lessen his interest till he gave me reason for it himself. It is unnecessary to repeat the solemn oaths he made never to love nor marry any other, for, as I did not approve of it then, so I will not now aggravate his crime by mentioning them. But there was nothing he left unsaid that could express a sincere virtuous true affection. Mr. T. (who with Moses and Miriam had all this time been so civil to us both as to retire at such a distance as not to hear what we said) came and interrupted him, and desired him to take his leave, lest longer stay might be prejudicial to us all. I called for a bottle of wine, and giving Mr. T. thanks for his civility and care, drunk to him, wishing a good and happy journey to Mr. H. So taking a farewell of them both, I went up the way I came, and left them to Moses' care to conduct them out quietly as he led them in.

This was not so secretly done but some of the house observed more noise than ordinarily used to be at that time of night, and by satisfying their curiosity in looking out discovered the occasion of it; but they were all so just as none of them ever acquainted my mother with it, though I did not conceal it from my sister the first opportunity I had to be alone with her. I was in hopes, after some time that Mr. H. was gone, my mother would have received me into her favor again, but the longer time she had to consider of my fault the more she did aggravate it. And though my Lord H. (who returned shortly after with his daughter) and my sister did use all the arguments imaginable to persuade her to be reconciled to me, yet nothing would prevail, except I would solemnly promise never to think more of Mr. H. and that I would marry another whom she thought fit to propose; to which I begged her pardon, for till Mr. H. was first married I was fully determined to marry no person living. She asked me if I was such a fool as to believe he would be constant. I said I did; but if he were not, it should be his fault, not mine, for I resolved not to make him guilty by example. Many were employed to speak to me. Some used good words, some ill; but one that was most severe, after I had heard her with much patience rail a long time, when she could say no more I gave a true account how innocent I was from having any design upon Mr. H. and related what I have already mentioned of the progress of his affection; which when she heard, she sadly wept and begged my pardon, and promised to do me all the service she could; and I believe she did, for she had much influence upon my Lord H. (having been with his lady from a child), and did give so good a character of me and my proceedings in that affair with his son, that he again made an offer to my mother to send for his son if she would consent to the marriage; but she would not hear it spoken of, but said she rather I were buried than bring so much ruin to the family she honored.

My mother's anger against me increased to that height, that for fourteen months she never gave me her blessing, nor never spoke to me but when it was to reproach me; and one day said with much bitterness she did hate to see me. That word, I confess, struck deeply to my heart, and put me to my thoughts what way to dispose of myself to free my mother from such an object. After many debates with myself, and inquiries what life I could take to that was most innocent, I resolved and writ to Sir Patrick Drumond, a cousin of my mother's, who was Conservator in Holland, to do me the favor to inform me if it was true that I had heard that there was a nunnery in Holland for those of the Protestant religion, and that he would inquire upon what conditions they admitted any to their society, because if they were consistent with my religion, I did resolve upon his advertisement immediately to go over; and desired him to hasten an answer, and not divulge to any what I had writ to him.

About a fortnight after, my mother sent for me one morning into her chamber, and examined me what I had writ to Sir Patrick Drumond. I ingenuously gave her an account, and the reason of it, for, since I found nothing would please her that I could do, I was resolved to go and so free her from the sight she hated, and since it was upon that consideration I did not doubt the obtaining her consent. It seems Sir Patrick Drumond, who was a wise and honest gentleman, apprehending discontent had made me take that resolution which I had writ to him about, instead of answering my letter, writes to my mother a very handsome serious letter, acquainting her with my intention, and concluded it could proceed from nothing but her severity, perhaps upon unjust

grounds, and therefore used many arguments to persuade her to return
to that wonted kindness which she had ever showed to all her children,
and what he was sure I would deserve, whatever opinion she had lately
entertained to the contrary. This he pressed with so much of reason and
earnestness that it prevailed more with my mother than whatever had
been said before, and from that time she received me again to her favor,
and ever after used me more like a friend than a child. In the meantime
all care was used that might prevent Mr. H.'s correspondence and
mine. But he found an excuse for sending home his man, believing him
honest and faithful to him, and with him he writ and sent me a present,
but instead of delivering them to me gave them to his father, who otherwise disposed of them. Yet in requital I sent back with him a ring with
five rubies, and gave him something for his pains, when he came to me
and endeavored to vindicate himself by protesting that unexpectedly he
was searched as soon as ever he entered his lord's house, and all was
taken from him; but I found afterwards he was not so honest as I
believed, for he never delivered my ring to his master, nor anything I
entrusted him with.

At this time my Lord H. had a sister in France, who gloried much of
her wit and contrivance, and used to say she never designed anything
but she accomplished it. My Lord H. thought she was the fittest person
to divert his son from his amour, and to her he writes, and recommends
it to her management; who was not negligent of what she was entrusted
with, as appeared in the conclusion, though her carriage was a great
disappointment to Mr. H., for he expected by her mediation to have
obtained what he desired, and that made him the more willing to comply with her, who designed her own advantage by this to oblige her
brother, who might be the more useful to her in a projected marriage
she had for her own son.

Upon Thursday the 13. of February 1646, word was brought to my
mother that the Countess of B. was come out of France, and Mr. H.
with her, which was a great surprise to her and all his relations. My
mother examined me if I had sent for him, or knew anything of his
coming; which I assured her I had not, and she said not much more.
But I was as much disturbed as any, sometime thinking he was come
with an assurance from his aunt that she would accomplish what he had
so passionately desired, or else that he had laid all thoughts of me aside,
and was come with a resolution to comply with his father's desires. The
last opinion I was a little confirmed in, having never received any word

or letter from him in ten days after his return, and, meeting him accidentally where I was walking, he crossed the way, and another time was in the room when I came in to visit some young ladies, and neither of these times took any notice of me more than of one I had never seen. I confess I was a little disordered in it, but made no conclusions till I saw what time would produce.

Upon Tuesday the 4. of March, my Lady Anne W., his cousin, came to my mother's, and having stayed a convenient time for a visit with my mother (for then it was not usual for mothers and daughters to be visited apart), I waited on her down, and taking me aside, she told me she was desired by her cousin T. H. to present his most faithful service to me, and to desire me not to take it ill that he did not speak to me when he met me, for finding his aunt not his friend as he expected, he seemed to comply with her desire only to have the opportunity of coming home with her, and had resolved for a time to forbear all converse with me, and to make love to all that came in his way, but assured me it was only to make his friends think he had forgotten me, and then he might with the less suspicion prosecute his design, which was never to love or marry any but me, and this she said he confirmed with all the solemn oaths imaginable. In pursuance of this he visited all the young ladies about the town, but an Earl's daughter gave him the most particular welcome, whose mother, not allowing him to come as a pretender, she made appointment with him and met him at her cousin's house frequently, which I knew, and he made sport of.

The summer being now advancing, my mother and her family went with my sister to her house in the country; which being not far from London, we heard often how affairs went there, and amongst other discourse that it was reported Mr. H. was in love with my Lady E. M. and she with him, at which some smiled and said it might be her wit had taken him but certainly not her beauty (for she had as little of that as myself). Though these reports put me upon my guard, yet I confess I did not believe he was real in his address there, neither did his sister, who was sometimes a witness of their converse and gave me account of it; but I approved not of his way, for I thought it could not but reflect upon himself, and injure either that lady or me. But she took a way to secure herself; for upon the last Tuesday in July 1646, a little before supper, I received a letter from Mrs. H., a particular friend of mine, who writ me word that upon the Tuesday before Mr. H. was privately married to my Lady E. M., and the relations of both sides was unsatisfied.

I was alone in my sister's chamber when I read the letter, and flinging myself down upon her bed, I said, "Is this the man for whom I have suffered so much? Since he hath made himself unworthy my love, he is unworthy my anger or concern"; and rising immediately I went out into the next room to my supper as unconcernedly as if I had never had an interest in him, nor had never lost it. A little after my mother came to the knowledge of it from my Lord H., who was much discontented at his son's marriage, and often wished he had had his former choice. Nothing troubled me more than my mother's laughing at me, and perhaps so did others, but all I said was, "I thought he had injured himself more than me, and I much rather he had done it than I"; and once, I confess, in passion, being provoked by something I had heard, I said with too much seriousness, "I pray God he may never die in peace till he confess his fault, and ask me forgiveness." But I acknowledge this as a fault, and have a hundred times begged the Lord's pardon for it; for, though in some respects it might be justified as wishing him repentance, yet many circumstances might make it impossible for me to be a witness of it. And God forbid that any should want peace for my passion! When Miriam first heard he was married, she lifted up her hands and said, "Give her, O Lord, dry breasts, and a miscarrying womb!" which I reproved her for; but it seems the Lord thought fit to grant her request, for that lady miscarried of several children before she brought one to the full time, and that one died presently after it was born, which may be a lesson to teach people to govern their wishes and their tongue, that neither may act to the prejudice of any, lest it be placed on their account at the day of reckoning. Not only was this couple unfortunate in the children, but in one another, for it was too well known how short a time continued the satisfaction they had in one another. . . .

Towards the winter he [Sir James Halkett] stayed most constantly at Edinburgh, and then grew so impertinent with me, not to allow his address, but to give him hopes that it should be successful, that to put him past all further pursuit I told him I looked upon it as an addition of my misfortune to have the affection of so worthy a person, and could not give him the return he deserved, for he knew I had the tie upon me to another that I could not dispose of myself to any other if I expected a blessing, and I had too much respect to him to comply with his desire in what might make him unhappy and myself by doing what would be a perpetual disquiet to me. He urged many things to convince me that I was in an error, and therefore that made it void; but when he saw nothing could prevail, he desired for his satisfaction that I would propose it to Mr. David Dickson (who was one he knew I had a great esteem of his judgment), and rely upon his determination. This I was content to do, not doubting but he would resolve the question on my side.

The first time Mr. Dickson came to me (which he usually did once in a week), being alone, I told him I was going to communicate something to him which hitherto I had concealed, but now would entrust him with it under promise of secrecy, and being impartially ingenuous in giving me his opinion in what I was to acquaint him with; which he promising, I told him I did not doubt but he and his wife and many others in Edinburgh did believe Sir Ja. Halkett's frequent visits to me was upon design of marriage, and I would avow to him that it was what he had oft with great importunity proposed, and had a long time evidenced so real an affection for me, that I could not but acknowledge if any man alive could prevail with me it would be he; but I had been so far engaged to another that I could not think it lawful for me to marry another; and so told him all the story of my being unhappily deceived, and what length I had gone, and rather more than less. He heard me very attentively, and was much moved at the relation, which I could not make without tears. He replied, he could not but say it was an unusual trial I had met with, and what he prayed the Lord to make useful to me. But withal he added that, since what I did was supposing C. B. [Colonel Bamfield] a free person, he not proving so, though I had been publicly married to him and avowedly lived with him as his wife, yet, the ground of it failing, I was as free as if I had never seen him; and this, he assured me, I might rely upon, that I might without offense either to the laws of God or man marry any other person whenever I found it convenient; and that he thought I might be guilty of a fault if I did not when I had so good an offer. He used many arguments to confirm his opinion; which though I reverenced coming from him, yet I was not fully convinced but that it might be a sin in me to marry, but I was sure there was no sin in me to live unmarried.

I was very just to Sir James in giving him an account what Mr. Dickson had said, though not till he urged to know it. And being determined on what he had often pleaded, for he hoped now I would have nothing more to object, I told him, though he had made [it] appear lawful to me, yet I could not think it convenient, nor could I consent to his desire of marrying without doing him so great prejudice as would make me appear the most ungrateful person to him in the world. I acknowledged his respect had been such to me that were I owner of what I had just right to, and had never had the least blemish in my reputation (which I could not but suffer in considering my late misfortune), I thought he deserved me with all the advantages was possible for me to bring him; but it would be an ill requital of his civilities not only to bring him nothing but many inconveniences by my being greatly in debt, which could not but be expected, having (except a hundred pound) never received a penny of what my mother left me, and had been long at law both in England and Scotland, which was very expensive, and I gave him a particular account what I was owing. Yet all this did not in the least discourage him, for he would have been content at that time to have married me with all the disadvantages I lay under; for he said he looked upon me as a virtuous person, and in that proposed more happiness to himself by enjoying me than in all the riches of the world. Certainly none can think but I had reason to have more than an ordinary esteem of such a person, whose eyes were so perceptible as to see and love injured virtue under so dark a cloud as encompassed me about.

When I found he made use of all the arguments I used to lessen his affection as motives to raise it higher, I told him since he had left caring for himself, I was obliged to have the more care of him, which I could evidence in nothing more than in hindering him from ruining himself; and therefore told him I would be ingenuous with him, and tell him my resolution was never to marry any person till I could first put my affairs in such a posture as that if I brought no advantage where I married, at least I would bring no trouble, and whenever I could do that, if ever I did change my condition, I thought he was the only person that deserved an interest in me. And I did resolve as soon as the winter session was done, which I expected would put a close to my lawsuit here, I would go to London, and vindicate myself from the supposed guilt I was charged with, and then try what I could persuade my brother to do in order to the paying what I owed. I acquainted Sir James with my intention, which he approved of, since he could not persuade me to nothing else. . . .

About a week after he was gone I fell into a feverish distemper, which continued some time, so that I found it necessary to send for Doctor Cuningham, which gave occasion to some people to say that I fell sick with heartbreak because Sir James H. was gone to London to marry my Lady Morton; which report went current amongst some, though not believed by any that was well acquainted with any of the three; but this acquainted me with the humor of some people, that use to make conclusions of their own rather than seem ignorant of anything. By the speedy return Sir James made, he convinced them of their folly who raised the reports, and brought much satisfaction to me by the assurance I had from my sister of being very welcome to her whenever it was convenient for me to come, and till then she thought it best to delay speaking of any particular to my brother; but for her husband I might be secure of his kindness to be ever the same I had found it. . . .

After this money was received and paid where it was most necessary, and that I had satisfied all that I knew anything was due to, I went to London for some few days, where Sir James came to me in order to conclude our marriage, which I could not now in reason longer defer, since the greatest objections I had made against it was removed, and that I was fully convinced no man living could do more to deserve a wife than he had done to oblige me; and therefore I intended to give him myself, though I could secure him of nothing more, and that was my regret that I could not bring him a fortune as great as his affection to recompense his long expectation. It was not without many debates with myself that I came at last to be determined to marry, and the most prevalent argument that persuaded me to incline to it was the extraordinary way that Sir James took even in silence to speak what he thought necessary to conceal till it appeared to be fit for avowing, and then not to be discouraged from all the inconveniences that threatened his pursuit was what I could not but look upon as ordered by the wise and good providence of the Almighty, whom to resist or not make use of so good an opportunity as by his mercy was offered to me I thought might be offensive to his divine Majesty, who in justice might deliver me up to the power of such sins as might be a punishment for not making use of the offer of grace to prevent them. And this consideration being added to Sir James' worth ended the controversy. However, lest I might have been mistaken, or Mr. D. Dickson in his opinion, who thought it lawful for me to marry, I entered not into that state without most solemnly seeking the determined will of God, which by fasting and prayer I supplicated to be evidenced to me, either by hedging up my way with thorns that I might not offend him, or that he would make my way plain before his face, and my paths righteous in his sight. And as I begged this with the fervor of my soul, so it was with an entire resignation and resolution to be content with whatever way the Lord should dispose of me. To this I may add St. Paul's attestation, "The God and Father of our Lord Jesus Christ, which is blessed forevermore, knoweth that I lie not" (2 Cor. xi. 31).

After this day's devotion was over, everything that I could desire in order to my marriage did so pleasingly concur to the consummation of it, and my own mind was so undisturbed and so freed of all kind of doubts, that with thankfulness I received it as a testimony of the Lord's approbation, and a presage of my future happiness; and, blessed be his name! I was not disappointed of my hope. Upon Saturday the first of March, 1656, Sir James and I went to Charleton, and took with us Mr. Gaile, who was chaplain to the Countess of Devonshire, who preached (as he sometimes used to do) at the church the next day, and after supper he married us in my brother Newton's closet, none knowing of it in the family or being present but my brother and sister and Mr. Neale; though, to conform to the order of those that were then in power, who allowed of no marriage lawful but such as were married by one of their Justices of Peace, that they might object nothing against our marriage, after the evening sermon my sister pretending to go see Justice Elkonhead who was not well, living at Woolwitch, took Sir James and me with her in the coach, and my brother and Mr. Neale went another way afoot and met us there, and the Justice performed what was usual for him at that time, which was only holding the Directory in his hand, asked Sir James if he intended to marry me, he answered Yes; and asked if I intended to marry him, I said Yes. Then says he, "I pronounce you man and wife." So calling for a glass of sack, he drank and wished much happiness to us; and we left him, having given his clerk money, who gave in parchment the day and witnesses, and attested by the Justice that he had married us. But if it had not been done more solemnly afterwards by a minister, I should not have believed it lawfully done.

20

SOME SPECIALITIES
IN THE LIFE OF M. WARWICK

(Diary, 1666–1673) *

Mary Boyle Rich, Countess of Warwick

I was born November the 8th, 1625, at Yohall, in Ireland; my father was Richard Boyle Earl of Cork, my mother was Katheren Fentone. My father was second son to Mr. Roger Boyle, my mother was only daughter to Sir Jefrey Fentone.

My father, from being a younger brother of a younger brother, who was only a private gentleman of Herefordshire, was by his mother's care, after his father's death, bred by her at Cambridge, and afterwards at the inns of court, and from thence, by the good providence of God, brought into Ireland, where when he landed he was master of but twenty-seven pounds and three shillings in the world, and afterwards God so prospered him there that he had in that country about twenty thousand pound a-year coming in, and was made Lord Treasurer of Ireland, and one of the two Lord Justices of the government of that kingdom.

My wise, and as I have been informed pious, mother died when I was about three years old; and some time after, by the tender care of my indulgent father, that I might be carefully and piously educated, I was sent by him to a prudent and virtuous lady, my Lady Claytone, who never having had any child of her own, grew to make so much of me as if she had been an own mother to me, and took great care to have me soberly educated. Under her government I remained at Mallow, a town in Munster, till I was, I think, about eleven years old, and then my

*Printed for the Percy Society, London, 1848; pp. 1–17.

father called me from thence (much to my dissatisfaction), for I was very fond of that, to me, kind mother. Soon after my father removed, with his family, into England, and dwelt in Dorsetshire, at a house he had purchased there; which was called Stalbridge; and there, when I was about thirteen or fourteen years of age, came down to me one Mr. Hambletone, son to my Lord Clandeboyes, who was afterwards earl of Clanbrasell, and would fain have had me for his wife. My father and his had, some years before, concluded a match between us, if we liked when we saw one another, and that I was of years of consent; and now he being returned out of France, was by his father's command to come to my father's, where he received from him a very kind and obliging welcome, looking upon him as his son-in-law, and designing suddenly that we should be married, and gave him leave to make his address, with a command to me to receive him as one designed to be my husband. Mr. Hambletone (possibly to obey his father) did design gaining me by a very handsome address, which he made to me, and if he did not to a very high degree dissemble, I was not displeasing to him, for he professed a great passion for me. The professions he made me of his kindness were very unacceptable to me, and though I had by him very highly advantageous offers made me, for point of fortune (for his estate, that was settled upon him, was counted seven or eight thousand pound a-year), yet by all his kindness to me nor that I could be brought to endure to think of having him, though my father pressed me extremely to it; my aversion for him was extraordinary, though I could give my father no satisfactory account why it was so.

This continued between us for a long time, my father showing a very high displeasure at me for it, but though I was in much trouble about it, yet I could never be brought either by fair or foul means to it; so as my father was at last forced to break it off, to my father's unspeakable trouble, and to my unspeakable satisfaction, for hardly in any of the troubles of my life did I feel a more sensible uneasiness than when that business was transacting. Afterwards I apparently saw a good providence of God in not letting me close with it, for within a year after my absolute refusing him he was, by the rebellion of Ireland, impoverished so that he lost for a great while his whole estate, the rebels being in possession of it; which I should have liked very ill, for if I had married him it must have been for his estate's sake, not his own, his person being highly disagreeable to me.

After this match was off, my father removed to London, and lived at a house of Sir Thomas Staford's. When we were once settled there, my father, living extraordinarily high, drew a very great resort thither, and the report that he would give me a very great fortune made him have for me many very great and considerable offers, both of persons of great birth and fortune; but I still continued to have an aversion to marriage, living so much at my ease that I was unwilling to change my condition, and never could bring myself to close with any offered match, but still begged my father to refuse all the most advantageous proffers, though I was by him much pressed to settle myself.

About this time my fourth brother, Mr. Francis Boyle then (afterwards Lord Shannon), was by my father married to Mrs. Elizabeth Kilegrew, daughter to my Lady Staford; and my brother being then judged to be too young to live with his wife, was a day or two after the celebrating the marriage (which was done before the King and Queen) at Whitehall (she being then a maid of honor to the Queen) sent into France to travel, and his wife then brought home to our house, where she and I became chamber-fellows, and constant bedfellows; and there then grew so great a kindness between us, that she soon had a great and ruling power with me; and by her having so brought me to be very vain and foolish, enticing me to spend (as she did) her time in seeing and reading plays and romances, and in exquisite and curious dressing.

When she was well settled in our family (but much more so in my heart) she had many of the young gallants that she was acquainted with at Court that came to visit her at the Savoy (where we lived); amongst others there came one Mr. Charles Rich, second son to Robert Earl of Warwick, who was a very cheerful, and handsome, well-bred, and fashioned person, and being good company was very acceptable to us all, and so became very intimate in our house, visiting us almost every day. He was then in love with a maid of honor to the Queen, one Mrs. Hareson, that had been chamber-fellow to my sister-in-law whilst she lived at Court, and that brought on the acquaintance between him and my sister. He continued to be much with us, for about five or six months, till my brother Broghil then (afterwards Earl of Orrery), grew also to be passionately in love with the same Mrs. Hareson. My brother then having a quarrel with Mr. Thomas Howard, second son to the Earl of Berkshire, about Mrs. Hareson (with whom he also was in love), Mr. Rich brought my brother a challenge from Mr. Howard, and was second to him against my brother when they fought, which they did without any great hurt of any side, being parted. This action made Mr.

Rich judge it not civil to come to our house, and so for some time forbore doing it, but at last my brother's match with Mrs. Hareson being unhandsomely (on her side) broken off, when they were so near being married as the wedding clothes were to be made, and she after married Mr. Thomas Howard (to my father's very great satisfaction, who always was averse to it, though to comply with my brother's passion he consented to it).

My brother being thus happily disengaged from that amour, brought again Mr. Rich to our family, and soon after he grew again as great among us, as if he had never done that disobliging action to us. By this time, upon what account I know not, he began to withdraw his visits to Mrs. Hareson (for that name she continued to have not being married to Mr. Howard in a good considerable time after), and his heart too; and in being encouraged in his resolution by my sister Boyle, began to think of making an address to me, she promising him all the assistance her power with me could give him to gain my affection, though she knew by attempting it she should lose my father's and all my family, that she believed would never be brought to consent to my having any younger brother; my father's kindness to me making him, as she well knew, resolved to match me to a great fortune. At last, one day she began to acquaint me with Mr. Rich's, as she said, great passion for me; at which I was at the first much surprised, both at his having it for me, and at her telling it to me, knowing how much she hazarded by it, if I should acquaint my father with it. I confess I did not find his declaration of his kindness disagreeable to me, but the consideration of his being but a younger brother made me sadly apprehend my father's displeasure if I should embrace any such offer, and so resolved, at that time, to give her no answer, but seemed to disbelieve his loving me at the rate she informed me he did, though I had for some time taken notice of his loving me, though I never thought he designed trying to gain me.

After this first declaration of his esteem for me by my sister, he became a most diligent gallant to me, seeking by a most humble and respectful address to gain my heart, applying himself, when there was no other beholders in the room but my sister, to me; but if any other person came in he took no more than ordinary notice of me; but to disguise his design addressed himself much to her; and though his doing so was not well liked in our family, yet there was nothing said to him about their dislike of it; and by this way his design became unsuspected, and thus we lived for some months, in which time, by his more than ordinary humble behavior to me, he did insensibly steal away my heart, and got a greater possession of it than I knew he had. My sister, when he was forced to be absent for fear of observing eyes, would so plead for him, that it worked, too, very much upon me. When I began to find, myself, that my kindness for him grew and increased so much, that though I had in the time of his private address to me, many great and advantageous offers made me by my father, and that I could not with any patience endure to hear of any of them, I began with some seriousness to consider what I was engaging myself in by my kindness for Mr. Rich, for my father, I knew, would never endure me, and besides I considered my mind was too high, and I too expensively brought up to bring myself to live contentedly with Mr. Rich's fortune, who would never have, when his father was dead, above thirteen or fourteen (at the most) hundred pounds a-year. Upon these considerations I was convinced that it was time for me to give him a flat and final denial; and with this, as I thought, fixed resolution, I have laid me down in my bed to beg my sister never to name him to me more for a husband, and to tell him from me, that I desired him never more to think of me, for I was resolved not to anger my father: but when I was upon a readiness to open my mouth to utter these words, my great kindness for him stopped it, and made me rise always without doing it, though I frequently resolved it; which convinced to me the great and full possession he had of my heart, which made me begin to give him more hopes of gaining me than before I had done, by anything but my inducing him to come to me after he had declared to me his design in doing so, which he well knew I would never endure from any other person that had offered themselves to me.

Thus we lived for some considerable time, my duty and my reason having frequent combats within me with my passion, which at last was always victorious, though my fear of my father's displeasure frighted me from directly owning it to Mr. Rich; till my sister Boyle's taking sick of the measles (and by my lying with when she had them, though I thought at first it might be the smallpox, I got them of her), my kindness being then so great for her, that though of all diseases the smallpox was that I most apprehended, yet from her I did not anything, and would have continued with her all her illness, had I not by my father's absolute command been separated into another room from her; but it was too late, for I had got from her the infection, and presently fell most dan-

gerously ill of the measles too, and before they came out I was removed
into another house, because my sister Dungarvan, in whose house I
was, in Long Acre, was expecting daily to be delivered, and was apprehensive of that distemper. Mr. Rich then was much concerned for me,
and he was most obligingly careful of me; which as it did to a great
degree heighten my passion for him, so it did also begin to make my
family, and before suspecting friends, to see that they were by a false
disguise of his kindness to my sister abused, and that he had for me, and
I for him a respect which they feared was too far gone.

This made my old Lady Staford, mother to my sister Boyle (who was
a cunning old woman, and who had been herself too much and too long
versed in amours), begin to conclude the truth, and absolutely to believe that her daughter was the great actor in this business, and that her
being confidant with us, would ruin her with my father; and therefore
having some power with him, to prevent the inconveniences that would
come to her daughter, resolved to acquaint my father with Mr. Rich's
visiting me when I had the measles, and of his continuing to do so at the
Savoy,—whither I was, after my recovery, by my father's order, removed,
and where by reason of my being newly recovered of an infectious
disease, I was free from any visits. After she had with great rage chid
her daughter, and threatened her that she would acquaint my father
with it (to keep me, as she said, from ruining myself), she accordingly,
in a great heat and passion, did that very night do it. My sister presently acquainted both Mr. Rich and me with her mother's resolution,
and when she had Mr. Rich alone, told him if he did not that very night
prevail with me to declare my kindness for him and to give him some
assurance of my resolution to have him, I would certainly the next day
by my father be secured from his ever speaking to me, and so he would
quite lose me. This discourse did make him resolve to do what she
counseled him to; and that very night, when I was ill and laid upon my
bed, she giving him an opportunity of being alone with me, and by her
care keeping anybody from disturbing us; he had with me about two
hours' discourse, upon his knees, by my bedside, wherein he did so
handsomely express his passion (he was pleased to say he had for me),
and his fear of being by my father's command separated from me, that
together with as many promises as any person in the world could make,
of his endeavoring to make up to me the smallness of his fortune by the
kindness he would have still to me, if I consented to be his wife; that
though I can truly say, that when he kneeled down by me I was far from

having resolved to own I would have him, yet his discourse so far prevailed that I consented to give him, as he desired, leave to let his father mention it to mine; and promised him that, let him make his father say what he pleased, I would own it.

Thus we parted, this evening, after I had given away myself to him, and if I had not done so that night, I had been, by my father's separating us, kept from doing it, at least for a long time; for in the morning my father, upon what the night before had been told him by my Lady Staford, came early to me, and with a very frowning and displeasing look, bid me go (as I had before asked to do) into the country to air myself, at a little house near Hampton Court, which Mrs. Katheren Kilegrew, sister to my sister Boyle, then had; and told me that he was informed that I had young men who visited me, and commanded me if any did so, where I was now going, I should not see them. This he said in general, but named not Mr. Rich in particular, which I was glad of; and so after my father had dismissed me, with this unkind look (and I thought severe command), I was presently, by my brother Broghil, in his coach, conveyed to a very little house at Hampton, which was at that time though much more agreeable to me than the greatest and most stately one could be, because it did remove me from my father some distance, which I thought best for me, till his fury was in some measure over, which I much apprehended. That very day I removed into the country, my Lord Goreing, afterwards Earl of Norwich, was by my Lord of Warwick and my Lord of Holland's appointment chose to be the first person that should motion the match to my father, and acquaint him with my esteem for Mr. Rich; he was chose by them, and approved of by me to do it, because his son having married one of my sisters, there was a great friendship between them, and he had a more than ordinary power with my father with what he was designed to do: but though he did it very well, my father was so troubled at it that he wept, and would by no means suffer him to go on.

The next day, as I remember, my Lord of Warwick and my Lord of Holland visited him, and mentioned it with great kindness to him; he used them with much respect, but told them he hoped his daughter would be advised by him, and he could not but still hope she would not give herself away without his consent, and therefore he was resolved to send to me to know what I said the next morning, which accordingly he did; and the persons he fixed upon to do it by were two of my brothers,— my eldest brother, Dungarvan, and my then third brother, Broghil, who came early down to me (but I was before informed by Mr. Rich of their coming), yet for all that I was disordered at their sight, knowing about what they came; but the extraordinary great kindness I had for Mr. Rich made me resolve to endure anything for his sake, and therefore when I had by my brothers been informed that they were, by my father's command, sent to examine me, what was between Mr. Rich and I, and threatened, in my father's name, if I did not renounce ever having anything more to do with him, I made this resolute, but ill and horribly disobedient answer, that I did acknowledge a very great and particular kindness for Mr. Rich, and desired them, with my humble duty to my father, to assure him that I would not marry him without his consent, but that I was resolved not to marry any other person in the world; and that I hoped my father would be pleased to consent to my having Mr. Rich, to whom, I was sure, he could have no other objection, but that he was a younger brother; for he was descended from a very great and honorable family, and was in the opinion of all (as well as mine) a very deserving person, and I desired my father would be pleased to consider, I only should suffer by the smallness of his fortune, which I very contentedly chose to do, and should judge myself to be much more happy with his small one, than with the greatest without him.

After my two brothers saw I was unmovable in my resolution, say what they could to me, they returned highly unsatisfied from me to my father; who, when he had it once owned from my own mouth, that I would have him, or nobody, he was extraordinarily displeased with me, and forbid my daring to appear before him. But after some time he was persuaded, by the great esteem he had for my Lord of Warwick and my Lord of Holland, to yield to treat with them, and was at last brought, though not to give me my before designed portion, yet to give me seven thousand pounds, and was brought to see and be civil to Mr. Rich, who was a constant visitor of me at Hampton, almost daily; but he was the only person I saw, for my own family came not at me: and thus I continued there for about ten weeks, when I was at last, by my Lord of Warwick and my Lord Goreing led into my father's chamber, and there, upon my knees, humbly begged his pardon, which after he had, with great justice, severely chid me, he bid me rise, and was by my Lord of Warwick's and my Lord Goreing's intercession reconciled to me, and told me I should suddenly be married. But though he designed I should be so at London, with Mr. Rich and my friends at it, yet being a great enemy always to a public marriage, I was, by that fear, and Mr. Rich's earnest solicitation, prevailed with, without my father's knowledge, to be privately married at a little village near Hampton Court, on the 21st July 1641, called Shepertone; which when my father knew he was again something displeased at me for it, but after I had begged his pardon, and assured him I did it only to avoid a public wedding, which he knew I had always declared against, his great indulgence to me made him forgive me that fault also, and within few days after I was carried down to Lees, my Lord of Warwick's house in the country, but none of our friends accompanied me, but my dear sister Ranelagh, whose great goodness made her forgive me, and stay with me some time at Lees, where I received as kind a welcome as was possible from that family, but particularly from my good father-in-law.

Here let me admire at the goodness of God, that by His good providence to me, when I by my marriage thought of nothing but having a person for whom I had a great passion, and never sought God in it, but by marrying my husband flatly disobeyed His command, which was given me in His sacred oracles, of obeying my father; yet was pleased by His unmerited goodness to me to bring me, by my marriage, into a noble and, which is much more, a religious family; where religion was both practiced and encouraged; and where there were daily many eminent and excellent divines, who preached in the chapel most edifyingly and awakeningly to us. Besides a famous household chaplain, my father-in-law had Doctor Gawden there, afterwards Lord Bishop of Worcester. I could not, as young as I was when I came to the family, being but fifteen years old, and as much as between the 8th of November and 21st of July, but admire at the excellent order there was in the family, and the great care that was had that God should be most solemnly worshiped and owned in that great family, both by the lord and lady of it. My mother-in-law was not my husband's own mother, she (Hatton) being dead, after she had brought her husband many fine children, and the greatest estate any woman had done for many years to a family. And my lord after her decease was married again to a rich woman, one Alderman Holiday's widow, of the City, who because she was a citizen was not so much respected in the family as in my opinion she deserved to be; for she was one that assuredly feared God; but she was at my first coming to Lees removed to her daughter Hungerford's, near the Bath, where she was resolved to stay till she was by some person she credited, informed whether my humor were such as would make her to live comfortably with me; for by reason of some former disputes with my first Lady Rich (a daughter of Earl Devonshire), that had been between them, she was almost come to a resolution of never more living with any daughter-in-law. But my Lady Roberts, that was my lord's sister, and a very pious woman, was pleased to assure her I would be dutiful to her, and at last did prevail with her to come down to Lees, where I then was, and I was so fortunate as I gained so much of her kindness, that for about five years that I lived constantly with her I did never displease her, or ever had any unkindness from her, but found her as obliging to me as if she had been my own mother, and she would always profess she loved me at that rate, and I did when God called her away mourn much for my losing her.

After her death my Lord of Warwick married again, to the Countess of Sussex (widow of Thomas Savil, Earl of Sussex), with whom I had, too, the great happiness of living as lovingly as it was possible for an own mother and daughter to live, for about eleven years, in some of which time I went on in a vain kind of life, only studying to please my husband and the family I was matched into; but, alas, too much neglected the studying to please God, and to save my immortal soul; yet in this time of my vanity conscience would often speak to me, but yet I went on, regardless, though I was allured by God with many mercies, and had afflictions too.

In the first year I was married, God was pleased to give me a safe delivery of a girl, which I lay in with at Warwick House. And soon after the second year, I was brought abed of a boy, in September 28th, 1643. The girl was named Elizabeth, and the boy Charles. The girl God was pleased to take from me by death, when she was not a year and a quarter old. For which I was much afflicted; but my husband as passionately so as ever I saw him; he being most extraordinarily fond of her. When I lay in with my son, the ill news of my father's death was brought to my husband; but by his care of me, it was concealed from me till I was up again; and then it was told me first by my mother-in-law. I was much afflicted, and grieved at the loss of one of the best and kindest of fathers in the world: but I being young and inconsiderate, grief did not stick long with me.

21

THE MOTHERS BLESSING

*OR The godly counsaile of a gentlewoman
not long since deceased, left behind her for her children* *

Dorothy Leigh

**To My Beloved Sons, George, John, and William Leigh,
All Things Pertaining to Life and Godliness**

My children, God having taken your father out of this vale of tears to
his everlasting mercy in Christ, myself not only knowing what a care he
had in his lifetime that you should be brought up godlily, but also at his
death being charged in his will by the love and duty which I bore him,
to see you well instructed and brought up in knowledge, I could not
choose but seek (according as I was by duty bound) to fulfill his will in
all things, desiring no greater comfort in the world than to see you grow
in godliness, that so you might meet your father in heaven, where I am
sure he is, myself being a witness of his faith in Christ. And seeing
myself going out of the world, and you but coming in, I know not how to
perform this duty so well, as to leave you these few lines, which will
show you as well the great desire your father had both of your spiritual
and temporal good, as the care I had to fulfill his will in this, knowing it
was the last duty I should perform unto him. . . .

Choice of Wives

Now for your wives, the Lord direct you; for I cannot tell you what is
best to be done. Our Lord saith, "First seek the kingdom of God and his

*London, 1616. STC 15402, Reel 1455, pp. 49, 53–58.

righteousness, and all things else shall be ministered unto you." First,
you must seek a godly wife, that she may be a help to you in godliness:
for God said, "It is not good for man to be alone, let him have a helper
meet for him" (Gen. 2:18); and she cannot be meet for him except she be
truly godly; for God counteth that the man is alone still if his wife be not
godly. . . .

It Is Great Folly for a Man to Mislike His Own Choice

Methinks I never saw a man show a more senseless simplicity than in
misliking his own choice, when God hath given a man almost a world of
women to choose him a wife in. If a man hath not wit enough to choose
him one whom he can love to the end, yet methinks he should have
discretion to cover his own folly; but if he want discretion, methinks he
should have policy, which never fails a man to dissemble his own simplicity in this case. If he want wit, discretion, and policy, he is unfit to
marry any woman. Do not a woman that wrong as to take her from her
friends that love her, and after a while to begin to hate her. If she have
no friends, yet thou knowest not, but that she may have a husband that
may love her. If thou canst not love her to the end, leave her to him that
can. Methinks my son could not offend me in anything if he served
God, except he chose a wife that he could not love to the end. I need not
say, if he served God, for if he served God, he would obey God, and
then he would choose a godly wife and live lovingly and godlily with
her, and not do as some man who taketh a woman to make her a
companion and fellow, and after he hath her, he makes her a servant
and drudge. If she be thy wife, she is always too good to be thy servant,
and worthy to be thy fellow. If thou wilt have a good wife, thou must go
before her in all goodness and show her a pattern of all good virtues by
thy godly and discreet life: and especially in patience, according to the
counsel of the Holy Ghost, "Bear with the woman, as with the weaker
vessel." Here God showeth that it is her imperfection that honoreth
thee, and that it is thy perfection that maketh thee to bear with her;
follow the counsel of God, therefore, and bear with her.

God willed a man to leave Father and Mother for his wife. This
showeth what an excellent love God did appoint to be between man and
wife. In truth I cannot by any means set down the excellency of that
love: but this I assure you, that if you get wives that be godly and you

love them, you shall not need to forsake me; whereas if you have wives that you love not, I am sure I will forsake you. Do not yourselves that wrong as to marry a woman that you cannot love: show not so much childishness in your sex as to say, you loved her once, and now your mind is changed: if thou canst not love her for the goodness that is in her, yet let the grace that is in thyself move thee to do it; and so I leave thee to the Lord, whom I pray to guide both thee and her with his grace, and grant that you may choose godlily, and live happily, and die comfortably, through faith in Jesus Christ.

PART FIVE

WOMEN TAKING CHARGE
OF HEALTH CARE

ॐ

Introduction

"A midnight industry . . ."

Women—especially those with husbands, children, and extended house-holds—had to function as primary health caregivers in their homes and in their communities. Large country estates and small villages were geographically too far removed from urban centers for access to professional medical care. It would take days for a physician to be notified of illness and days for the physician to arrive to treat the sick. The poor, of course, no matter where they lived, could not afford professional medical care and had to rely almost exclusively on the female health caregivers.

The medical profession in England in the sixteenth and seventeenth centuries was a male-only profession, although there were a few women without academic credentials who were licensed to practice medicine. The profession kept itself male by writing medical textbooks in a language that most women had not been taught to read—Latin—and by restricting formal academic medical education to males. Medical writing did occasionally appear in the English vernacular and in translation, but those books were relatively rare and hard to come by. Herbals, however, were standard household possessions, and women consulted Turner, Lyte, Gerard, and Parkinson regularly. A few vernacular and translated medical textbooks were owned and read by women practitioners.

Because they were denied medical training, women had to establish their own health-care delivery systems. They had to learn basic anatomy and physiology from other women. They had to gain practical pharmaceutical knowledge from other women and exchange with one another a wide range of remedies and palliatives. They had to teach one another about menstruation, coition, pregnancy, delivery of babies, care of infants, and menopause; about sexually transmitted diseases; about wounds and cuts and broken bones; about diet.

Networking was the best way for women to instruct other women. Networking could be oral or written or even a personal delivery system.

173

For those who could not read, oral communication and apprenticeship participation in the care of the sick were the only means available for medical instruction. For those who could read, women recorded their medical information and accumulated knowledge in their diaries, "receipt books," medical handbooks, and midwives' books. Networking also became a delivery system when women sent their own homemade pharmaceutical preparations to those who required remedies or alleviation of suffering and pain. Often women themselves traveled extensively to treat the sick, personally administering their own preparations and supervising the care of the sick.

In order to disseminate medical information to their sister health caregivers, and ultimately to promote better health in their homes and communities, women felt the need to reach beyond conversation, observation, anecdotal transmission of experience, and personal attendance of the sick. Barred from academic medicine, women took to educating themselves by writing their own medical and pharmaceutical handbooks and their own textbooks for the delivery of babies and postpartum care of mother and infant. Not all of these books were published in their day; some were circulated in manuscript and remained in manuscript for centuries.

The unpublished journal of Lady Grace Mildmay (c. 1570–1620), for example, acknowledges the role her father's niece played in her medical education: "[She] let me read in Dr. Turner's Herbal and Bartholomew Vigoe [*The most excellent works of chirurgerye made and set forth by Maister J. Vigon*, 1543]" (Nagy, 121). Lady Mildmay also instructed herself in medical theory and practice: "Every day I spent some time in the Herbal and books of physic, and in ministering to one or other by the directions of the best physicians of my acquaintance and ever God gave a blessing thereunto" (Nagy, 125). Like so many of the women of her day, Lady Mildmay kept a book of prescriptions for the use of women who followed her. She records her indebtedness to those who passed on prescriptions to her: "A medicine for the falling sickness taught by Mrs. Stacey" and "A very good receipt against the jaunders, taught by old Mistress Bash" (Nagy, 131).

In *Popular Medicine in Seventeenth-Century England* Doreen Evenden Nagy records the extensive use of receipt books in female health care delivery systems:

> While country herb women or wise women depended for the most part on orally transmitted knowledge, many women of gentle birth could

claim some degree of literacy and kept their own collections of "receipts" in personal "Receit Books." The practice of writing and preserving such books must have been widespread. For example, the Bedfordshire Record Office contains at least ten recipe books belonging to women; at least three are from the seventeenth century and four or five from the eighteenth century. . . . Several notable examples of female receipt books in manuscript can be found in the British Library, such as "Mary Doggett: Her Book of Receipts, 1682" and "My Lady Ranelagh's Choice Receipts" (undated), and in private collections. Of the latter, "The Lady Sedley's Receipt Book 1686" is a fine example. . . .

These receipt books were highly valued by their owners and contained prescriptions from a variety of sources: mothers, relatives, friends, servants, professional practitioners and authorities such as Gerard, author of the well-known herbal. One receipt book is known to have been passed down through six successive generations of females in a matriarchally linked family. . . . Additions had been made by other women in the family as it was passed from mother to daughter for almost 120 years. (67)

For those women who decided to have their medical books published, their commitment to the alleviation of suffering and the improvement of health outweighed their doubts about the propriety of women going into print. In their prefaces, they apologized vigorously, though not abjectly, for writing.

A typical apology, found even in a fringe medical textbook, was written by Sarah Jinner in *An Almanack or Prognostication for Women* (1658). "You may wonder," she says in her book, which contains medical information along with astrological charts of propitious times for administering medications, "to see one of our sex in print. . . . But, why not women write, I pray? Have they not souls as well as men?" Jinner continues with her defense of women writing for publication by attacking the prevailing medical and philosophical notion that women are anatomically imperfect men—with undescended testicles and inverted male anatomy. Attempting to prove that women are more than "imperfect men," she focuses on women whose contributions to society's health care equaled those of men. She includes "the virtuous Queen Elizabeth" and "many more that have been famous in philosophy and physic [medicine] as the Countess of Kent, and others." She urges women to make contributions in print and concludes, "Let us scour the rust off, by ingenious endeavoring the attaining higher accomplishments."

This section does not comment on or evaluate medicine in the sixteenth and seventeenth centuries, whether practiced by females or males. There is no need, for example, to point out to the twentieth-century reader that an ophthalmologist today would not use head lice to remove a cloudy film from the eye of a patient. But the documents reprinted here do show that women in those centuries were involved in and knowledgeable in all aspects of health care, that they were not simply ancillary to male physicians and surgeons.

Whether or not Elizabeth Grey, countess of Kent, intended to have her manual of pharmaceutical preparations published during her lifetime cannot be determined. First published in 1651 after her death, it went into nineteen editions over a period of thirty-four years. The manual reflects the state of health care of her day and the continuing suitability of her remedies for more than three decades following her death. It includes prescriptions for measles, plague, dysentery; for cardiac and pulmonary diseases; for syphilis and gonorrhea; for pre- and post-surgical conditions; and for many forms of mental illness, especially depression.

An illness that received considerable attention in the countess of Kent's day was known as green sickness or chlorosis, a condition observed in anemic amenorrheic young women. Long before Dr. Thomas Sydenham (1624–1689) prescribed steel pills or powder for female anemia, the countess of Kent had a recipe for anemia using steel pills or powder, although Dr. Sydenham is usually credited with recognizing the need for iron in such cases. The countess of Kent also included remedies for "the mother," a hysteric or hypochondriac condition (of females, but also of males, as we remember the complaint of King Lear, "O how this mother swells up toward my heart" [II.iv.56]), which is much discussed in medical textbooks written by males.

Lady Margaret Hoby began her diary three years after her third marriage (1599) and stopped writing in it in 1605. Spending most of her married life in Hackness, Yorkshire, she used the diary to chart her medical work in her home and community. Lady Hoby spent a part of each day making the rounds of her patients: she dressed wounds and attended to sores, cuts, bruises, and broken bones; helped those who were suffering from mental illness; and, although she had no children of her own, was called out for "midnight service" in the delivery of babies. Her diary includes no recipes, no prescriptions, no antidotes: she simply records administering prescriptions to those who needed them—

whether a salve for an inflamed breast or a purgative mixture for an ailing servant. Her knowledge of medicine and pharmacy came from the herbals, from Timothy Bright's *A Treatise of Melancholy,* and from other women. Included in the diary are references to her own acute dental pain and her own mental depression. In the midst of mortality, she records a shocking figure that was reported to her: 3,200 people died of the plague in London in one week in 1603. Published in 1930, three and a quarter centuries after it was written, the original diary is in manuscript form in the British Library (Egerton, 2614).

Wartime calls for medical skills. Women usually bring nursing (supportive) skills to the field and to the hospital; men diagnose, prescribe, and perform surgery. In seventeenth-century Britain, many women had to be more than nurses during the English Civil War. The wounded were everywhere, and they needed acute care. Lady Anne Halkett, while traveling in Scotland, met soldiers whose wounds were untreated, stinking, bleeding. They were the walking dead—with deep chest wounds, severed limbs, and head injuries. Their bodies were crawling with lice; their clothes were verminous. One head injury—the man was walking—was so severe that Lady Halkett could see his exposed brain. Acting as both physician and surgeon, she treated more than thirty-six soldiers at the home of the countess of D., where she applied her own medications and surgery to their wounds. She not only performed the task of a physician but was able to operate in the environment of vermin. Lady Halkett was officially recognized by King Charles II for her medical services to soldiers. Without her many of them would have died.

Lady Halkett trained herself in the preparation of medicaments in what seems to have been an extensive practice. Soldiers were not her first patients. Her *Autobiography* records her medical services to many patients: to one woman whose face was being progressively destroyed by cancer; to a man who had a horn growing from his head.

The countess of Kent, Lady Hoby, and Lady Halkett are representative of the females who were primary health caregivers in their day. Names such as Lady Ann Howard, Prudence Potter, Alice Thornton, Lady Anne Clifford, the Barrington women, Lady Warwick, Dorothy Lawson, Lady Honeywood, Mrs. Josselin, Hannah Wolley, Sara Fell, the Ferrar women, Elizabeth Walker, and Lady Nevill must be added to the ranks of women medical practitioners (see Nagy, chap. 5).

Mary Trye was a chemical physician. Her father, the chemical physician Dr. Thomas O'Dowd, taught her everything he knew and took her on his daily rounds. When he died of plague, she took over his practice. Fearless in defense of his anti-Galenic approach to medicine, Trye took on the male medical establishment in her book *Medicatrix, or The Woman Physician.* One section of this book contains Dr. O'Dowd's pharmaceutical recipes and other chemical remedies for a number of illnesses.

Throughout his life her father had been attacked by Dr. Henry Stubbe, a physician whose practice depended largely on the use of surgical instruments and phlebotomy. Dr. Stubbe continued his abusive attacks on chemical medicine and the practice of it after O'Dowd's death. Mary Trye, undaunted by the malicious attacks, forcefully challenged Stubbe, explaining in detail her own approach to medicine and healing. She cites case histories of her successful treatments and cures. Then she dared him to a duel: for every one patient that he cured with surgical instruments (lancet, probe, knife), she would cure two patients by pharmaceutical means. Needless to say, the dare was ignored by Stubbe.

Mary Trye coped with these attacks on her kind of medical practice by identifying her sufferings with those that Christ endured at the hands of enemies who used diabolical language to condemn his unconventional healings of the sick.

Jane Sharp was the first Englishwoman to write a medical handbook for midwives in English. Since midwives were accused of being medically uneducated, ignorant in the anatomy of the reproductive system, contributors to infant mortality, and rivals to the "man midwife," Jane Sharp wanted to share her thirty years' experience as a midwife with her sister midwives by instructing them in the art of delivery of babies and in basic anatomy.

"Sisters," she says in her introduction to *The Midwives Book* (1671), "I have often sat down sad in consideration of the many miseries women endure in the hands of unskillful midwives; many professing the art (without any skill in anatomy, which is the principal part effectually necessary for a midwife) merely for lucre's sake. I have been at great cost in translations for all books, either French, Dutch, or Italian, of the kind. All which I offer with my own experience; humbly begging Almighty God to aid you in this great work; and am your affectionate friend, Jane Sharp."

Apologizing for using English words to describe the reproductive organs of both females and males, she defends her use of the common language: "I shall proceed to set down rules and method concerning this art as I think needful, and that as plainly and briefly as possibly I can, and with as much modesty in words as the matter will bear . . . desiring the Courteous Reader to use as much modesty in the perusal of it, as I have endeavored to do in the writing of it, considering that such an art as this cannot be set forth, but that young men and maids will have much just cause to blush sometimes, and be ashamed of their own follies, as I wish they may if they shall chance to read it, that they may not convert that into evil that is really intended for a general good" (4–5).

What troubled Jane Sharp—and this troubled all the writers of medical textbooks in the vernacular—was a general resistance to anglicizing the vocabulary used to describe the genitals and the process of reproduction. The language of sexuality in most textbooks remained Latinate (as it does today). At considerable risk of ridicule, of being accused of being unprofessional, of being a promoter of bawdry, Jane Sharp talked about the *neck* or *mouth* of the *womb* "which will open and shut like a purse," used the English word *yard* instead of the Latin *penis,* and compared the womb's shape to that of a pear.

Her book of 418 pages continued to be published during her life and after her death, the last edition being published in 1725 and titled *The Compleat Midwife's Companion.* The publisher of the fourth edition paid her this tribute: "The constant and unwearied industry of this ingenious and well-skilled midwife, Mrs. Jane Sharp, together with her great experience of anatomy and physic, by the many years of her practice in the art of midwifery, hath sufficiently recommended her labors, and made them more than ordinarily useful, and much desired by all that either knew her person and experienced her artful skill, or ever read this book, which of late by its *scarceness* hath been so much inquired after, will, I question not, be so much valued, and esteemed by all as to have many after impressions."

There is notoriety connected with the life of Elizabeth Cellier, who had high visibility in her day. Arrested for treason, she defended herself brilliantly and was acquitted. She was rearrested for statements that she had made in a book called *Malice Defeated* (1680), found guilty, ordered to be imprisoned until she paid a fine of £1,000, and, finally, was to be put in the pillory on three separate days in three separate places in London.

In the document reprinted in this section, she answers queries concerning the college of midwives that she had proposed to the king. Her original proposal, dated June 1687, was found in the papers of James II in a folio manuscript titled: "A scheme for the foundation of a Royal hospital and raising a revenue of five or six thousand pounds a year, by and for the maintenance of a corporation of skillful midwives, and such foundlings or exposed children as shall be admitted therein." Cellier uses statistics to prove the need for such a college. Hers is an early attempt to professionalize midwifery by elevating the practice to its rightful place in medical education:

. . . that within the space of twenty years last past, above six thousand women have died in childbed for want of due skill and care in those women who practice the art of midwifery; to remedy which it is humbly proposed that your Majesty will be graciously pleased, by your Royal authority, to unite the whole number of skillful midwives, now practicing within the limits of the weekly bills of mortality, into a corporation under the government of a certain number of the most able and matronlike women among them. . . . That such a number so admitted shall not exceed a thousand at one time. . . . That every woman so admitted as a skillful midwife may be obliged to pay for her admittance the sum of five pounds, and the like sum annually by quarterly payments for and towards the pious and charitable uses hereafter mentioned. . . .

The principal physician or man midwife [shall] examine all extraordinary accidents, and once a month at least read a public lecture to the whole society of licensed midwives, who are all obliged to be present at it, if not employed in their practice; and he shall deliver a copy of such reading, to be entered into the books to be kept for that purpose. . . .

That no men shall be present at such public lectures on any pretense whatsoever, except such able doctors or surgeons as shall enter themselves students in the same art, and pay for such their admittance ten pounds. . . . That all physicians and surgeons so admitted students and practitioners in the art of midwifery shall be of council with the principal man midwife. (Aveling, 76–82)

Apparently King James II endorsed Cellier's proposal and physicians took her seriously, although the query by a physician to which she responded is not extant. Cellier's reply to the physician is not an elaboration of her proposal for a college of midwives but a defense of female midwives—and female physicians. She cites historical precedents for midwives, beginning with Exodus and the delivery of Hebrew children in Egypt by midwives; goes to ancient Greece to prove that a woman disguised as a physician healed women when male physicians had failed to heal them; to pre-Roman Britain for evidence that women practiced medicine there; and to contemporary Britain where women were licensed as midwives (after passing medical examinations) but where, after the Act of Uniformity of 1642, medical instruction was denied midwives and only an oath demanded from them. She concludes her argument by saying that where male physicians had pronounced the queen infertile, she had supervised a regimen that made the queen fertile, showing that fertility and infertility were included in the practice of midwifery.

Her college of midwives was not established. Although the college would have been on shaky financial foundations, it failed not because of its economic impracticability but because James II, its endorser, fled from England. Cellier's fertility methods had proved too successful: the queen gave birth to a male successor to the throne who would (like his father the king and his mother the queen) be of the Roman Catholic faith. Protestant England could not accept a Roman Catholic successor; the hopes of a college of midwives died with his birth.

Although a wealthy woman might wish to nurse her newborn child and be directly involved in its nutritional and emotional well-being, the prevailing opinion in upper-class society was against breast-feeding by the mother. Husbands expressed a dislike for seeing their wives with a nursing infant at the breast. Since it was believed that a mother's milk could be contaminated in sexual intercourse, husbands would be under a prohibition on marital sex. Frowning upon this prohibition and interruption in their sexual lives, upper-class husbands exercised their male authority by insisting that their wives employ wet-nurses for the newborn.

After giving birth to eighteen children, none of whom she nursed, the countess of Lincoln wrote a tract to women trying to persuade them to breast-feed their infants. Two of the countess's babies had died in the care of a wet nurse; she considered her failure to nurse them a contributing factor in their deaths. With prevailing opinion against breast-feeding, however, the countess had to adduce more than her own personal loss to bolster her argument.

Published in 1622, the tract was dedicated to her daughter-in-law, who was breast-feeding her baby. Seeing her suckling her child, the countess muses on biblical examples of women who also nursed their infants—Eve, Sarah, the Virgin Mary, among others. After citing these powerful examples from the scriptures, the countess moved to another argument. She discovers a theological imperative for breast-feeding: God gives milk to mothers; the breast exists to nourish the young; hence mothers must use that breast for its natural purpose. Breast-feeding, she argues, is natural because God ordained it and is essential to the health of the infant. To dry up the breasts is to defy the natural order.

Why, then, her readers might ask, did the countess not nurse her own children? The answer comes in her statement about male authority: "partly I was overruled by another's authority"—presumably her husband's. The tract is addressed to women—is an appeal to women—but the subtext may well have been a challenge to men. The countess demonstrates that God is the final authority in all of life. Husbands have a derived authority: it is received from God. If husbands forbid women to breast-feed their young, they are contradicting God's authority—to the peril of the health of their infant children. In her judgment, the biblical examples of breast-feeding and the scriptural evidence for the God-created natural order show that the health of the infant takes precedence over the sexual expectations of the husband.

The countess concludes with regrets and repentance. She firmly believed that as a primary health caregiver, she had to proclaim the significance of breast-feeding in the health of the newborn and of the mother. Only the mother of the newborn could be the ultimate health caregiver.

Suggested Readings

Aveling, J. H. *English Midwives*. London: J. and A. Churchill, 1872.

Debus, Allen G., ed. *Medicine in Seventeenth-Century England*. Berkeley: University of California Press, 1975.

Eccles, Audrey. *Obstetrics and Gynaecology in Tudor and Stuart England*. London: Croom Helm, 1982.

Forbes, Thomas. "The Registration of English Midwives in the Sixteenth and Seventeenth Centuries." *Medical History* 8 (1964): 235–44.

Fraser, Antonia. *The Weaker Vessel*. New York: Knopf, 1984.

Guthrie, Leonard. "The Lady Sedley's Receipt Book, 1686, and Other Seventeenth-Century Receipt Books." *Proceedings of the Royal Society of Medicine* 6 (1913): 150–70.

Guy, John R. "The Episcopal Licensing of Physicians, Surgeons, and Midwives." *Bulletin of the History of Medicine* 56 (1982): 528–42.

Nagy, Doreen Evenden. *Popular Medicine in Seventeenth-Century England*
Bowling Green, Ohio: Bowling Green State University Press, 1988.
Smith, Snell Donna. "Tudor and Stuart Midwifery." Ph.D. diss., University of Kentucky, 1980.
Weigall, Rachel. "An Elizabethan Woman: The Journal of Lady Mildmay." *Quarterly Review* 215 (1911): 119–38.

22

A CHOICE MANUALL

*OR Rare and select secrets in physick**

Elizabeth Grey, Countess of Kent

For a pin or web in the eye. Take two or three lice out of one's head, and put them alive into the eye that is grieved, and so close it up, and most assuredly the lice will suck out the web in the eye, and will cure it, and come forth without any hurt.

A powder for the green sickness, approved with very good success upon many. Take of cloves, mace, nutmegs, of each one quarter of an ounce, beat them severally, and then altogether very well, fine sugar very small beaten and one quarter of a pound, and then mix and beat them all four together, pearl the sixth part of half an ounce very finely beaten, mingle it with the rest, and beat them altogether again, the filing of steel or iron one ounce and a quarter, sift it very fine, and mingle it with the rest, but if so small a quantity will not serve, add a quarter more of the metal, let it be sifted before you weigh it, but if all this will not serve the turn, put in a rhubarb, or a little Alexakatrina [culinary plant].

The manner of using this powder. In the morning when you rise take half a spoonful of it, take as much at four o'clock in the afternoon, and as much when you go to bed, walk or stir much after the first takings of it, or more, and then eat some sugar sops or thin broth.

The patient's diet. She must forbear oatmeal in broth or any other thing, cheese, eggs, custards, or any stopping meat [constipating food]. Take care that this be not given to any woman that hath conceived, or is with child.

For a dead child in a woman's body. Take the juice of hyssop, temper it in warm water, and give it to the woman to drink.

*Second edition, London 1653. Wing K311, Reel 152, pp. 41, 77, 80–82, 87–88, 90, 114, 127, 145.

For a woman that hath her flowers too much [frequent menstruation] Take a hare's foot, and burn it, make powder of it, and let her drink it with stale ale.

To cause a woman to have her sickness [menstruation]. Take agrimonye, motherwort, avens, and parsley, shred them small with oatmeal, make pottage of them with pork, let her eat the pottage, but not the pork.

For the mother [for suffocation of the womb; hysteria]. Take three or four handfuls of fern that groweth upon a house, seethe it in Rhenish wine till it be well sodden, then put it in a linen cloth, and lay it to her navel, as hot as she may suffer it, four or five times.

To deliver a child in danger. Take a date stone, beat it into powder, let the woman drink it with wine, then take polipody [wallfern] and emplaster it to her feet, and the child will come whether it be quick or dead; then take centory [centaury], green or dry, give it to the woman to drink in wine, give her also the milk of another woman.

A remedy for the mother. When the fit beginneth to take them, take the powder of white amber, and burn it in a chafing dish of coals, and let them hold their mouths over it, and suck in the smoke, and anoint their nostrils with the oil of amber, and if they be not with child, take two or three drops of the oil of amber in white wine warm or cold, but the oil of amber must be taken inward but once a day, and outward as often as the fit taketh them.

23

DIARY OF LADY MARGARET HOBY*

(1599–1605)

January 30, 1599, the 3rd day of the week

After I had prayed privately I dressed a poor boy's leg that came to me, and then brake my fast with Mr. Hoby: after, I dressed the hand of one of our servants that was very sore cut . . . after to supper, then to the lector: after that I dressed one of the men's hands that was hurt, lastly prayed, and so to bed.

The fourth day of the week, 31

After I was ready I prayed, then I went about the house and dressed two that was hurt. . . .

The fifth day of the week, February 1

After I was ready I went about the house and then prayed, brake my fast, dressed a poor boy's leg that was hurt, and Jurden's hand. . . .

The sixth day of the week, 2

After I had prayed I dressed the sores that came to me. . . .

The Lord's Day, 3

After private prayers I did eat my breakfast, and then dressed the sores that I had undertaken . . . came to private examination and prayer, and then to supper: after, to the Repetition and, when I had dressed some sores, I went to private prayer and so to bed.

The first day of the week, 4

. . . at 5 o'clock I dressed my patients . . . .

*Ed. Dorothy M. Meads (London: George Routledge and Sons, 1930), pp. 100–101, 102, 168–170, 197, 201, 204–5.

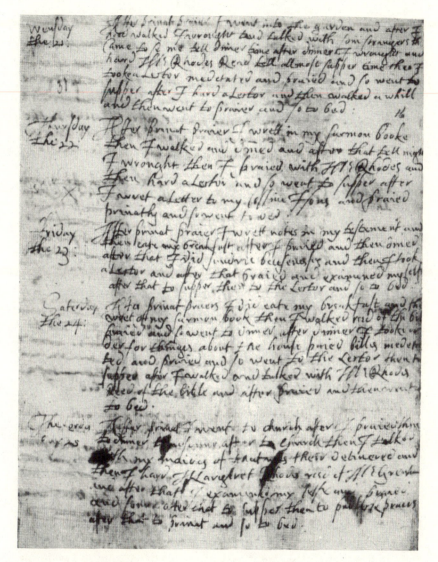

Figure 7. Folio 16A from *The Diary of Lady Margaret Hoby.*

The Lord's Day, 10

After private prayer I did eat my breakfast, then went to church: after I came home, I dressed my patients, then dined: after dinner I talked with some of my neighbors that came to me till church time: then, after the sermon, I dressed other poor folks. . . .

The 17 day, 1601

This day Blakeborn cut his foot with a hatchet.

The 18th day

This day I finished my work, wrote letters to London, talked with Mr. Stillington, prayed at my accustomed times, and dressed Thomas Blakeborn's foot. . . .

The Lord's Day, 26

After I was ready I went to the church, and after prayers and sermon, I came home and dressed Blakeborn's foot . . . after, I went to the church, and after sermon, I dressed a poor man's hand. . . .

The 27th day

After private prayer I was busy about the house, and dressed my servant's foot and another poor man's hand, and talked with others that came to ask my counsel: after I went into the garden and gave some herbs unto a good wife of Erley for his [*sic*] garden. . . .

May, the 9th day

This day I kept my chamber and took physic, being all the night before pained in my teeth so that I neither slept nor took rest.

The 10th day

I was for my pain eased, but my face was swollen, and so I kept my chamber, save that I went to the church. . . .

The 6th day, 1602

I praise God I had health of body: howsoever justly God hath suffered Satan to afflict my mind, yet my hope is that my Redeemer will bring my soul out of troubles, that it may praise his name: and so I will wait with patience for deliverance: from the 6th unto the 20th, I praise God, I continued well, and found God's mercy in vouchsafing me comfort every way: and now I beseech thee, O Lord, give me power to render unto thee the calves of my lips [Hosea 14:2], and with my whole heart to follow righteousness.

The 23rd of March, 1603, which day the Queen departed this life

August the 24th

Came Robert Netelton from York and told us that the number of those that died of the plague at London: 124; that Newcastle was grievously visited with a sore plague, likewise Hull: the King took about this time his journey into Wales with the Queen and the young prince.

September 4th

We heard that the plague was spread in Whitby, and that there died at London 3200 a week.

The 23rd of September

Mr. Hunter came and kept us company at dinner, who told us of the exercise that should be held for this great mortality, which was not only at London but almost dispersed through all the realm of England: God of his mercy pardon our sins, for Christ's sake, Amen.

24

THE AUTOBIOGRAPHY OF
LADY ANNE HALKETT*

1650

Upon Saturday the 7. of September we left Dunfermline, and came that night to Kinrose, where we stayed till Monday. I cannot omit to insert here the opportunity I had of serving many poor wounded soldiers, for as we were riding to Kinrose I saw two that looked desperately ill, who were so weak they were hardly able to go along the highway; and inquiring what ailed them, they told me they had been soldiers at Dunbar, and were going towards Kinrose if their wounds would suffer them. I bid them when they came there inquire for the Countess of D. lodging, and there would be one there would dress them. It was late it seems before they came, and so till the next morning I saw them not, but then they came attended with twenty more, and betwixt that time and Monday that we left that place I believe threescore was the least that was dressed by me and my woman and Ar. Ro. who I employed to such as was unfit for me to dress; and besides the plasters or balsam I applied, I gave every one of them as much with them as might dress them 3 or 4 times, for I had provided myself very well of things necessary for that employment, expecting they might be useful. Amongst the many variety of wounds amongst them two was extraordinary: one was a man whose head was cut so that the [blank] was very visibly seen, and the water came bubbling up, which when Ar. Ro. saw he cried out, "Lord have mercy upon thee! for thou art but a dead man." I seeing the man who had courage enough before begin to be much disheartened, I told him he need not be discouraged with what he that had no skill said, for if it pleased God to bless what I should give him he might do well enough; and this I said more to hearten him up than otherwise, for I

*Printed for the Camden Society, London, 1875; pp. 62–64, 66–67.

saw it a very dangerous wound; and yet it pleased God he recovered, as I heard afterwards, and went frankly from dressing, having given him something to refresh his spirits. The other was a youth about 16 that had been run through the body with a tuke [rapier]. It went in under his right shoulder and came out under his left breast, and yet [he] had little inconvenience by it; but his greatest prejudice was from so infinite a swarm of creatures that it is incredible for any that were not eyewitnesses of it. I made a contribution and bought him other clothes to put on him, and made the fire consume what else had been impossible to destroy. Of all these poor soldiers there was few of them had ever been dressed from the time they received their wounds till they came to Kinrose, and then it may be imagined they were very noisome; but one particularly was in that degree who was shot through the arm that none was able to stay in the room, but all left me. Accidentally a gentleman came in, who seeing me (not without reluctancy) cutting off the man's sleeve of his doublet, which was hardly fit to be touched, he was so charitable as to take a knife and cut it off and fling it in the fire.

When I had dressed all that came, my Lady D. was by this time ready to go away, and came to St. Johnston that night, where the King and Court was. My La. A. A. and I waited upon my Lady into her sister the C. of Kinowle, and there my Lord Lorne came to me, and told me that my name was often before the Council that day. I was much surprised, which his Lord P. seeing kept me the longer in suspense; at last he smiling told me there was a gentleman (which it seems was he that had cut off the man's sleeve) that had given the King and Council account of what he had seen and heard I had done to the poor soldiers, and representing the sad condition they had been in without yet relief, there was presently an order made to appoint a place in several towns, and surgeons to have allowance for taking care of such wounded soldiers as should come to them. And the King was pleased to give me thanks for my charity. I have made this relation because it was the occasion of bringing me much of the divertissement I had in a remoter place. . . .

The variety of distempered persons that came to me was not only a divertissement, but a help to instruct me how to submit under my own crosses, by seeing how patient they were under theirs, and yet some of them intolerable by wanting a sense of faith which is the greatest support under afflictions. There was three most remarkable of any that came to me: one, Isbell Stevenson, who had been three years under a discomposed spirit; the other was a young woman who had been very beautiful, and her face became loathsomely deformed with a cancerous humor that had overspread it, which deprived her of her nose and one of her eyes, and had eaten much of her forehead and cheeks away; the third was a man that had a horn on the left side of the hinder part of his head, betwixt 4 and 5 inches about and 2 inches long, and his wife told me she had cut the length of her finger off (as she usually did) when two or three days before he came to me, because the weight of it was troublesome.

25

MEDICATRIX

OR The woman physician *

Mary Trye

*Vindicating Thomas O'Dowd, a Chemical Physician
and Royal Licentiate; and chemistry; against the calumnies
and abusive reflections of Henry Stubbe, a physician at Warwick.*

*The Epistle Dedicatory: To the glory of her sex, the honor of her country, and the
most accomplished Lady, the Lady Fisher, Wife of Sir Clement Fisher, Knight
and Baronet of Packington-Hall in the County of Warwick.*

. . . I think it may modestly be said that you will find some things
herein not very common . . . and that is that one of the feminine degree, in a medicinal contest, hath now encountered a rhetorical and
physical hector, an expression I confess too generous for one that deserves so little.

But that my pen may not altogether surprise your Ladyship by these
occasional and vindicatory papers . . . 'twill be civil and requisite to let
you know that abiding the late great and never-to-be-forgotten pestilen-
tial calamity of this city, and undergoing that mortal stroke, in which I
lost two of my dearest friends, my father and mother, but surviving
them myself, I received a medicinal talent from my father, which by the
instruction of so excellent a tutor as he was to me, and my constant
preparation and observation of medicines, together with my daily experience by reason of his very great practice; as also being mistress of a
reasonable share of that knowledge and discretion other women attain;
I made myself capable of disposing such noble and successful medicines, and managing so weighty and great a concern.

*London, 1675. Wing T3174, Reel 1296, pp. 55–60, 113–15.

In process to the strict commands and deathbed injunction of so good a father, which was, that his medicines being of that value and incomparable benefit to the world, that no man in this kingdom was master of the like (notwithstanding the high malice of his enemies and pitiful detractors), I should never suffer them to fall to the ground, or to die and be buried in oblivion, nor never to stop my ears from the cry of the poor, languishing for want of such medicines. . . . I have continued his medicines to this day (though not in this city) to the succor of many hundreds, more out of charity than my private interest to the bright glory of these chemical, and not-to-be-paralleled medicines, and to the shame and odium of his Galenical opposers. . . . [Signed Mary Trye, From the Feathers, in the Old Pell-Mell near Saint James's, 1 December 1674]

* * *

. . . I confess, I have good divinity, and reason to content me; since I do firmly believe that there was once the Son of God upon earth that patiently endured his temporary course under the greatest passion and bitter malediction imaginable; and that not only in the general deportment of his life, but even in this particular fact of healing, the Savior of the world was condemned and assaulted with the language of devils.

And since I must take liberty to tell Mr. Stubbe that I am satisfied there is ability enough in my sex, both to discourse his envy and equal the arguments of his pen in those things that are proper for a woman to engage: and what is more, that knowledge and skill in chemistry so far as to obtain those medicines that neither the Medicus at Warwick, nor all his authors he pretends he hath perused, if not conjured together, could ever parallel or procure: Neither is this so great a mystery, nor shall I seem immodest if it be considered that Mr. Stubbe abominates experiment and all such _____. . . . in sum, his rude, idle paper blotted with folly, and uncivilly reflecting on this deceased physician I have mentioned, together with some other bold and intolerable errors, imposed on the world by Mr. Stubbe, provokes, and therefore I proceed thus to defense and challenge.

* * *

. . . His [her father's] death was after this manner, the week before the sickness was at the highest pitch, which was in August 1665. My father, passing over to Chelsea to visit a gentlewoman sick there, and taking me with him, as we went near the neat houses, he made his servant fetch him a muskmelon, which he had a more than ordinary desire for . . . and he was himself afterwards satisfied was the original cause of his mortal seizure; and I doubt not but those chemical physicians that abided the pest, by their public and free practice amongst all patients, easily saw that any light surfeit was the inlet and retainer of that nimble, devouring mortal guest, the Plague; and such a plague that I think could not be fiercer or more destructive. . . . Next morning he seemed somewhat discomposed. . . . That morning he was engaged to attend a person, as I remember, near Charing Cross . . . to whom some application . . . was made about a botch, or carbuncle; the poisonous matter thereof so unexpectedly flew about the room, the patient being very corpulent, that I heard say occasioned the most horrid stench he ever smelt. . . .

Yet for all this, although minded and desired to take medicines to rectify and prevent, his business so pressed him that he was forced to put off and defer the taking anything several days, as I think from Wednesday to Monday; and delays in those cases, and at that time, those that understand it, well know was not very safe. But indeed the great burden and care of the sick that was then upon him would not permit him any leisure, till at last he was so far spent and seized that he was entangled and taken captive by the ill effects and misery of that malignant and monstrous disease. . . . he could not be ever prevailed with to take one medicine of his own, or anybody's else . . . but in a few hours he saw his infallible messengers, and in two hours more, he pleasantly, sensibly, and most willingly resigned himself into the hands of him who can best judge of his merit. . . .

This terrible sickness now prevailing to the amazement of all, and so outrageous, that woeful and lamentable were the shrieks, the cries, and groans of poor creatures, and some of their needs so great that, our house being shut up, we had much ado to prevent the doors and windows from being broken open . . . yet with what conveniences I could, I conveyed medicines to many of those that wanted.

The next Friday after the death of my father, I fell ill myself of this raging disease, and by the goodness of God, and the medicines of my father, directed by my own order and instruction, I recovered; three of our family more were likewise presently smitten with the same stroke, but all of them I preserved with my father's medicines. . . .

* * *

I will give him [Mr. Stubbe] one example in full answer to him and all his assertions, which was a cure performed on an apoplectic person [one who has suffered a stroke], to the view and notice of all the country round him; the patient was one Major Abrell, a gentleman of good fortune, and well known in the county where he lives, who fell ill one night of an apoplexy. I being then in the country within two or three miles of him, his Lady sent earnestly to press my coming to him; but because I was at that time indisposed, and not willing to take the trouble of the country in such affairs, I desired to be excused, and advised their sending for some other. . . . But I denied and refused as before, till at last by their undeniable importunity, and the persuasions of some of my own relations in the same family with me, I went, and found him in his bed, in a desperate and sad condition, having lain so for several hours, speechless and insensible, his mouth displaced by a strong convulse, and foaming thereat, with difficulty of breathing, and a rattling in his throat, as if ready to be choked. . . . So soon as I had told them what was to be done, I ordered the patient to be placed in that posture, as I thought fit, for the reception of that medicine I had carefully and particularly prepared for him; and his mouth being with some trouble opened, I gave him a small quantity of this liquid medicine, some of which took place, and immediately, in as little time as I could walk the room to and fro, the convulse ceased: And in less than a quarter of an hour, Nature began to be enlivened, assisted, and roused up; and the patient moved, discharging half a pint or more (in a short space) of the offensive and apoplectic matter; and in an hour he began to look about and came to utter many words, and in half an hour more spoke sensibly. Now having secured his life from any fear of danger, I left him, leaving my directions.

. . . before night (I was informed after) he rose out of his bed and sat up: And with three or four medicines more which I sent him, he was recovered perfect well; and his head and body, not only cleansed and disburdened of this ill guest, but of some other troublesome indispositions he had for some years been oppressed with. . . .

And now Mr. Stubbe may see . . . and whether this course where there are such noble, amicable, safe, effectual remedies to be had, is not better, less tedious, more certain and quick to prevent the great hazard and danger of delay in this sickness than his impertinent lancet, shavings, burnt feathers, snuff, tickling the nose, pinching the fingers and toes, whooping in the ears, touching the lute, frictions, ligatures, and a long list more. . . . I have by this example contradicted the bold, erroneous doctrine of the Physician at Warwick. . . .

26

THE MIDWIVES BOOK*

Jane Sharp, Practitioner in the Art of Midwifery above Thirty Years

Of the Generation or Privy Parts in Women

Man in the act of procreation is the agent and tiller and sower of the ground, woman is the patient or ground to be tilled, who brings seed also as well as the man to sow the ground with. I am now to proceed to speak of this ground or field which is the woman's womb, and the parts that serve to this work: we women have no more cause to be angry, or be ashamed of what Nature hath given us than men have; we cannot be without ours no more than they can want theirs. The things most considerable to be spoken to are, 1. The neck of the womb or privy entrance. 2. The womb itself. 3. The stones. 4. The vessels of seed. At the bottom of the woman's belly is a little bank called a mountain of pleasure near the wellspring and the place where the hair coming forth shows virgins to be ready for procreation, in some far younger than others; some are more forward at twelve years than some at fifteen years of age, as they are hotter and riper in constitution. Under this hill is the springhead, which is a passage having two lips set about with hair as the upper part is: I shall give you a brief account of the parts of it, both within and without, and of the likeness and proportion between the generative parts in both sexes. . . .

Of the Womb Itself or Matrix

The womb is that field of nature into which the seed of man and woman is cast, and it hath also an attractive faculty to draw in a magnetic

*London, 1671; pp. 33–34, 63–80.

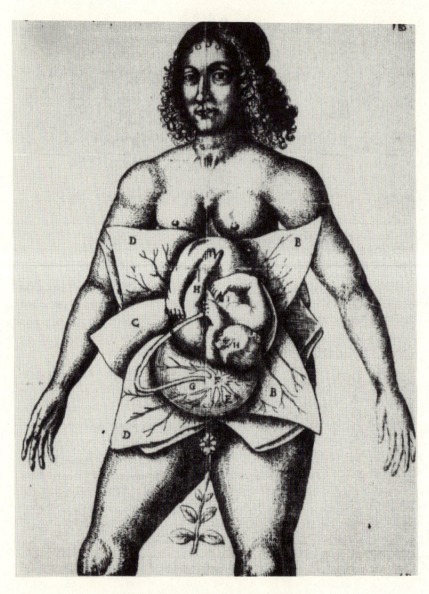

Figure 8. Illustration from *The Midwives Book,* by Jane Sharp.

quality, as the lodestone draweth iron, or fire the light of the candle; and to this seed runs the woman's blood also, to beget, nourish, increase and preserve the infant till it is time for it to be born; for the natural and vegetable soul is virtually in the seed, and runs through the whole mass, and is brought into act by the virtue and heat of the woman that receives the seed, and by the forming faculty which lies hid in the seed of both sexes, and in the disposition of the womb both seeds are well mingled together at the same time in all parts of the body, I mean as to the parts made of seed, but as for the parts made with blood, they are made at several times, as they can sooner or later procure nourishment and spirits. The parts therefore next the liver are sooner made than those that are far from it, and those are first made that the mother's blood first runs to, that is first the navel vein, and that being first made, by that the blood is carried to other parts.

The womb is like a bottle or bladder blown when the infant is in it, and it lieth in the lower belly, and in the last place amongst the entrails by the watercourse, because this is easily enlarged as the child grows in the womb; and the child is by this means more easily begot, and the woman delivered of it; nor is it any hindrance to the parts of nutrition while the woman continues with child; but had the womb where the infant lieth been seated in the middle or upper belly, the child would have been soon stifled, for the womb could not have stretched wider according to the growth of the child, because the bones that compass the upper belly would have hindered it.

The hollow part of the belly where the womb lieth is called the bason, and it is placed between the bladder and the right gut; the bladder stands before it, and is a strong membrane to defend it, and the right gut lieth behind it as a pillow to keep off the hardness of the backbone, so that the womb lieth in the middle of the lowest belly to balance the body equally, and to contain the womb: the bason is larger in women than in men, as you may see by their larger buttocks. As the child grows, the bottom of the womb which lieth uppermost, lying at liberty and not tied, grows upward towards the navel, and so leans upon the small guts, and so fills all the hollow of the flanks when women are near the time to bring forth.

The womb is fastened and tied partly by the substance of it, and also by four ligaments, two above, and two beneath, but the bottom is not tied neither before, nor behind, nor above, but is free and at liberty, that it can stretch as need requires in copulation or childbearing, and it hath

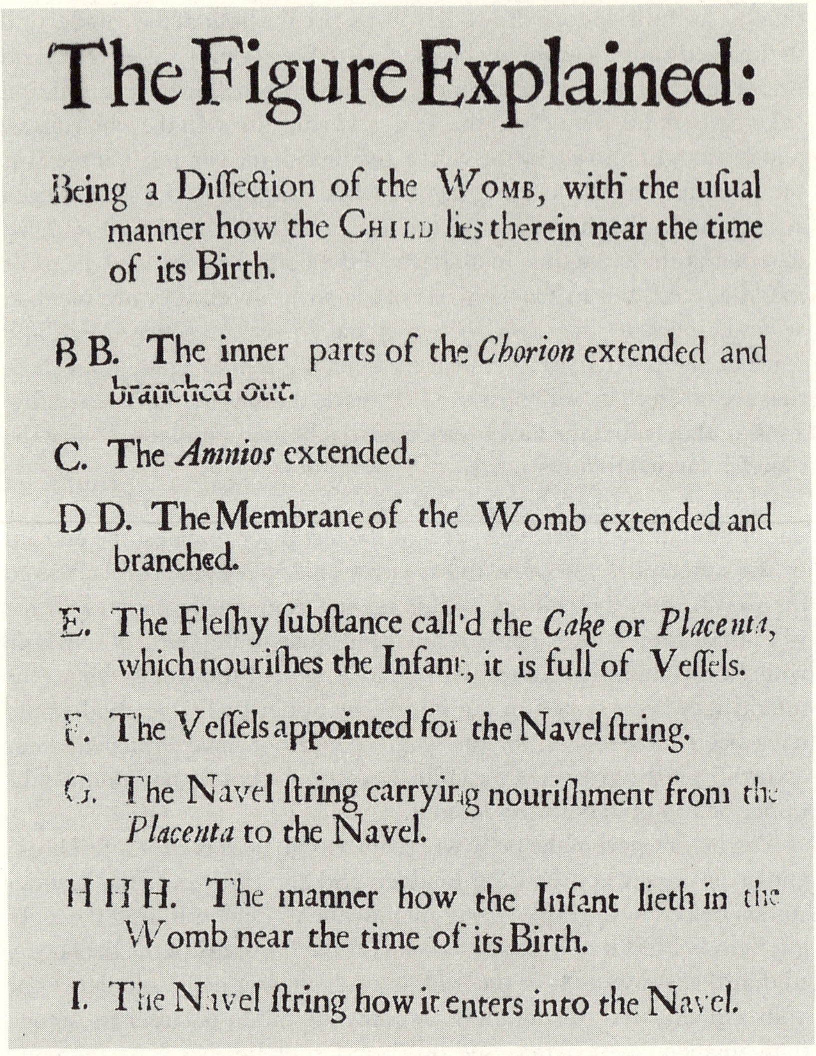

The Figure Explained:

Being a Diffection of the Womb, with the ufual manner how the Child lies therein near the time of its Birth.

B B. The inner parts of the *Chorion* extended and branched out.

C. The *Amnios* extended.

D D. The Membrane of the Womb extended and branched.

E. The Flefhy fubftance call'd the *Cake* or *Placenta*, which nourifhes the Infant, it is full of Veffels.

F. The Veffels appointed for the Navel ftring.

G. The Navel ftring carrying nourifhment from the *Placenta* to the Navel.

H H H. The manner how the Infant lieth in the Womb near the time of its Birth.

I. The Navel ftring how it enters into the Navel.

Figure 9. Page from *The Midwives Book,* by Jane Sharp.

a kind of animal motion to satisfy its desire. Galen saith that the sides are fastened to the haunch-bone by membranes and ligaments, coming from the muscles of the loins, and interwoven ofttimes with fleshy fibers, and carried to other parts of the womb to hold it fast.

The neck of the womb is tied, but not every side, to the parts that lie near it; at the sides it is loosely tied to the peritoneum by certain membranes that grow to it, and on the back part it is fastened with thin fibers, and a little fat to the right gut and the holy-bone, it lieth upon that fat all along that passage, and it grows into one with the fundament, above the lap, to which it is joined before; if the fundament chance to be ulcerated within, the dung hath been seen to fall out at the lap.

The forepart is knit to the neck of the bladder, and because the womb's neck is broader than the neck of the bladder, some part of it is fastened by membranes coming from the peritoneum to the share-bone; from hence it happens that when the womb is inflamed, the woman hath a great desire to go to stool and to make water, but cannot.

The lower strings that fasten the womb are two also, called the horns of the womb; they are sinewy, round, reddish, and hollow, chiefly at their ends, like to the husky membrane; and sometimes this hollowness is full of fat; these horns come from the side of the womb, and at their first coming forth they touch the seed-carrying vessels.

Fleshy fibers are joined to these productions after they come forth of the abdomen and they are small muscles called holders-up in women. They belong not to the stones as they do in men, because they join in men to the seed vessels. When these ligaments come at the share-bone, they change into a broad sinewy slenderness, mingled with a membrane which toucheth and covers the forepart of the share-bone, and upon this the clitoris cleaveth and is tied, which being nervous, and of pure feeling, when it is rubbed and stirred it causeth lustful thoughts, which being communicated to these ligaments, it passeth to the vessels that carry the seed. Yet these holders-up serve for other uses, for as they are muscles that hold up the stones in men, so they hold up the womb in women that it may be kept from falling out at the lap.

The parts then of the womb are two: The neck or mouth, and the bottom. The neck is the entrance into it, which will open and shut like a purse, for in the act of copulation it receives the yard into it, but after conception the point of a bodkin cannot pass; yet when the time comes for the child to come forth, it will open and make room enough for the greatest child that is conceived. This made Galen wonder, and so should we all, to consider how fearfully and wonderfully God hath made us as the Psalmist saith, "The works of the Lord are wonderful, to be sought out of all those that take pleasure therein."

The form of the womb is exactly round, and in maids it is no bigger than a walnut, yet it will stretch so after conception that it will easily contain the child and all that belongs to it; it is small at first to embrace the seed that is but little cast into it. It is made of two skins, an outward and an inward skin; the outward is thick, smooth, and slippery, excepting those parts where the seed vessels come into the womb; the inward skin is full of small holes.

It is far different from the matrix of beasts which Galen knew not, for the Grecians in those days held it an abomination to dissect any man or woman though they were dead; all the knowledge of anatomy they learned was by dissecting apes and such creatures that were the most like to mankind, but the inside of men or women they saw not, and so were ignorant of the difference between them. Whence it is confirmed that they knew not the seat of some diseases so well as we do, and therefore must need fall short of the cure; nor would they use the means to find out what disease they died of, which true anatomy would have made known to them, and would have been a great furtherance to preserve others that were sick of the same diseases that others died of before. . . .

. . . the beginning of conception is not so soon as the seed is cast into the womb, for then a woman would conceive every time she receives it. But the perfect mixing of the seed of both sexes is the beginning of conception, and it is hard to believe that the womb that is so small at first that it will hardly hold a bean, and having but one cell, can mingle the man and woman's seed together exactly in two places at the same time, and it is certain it shuts so close that no place is left for the air to enter in. . . .

Of the Fashion and Greatness of the Womb, and of the Parts It Is Made Of

The womb is of the form of a pear, round toward the bottom and large, but narrow by degrees to the neck; the roundness of it makes it fit to contain much, and it is therefore less subject to be hurt. When women are with child the bottom is broad like a bladder, and the neck narrow; but where they are not with child, the bottom is no broader than the neck. Some women's wombs are larger than others, according to the age, stature, and burden that they bear; maid's wombs are small and less than their bladders; but women's are greater, especially after they have once had a child, and so it will continue. It stretcheth after they have conceived, and the larger it extends the thicker it grows.

It hath parts of two kinds: the simple parts it is made of are membranes, veins, nerves, and arteries.

The compound parts are four: the mouth, the bottom, the neck, and the lap or lips. The membranes are two as I said, one outward and the other inward, that it may open and shut at pleasure; the outward membrane is sinewy, and the thickest of all the membranes that come from the peritoneum; it is strong and doubled, and clothes the womb to make it more strong, and grows to it on both sides. The inward membrane is double also, but can scarce be seen but in exulcerations of the womb. When the woman conceives, it is thick and soft, but it grows thicker daily, and is thickest when the time of birth is. Fibers of all kinds run between these membranes to draw and keep the seed, and to thrust forth the burden, and the flesh of the womb is chiefly made up of fleshy fibers.

The three sorts of fibers for seed do plainly appear after women have gone long with child; those that draw the seed are inward, and are not many. Because the seed is most cast into the womb by the yard, the thwart fibers are strongest, and most, and they are in the middle, but the fibers that lie transverse are strong also, and lie outward, because it is great force that is required in time of delivery.

The veins and arteries that pass through the membranes of the womb come from divers places, for two veins and two arteries come from the seed vessels, and two veins and two arteries from the vessels in the lower belly, and run upward, that from all the body, both from above and under, blood of all sorts might be conveyed, to bring nourishment for the womb, and for the infant in it; also they serve as scavengers to purge out the terms every month. The twigs of the vein that is in the lower belly mingle in the womb with the branches of the seed veins, and the mouths of them reach into the hollow of the womb, and they are called cups; through these comes more blood always than the infant needs, that the child may never want nutriment in the womb, and there may be some to spare when the time comes for the child to be born; but after the birth, this blood comes not hither but goes to the breasts to make milk; but at all other times it is cast out monthly what is superfluous, and if it be not, it corrupts and causeth fits of the mother; yet they come more often from the seed corrupted and staying there than they do from blood.

It is not only blood is voided by the terms, but multitude of humors and excrements, and these purgations last sometimes three or four days, sometimes a week, and young folk have them when the moon changeth, but women in years at the full of the moon; which is to be observed, that we may know when to give remedies to maids whose terms come not down, for we must do it in the time when the moon is new or ready to change, and to elder women about the time that nature uses to send them forth, because a physician is but a helper to nature, and if he observe not nature's rules, he will sooner kill than cure.

The sinews of the womb are small but many, and interwoven like network, which makes it quick of feeling; they come to the upper part of the bottom from the branches of the nerves of the sixth conjugation, which go to the root of the ribs, and to the lower part of the bottom, and to the neck of the womb from the marrow of loins and the great bone. Thus they by their quick feeling cause pleasure in copulation and expulsion of what offends the part; they are most plentiful at the bottom of the womb, to quicken and strengthen it in attracting and embracing the seed of man.

There is but one continued passage from the top or lap to the bottom of the womb; yet some divide it into four parts; namely into 1. The upper part, or bottom, for that lieth uppermost in the body. 2. The mouth or inward orifice of the neck. 3. The neck. 4. The outward lap, lips, or privity.

The chief part of these, which is properly the womb or matrix, is the bottom; here is the infant conceived, kept, formed and fed until the rational soul be infused from above, and the child born. The broader part or bottom is set above the share-bone that may be dilated as the child grows; the outside is smooth and overlaid with a watery moisture: there is a corner on each side above, and when women are not with child, the seed is poured out into these, for the carrying vessels for seed are planted into them. They are to make more room for the child, and at first it is so small that the parents' seed fills it full, for it embraceth it, be it never so little, as close as 'tis possible: the bottom is full of pores, but they are but the mouths of the cups by which the blood in childbearing comes out of the veins of the womb into the cavity. The corners of the womb's bottom are wrinkled; the bottom is softer than the neck of it, yet harder than the lap and more thick. From the lower part of the bottom comes a piece an inch long like the nut of the man's yard, but small as one's little finger, and a pin's point will but enter into it, but it is rough to keep the seed from recoiling after it is once attracted, for when the parts are overslippery the humors are peccant, and those women are barren. Hippocrates saith, that sometimes part of the kall [membrane] falls between the bladder and the womb and makes women fruitless.

This part may well be reckoned for another part of the womb, for it lieth between the beginning of the bottom and the mouth, and there is a clear passage in it. The womb hath two mouths, the inward mouth and the outward; by the inward mouth the bottom opens directly into the neck, this mouth lieth overthwart like the mouth of a plaice, or the passage of the nut of the yard; the whole orifice with the slit transverse is like the Greek letter theta Θ: it is so little and narrow that the seed once in can scarce come back, nor any offensive thing enter into the hollow of the womb. The mouth lieth directly against the bottom, for the seed goeth in a straight line from the neck to the bottom.

The womb is always shut but in time of generation, and then the bottom draws in the seed, and it presently shuts so close that no needle, as I saith, can find an entrance, and thus it continues till the time of delivery, unless some ill accident, or disease force it to open; for when women with child are in copulation with men, they do give seed forth, but that seed comes not from the bottom, as some think, but by the neck of the womb. It must open when a child is born so wide as to give passage for it by degrees, because the neck of the womb is of a compact thick substance, and thicker when the birth is nigh; wherefore there cleaves to it a body like glue, and by that means the mouth opens safely without danger of being torn or broken; and as often as the passage is open, it comes away like a round crown, and midwives call it the rose, the garland, or the crown. If this mouth be too often and unreasonably opened by too frequent coition, or in overmoist bodies, or by the whites, it makes women barren, and therefore whores have seldom any children; it is the same reason if it grow too hard or thick or fat, also the cancer and the scirrhus, two diseases incurable, which happen but seldom till the courses fail, are bred here.

Thus I have as briefly and as plainly as I could, laid down a description of the parts of generation of both sexes, purposely omitting hard names, that I might have no cause to enlarge my work, by giving you the meaning of them where there is no need, unless it be for such persons who desire rather to know words than things.

27

TO DR. _____ AN ANSWER TO HIS QUERIES,
CONCERNING THE COLLEGE OF MIDWIVES*

Elizabeth Cellier

To answer your query, Doctor, Whether ever there were a College of Midwives in any part of the world? According to my promise made the 12th instant, I will now prove there was some hundreds, if not thousands of years before you can prove one of physicians: as appears both by sacred and profane histories. I will begin with the first; and desire you to read the first chapter of Exodus.

> Verse 15. And the King of Egypt spake to the Hebrew midwives, of which the name of the one was Shiprah, and the other Puah.
> Verse 16. And he said unto them, When ye do the office of a midwife to the Hebrew women, and see them upon the stools; if it be a son, you shall kill him: but if it be a daughter, then she shall live.
> Verse 17. But the midwives feared God, and did not as the King of Egypt commanded them, but saved the men children alive.
> Verse 20. Wherefore God dealt well with the midwives: and the people multiplied, and waxed very mighty.
> Verse 21. And it came to pass, because the midwives feared God, that he made them houses.

I believe no rational person will think that these two women could in their own persons act as midwives to all the women of that mighty people, who about 100 years after went up out of Egypt 600,000 fighting men, besides women and children, and a great mixed multitude, but rather that they were the governesses and teachers of other midwives,

*London, 1688. Wing C1663, Reel 1457.

which could not be a few; and as I am informed by a learned Rabbi, now in town, their names signify the same.

And the Apostle saith, That God built them houses, and blessed them.

Now if it were, as some think, that these were not Israelites but Egyptians, appointed governesses over such as should assist the Hebrew women, who by conversation among them learned the knowledge of the only true God, and fearing him, did not impose those bloody orders of destroying the males.

Then it was plain that the government of that art was regular, under superiors, as the magi and priesthood of that nation was, and must have some certain place for consulting in, from whence they might issue their directions. Which, by your leave, Doctor, without absurdity in the language of these times, might well be called a college.

But for the piety of the ruling midwives God built them houses: that is, they were incorporated into the body of the Jews, and reckoned honorable families among them: as Rahab and others for their singular service to that nation afterwards were. Which families of the faithful midwives, some Hebrews say, continue in honor among them at Thessalonica to this day.

And such a favor from God of building houses for them, we do not read the physicians ever received; nor was physic then a regular study, nor brought under government in that learned nation of Egypt, in Herodotus his time, which put together, proves the antiquity of the midwives' government so much ancienter than that of the doctors.

For your further satisfaction be pleased to read Origen, his 11th Homily upon Exodus, which will inform you that Shiprah and Puah were not only the governesses of the midwives, but also women of great learning, and excellently skilled in physic, which was then practiced by women to women.

And you cannot deny at our last conference, but that Hippocrates swears by Apollo and Escalapius, and by Hygeia and Panacea, the gods and goddesses of Physic: And pray, Doctor, who were the gods and goddesses of antiquity, but men and women, who first found out and taught arts and mysteries so beneficial to mankind, as made them think they could not but be guided by a divine spirit to the knowledge of things so useful and so far above the vulgar [common] capacities this? Hippocrates is so ingenuous as to confess, and doth not part the gods and goddesses, but had them in equal veneration, as appears by his oath, to which I refer you, because I perceive you have forgot it; for he swears he will not cut those that have the stone, but will leave it to the skillful in that practice. But you, though you understand nothing of it, pretend to teach us an art much more difficult (and which ought to be kept as a secret amongst women as much as is possible).

'Tis true among the subtle Athenians, some physicians being gotten into the government, and miscarriages happening to some noble women about that time, they obtained a law, that for the future no woman should study or practice any part of physic on pain of death. This law continued some time, during which many women perished, both in childbearing, and by private diseases; their modesty not permitting them to admit of men either to deliver or cure them.

Till God stirred up the spirit of Agnodicea, a noble maid, to pity the miserable condition of her own sex, and hazard her life to help them, which to enable herself to do, she cut off her hair, appareled herself like a man, and became the scholar of Hyrophilus, the most famous physician of that time; and having learned the art, she found out a woman that had long languished under private diseases, and made proffer of her service to cure her, which the sick person refused, thinking her to be a man, but when Agnodicea had discovered that she was a maid, the woman committed herself into her hands, who cured her perfectly. And after her many others with the like skill and industry. So that in a short time she became the successful and beloved physician of the whole sex, none but she being called to assist them.

This so incensed the physicians that they conspired her ruin, saying she shaved off her beard to abuse the women, who feigned themselves sick to enjoy her company; and there being witnesses to be found then (as of late years, that would swear anything for money), she was upon their testimony condemned to death for committing adultery with Agisilea, one of the Areopagites' wives; it being easy to make old men, who had beautiful wives, believe anything of so young and handsome a doctor.

This forced Agnodicea to discover her sex to save her life; and then the enraged physicians accused her of transgressing the law, which forbid women to study or practice physic. And for this crime she was like to be condemned to death; which coming to the ears of the noble women, they ran before the Areopagites, which were the chief magistrates, and the house being encompassed by most women of the city, the ladies entered before the judges, and told them they would no longer account them for husbands or friends, but for cruel enemies, that condemned her to death, who restored them to their healths; protesting they would all die with her if she were put to death.

This caused the magistrates to disannul that law, and make another, which gave gentlewomen leave to study and practice all parts of physic to their own sex, giving large stipends to those that did it well and carefully, and imposing severe penalties upon the unskillful and negligent. And there were many noble women who studied that practice, and taught it publicly in their schools as long as Athens flourished in learning.

But Phanarota, the mother of wise Socrates, who was a woman of great learning and skill, deserves a particular remembrance, both for her own, and her son's sake; who, as it is believed by many, was a martyr, being put to death for professing there was but one God, which Wisdom himself saith he learned of his mother. Thus, Doctor, it appears, even that learned idolatrous city had in it a midwife that knew and feared the true God. Though, as the Apostle saith, there was an altar therein dedicated to the unknown God.

This Ambrose Perre [Paré], counselor and surgeon to the king of France, and his ingenuous disciple Gulielmus, prove fully: and that is as far as my small learning and weak capacity goes. But you, Doctor, may prove it more at large when you please, by the Hebrew, Greek, Latin and Arabic books which treat on these subjects; in which times the three parts of physic, midwifery, surgery, and the making up and administering of medicines, were all one, though the last, which was then the servile part, hath now usurped upon the other two; but we pretend only to the first, as being the most ancient, honorable, and useful part. Wherein we desire you not to concern yourselves, until we desire your company, which we will certainly do as often as we have occasion for your advice in anything we do not understand, or which doth not appertain to our practice.

But to come into our own country, it is not hard to prove by ancient British books and writings, that before the Romans came hither here were colleges of women practicing physic, dedicated to some of the female deities; but whether so ancient as the bards, I cannot tell, though some old British songs written in praise of the goddess Trawth, seem to prove it; but they were in the time of the Druids, as appears both by British and French books, and the name of Wise Women, by which midwives are still called in France, and most of the western parts, as they are by that of Wise Mother in the Low Countries, Germany, and most of the northern parts of the world.

And here in London were colleges of women about the Temple of Diana, who was goddess of midwives here, as well as at Ephesus. From whence the Grecians say, she was absent at Queen Olympia's labor, who was that night delivered of Alexander the Great; where she was so fully employed that she could not defend her stately temple, which was burned down by Herostrateus the shoemaker, to perpetuate his name.

Nor did the bishops pretend to license midwives till Bishop Bonner's time, who drew up the form of the first license, which continued in full force till 1642, and then the physicians and surgeons contending about it, it was adjudged a surgical operation, and the midwives were licensed at Surgeons-Hall, but not till they had passed three examinations, before six skillful midwives, and as many surgeons expert in the art of midwifery. Thus it continued until the Act of Uniformity passed, which sent the midwives back to Doctors Commons, where they pay their money (take an oath which is impossible for them to keep) and return home as skillful as they went thither.

I make no reflections on those learned gentlemen the licensers, but refer the curious for their further satisfaction to the yearly bills of mortality, from 1642 to 1662, collections of which they may find at Clerks-Hall: Which if they please to compare with these of late years, they will find there did not then happen the eighth part of the casualties, either to women or children, as do now.

I hope, Doctor, these considerations will deter any of you from pretending to teach us midwifery, especially such as confess they never delivered women in their lives, and being asked what they would do in such a case? reply they have not yet studied it, but will when occasion serves. This is something to the purpose, I must confess, Doctor. But I doubt it will not satisfy the women of this age, who are so sensible and impatient of their pain, that few of them will be prevailed with to bear it, in complement to the doctor, while he fetches his book, studies the case, and teaches the midwife to perform her work, which she hopes may be done before he comes.

I protest, Doctor, I have not power enough with the women to hope to prevail with them to be patient in this case, and I think if the learnedest of you all should propose it whilst the pains are on, he would come off with the same applause which Phormio had, who having never seen a battle in his life, read a military lecture to Hannibal the Great.

But let this pass, Doctor, as I do the discourses you have often made to me on this subject, and I will tell you something worthy of your most serious consideration: Which is,

That in September last, our gracious Sovereign was pleased to promise to unite the midwives into a corporation, by his Royal Charter, and also to found a cradle-hospital, to breed up exposed children, to prevent the many murders, and the executions which attend them, which pious design will never want a suitable return from God, who no doubt will fully reward his care for preserving so many innocents as would otherwise be lost.

And I doubt not but one way will be by giving him a prince by his royal consort, who like another Moses may become a mighty captain for the nation; and lead to battle the soldiers which the hospital will preserve for him.

And now, Doctor, let me put you in mind, that though you have often laughed at me, and some doctors have accounted me a mad woman these last four years, for saying Her Majesty was full of children, and that the Bath would assist her breeding: 'Tis now proved so true that I have cause to hope myself may live to praise God, not only for a Prince of Wales and a Duke of York, but for many other royal babes by her; and if the overofficious will but be pleased to let them live, I hope in a few years to see them muster their little soldiers: Which joyful sight, I believe, is the hearty desire of all loyal subjects, of what persuasion soever, as it is the daily and fervent prayer of,

Your Servant,

Elizabeth Cellier

From my house in Arundel-Street,
near St. Clement's Church
in the Strand. Jan. 16, 1687

Where the word of a king is, there is power: and who shall say unto him, What doest thou? Eccles. 8:4.

28

THE COUNTESS OF LINCOLN'S NURSERY*

Elizabeth Clinton, Countess of Lincoln

Because it hath pleased God to bless me with many children and so caused me to observe many things falling out to mothers and to their children, I thought good to open my mind concerning a special matter belonging to all childbearing women seriously to consider of, and to manifest my mind the better, even to write of this matter, so far as God will please to direct me; in sum, the matter I mean is, the duty of nursing, due by mothers to their own children.

In setting down whereof I will, first, show that every woman ought to nurse her own child; and, secondly, I will endeavor to answer such objections as are used to be cast out against this duty, to disgrace the same.

The first point is easily performed, for it is the express ordinance of God that mothers should nurse their own children, and, being his ordinance, they are bound to it in conscience. This should stop the mouths of all repliers, for God is most wise and therefore must needs know what is fittest and best for us to do; and, to prevent all foolish fears or shifts, we are given to understand that he is also all-sufficient, and therefore infinitely able to bless his own ordinance and to afford us means in ourselves (as continual experience confirmeth) toward the observance thereof.

If this, as it ought, be granted, then how venturous are those women that dare venture to do otherwise, and so to refuse, and, by refusing, to despise that order which the most wise and Almighty God hath appointed, and instead thereof to choose their own pleasures? O what peace can there be to these women's consciences, unless, through the darkness of their understanding, they judge it no disobedience?

*Oxford, 1622. STC 5432, Reel 984.

And then they will drive me to prove that this nursing and nourishing of their own children in their own bosoms is God's ordinance. They are very willful, or very ignorant, if they make a question of it. For it is proved sufficiently to be their duty, both by God's word and also by his works.

By his word it is proved, first, by examples: namely, the example of Eve. For who suckled her sons Cain, Abel, Seth, etc. but herself? Which she did not only of mere necessity, because yet no other woman was created, but especially because she was their mother, and so saw it was her duty; and because she had a true natural affection which moved her to do it gladly. Next, the example of Sarah, the wife of Abraham; for she both gave her son Isaac suck, as doing the duty commanded of God, and also took great comfort and delight therein, as in a duty well pleasing to herself; whence she spoke of it, as of an action worthy to be named in her holy rejoicing. Now if Sarah, so great a princess, did nurse her own child, why should any of us neglect to do the like, except (which God forbid) we think scorn to follow her, whose daughters it is our glory to be, and which we be only upon this condition, that we imitate her well-doing. Let us look therefore to our worthy pattern, noting withal, that she put herself to this work when she was very old, and so might the better have excused herself, than we younger women can, being also more able to hire and keep a nurse than any of us. But why is she not followed by most in the practice of this duty? Even because they want her virtue and piety. This want is the common hindrance to this point of the woman's obedience; for this want makes them want love to God's precepts, want love to his doctrine, and, like stepmothers, want due love to their own children. . . .

To proceed, take notice of one example more: that is, of the blessed Virgin; as her womb bare our blessed Savior, so her paps gave him suck. Now who shall deny the own mother's suckling of their own children to be their duty, since every godly matron hath walked in these steps before them. . . .

So far for my promise to prove, by the word of God, that it is his ordinance that women should nurse their own children; now I will endeavor to prove it by his works: First, by his works of judgment; if it were not his ordinance for mothers to give their children suck, it were no judgment to bereave them of their milk; but it is specified to be a great judgment to bereave them hereof, and to give them dry breasts; therefore it is to be gathered, even from hence, that it is his ordinance, since to deprive them of means to do it is a punishment of them.

I add to this, The work that God worketh in the very nature of mothers, which proveth also that he hath ordained that they should nurse their own children; for by his secret operation the mother's affection is so knit by nature's law to her tender babe, as she finds no power to deny to suckle it, no not when she is in hazard to lose her own life by attending on it; for in such a case it is not said, Let the mother fly, and leave her infant to the peril, as if she were dispensed with; but only it is said, Woe to her, as if she were to be pitied, that for nature and her child she must be unnatural to herself; now if any then being even at liberty and in peace, with all plenty, shall deny to give suck to their own children, they go against nature; and show that God hath not done so much for them as to work any good, no not in their nature, but left them more savage than the dragons, and as cruel to their little ones as the ostriches.

Now another work of God, proving this point, is the work of his provision for every kind to be apt and able to nourish their own fruit; there is no beast that feeds their young with milk but the Lord, even from the first ground of the order of nature, Grow and multiply, hath provided it with milk to suckle their own young, which every beast takes so naturally unto, as if another beast come towards their young to offer the office of a dam unto it, they show, according to their fashion, a plain dislike of it, as if nature did speak in them and say it is contrary to God's order in nature, commanding each kind to increase and multiply in their own bodies, and by their own breasts, not to bring forth by one dam, and to bring up by another; but it is his ordinance that every kind should bring forth, and also nurse its own fruit.

Much more should this work of God prevail to persuade women made as man in the image of God, and therefore should be ashamed to be put to school to learn good nature of the unreasonable creature. In us also, as we know by experience, God provideth milk in our own breasts against the time of our children's birth, and this he hath done ever since it was said to us also, Increase and multiply; so that this work of his provision showeth that he tieth us likewise to nourish the children of our own womb, with our own breasts, even by the order of nature; yea it showeth that he so careth for and regardeth little children, even from the womb, that he would have them nursed by those that in all reason will look to them with the kindest affection, namely their mothers; and in giving them milk for it, he doth plainly tell them that he requires it.

Oh consider, how comes our milk? Is it not by the direct providence of God? Why provides he it but for the child? The mothers then that refuse to nurse their own children, do they not despise God's providence? Do they not deny God's will? Do they not as it were say, I see, O God, by the means thou hast put into me, that thou wouldst have me nurse the child thou hast given me, but I will not do so much for thee. Oh impious and impudent unthankfulness; yea monstrous unnaturalness, both to their own natural fruit born so near their breasts and fed in their own wombs, and yet may not be suffered to suck their own milk.

And this unthankfulness and unnaturalness is oftener the sin of the higher and the richer sort than of the meaner and the poorer, except some nice and proud idle dames, who will imitate their betters, will make their poor husbands beggars. And this is one hurt which the better rank do by their ill example egg and embolden the lower ones to follow them to their loss. Were it not better for us greater persons to keep God's ordinance and to show the meaner their duty in our good example? I am sure we have more helps to perform it and have fewer probable reasons to allege against it than women that live by hard labor and painful toil. If such mothers as refuse this office of love and of nature to their children should hereafter be refused, despised, and neglected of those their children, were they not just requited according to their own unkind dealing? I might say more in handling this first point of my promise, but I leave the larger and learneder discourse hereof unto men of art and learning; only to speak of so much as I read and know in my own experience, which, if any of my sex and condition do receive good by, I am glad; if they scorn it, they shall have the reward of scorners. I write in modesty, and can reap no disgrace by their immodest folly.

And so I come to my last part of my promise which is, to answer objections made by divers against this duty of mothers to their children.

First, it is objected that Rebecca had a nurse, and that therefore her mother did not give her suck of her own breasts, and so good women in the first ages did not hold them to this office of nursing their own children. To this I answer that if her mother had milk and health, and yet did put this duty from her to another, it was her fault, and so proved nothing against me; but it is manifest that she that Rebecca called her nurse was called so either for that she most tended her while her mother suckled her, or for that she weaned her, or for that, during her nonage and childhood, she did minister to her continually such good things as delighted and nourished her up. For to any one of these the name of a nurse is fitly given; whence a good wife is called her husband's nurse; and that Rebecca's nurse was only such a one, appeareth, because afterwards she is not named a nurse but a maid, saying: Then Rebecca rose, and her maids; now maids give not such out of their breasts, never any virgin or honest maid gave such, but that blessed one from an extraordinary and blessed power.

Secondly, it is objected that it is troublesome, that it is noisome to one's clothes, that it makes one look old, etc. All such reasons are uncomely and unchristian to be objected, and therefore unworthy to be answered; they argue unmotherly affection, idleness, desire to have liberty to gad from home, pride, foolish fineness, lust, wantonness, and the like evils. Ask Sarah, Hannah, the blessed Virgin, and any modest loving mother, what trouble they accounted it to give their little ones suck? Behold most nursing mothers, and they be as clean and sweet in their clothes and carry their age and hold their beauty as well as those that suckle not, and most likely are they so to do because, keeping God's ordinance, they are sure of God's blessing; and it hath been observed in some women that they grow more beautiful and better favored, by very nursing their own children.

But there are some women that object fear, saying that they are so weak, and so tender, that they are afraid to venture to give their children such lest they endanger their health thereby. Of these I demand, why then did they venture to marry and so to bear children? And if they say they could not choose, and that they thought not that marriage would impair their health, I answer, that for the same reasons they should set themselves to nurse their own children, because they should not choose but to do what God would have them do; and they should believe that this work will be for their health also, seeing it is ordinary with the Lord to give good stomach, health, and strength to almost all mothers that take this pains with their children. . . .

Now if any reading these few lines return against me, that it may be I myself have given my own children such and therefore am bolder and more busy to meddle in urging this point, to the end to insult over and to make them to be blamed that have not done it. I answer, that whether I have or have not performed this my bounden duty, I will not deny to tell my own practice. I know and acknowledge that I should have done it and, having not done it, it was not for want of will in myself, but partly I was overruled by another's authority and partly deceived by some ill counsel, and partly I had not so well considered of my duty in this motherly office as since I did, when it was too late for me to put it in execution. Wherefore, being pricked in heart for my undutifulness, this way, I study to redeem my peace, first by repentance towards God, humbly and often craving his pardon for this my offense; secondly, by studying how to show double love to my children, to make them amends for neglect of this part of love to them, when they should have hung on my breasts and been nourished in my own bosom; thirdly, by doing my endeavor to prevent many Christian mothers from sinning in the same kind, against our most loving and gracious God. . . .

PART SIX

WOMEN DESCRIBING CHILDBIRTH, SICKNESS, AND DEATH

Introduction

"All my pretty ones?"

Home. The place where females participated more intensely than males in the life-death cycle. Females were born there, and they married, conceived, miscarried, gave birth, and died there. There they attended their families in sickness, often seeing their children die from smallpox, measles, plague, worms, tetanus, accidental overlying—from "the thousand natural shocks that flesh is heir to." There women experienced firsthand the destructibility of human life.

In the sixteenth and seventeenth centuries, society regarded the bearing of children as woman's primary calling and children as her primary contribution to the family and the state. In most instances women did not resist their calling. If a woman was an Anglican, she agreed, when she assented to the form for the Solemnization of Marriage, that marriage was ordained first "for the procreation of children" and second as "a remedy against sin, and to avoid fornication" for those persons who did not have the "gift of continency." Alice Thornton affirmed this in her autobiography: "It pleased God to enrich my father and mother with (the chief end for which marriage was ordained) the blessing of children." If a woman was a Puritan, she might have entertained doubts about the primary end of marriage, since Puritan divines skirmished on this territory: some argued that mutual solace was the primary end of marriage, others that procreation was the primary end.

But whether they were Anglican, Puritan, Nonconformist, or Roman Catholic, most women regarded children as a blessing sent from God in a life in which the vulnerability of their children to diseases and accidents was a constant presence. A new child was one more stratagem for staving off grief and staking out claims to perpetuity.

For most pregnant women, the approaching time of childbirth held surreal terrors. Women were acutely aware of prolonged labor, breech birth, stillbirth, deformed children, and of the possibility of dying. Eliz-

abeth Joceline ordered a shroud in the last days of pregnancy and wore
it in a predeath premonitional ceremony; she died nine days after the
birth of her child. Ann More, who married John Donne in 1601, was
typical of the women of her day. She gave birth to twelve children in the
period from 1603 to 1617. She was buried with her stillborn child on
August 16, 1617, at the age of thirty-three. Her husband and seven children survived her. The parish records contain notations for her burial
fee and for the ringing of the death knell and the passing bell. Her
epitaph, written by her husband (and carved by Nicholas Stone for her
burial at the Church of St. Clement Danes), traces her lineage through
the males in her family: Georgi, Robert, Willelm, and Christophor.
Her mother's name does not appear on the epitaph.

Ann Donne is not an isolated statistic, although statistics for deaths
in childbirth are difficult to come by in the parish records. Elizabeth
Cellier, however, reported 6,000 deaths of women in childbirth and
13,000 deaths of infants at birth or shortly thereafter in a twenty-year
period (see part 5). In a discussion about the absence of conclusive data
on deaths in childbirth Antonia Fraser (*The Weaker Vessel*) concludes:
"One estimate gives a figure varying from 125 to 158 per 1,000 in the first
half of the seventeenth century and from 118 to 147 in the second half.
Research among aristocratic women has produced the statistics that
45 percent died before the age of fifty, one quarter from the complica-
tions of childbirth; these figures do not however allow for the debilita-
tions caused by constant parturition. Many women must have died . . .
worn through by ceaseless child-bearing, who did not actually die in labour" (76).

If women escaped death in childbirth or as the consequence of childbirth, they were always close to death with their children. Social historian Lawrence Stone argues in *Family, Sex and Marriage in England,
1500–1800* that the high mortality rate of infants inured mothers to grief
and deadened maternal sorrow. In *Mystical Bedlam*, a study of the medical practice of the seventeenth-century physician Richard Napier,
Michael MacDonald observes quite the contrary:

> The searing grief experienced by bereaved mothers among Napier's
> patients and the desperation of the childless show that the idea that
> intimate relationships should and did exist between mothers and chil-
> dren was not merely a literary artifact. Of the 134 cases of disturbing
> grief, 58 were attributed to children's death, and 51, or 88%, of these

sufferers were mothers   Mistress Judith Gostick "took grief" when her four-year-old died of the pox, and her misery was worsened when an accidental gunshot killed another child. The mistress of the Red Lion Inn was "ever leaden with grief" because she believed that a careless neighbor had killed her child of four, and she found no consolation in the infant she was nursing. . . . Nor did Napier think that grieving the death of a child was itself a sign of mental instability; it was instead a source of profound distress, which might cause emotional disturbances or physical illnesses. (82)

The scene played over and over, with women and children as the chief actors in the mortality play. John Graunt, an early medical statistician, attempted in 1662 to quantify deaths from the mortality bills for the preceding twenty years. Graunt discovered that eighty-one causes of death appeared in these bills. Among the leading causes were consumption and cough, 44,487 deaths; chrisom children and infant deaths, 32,106; ague and fever, 23,784; teething and worms, 14,236; and smallpox, 10,576. Plague was fourth on the mortality lists, causing 16,384 deaths. For the twenty-year period that Graunt charted, a third of the deaths were infant mortalities, two-ninths from "chronical diseases" (Cassedy, 296).

Both fathers and mothers grieved at the death of a child. Ben Jonson, for example, wrote tender elegies on the death of a child. John Milton, although not a father at the time, wrote an elegy to console his sister in the loss of a child who died of a cough and reassured her that her new pregnancy would assuage her grief. "On the Death of My First and Dearest Child . . . , 1655," an elegy by Katherine Philips penetrates more deeply into the female heart:

> Twice forty months in wedlock I did stay,
> Then had my vows crown'd with a lovely boy.
> And yet in forty days he dropped away;
> O! swift vicissitude of human joy!
>
> I did but see him, and he disappeared,
> I did but touch the Rose-bud, and it fell. . . .

Males, and especially clergymen, were inclined to give women advice and instructions on how to cope with suffering and grief and how to handle childbirth, sickness, and death. They warned women about indulging in excessive and prolonged grief. Women's writings on these topics can thus be seen as a response to male coercion and restraint.

Women knew—and their writings reveal—that in the realm of suffering and death theirs was the primary experience; males' experience in this area was secondary. To be sure, no males were excluded from suffering; no human being is. But no male gave birth. No male knew the trauma of a stillbirth. No male nursed a child and watched it die. Women's poems, memoirs, diaries, narratives, and testimonies were their claim to space, space which was in the home, the birthing bed, the crib and cradle, and in the coffin. It is interesting to observe that in twentieth-century studies of sixteenth- and seventeenth-century suffering women's writings have been largely ignored.

As the documents in this section demonstrate, women's perceptions of suffering and grief sprang from their femaleness. Those women who recorded their perceptions and feelings played out the drama of primary experience in language, often day by day. They did not flirt with language: it was for them organic discourse. They used language as they did a child: they loved it. The patience and endurance that they achieved and the equanimity that springs from their pages were not male-generated. Even though at certain stages women were overcome by suffering and death, language enabled them to acknowledge the benignity of the universe and the goodness of God.

When Lady Mary Carey was pregnant with her eighth child, she miscarried. She looked at the dead embryo and then grieved for the "dead formless babe," which apparently aborted before its quickening. In her poem she attempts to discover why God chose to punish her with a dead embryo rather than to bless her with a full-term living child. She sallies back and forth in the poem—acquiescing to the will of her "sweet God" and demanding an explanation from Him.

She initiates a dialogue with God, something not many women did. "Methinks," she says, "I hear God's voice." (This is not unlike George Herbert in "The Collar": "Me thoughts I heard one calling, *Child*! / And I reply'd, *My Lord*.") God calls Mary Carey "my child," and he responds to her questioning by reminding her that the dead embryo is not different from the dead embryonic spiritual fruits she regularly brings him. Recognizing that the abortion of the embryo in her physical life is the image of the premature dead fruits in her spiritual life, she achieves clarity in the dialogue. By using female reproductive metaphors throughout the poem (womb, miscarrying, quickening, fruition), she establishes her female identity, and although birth and fruition images were not foreign to males, it is metaphor in her direct appeal to the Holy Spirit that brings her female experience into an area free from male mediation: "Let not my heart (as doth my womb) miscarry."

In three small volumes covering the years 1629–1669, Alice Thornton chronicled her deliverances from measles, smallpox, drowning, fire, falling, shipwreck, hemorrhaging, wounds, and childbirth. The excerpts that appear in this section (see also part 1) may look like a catalog of suffering by one who was aspiring to martyrdom. It is important to note, however, that Alice Thornton was writing her history of deliverance, not, technically speaking, an autobiography.

Her writing style is clinical and biblical. By providing gynecological, obstetrical, pediatric, and geriatric data from her own life, she shows the primacy of the female experience. Called to attend her sister on her deathbed, Alice Thornton describes her sister's prolonged dying after a breech delivery of her sixteenth child; six of her offspring were still-born. Attending her mother in her last sickness and death, Alice Thornton charts her mother's physical symptoms. While her tongue and mouth turned black, then white, then bled profusely and a lump in her throat prevented her from swallowing, her invincible spirit triumphed as it drew on the history of salvation. Alice Thornton portrays her mother's life and death as the center of charity and hope. Her account of her mother's death prevented her mother's life from being buried and lost in the hazy memory of orality, as female lives were apt to be.

Alice Thornton's complete history of her own pregnancies is a construct of the female self. Each clinical detail—miscarriage, labor, breech birth, hemorrhaging, fear of barrenness—separates her from the male world and gives her a distinctly female identity. She intertwines the clinical with the biblical. Female terror is blended with the biblical promise of deliverance. She rescued the uniquely female reproductive experience from its secondary role in society and boldly placed herself in the long biblical tradition of suffering and deliverance from it. Without flinching, she appropriated the language of the prophets, the psalmist, the apostles, and of the medical profession and, by using it, snatched it away from its domination by male experience.

In contrast with Alice Thornton's account of her deliverances, Elizabeth Freke's diary lists "some few remembrances of my misfortunes which have attended me in my unhappy life since I were married: which was November the 14, 1671." (For an account of her unhappy marriage see part I.) Even though she suffered excruciating pains in the birth of her first child, she did not number childbirth among her misfortunes. She is cryptic in describing her four- to five-day labor and the delivery of her first child by a skilled midwife, Mrs. Mills, after a "man midwife" had failed. Among the misfortunes that she catalogs are her miscarriage in Ireland, where she was treated harshly by her mother-in-law; the injury to her son's leg caused by the carelessness of his nurse; and the birth of a dead son in London.

Religious melancholy, the name given by Robert Burton in his *Anatomy of Melancholy* to a species of mental illness, made no gender distinctions. Males and females suffered acutely from deep depressions that alienated them from God especially, and inevitably from their families and friends. These people were frequently suicidal, in spite of the fact that they knew that suicides were denied Christian burial in church or churchyard, that the funeral rites were aborted, and that a stake was driven through the heart and the body buried in a crossway on a highway where people walked and rode over it (Forbes, 164–65). The ignominy of murdering oneself became a mode of instruction in the community and was to serve as a deterrent to those who might be contemplating suicide.

In light of the legal, ecclesiastical, and social practices of the day, it is startling to discover an account by Hannah Allen of at least five attempts at suicide. Not many wished to reveal such a weakness by writing about their inclination toward self-murder. Allen describes in detail her suicide attempts: to acquire opium and to overdose on it; to use a pair of scissors for stabbing and consequent hemorrhaging; to untie the tourniquet applied after phlebotomy in order to unstanch the bleeding; to smoke spiders with tobacco and so to poison herself; to stop eating and starve to death.

Allen also describes the various stages of her religious melancholy. She denounced God, Christian counsel, attendance at worship services, and the Bible; she perceived herself as reprobate and felt acutely the potency of the devil's malicious suggestion that she was destined for hell. Her narrative's alternative title, *Satan His Methods and Malice Baffled,* indicates how closely mental illness in the seventeenth century was associated with Satan's invasion of a life and the disequilibrium that was attributed to his intervention.

Hannah Allen's narrative emphasizes the fact that it was not religion that had failed her nor God who had abandoned her. The narrative is an attempt by a female to disclose what an individual, a family, and a community would wish to keep hidden. Although physicians recorded cases of mental illness (MacDonald, *Mystical Bedlam*), not many sufferers put in writing their struggles with bouts of mental illness. Cured by counseling and medication by a Mr. Shorthose after a period of about three years, Allen wrote her mental history, perhaps initially to serve as therapy but also to help her readers who might be experiencing similar doubts, depression, and temptations to suicide. What emerges from her courageous seventy-page book is a woman whose depression, anti-God pronouncements, and suicide attempts did not result in self-condemnation. Her experiences and healing were vindication for sufferers from mental illness. She gave hope to those in despair.

Funeral sermons, elegies, books on dying, and reflections on mortality were largely in the masculine domain, though women were frequently eulogized in them. Jeremy Taylor's *Holy Dying* (1651), for example, was written for Lady Carberry. After the Restoration women joined the genre, writing firsthand accounts of dyings, not out of morbid interest in the process but as interpretations of the life and death of someone they loved. Since Quaker women were permitted to participate orally in religious meetings, they were less hesitant about writing eyewitness accounts of a death than were women in other religious communities. They left simple but eloquent descriptions of the death of a child, a husband, a friend. A time of dying was a time for family and members of the religious community to gather at a deathbed, and a written account of a death could then be verified by those in attendance. By printing such accounts, Quaker women attested to the holy living and dying of one in their community.

Sarah Featherstone Browne, a Quaker, records the dying of her last child. Nine of her children predeceased this last daughter. The daughter died with equanimity, being unconcerned about the place of her burial. The mother's hidden protest on the death of her child is found in the lines she borrows from King David, who lamented the death of his son Absalom: both wished that they had died instead of their child.

It was rumored in the Quaker community that a young woman, Susannah Whitrow, was dying of love melancholy, not of a physical disease. Susannah was accused of dying of unrequited love. Since Susannah's reputation in the community and her personal happiness were of deep concern to her mother, it was necessary for her mother to question her about the nature and cause of her illness. (The seventeenth century was apt to confuse mental and physical illness [Babb, *Eliz-abethan Malady*].) In a document taken as a testimony on her deathbed by female witnesses, Susannah testifies that she voluntarily withdrew from a marriage proposal and that her illness, in no way related to the proposal, is terminal.

Susannah speaks on her deathbed in the language of the scriptures, which she had absorbed in her home and religious community. She blesses and thanks her mother for the concern she showed for the religious health of her family. Susannah also reverses her previously held opinion that women should not speak in religious meetings. Recognizing now the power of women in the religious community, Susannah wishes the community to know that she now affirms the right of women to have speaking roles in the meetings and the need for the community to hear them.

It was unusual for a woman in the seventeenth century to be a professional traveler. Celia Fiennes, an early forerunner of the twentieth-century journalist, traveled over 3,000 miles in the last decade of the seventeenth century, mostly on horseback and accompanied only by a few male servants. She recorded her observations on the places and persons she visited with scrupulous attention to detail.

In this section Fiennes describes the intricacies of the ceremonies attendant upon the death of Queen Mary. With a reportorial style that omits no aspect of death, lying in state, and funeral at Westminster Abbey, she concludes her report with the breaking of white staves by the officers of the queen and the flinging of their keys into the tomb. Her language is poignant in its simplicity and directness. Completing her description of the queen's death and burial, Fiennes candidly informs her readers that "if it be Kings' then the ladies attend not"—in which case the funerals of kings would have gone unwitnessed by the cinematic eye of this female reporter.

Suggested Readings

Babb, Lawrence. *Elizabethan Malady.* East Lansing: Michigan State University Press, 1951.

Bald, R. C. *John Donne: A Life.* Oxford: Clarendon Press, 1970.

Burton, Robert. *The Anatomy of Melancholy.* 3 vols. Ed. A. R. Shiletto. London: G. Bell and Sons, 1912.

Cassedy, James H. "Medicine and the Rise of Statistics." In *Medicine in Seventeenth-Century England,* ed. Allen G. Debus. Berkeley: University of California Press, 1975.

Dobbie, B. Willmott. "An Attempt to Estimate the True Rate of Maternal Mortality in the Sixteenth to Eighteenth Centuries." *Medical History* 26 (1982): 79–90.

Eccles, Audrey. *Obstetrics and Gynaecology in Tudor and Stuart England.* London: Croom Helm, 1982.

Forbes, Thomas Rogers, ed. *Chronicle from Aldgate.* New Haven: Yale University Press, 1971.

Fraser, Antonia. *The Weaker Vessel.* New York: Knopf, 1984.

Graunt, John. *Natural and Political Observations . . . upon the Bills of Mortality.* London: 1662.

Greer, Germaine, et al., ed. *Kissing the Rod: An Anthology of Seventeenth-Century Women's Verse.* London: Virago Press, 1988.

Hobby, Elaine. *Virtue of Necessity: English Women's Writing 1649–88.* Ann Arbor: University of Michigan Press, 1989.

Joceline, Elizabeth. *The Mothers Legacie to Her Unborne Childe.* London, 1624.

MacDonald, Michael. *Mystical Bedlam.* Cambridge: Cambridge University Press, 1981.

Mendelson, Sara Heller. "Stuart Women's Diaries and Occasional Memoirs." In *Women in English Society 1500–1800,* ed. Mary Prior. London and New York: Methuen, 1985.

Rose, Mary Beth. "Gender, Genre, and History: Seventeenth-Century English Women and the Art of Autobiography." In *Women in the Middle Ages and the Renaissance,* ed. Mary Beth Rose. Syracuse, N.Y.: Syracuse University Press, 1986.

Stone, Lawrence. *Family, Sex and Marriage in England, 1500–1800.* New York: Harper and Row, 1977.

Taylor, Jeremy. *Holy Dying.* London, 1651.

29

UPON THE SIGHT OF MY ABORTIVE BIRTH
THE 31ST OF DECEMBER 1657*

Mary Carey

What birth is this; a poor despised creature?
   A little embryo, void of life and feature.
Seven times I went my time; when mercy giving
   deliverance unto me; and mine all living:
Strong, right-proportioned, lovely girls and boys,
   their father's, mother's present hoped-for joys.
That was great wisdom, goodness, power, love, praise
   to my dear Lord; lovely in all his ways:
This is no less; the same God hath it done;
   submits my heart, that's better than a son:
In giving, taking, stroking, striking, still;
   his glory and my good; is, his, my will.
In that then; this now; both good God most mild,
   his will's more dear to me than any Child.
I also joy that God hath gained one more,
   to praise him in the heavens, than was before:
And that this babe (as well as all the rest),
   since 't had a soul, shall be forever blest:
That I'm made instrumental to both these,
   God's praise, babe's bliss, it highly doth me please.

* * *

As limners draw dead shades for to set forth
   their lively colors and their pictures' worth,

*Autograph, pp. 195–201. In *Kissing the Rod: An Anthology of Seventeenth-Century Women's Verse,* ed. Germaine Greer et al. (London: Virago Press, 1988), pp. 158–61. MS. in possession of Dame Alix Meynell.

So doth my God in this, as all things, wise,
    by my dead formless babe teach me to prize
My living pretty pair, Nat and Bethia,
    the children dear (God yet lends to Maria).
Praised be his name, these two's full compensation
    for all that's gone, and that in expectation:
And if herein God hath fulfilled his will,
    his handmaid's pleased, completely happy still:
I only now desire of my sweet God
    the reason why he took in hand his rod?
What he doth spy; what is the thing amiss
    I fain would learn, whilst I the rod do kiss?

* * *

Methinks I hear God's voice, this is the sin,
    and conscience justifies the same within:
Thou often dost present me with dead fruit;
    Why should not my returns thy presents suit:
Dead duties; prayers; praises thou dost bring,
    affections dead; dead heart in everything.

* * *

Mend now my child, and lively fruit bring me;
    so thou advantaged much by this wilt be.

* * *

But, Lord, since I'm a child by mercy free,
    let me by filial fruits much honor thee.

* * *

Let not my heart (as doth my womb) miscarry,
    but precious means received, let it tarry
Till it be formed, of Gospel shape, and suit;
    my means, my mercies, and be pleasant fruit:
In my whole life; lively do thou make me:
    for thy praise and name's sake, O quicken me.

* * *

And since my heart thou'st lifted up to thee;
    amend it, Lord, and keep it still with thee.

        Saith Maria Carey, always in Christ happy.

January 12, 1657

30

THE AUTOBIOGRAPHY OF
MRS. ALICE THORNTON
(1645–1662)*

The death of my sister Danby, Sept. 30, 1645,
at her house at Thorpe

About this year, my dear and only sister, the Lady Danby, drew near her time for delivery of her sixteenth child. Ten whereof had been baptized, the other six were stillborn, when she was above half gone with them, she having miscarried of them all upon frights by fire in her chamber, falls, and such like accidents happening. All her children were sons, saving my two nieces, Katherine and Alice Danby, and most sweet, beautiful, and comely were they all. The troubles and distractions of those sad times did much afflict and grieve her, who was of a tender and sweet disposition, wanting the company of her husband, Sir Thomas, to manage his estate and other concerns. But he, being engaged in his king's service, was not permitted to leave it, nor come to Thorpe but seldom, till she fell sick. These things, added to the horrid rudeness of the soldiers and Scots quartered then amongst them, which vexing and troubling her much with frights, caused her to fall into travail sooner than she expected, nor could she get her old midwife, being then in Richmond, which was then shut up, for the plague was exceeding great there, so that all the inhabitants that could get out fled, saving those had the sickness in their houses. At this time did my dear mother and whole family receive grand preservation from the Divine Providence in delivering us from the arrow that flieth by day, when as hundreds died so near us, and thousands fell at noonday; nay, all that

*Published for the Surtees Society, Durham, London, Edinburgh, 1875; pp. 49–53, 84–117, 123–27, 139–42.

town was almost depopulated. How did our good and great Lord preserve all us at Hipswell, so that no infection seized upon anyone that belonged us, although the malice of the beggars was great to have done harm by rags, notwithstanding all her [Thornton's mother's] charitable relief daily with much meat and money. Blessed be the great and ever merciful Father, who did rebuke the destroying angel, and at last stayed this plague in Richmond.

But to return to my poor sister, whose extremity called her friends to her assistance. She had been very ill long time before her delivery, and much altered in the heat of her body, being feverish. After exceeding sore travail she was delivered of a goodly son about August 3rd, by one dame Sworre. This boy was named Francis, after another of that name, a sweet child that died that summer of the smallpox. This child came double into the world, with such extremity that she was exceedingly tormented with pains, so that she was deprived of the benefit of sleep for fourteen days, except a few frightful slumbers; neither could she eat anything for her nourishment as usual. Yet still did she spend her time in discourse of goodness excellently pious, godly, and religious, instructing her children and servants, and preparing her soul for her dear Redeemer, as it was her saying she should not be long from Him. That week when I was left with her, after my Lady Armitage, and my aunt Norton was gone, though she could not get rest, yet all her discourse was very good and profitable to the hearers, patience, humility, and all how to entertain the pleasure of God with contentedness, making so excellent a confession of faith and other Christian virtues and graces that Mr. Siddall exceedingly admired her parts and piety, giving her as high a character as could be. She did entreat Sir Thomas, her husband, to send for Mr. Farrer, and to join with her in the receiving of the Holy Sacrament, but he would not give leave, which was to my knowledge a great grief and trouble to her thoughts.

That night she poured out her soul in prayer with such comprehensive and good expressions that could be for her own soul, for pardon and remission of her sins, for grace and sanctification from the Spirit, faith, and assurance; and then for her husband, children, mother, and all her other relations and myself; for the restoration of the king, the church, and the kingdom's peace; with such pathetical and zealous expressions that all did glorify God for [the] things He had done for her. After which, she did in a manner prophesy that God would humble the kingdom by afflictions for their sin and security; but after that when we were humbled and reformed, whosoever should live to see it (for she should not) should enjoy happy days for church and state. Thus, she continued, and with prayers for our enemies, and because they stood in need of our prayers for the forgiveness of all their evils, she called her children, exhorted them abundantly to fear God, serve Him, and love one another, be obedient to their father, with admonishing them and her family. She was kind and dearly affectionate to her husband, to whom, under God, she left the care of her seven young children. Sometimes she did express abundant joy in God, and would sweetly, with a melodious voice, sing aloud His praise and glory in anthems and psalms proper for her condition, with many sweet verses praising Him for all things; nor was she in the least concerned to part with her husband or children, nor anything in this world, having her hopes and desires fixed upon God, leaving her children freely to the providence of her God, who had relieved her soul out of all her distress, who had promised to be a father to the fatherless. All her words were full of sweetness and affection, giving me many hearty thanks for all my pains and care I took with her, and watching a whole week together; if she lived she would requite my love; with an abundance of affectionate expressions to this purpose.

My grief and sorrow was so great for her, that I had brought myself into a very weak condition, in so much as my mother came to Thorpe with Dafeny Lightfoote, a careful servant, to help with my sister, and sent me home who was almost spent in that time. At which time I took my last leave of my dearest and only sister, never could get to see her for my own illness afterwards. But she, waiting her Lord's time to be called, was fitting her soul and heart for Him. As the disease increased of the fever, notwithstanding what could be done for her in that condition, it did to her as many others in such extremity, deprive her (for want of sleep and food, which she could not take by reason of a sore throat) of part of the use of understanding for a little while when its fury lasted. But Dafeny was always with her, who she had a great love for, and as she grew weaker after a month's time of her delivery, holding her head on her breast, said to her in a faint, weak voice, "I am going to God, my God, now." Then said Dafeny, "Nay, madam, I hope God will please to spare your life to live amongst your sweet children, and bring them up." "How can that be?" answered my sister, "for I find my heart and vitals all decayed and gone. No; I desire to be dissolved and to be with Christ, which is best of all. I have made my peace with God." And immediately she said with as strong a voice as she could, "Lord Jesus, receive my spirit"; then, giving a little breathing sigh, delivered up her soul into the hands of her Savior, sweetly falling asleep in the Lord.

And thus ended that sweet saint her weary pilgrimage, having her life interwoven with many cares and afflictions. Although she was married to a good estate, yet did she enjoy not much comfort, and I know she received her change with much satisfaction, being, she hoped, to be freed, as she said, from a wicked world, and all the evils therein. Thus departed that good soul, having been young called to walk in the ways of God, and had made His service her continual practice. The Lord sanctify this sad loss of this virtuous sister of ours to the whole family, and that, as she lived the ways of godliness from her youth, so she may be a godly example to all her children. She was a most obedient child to her parents, loving and loyal, affectionate and observant to her husband, a tender and prudent mother to her children, bringing them up in the severities of Christian duties, yet enough indulgent over them with a Christian moderation: a wise and discreet mistress towards her servants, who loved and honored her in their obedience, truly affectionate to all her relations in general, and courteously affable to all neighbors and friends. And, indeed, a great loss to all amongst whom she lived, doing much good and employing her time in helping the diseased, and doing many cures, following the example of my mother in all these things. She lived, after the birth of this child, about a month, dying on the 30th of September, 1645, and was buried that night at Sir Thomas Danby's own town, in Massam Church, in the night, by reason of the Parliament set and Scots, who would not let a sermon be preached. But there was great lamentation made for her death.

The death of my cousin, John Norton, 1646

My cousin John Norton died of a consumption, long in a languishing condition, but at length it pleased God to take him to himself in the year 1646. He was a sweet good-natured youth; he died at St. Nicholas.

* * *

Meditations upon my deliverance of my first child, and of the great sickness followed for three quarters of a year; August 6, 1652, lasted till May 2, 1653.

About seven weeks after I married it pleased God to give me the blessing of conception. The first quarter I was exceeding sickly in breeding, till I was with quick child; after which I was very strong and healthy, I bless God, only much hotter than formerly, as is usual in such cases from a natural cause, insomuch that my nose bled much when I was about half gone, by reason of the increase of heat. Being helped more forward in the distemper by the extreme heat of the weather at that time, when the extreme great eclipse of the sun was in its height, and a great and total eclipse fell out this year 1652. At which time I was big with child, and the sight of it much affrighted me, it being so dark in the morning that [one] could not see to eat his breakfast without a candle. But this did amaze me much, and I could not refrain going out into the garden and look on the eclipse in water, discovering the power of God so great to a miracle, who did withdraw His light from our sun so totally that the sky was dark, and stars appeared, and a cold storm for a time did possess the earth. Which dreadful change did put me into most serious and deep consideration of the day of judgment which would come as sudden and as certainly upon all the earth as this eclipse fell out, which caused me to desire and beg of His Majesty that He would prepare me for this great day in repentance, faith, and a holy life, for the judgments of God was just and certain upon all sins and sinners. O prepare me, O God, for all Thy dispensations and trials in this world, and make me ready and prepared with oil in my lamp, as the wise virgins, against the coming of the sweet Bridegroom of my soul.

About a month after, Mr. Thornton desired and his relations that I should go to see them both at Crathorne, Buttercrambe, York, and at Hull and Beverley, at Burn Park where his mother lived then . . . and by God's mercy did I go to all those places where his friends lived, and [was] most kindly received and entertained. I bless God who gave me favor in the eyes of my husband's friends. When I came to Hull, Dr. Witty would have had me advised to be let blood. . . . In my return home by Newton when I saw the old house the remains of it, as I was in the great chamber, the door into a little room was so low as I got a great knock on my forehead which struck me down, and I fell with the force of the blow, at which my husband was troubled. But I recovering my astonishment (because he should not be too much concerned), smiled, said I hoped I was not much worse, but said I had taken possession, which made him smile, and said it was to my hurt, and indeed so it was many ways. For in my going homeward he carried me to that place of the great rocks and cliffs which is called Whitson Cliff. . . . But this my husband would not have had me go down this way, but by Ampleford, about, and plain way, but for Mr Bradley, who told him it would not do me no hurt, because his wife went down that way and was no worse. However, the effect to me was contrary, for I being to go to my cousin Ascough's, she did admire that I came that way, and wished I might get safe home. It was indeed the good pleasure of my God to bring me safe home to my dear mother's house, Hipswell.

But my dangerous journey the effects of it did soon appear on me, and Dr. Witty's words came true. For as soon as I got home I fell into the most dreadful sickness that ever any creature could possibly be saved out of, and by a strong and putrid fever, which was on me eleven days before Dr. Witty came from Hull, had so putrified my whole blood that both myself and poor infant was like to go. . . . The more particular description of this great and long-lasting sickness I have related in my first book of my Life, and with the miraculous deliverance was towards me in all that time. Mr. Thornton had a desire that I should visit his friends, in which I freely joined, his mother living about fifty miles from Hipswell, and all at Newton and Buttercrambe. In my passage thither I sweat exceedingly, and was much inclining to be feverish wanting not eight weeks of my time, so that Dr. Witty said that I should go near to fall into a fever, or some desperate sickness, if I did not cool my blood, by taking some away, and if I had stayed but two days longer, I had followed his advice. In his return home from Newton, his own estate, I was carried over Hambleton towards Sir William Ascough's house, where I passed down on foot a very high wall betwixt Hudhill and Whitson Cliff, which is above a mile steep down, and indeed so bad that I could not scarce tread the narrow steps, which was exceeding bad for me in that condition, and sore to endure, the way so straight and none to lead me but my maid [Susan Gosling], which could scarce make shift to get down herself, all our company being gone down before. Each step did very much strain me, being so big with child, nor could I have got down if I had not then been in my full strength and nimble on foot. But, I bless God, I got down safe at last, though much tired, and hot and weary, finding myself not well, but troubled with pains after my walk. Mr. Thornton would not have brought me that way if he had known it so dangerous, and I was a stranger in that place; but he was advised by some to go that way before we came down the hill.

This was the first occasion which brought me a great deal of misery, and killed my sweet infant in my womb. For I continued ill in pain by fits upon this journey, and within a fortnight fell into a desperate fever at Hipswell. Upon which my old doctor, Mr. Mahum, was called, but could do little towards the cure, because of being with child. I was willing to be ordered by him, but said I found it absolutely necessary to be let blood if they would save my life, but I was freely willing to resign my will to God's, if He saw fit for me, to spare my life, yet to live with my husband; but still with subserviency to my Heavenly Father. Nor was I wanting to supplicate my God for direction what to do, either for life or death. I had very often and frequent impressions to desire the latter before the former, finding no true joy in this life, but I confess also that which moved me to use all means for my recovery, in regard of the great sorrow of my dear and aged mother and my dear husband took for me, far exceeding my deserts, made me more willing to save my life for them, and that I might render praises to my God in the land of the living. But truly, I found my heart still did cleave to my Maker that I never found myself more desirous of a change to be delivered from this wicked world and body of sin and death, desiring to be dissolved and to be with Christ. Therefore endured I all the rigors and extremity of my sickness with such a share of patience as my God gave me.

As for my friends, they were so much concerned for me that, upon the importunity of my husband, although I was brought indeed very weak and desperately ill about eleventh day of my sickness, I did let him send for Dr. Witty, if it were not too late. The doctor came post the next day, when he found me very weak, and durst not let me blood that night, but gave me cordials, etc., till the next day, and if I got but one hour's rest that night, he would do it the morning following. That night the two doctors had a dispute about the letting me blood. Mr. Mahum was against it, and Dr. Witty for it; but I soon decided that dispute, and told them, if they would save my life, I must bleed. So the next day I had six or seven ounces taken which was turned very bad by my sickness, but I found a change immediately in my sight, which was exceeding dim before, and then I see as well as ever clearly, and my strength began a little to return; these things I relate that I may set forth the mercy of my ever-gracious God, who had blessed the means in such manner. Who can sufficiently extol his Majesty for his boundless mercies to me his weak creature, for from that time I was better, and he had hopes of my life.

The doctor stayed with me seven days during my sickness; my poor infant within me was greatly forced with violent motions perpetually, till it grew so weak that it had left stirring, and about the 27th of August I found myself in great pains as it were the colic, after which I began to be in travail, and about the next day at night I was delivered of a goodly daughter, who lived not so long as that we could get a minister to baptize it, though we presently sent for one. This my sweet babe and first child departed this life half an hour after its birth, being received, I hope, into the arms of Him that gave it. She was buried that night, being Friday, the 27th of August, 1652, at Easby Church.

The effects of this fever remained by several distempers successively, first, after the miscarriage I fell into a most terrible shaking ague, lasting one quarter of a year, by fits each day twice, in much violency, so that the sweat was great with faintings, being thereby weakened till I could not stand or go. The hair on my head came off, my nails of my fingers and toes came off, my teeth did shake, and ready to come out and grew black. After the ague left me, upon a medicine of London treacle, I fell into the jaundice, which vexed me very hardly one full quarter and a half more. I finding Dr. Witty's judgment true, that it would prove a chronical distemper; but blessed be the Lord, upon great and many means used and all remedies, I was at length cured of all distempers and weaknesses, which, from its beginning, had lasted three quarters of a year full out. Thus had I a sad entertainment and beginning of my change of life, the comforts thereof being turned into much discomforts and weaknesses, but still I was upheld by an Almighty Power, therefore will I praise the Lord my God. Amen.

* * *

Upon the birth of my second child and daughter, born at Hipswell on the 3rd of January in the year 1654.

Alice Thornton, my second child, was born at Hipswell near Richmond in Yorkshire the 3rd day of January, 1654, baptized the 5th of the same. Witnesses, my mother the Lady Wandesforde, my uncle Mr. Major Norton, and my cousin York his daughter, at Hipswell, by Mr. Michell Siddall, minister then of Caterick.

It was the pleasure of God to give me but a weak time after my daughter Alice her birth, and she had many preservations from death in the first year, being one night delivered from being overlaid by her nurse, who laid in my dear mother's chamber a good while. One night my mother was writing pretty late, and she heard my dear child make a groaning troublesomely, and stepping immediately to nurse's bedside she saw the nurse fallen asleep, with her breast in the child's mouth, and lying over the child; at which she, being affrighted, pulled the nurse suddenly off from her, and so preserved my dear child from being smothered. . . .

* * *

After I was delivered [of her third child, Elizabeth], and in my weary bed and very weak, it fell out that my little daughter Alice, being then newly weaned, and about a year old, being asleep in one cradle and the young infant [Elizabeth] in another, she fell into a most desperate fit, of the convulsions as supposed to be, her breath stopped, grew black in her face, which sore frighted her maid Jane Flouer. She took her up immediately, and with the help of the midwife, Jane Rimer, to open her teeth and to bring her to life again.

But still, afterwards, no sooner that she was out of one fit but fell into another fit, and the remedies could be by my dear mother and aunt Norton could scarce keep her alive, she having at least twenty fits; all friends expecting when she should have died. But I lying the next chamber to her and did hear her, when she came out of them, to give great shrieks and suddenly, that it frighted me extremely, and all the time of this poor child's illness I myself was at death's door by the extreme excess of those, upon the fright and terror came upon me, so great floods that I was spent, and my breath lost, my strength departed from me, and I could not speak for faintings, and dispirited so that my dear mother and aunt and friends did not expect my life, but overcome with sorrow for me. Nor durst they tell me in what a condition my dear Naly [Alice's nickname] was in her fits, lest grief for her, added to my own extremity, with loss of blood, might have extinguished my miserable life: but removing her in her cradle into the Blue Parlor, a great way off me, lest I hearing her sad shrieks should renew my sorrows. These extremities did so lessen my milk, that though I began to recruit strength, yet I must be subject to the changes of my condition. After my dear Naly was in most miraculous mercy restored to me the next day, and recruited my strength; within a fortnight I recovered my milk, and was overjoyed to give my sweet Betty suck, which I did, and began to recover to a miracle, blessed be my great and gracious Lord God, who remembered mercy towards me.

Meditations upon the birth of my third child.

Elizabeth Thornton, my third child, was born at Hipswell the 14th of February, 1655, being on Wednesday, half an hour after 11 o'clock in the forenoon. She was baptized the 16th of February, by Mr. Anthony; witnesses, my mother, my aunt Norton, and my brother, Christopher Wandesforde. Mrs. Blackburne stood for my mother, being sick then.

* * *

Meditation upon the birth of my fourth child, Katherine Thornton, June 12th, 1656, born at Hipswell June 12th, 1656.

Katherine Thornton, my fourth child, was born at Hipswell, near Richmond in Yorkshire, the 12th day of June, 1656, being on Thursday, about half an hour after four o'clock in the afternoon, and was baptized the 14th of June by Mr. Siddall; witnesses, my mother, my niece, Katherine Danby and Mr. Thornton.

My dear mother feared me much from those ill symptoms she saw in my labor, which caused her to pour out her humble petitions to heaven for me in a most excellent prayer of her own composure for that purpose, which is at large entered by me in my first book more at large, as also her humble thanksgiving for me after my safe deliverance.

Elizabeth Thornton's death, the 5th of September, 1656.

It pleased God to take from me my dear child Betty, which had been long in the rickets and consumption, gotten at first by an ague, and much gone in the rickets, which I conceived was caused by ill milk at two nurses. And notwithstanding all the means I used, and had her with Naly at St. Mungno's Well for it, she grew weaker, and at the last, in a most desperate cough that destroyed her lungs, she died.

That dear, sweet angel grew worse, and endured it with infinite patience, and when Mr. Thornton and I came to pray for her, she held up those sweet eyes and hand to her dear Father in heaven looked up, and cried in her language, "Dad, dad, dad" with such vehemency as if inspired by her holy Father in heaven to deliver her sweet soul into her heavenly Father's hands, and at which time we also did with great zeal deliver up my dear infant's soul into the hand of my heavenly Father, and then she sweetly fell asleep and went out of this miserable world like a lamb.

Elizabeth Thornton, my third child, died the 5th of September 1656, betwixt the hours of five and six in the morning. Her age was one year six months and twenty-one days. Was buried the same day at Catterick by Mr. Siddall.

Upon my great fall I had, being with child of my fifth,
Sept. 14, 1657, at Hipswell.
Meditations on the deliverance of my first son and fifth child
at Hipswell the 10th of December.

It pleased God, in much mercy, to restore me to strength to go to my full time, my labor beginning three days; but upon the Wednesday, the ninth of December, I fell into exceeding sharp travail in great extremity, so that the midwife did believe I should be delivered soon. But lo! it fell out contrary, for the child stayed in the birth, and came cross with his feet first, and in this condition continued till Thursday morning between two and three o'clock, at which time I was upon the rack in bearing my child with such exquisite torment, as if each limb were divided from other, for the space of two hours; when at length, being speechless and breathless, I was, by the infinite providence of God, in great mercy delivered. But I having had such sore travail in danger of my life so long, and the child coming into the world with his feet first, caused the child to be almost strangled in the birth, only living about half an hour, so died before we could get a minister to baptize him, although he was sent for.

I was delivered of my first son and fifth child on the 10th of December 1657. He was buried in Catterick church the same day by Mr. Siddall. This sweet goodly son was turned wrong by the fall. I most unfortunately going over the hall at Hipswell, my gown skirt wrapped about my feet and so twisted that I could not loose it before it cast me a desperate fall, which I fell upon my hands and knees to save my child . . . Sept. 14, 1657. My case was so ill that Dr. Witty was sent for, who used all his art to preserve myself and the child, saying that I was with child of a son he was confident, but should have difficult labor. He having used all his skill to preserve the stock, by the blessing of God I was preserved from death and marvelously restored to health and strength, being let blood and other remedies, which made me go to my full time I got in September before, nor had the midwife skill to turn him right, which was the cause of the loss of his life, and the hazard of my own. The weakness of my body was exceeding great, of long continuance, that it put me into the beginning of a consumption, not expecting for many days together that I should recover; and when I did recruit a little, then a new trouble seized on me by the loss of blood, in the bleeding of the hemorrhoids every day for half a year together. Nor did I recover the lameness of my left knee for one whole quarter of a year, in which I could not touch the ground with it. This I got in my labor, for want of the knee to be assisted. But, alas! all these miseries was nothing to what I have deserved from the just hand of God, considering the great failings of my duties as required both as to God and man. And though I am not given over to any sinful enormous crimes which thousands are subject to, yet am I not pure in the sight of God, for there is no man that liveth and sinneth not. What cause therefore have I to cry out, Oh, the height, the depth, the breadth, the length of the love of God, which had great compassion upon the weak handmaid of the Lord which was destined to destruction, and did show me mercy in the land of the living. The Lord Most High make me truly remember his goodness, and that I may never forget this above all his mighty and stretched-out hand of deliverances to me his vile creature. That I may extol and praise the Lord with all my soul, and never let go my hope from the God of my salvation, but live the remainder of my life he gives me to his honor and glory, and that, at the last, I may praise him eternally in the heavens. Bless the Lord, O my soul, and forget not all his benefits.

My cure of bleeding at Scarborough, August, 1659

It was the good pleasure of God to continue me most wonderfully, though in much weakness, after the excessive loss of blood and spirits, in childbed, with the continuance of lameness above twenty weeks after, and the loss of blood and strength by the bleeding of the hemorrhoids, which followed every day by siege, and was caused by my last travail and torment in childbirth, which brought me so low and weak that I fainted almost every day upon such occasions, when I daily lost about four or five ounces of blood. And it was the opinion of Dr. Witty that I was deeply gone in a consumption, and if it continued longer I should be barren; all which being considered by my dear husband and mother, they were resolved, from the doctor's opinion, that I should go to Scarborough Spa for the cure of the said distemper, and accordingly I went with Mr. Thornton, staying about a month there; in which time, upon drinking of the waters, I did by the blessing of God recover my strength after the stay of the former infirmity of bleeding, it leaving me within two days totally, and was cleared from those faintings this carried along with it, returning to Oswaldkirk by my sister Denton homewards.

After this great cure which the Spa wrought on me, for which I most humbly return my hearty and faithful acknowledgment of His mercy, we returned home to Hipswell, where we found my dear mother somewhat recovered of a very ill fit of the stone, in which she had been in great danger about two days before, and had sent for me home; her servant met me at my sister Crathorne's in my way to Hipswell. I was very joyful to find her any thing recruited [recovered] from her extremity, blessed be the Lord Most High, which had compassion on my dear mother in raising her from death, and easing her from those violent fits of pain and torment, giving her to me, and sparing my life also from that languishing sickness caused by my childbirth, and might have caused my death.

About this August, after our return from Scarborough, it pleased God to give me much strength and health so that I conceived with child, which after Mr. Thornton perceived, he with my mother greatly rejoiced, hoping that I might at length be blessed with a son. For four months together I enjoyed a great deal of comfort and health, being much stronger and lively when I was with sons than daughters, having great cause to admire the goodness of God, which ever contrary unto hope caused me to recover of that sad distemper wherewith I was afflicted, and giving me hopes to bring forth a son to be a comfort to my dear husband and us all.

* * *

A relation concerning my dear and honored mother the Lady Wandesforde, and of her death, December 10th, 1659.

My dear mother was sole daughter to Sir Hewet Osborne and Lady Joyce his wife, which Lady Joyce was eldest daughter to Sir Miles Fleetewood of London, in the reign of Queen Elizabeth, of happy memory. She was born at Sir John Payton's house, January 5th, 1591, at Islelome in Cambridgeshire, my grandfather and grandmother living then at my aunt's house at Islelome, being the eldest child of my grandfather's and intended by him to have inherited his estate, having so entailed it upon her at his first going beyond sea in Callis's voyage.

After some years he returned into England, and it pleased God to give them a gallant son and heir, which afterwards proved a most excellent, wise, and good man, Sir Edward Osborne, of Keveton, baronet. A faithful, prudent man, zealous for God, the king, and the church; of great abilities, to serve his king and country, being advanced to be Lord President of York; and lived and died in much honor and fame.

To return to my mother, who was bred up in her youth and infancy with much care and circumspect by the eye of my grandmother, a discreet and wise woman, giving her all the advantages of breeding and good education that the Court and those times could afford, which was indeed excellent for gravity, modesty, and piety, and other suitable qualities for her degree, as writing, singing, dancing, harpsicalls [harpsichord], lute, and what was requisite to make her an accomplished lady, as she did approve herself in all her time. At the age of twenty-one years she was married, by the consent of her mother, being then herself married to Sir Peter Frechvile, having lived seven years a widow since my grandfather's death. The portion which my father received was very fair in those days, being two thousand pounds, paid the next day of their marriage. Nor was she awanting to make a far greater improvement of my father's estate through her wise and prudential government of his family, and by her care was a means to give opportunity to increasing his patrimony, as my dear father is pleased to leave upon record in his own book, for her eternal honor, so that it might be said of her, "many daughters have done well, but thou exceedest them all."

It pleased God to enrich my father and mother with (the chief end for which marriage was ordained) the blessing of children, my mother bringing forth to him seven, hopeful enough to live, and to be comforts to their parents, four sons and three daughters. The eldest being Katherine; the second, Christopher, who died at six years old, was a wise and beautiful child, endowed with piety and parts, whose loss was very deeply resented by his parents. The third was George, whom I have had occasion to mention in this book. The fourth was Joyce, a sweet and comely child, died about four years old. The fifth, myself, Alice Thornton. The sixth, my brother Christopher Wandesforde, now heir to my father after my brother George's death. The seventh and last child was John, born at London before she went for Ireland, a sweet, beautiful and pregnant child and young man, an excellent scholar, and of piety and parts beyond his years.

My father being called over into Ireland to serve the king in the Roles Office in that kingdom, by reason of my mother's late weakness after her delivery of my brother John, went into Ireland one year before my mother and her family. After which she had a safe passage thither, living in much comfort and happiness all my father's life, doing much good to all people in each sphere wherein she acted, laying out herself to the best for her husband, whom she highly honored. Her children, friends, and servants found there, as in England, a perpetual effluence of all graces and virtues flowing from so full a spring which God had endowed her noble soul withal, lived in great peace, tranquility, and charity, full of meekness, humility, chastity, modesty, sobriety, and gravity; yea, she was endowed with great wisdom in the constant course of her life, of a sweet and pleasant composure of spirit, not sullenly sad, nor vainly light, but of an excellent temper in soul and body, neither of them wanting those due ornaments which might make her lovely in the eyes of God and man. And indeed exactly studious to advance the interest of her duties, in piety and religion, in herself and all her children, whose care was very sedulous for their souls' happiness as well as the embellishments of their persons, desiring to yield her accounts to God in righteousness and truth, according to the sincerity of her soul in his service. Thus were we happy and blessed, that we were children and offspring of such a holy and sanctified couple, whom God Almighty had filled with such a measure of his spirit, making them great ornaments of religion.

After my dear father's decease, she lived his widow till her death, which was the space of nineteen years and seven days, dying in that same month of December, and in old age. But she was not one of those that lived in pleasure, or spent her days in vanity, for what time could be spared from works of necessity and duty to her children and family, all the rest was given to the service of her God, either as works of piety and devotion, in private and public, or charity towards her brethren, whom she saw did stand in need and necessity. Especially having a due regard and compassion upon the clergy, which through the rigor of those times of oppression were banished from their own homes, wanting all manner of relief, with their families, very often and frequently found the bowels of a good Samaritan in hers, she opening her arms to receive Christ in his poor members, accounting it a great happiness that he vouchsafed her the honor to be instrumental for the relief and support of such as were precious in His sight.

I have formerly made a discourse of her travels and several accidents that befell her person and family after my father's death, till she came to live at her jointure at Hipswell, and also what troubles and trials, losses and crosses she underwent almost all the time she lived there, as well from the unnatural actions and unkindness of friends, which had repining thoughts that she should enjoy her jointure, as from the public enemies and disturbances from the public calamities of church and state.

All which she endured with a noble and invincible spirit, being fortified by her religion, and the testimony of a good conscience, that she laid out herself for God's service and glory, and the good of my father's whole family, and the general benefit of Christians amongst whom she lived; yea, even in those sad times of losing all, many hundreds were relieved and supplied at her door. For her exceeding kindnesses done for the help of the heir, younger children, and debtors of my father's, let her own narration, delivered from her in writing before witnesses, declare, what and how she expended upon that account, she being in a manner compelled to leave such a testimony from some unworthy prejudices which said she did not much from her estate for them. But it was requisite, for such an act of kindness which she did, spending all she received upon it, which should not be forgotten by that family who received so grand a blessing in her life and preservation, without the which it is too probable that we might have been made merchandise of. Should I forget her unparalleled wisdom, goodness, tenderness, love and parental affection by which she governed all her gracious actions towards us, in our maintenance and education, I should be worse than an infidel, who had forsaken the faith, and been ungrateful to that God which made them, and the very ox and ass which knows his owner's crib would rise up in judgment against me. Therefore do I desire in point of gratitude to God my Father, and that gracious mother whom he gave me, to mention those great mercies we received from her in general, and in particular for those exceeding goodness and favors wherein she extended her bounty towards me; who was pleased to provide an habitation for me after her decease, and disposed me in marriage, after which I, with my husband and children, did live with her eight years after my marriage, bringing forth four of my children in her house; and had all manner of charges, expenses, and household affairs, in sicknesses, births, christenings, and burials, of and concerning ourselves and children, with the diet, etc., of nurses, menservants and maids, and our friends' entertainments, all things done of her own cost and charges all her days while she lived, which could not be of less value to us clearly than £1600. And no small addition of help to my husband's estate was her disposal of her real estate in land, which she had purchased for £550, settling it upon myself and my children. Also her exceeding affection extended itself in her settling all her personal estate by deed of gift, and her last will and testament, saving her debts and legacies and funerals, in feoffees in trust for the use of myself, husband, and children. All which I confess far exceeding my merit, but not her entire affection, for my constant being with her in her sorrows and solitudes. . . .

It was very observable that she outlived those sad troubles upon the kingdom in part, though not till the restoration of our happy king Charles the Second, whose coming in was daily prayed for and heartily wished. And the last soldiers which quartered at Hipswell proved to be such as turned to General Monk from Lambert; and within a short time the mighty power and providence of God turned the minds and hearts of the people, as a mighty river towards its own channel, after her disease, which she had put up so many prayers to God for, and would have been a joyful day for her to have lived to see. But I hope God had prepared a great reward in heaven for her, for all her toil and sorrows she endured in this Baca and vale of tears, and after three weeks' sickness gave her the full fruition of her long-desired happiness.

The relation of her sickness here follows: It pleased God to visit my dear and honored mother, the Lady Wandesford, with her last sickness, upon Friday the 17th of November, 1659, beginning then with an exceeding great cough, which tormented her body with stitches in her breast, and troubled her with short breathing. These stitches continued about fourteen days together, hindering her from almost any sleep or rest, insomuch that it was wonderful how she could subsist. But upon the use of bags with fried oats, butter and chamomile chopped, laid to her sides, the stitches removed, and the cough abated, as to the extremity thereof. But then she was seized with a more dangerous symptom, of a hard lump contracted in her stomach, that laid on her heart, with great pain and rising up in her throat, almost stopping her breath, when she either swallowed anything or laid to sleep. Which lump was conceived to be contracted of wind and phlegm in the stomach for lack of voidance. She had also an exceeding sore throat and mouth, so that she was deprived of the benefit of eating or swallowing almost any kind of food, save a little drop of beer, being the most she took inwardly for four or five days, and that but with a syringe. Her tongue and mouth at first was black, then it turned white, so that with the pains my dear mother took in washing and cleansing, the skin came off, and was red till the blood came; this continuing till, in the end, her mouth grew white all over.

In this most sad condition of weakness was my dear mother, almost quite without food, rest, ease, or sleep for about a week. In which time, as also in all the rest of her sickness, she expressed extraordinary patience, still saying it was the Lord that sent it to her, and none else could take it from her, and if he pleased to see it fit, he could ease her, or give her patience to endure his hand. Often would she say that the way to heaven was by the gates of hell, and that the Lion of the tribe of Judah would deliver her. Likewise would she frequently break out and say with the sweet Psalmist of Israel, in the midst of her inexpressible pains and torments, "Why art thou so full of heaviness, oh my soul, and why art thou so disquieted within me? I will still hope in my God, and put my trust in the God of my salvation, who is the help of my countenance, and my God" (Psalms 42.11; 43.5). She frequently repeated the seventy-first Psalm, which she said was penned for old age. Surely she was a great example and patron of piety, faith, patience, of fortitude and resolution, to withstand all the fiery darts of Satan, which he, in her weakness, cast to affright and hinder her journey to heaven. But he in whom she put her whole confidence, and served from her youth up, did not now leave her in extremity, but so assisted her in soul and spirit that it was an heavenly sight to the beholders.

Even to her last period, and notwithstanding all her torments, still she put forth herself for the glory of God, and the good of her family and beholders, in good instructions, severe reproofs for all sins in general, with a continual praying to God and praising him in psalms suitable for her condition, speaking to God in his own phrase and word, saying that we could not speak to him from ourselves in such an acceptable a manner as by that which was dictated by his own most Holy Spirit. She often desired her friends to pray with her, and for her, and told them that she desired that they would not pray for her continuance in this life, for she was weary of it and desired to obtain a better, and to be fitted for it. . . .

Her desire was earnest to receive the Holy Sacrament, which she did with great comfort, on Thursday was sennight before her departure, from Mr. Peter Samois, although it was with great difficulty of swallowing, she never tasting dry bread after, for that excessive weakness. Her desire was to Mr. Kirton, he would preach her funeral sermon, the text to be out of the 14th of the Revelation, verse the 13th, *"Blessed are the dead that die in the Lord, for they rest from their labors."* This blessed soul had the gift from her God to continue till her last breath her perfect memory, understanding, and great wisdom and piety, ever preparing her soul for God and recommending herself in devout ejaculations, crying out with St. Paul, *"I desire to be dissolved, and to be with Christ"* (Phil. 1.23). And all that Friday night, before she departed, having this sweet saying her mouth, *"Come, Lord Jesus, come quickly"* (Rev. 22.20); she making Dafeny to pray with her that prayer of Dr. Smith made in his book for a person at the point to die; and took great notice of each petition, praying with zeal and ardency. It was very observable in all her sickness, as indeed she was not wanting of her gratitude to God for his exceeding testimony of his love and mercy to her in all her preservations and deliverances of her and her children, which she very often repeated and severally enumerated in her best health; so was it now in her grand weakness and torment, even till her death, still the subject of her discourse; calling to mind wonderful and infinite goodness of God to her even from her childhood, setting forth his favors to her soul, and spiritual mercies innumerable, which she particularly mentioned. And then she mentioned all her manifold preservations and deliverances of her person from death and destruction, making such an excellent catalog of all that it was a great consolation to the hearers, and proved by these things as a great argument of the support of her drooping spirits now at the hour of death; being a strong bar of defense against her spiritual adversaries, that God had appeared gloriously for her that was his servant, who had delivered her from time to time whenever she called on him; her Lord never forsaking her; but brought her to the gates of death in a happy old age, and to the sight of heaven, where she fain would be. . . .

She had made several times in her sickness, upon occasion of ministers visiting her, many very excellent confessions of her faith, and profession of those Christian foundations upon which our faith was built, and of her true zeal to the service of God in His holy ordinances of our most pious and Christian church of England. Wishing us, as we would escape the danger of damnation, not to dishonor that great God whom we served by renouncing that faith and profession which was taught us by the holy clergy and bishops of England; never to listen to the insinuations of any factious, new doctrines whatever, but serve God truly and sincerely therein; and he would accept of our souls, and we should be happy, if not in this world, yet hoped in a better. And that she did believe, that if we humbled ourselves for the abominable sins of this nation, and pray to God faithfully, and serve him sincerely in heart, God would return in mercy and restore his decayed church in England, and his servant's son, blessed King Charles the First's posterity, to rule in this nation. Praying heartily we might be delivered from popery, which these divisions and schisms might tend to, if not prevented by the all-wise providence of Almighty God. . . .

As to my own private concerns, she petitioned God that I might find comfort in my husband's family, and be rewarded with the same blessing that God had been graciously pleased to give me in my children (as she was pleased to say I had been to her); and that I might be strengthened by his grace to endure those afflictions with patience which I must find in this world after her death; and that I might have hope in God's mercy that he would lay no more on me than he would enable me to undergo; and that they were signs of his love to me; and that I must not grieve too much for her loss, since the Lord had continued her so long to me, for he could make up her loss in a greater comfort by giving me a son, which I wanted, and that I was then with child of one. Wished me continue as I had begun, and then we should receive each other with joy in heaven, which she was confident of, through the merits of Jesus Christ, according to his speech to St. John, *"Be thou faithful, and I will give thee a crown of life"* (Rev. 2.10): with abundance of other heavenly rich expressions that I am not able to write down. . . .

About Thursday night she sent for her children to take her last farewell in this life, when Mr. Thornton and myself came with our two children, Alice and Katherine, she desiring my husband to pray with and for her, as he had done several times; in which she was much pleased and satisfied, ever joining most devoutly, reverently praying with her heart and soul in each petition, finding great joy and refreshment upon such occasions. After which prayer, she embraced us all severally in her arms, and kissed us, pouring out many prayers and blessings for us all; like good old Jacob, when he gave his last blessing to his children, she begged of God Almighty for us all. After which I took the saddest last leave of my dear and honored mother as ever child did to part with so great and excellent a parent and infinite comfort. And yet the great grief I had was increased by reason of her exceeding torment which she endured, which made me more willingly submit to part with her, who I saw endured much pain and extremity, not desiring she should long endure that which it was the pleasure of God, for the exercise of her patience, to lay on her. Also when she saw me weep much, for this affliction of hers did indeed concern me nearly, she said, "Dear child, why will you not be willing to part with me to God? Has he not lent me to be a comfort to you long enough? O part with me freely, as I desire to enjoy my Savior in heaven. Do not be unwilling that I should be delivered from this miserable world; give me willingly and freely to him that lent me thus long, and be contented in everything. You never have been disobedient to me in all your life; I pray thee obey me in this, that you submit cheerfully to the wise and good determination of our Lord God. And fill your heart with spiritual comfort instead of this in me he takes to himself. And so the blessing of God Almighty be upon the head of you and yours forever. Amen."

Certainly the words of a dying friend prevails much; and I do believe the Lord had put words of persuasion into her mouth which prevailed more than all the world with me to moderate my excessive sorrow, and build me up in hopes, as she said, of our meeting again, never to part; which so happened, for I was after this even desirous that if it were the determinate pleasure of God to take her from my head, that I might patiently submit when he should free that sweet soul from all those burdens of pressures and extremities. It pleased God she continued till Saturday. About noon she spoke to my uncle Norton, and recommending myself and all her children to his care, with much good prayers for him and his, she then took her leave of him. About four o'clock my aunt Norton came to see her, when she saluted her gladly, bidding her "Welcome, dear sister, what comfort is it to me to see my dear and honored husband's sister" with her at that time, there ever having been a strict league of affection and friendship betwixt them; she was then come to see her make her last end and scene of her life, whom she had known near forty years, and so took her solemn farewell of her. I forgot to declare, that, about Wednesday before, she called for her last will, it being made a year before that, and ratifying the same, and publicly declared the same to be her last will and testament, before my husband and myself, and many other witnesses, making the same to be endorsed on the back of her will, etc.

To return to her last actions in this life. About six o'clock at night this sweet saint of God began to be speechless, having still all that time employed that tongue in nothing but prayers, praises, and petitions to God with most heavenly, spiritual, and pathetic recommendations of herself to the Lord, ever saying, "Come, Lord Jesus, make haste and receive my soul," and at the last immediately before her speech failed, "Lord Jesus, into Thy hands I commit my spirit." And when it failed, still lifting up to heaven her eyes and hands to God. And Dafeny perceived she drew her breath short, and going to depart, prayed her that she would give them that was with her some sign that she found the comfort of God's Spirit in her soul, with a taste of the joys of heaven, which she immediately did, to all their great comforts, for she lifted up both her eyes and hands steadfastly to heaven three times distinctly, one after another, and closing her eyes herself then laid down her head and her hands, this holy saint and patron of true piety sweetly fell asleep in the Lord, between the hours of eight and nine o'clock at night, upon Saturday, the 10th of December, 1659, being the day of her coronation, I hope, in heaven, with her Father, receiving that welcome of *"Come, ye blessed of my Father, receive the kingdom He has prepared for you. For I was hungry and ye fed me, naked and ye clothed me, sick and imprisoned, and ye ministered unto me. Inasmuch as ye did it unto these, ye did it unto me"* (Matt. 25.34ff.). And I hope she is now entered into the joy of her Lord.

My brother Christopher Wandesforde was then at London, where he was writ to inform him, both of her sickness and death. Her funeral was solemnized with as much handsomeness as those times would afford, and considering the condition we were in, the soldiers having been quartered amongst us, though not according to her worth and quality. She was interred upon Tuesday, the 13th of December following, in the chief place in her own choir at Catterick church, she having repaired the same all that summer, at her own charges, to the value of above twenty pounds. Her corpse was carried out of her house by the Lord D'arcy, his son Col. D'arcy, Sir Christopher Wivill, baronet, and divers other persons and kindred of quality. Then from Hipswell green her tenants took her, and so carrying her to the town of Catterick, where the ministers who were appointed by her own nomination carried her into the church; and after sermon laid her in her grave. The ministers' names were these: Mr. Peter Samois, Mr. Kirton, Mr. Ferrers, Mr. Edrington, Mr. Binlows, Mr. Robinson, Mr. Smith, Mr. Brockell, Mr. Parke. Infinite number of poor were served by dole at the door; above fifteen hundred; besides in the church of Catterick.

This blessed mother of mine was thus gathered into her grave, having lived many peaceable years together with my father, brought him a competent number of children, being the support of his house and family, preserving it and the branches under her care and prudence, living his chaste wife and widow for above nineteen years. Her whole age wherein she lived was threescore and seven years, and eleven months and odd days; so that she died in a good old age, full of good works and virtue and honor to all of her family and country. To the Lord's most infinite Majesty be all glory and praise, for his great goodness and mercy extended to me and us all, through this dear parent of ours. He make us to possess those graces and virtues which he bestowed upon her, that we may be the better capable to do him true and faithful service to our life's end. Amen.

My delivery of my son William, my sixth child,
and of his death, April the 17th, 1660, at St. Nicholas.

It was the good pleasure of God to continue me in the land of the living, and to bring forth my sixth child at St. Nicholas. I was delivered of a very goodly son, having Mrs. Hickeringgill with me, after hard labor and hazardous, yet, through great mercy, I had my life spared, and was blessed with a happy child about 3 or 4 o'clock in the morning upon Tuesday, the 17th of April, 1660. That day also was my child baptized by Mr. Kirton of Richmond, called William after his father. His sureties were my cousin John York, my cousin William Norton, and my cousin James Darcy lady of Richmond. Thus was I blessed with the life and comfort of my dear child's baptism, with its enjoyment of that holy seal of regeneration; and my pretty babe was in good health, sucking his poor mother to whom my good God had given the blessing of the breast as well as the womb, of that child to whom it was no little satisfaction, while I enjoyed his life; and the joy of it made me recruit [recover] faster, for his sake, that I might do my duty to him as mother. But it so pleased God to shorten this joy, lest I should be too much transported, that I was visited with another trial; for on the Friday sennight after, he began to be very angry and forward, after his dressing in the morning; so that I perceived him not to be well, upon which I gave him Gascoyne powder and cordial, lest it should be the Red Gum in children, usual at that time, to strike it out of his heart at morning after his dressing. And having had three hours' sleep, his face when he awaked was full of red round spots like the smallpox, being of the compass of a halfpenny, and all whealed white all over, these continuing in his face till night, and being in a slumber in my arms on my knee he would sweetly lift up his eyes to heaven and smile, as if the old saying was true in this sweet infant, that he saw angels in heaven. But then, whether through cold upon his dressing then, or what else was the cause, the Lord knoweth, the spots struck in, and grew very sick all night, and about nine o'clock on Saturday morning he sweetly departed this life, to the great discomfort of his weak mother, whose only comfort is that the Lord, I hope, has received him to that place of rest in heaven where little children behold the face of their heavenly Father, to his God and my God; whom I humbly crave to pardon all things in me which he sees amiss, and cleanse away my sins by the blood of my dearest Savior and Redeemer. And that my soul may be bettered by all these chastisements he pleaseth to lay upon me, his vile worm and unprofitable servant, under all his dispensations that hath laid heavy upon me for these many years, whereby he has corrected me, but not given me over to death and destruction, for which I humbly magnify his glorious name forever. And I most heartily beseech him to sanctify these fatherly rebukes, and make them profitable to my poor soul, to bring me in the possession of patience nearer to himself by a strict communion to see him with joy above all these earthly comforts or enjoyments, that so I may be better prepared for acting to his glory here and hereafter; even for Christ Jesus his Son's sake. Amen.

My son William Thornton was buried at Easby in the same grave with his elder sister, which died before baptized, by Mr. Kirton, he being scarce fourteen days old, near my Lady Wharton's grave at Easby, April 29th, 1660: his father being much troubled at his loss, whom the child was exceeding like in person, and also his eldest sister. . . .

Upon this sad affliction of the loss of so brave a delicate son who we took delight in, my Lady Francis Darcy coming to see me desired me to bear it as patiently as I could, for she was persuaded that God would at length give me a son to live (and my husband), but he was to be born at his house where God would make him the heir of, and the Lord would look in mercy upon me, and that I should not die without an heir. I was then resolved in my mind, if it should not please the Lord to grant me that blessing of a son, to be an upholder to my husband's family in its name, that I would freely give him unto the Lord as Hannah did to Samuel in the service of the Lord at his holy altar. But I only desired my will should be submissive to his heavenly pleasure; not my will but his be done in me and mine, and he should be dedicated unto the Lord my God from the womb. Amen.

After the death of my dear Willy Thornton I took the cross very sadly, that he died so soon, and had many sad thoughts of God's afflicting hand on me, and one day was weeping much about it. My dear Naly came to me, then being about four years old, and looked very seriously on me, said, "My dear mother, why do you mourn and weep so much for my brother Willy? Do you not think he is gone to heaven?" I said, "Yes, dear heart, I believe he is gone to heaven, but your father is so afflicted for his loss, and being a son he takes it more heavily, because I have not a son to live." She said again, "Mother, would you or my father have my brother to live with you, when as God has taken him to himself to heaven, where he has no sickness, but live in happiness? Would you have him out of heaven again, where he is in joy and happiness? Dear mother, be patient, and God can give you another son to live with you and my father, for my brother is in happiness with God in heaven." At which the child's speech I did much condemn myself, being instructed by the mouth of one of my own children, and begged that the Lord would give me patience and satisfaction in his gracious goodness, which had put such words into the mouth of so young a child to reprove my immoderate sorrow for him, and begged her life might be spared to me in mercy.

* * *

*Upon my deliverance of my son Robert Thornton, my seventh child,
born at East Newton, the first child that was born
in the new house, September 19, 1662.*

Almighty God, the wise disposer of all good things, both in heaven and earth, who seest what and how much of the comforts of this mortal life is conveniently fit for us to enjoy in this earth, hath at length had pity on my afflictions, and gave me such a mercy and dear enjoyment to myself and husband, after all his and my several troubles and losses of sons, as I could not hope for or expect; making me a joyful mother of a sweet son, born at full time, after five great trials and hazards of miscarriage when I was with him, the one of sickness, the second through grief at a strange accident that happened me when I was pretty big of him of a fright which caused a mark of blood upon his heart of most pure color and several shapes, continuing till he was about a year old, and seen by many persons at several times; the third, the trouble of Nettleton bailiffs; and the fourth, that before the settlement was made of his estate on my children; the fifth was a great danger I escaped of him by a fall I got down the stairs to preserve Celia Danby from hurt, when she tumbled down the whole stairs before me. The least of which mercies and deliverances were subject of a hearty praise and thanksgiving to the Lord of Lords. But it still pleased the Most High God to add this blessing when I was delivered, after great danger and peril of my life in travail of my son Robert Thornton, upon Friday, the 19th of September, 1662.

On Thursday my Lady Cholmely and my dear aunt Norton, my Lady York and Mrs. Wattson, with my sisters Denton and Frances Thornton, were with me and stayed till evening, then went home to Oswaldkirk. The next day came again. And I lay in bed while all the company was got together to view that goodly child and admire him, so large and big, newly born, and all so fond of him being a son, with great joy. My Lady York out of her fright came to my bedside and wept over me, and said: "My dear cousin, you that help every one to save them, cannot you tell me what do you good in this extremity to save your own?" On which it pleased my good God to enable me, she laying her ear to my mouth, to say only, "Go into closet, right-hand shelf, box, powder, syrup of cloves, give me." And by Divine Providence she got the box and powder which I told her of, and had laid ready for myself before my sickness, and told my midwife and maid of it, to give me in such a case, but they had forgotten it in their trouble for me.

He was born at East Newton, betwixt the hours of eight and nine o'clock at night, having been since the night before in strong labor of him till that time. But as though this grand mercy should not pass alone, without its severer monitor to my unbridled passion of joy, and that I might be cautioned not to set my affection too much on things below, be they never so necessary or desirable, it pleased the great God to lay on me, his weak handmaid, an exceeding great weakness, beginning a little after my child was born, by a most violent and terrible flux of blood, with such excessive floods all that night, that it was terrible to behold to those about me, bringing me into a most desperate condition, without hopes of life; spirits, soul, and strength seemed all gone from me. My dear husband, and children, and friends had taken their last farewell. In this deplorable condition lay I in for several hours together, not being able to utter one word. All the means could be was done in that fright, but did not prevail.

After five hours' torment it pleased my gracious Lord to have compassion on his languishing creature, and brought to my remembrance a powder which I used formerly to others, and with His blessing had good success in the like kind, and hardly could I get the name of it to my Lady York for my feebleness; but after she had given me some of it, through the mercy of my Savior, who healeth and helped all that came unto him, by it helped me, so that the flux stayed by degrees till Dr. Witty was come, when, after the use of other means, I was delivered and spared at that time from that death so nigh, but brought so exceeding weak that the effects lasted till Candlemas upon my body by fits; yet did I recover my milk again. But oh! O Lord, most high and loving Father, wherefore are thy miraculous favors and mercies extended thus to such a vile worm as myself, who am not able to recount the unmeasurable goodness, nor tell what thou didst for my soul. Doubtless to set forth thine Almighty power, glory, and infinite perfection, that canst raise from death and bring to the grave in a moment.

31

DIARY (1671–1714)*

Mrs. Elizabeth Freke

April 5, 1675

God took to himself my dear niece, Mrs. Ciceally Choute, of the small-pox, near a month after the death of my dear sister; which on her deathbed request was buried in her mother's grave in the chancel of Hollingbourne in Kent. She did die in London, as did my sister, both to my great grief.

June 2, 1675

Wednesday, June the second, my dear son, Mr. Ralph Freke, was born about three in the afternoon, at my father's at Hanington, and by him, with my Aunt Freke and Sir George Norton, he was christened Ralph Freke, of my dear father's name. I were four or five days in labor of him, and had for him four midwives about me when he was born, the man midwife affirming he had been long dead to my husband and aunt and sister Norton with my Lady Thinn, all who were with me several days in this my extremity.

My great and good God that never failed me or denied my reasonable request, raised me up a good woman midwife of my Lady Thinn's acquaintance, one Mrs. Mills, who came in at this juncture of time, and, by my God's mercy and providence to me, I was safely delivered, and though apparently of a dead child, my God raised him up to me so far as the same night to baptize him of my dear father's name, Ralph Freke, for which mercy to him and me I beg I may never forget to be thankful.

I put my son into the hand of a good surgeon for at least six weeks,

*Ed. Mary Carbery (Cork, Ireland: Guy and Company, 1913), pp. 24–27.

MRS. ELIZABETH FREKE, HER DIARY.

Raw silk heats and drys, Cheers the hartt, Comforts the vittall spirritts, both Nattureall, vittall, & Animall, & drives away Sadness.

Hony is off a Gallantt Clensing Quality, exceeding profytable In Inward Ulcers, in whatt partt of the Body soever; Itt opens the veins, and Clenses the Reyns and Blader; nor has itt any vice in Itt, butt thatt itt soon Turns to Choller.

St. John's wortt, worne aboutt one, keeps one from being hurtt by witches.

The Skull of a Man thatt was never Buryed, being Beatten to Powder and given Inwardly, the quantity of a dragme att a Time In Bettony Watter, helps Pallsyes & Falling sickness.

The Small Triangular Bone In the Skull of a Man, Called Ostriquetrum, soe absolutely Cures the Falling Sickness, thatt itt will never Come Againe, saith Paracellsas.

The Head of a Cole Black Catt, being Burntt to Ashes in a New pott or Crucible and some of the Ashes fine sifted, and blown Into the Eyes Every day, helps such as have a skinn grown over the sight; and Iff there be any Inflamation, Moysten an oake Leafe In Watter and Lay over the Eyes. Mizalldua saith by this one Medicyne hee hath Cured such as have bin Blind a Whole yeare.

The Head of a Young Kitte, being Burntt to Ashes, and the quantity of A dragme taken every morning in a Little watter, is an admirable Remedy against the Goute.

Crabbs eyes Break the Stone & opens stopings of the Bowles.

The Lungs of A fox well dryed is an admirable strengthener of the Lungs.

The Brains of A Hare, Rosted, hleps Trembling, & maks Children breed their Teeth easily, ther Gums Rubed with Itt; And helps scald heads And Falling off off The Haire, the Head being Anoynted Wth Itt.

Figure 10. Excerpt from the published diary of Elizabeth Freke.

who came every day from Highworth, a mile from my dear father's, I being almost all the time confined to my bed, and at last, by my God's great goodness and mercy to me, he recovered him, for which great God make me ever thankful for sparing my child and raising up his poor servant, Elizabeth Freke.

In July my son was taken with a thrush in his mouth with which he was again given over for dead, and carried away from me in order to a burial; but from this misfortune my God raised him up again, I hope to be his servant, and a comfort to me, his poor afflicted mother, instead of my dear sister Choutt, whom God took from me about two months before. She was to have been with me in all this my troubles of lying-in. My sister Norton and a great many of my friends were met together at my dear father's to be merry, which mirth my God soon turned to mourning, by the death of my sister and her daughter.

About the middle of September I set out again from Bristol Fair for Ireland, the first time of my going over thither, and I left my only son (with my dear father's care over him) at Highworth at nurse, he being then about ten weeks old.

I landed at Youghhall in the County of Waterford, where when I came I had no place fit to put my unfortunate head in. From Youghhall Mr. Freke and his mother carried me to Rustillian, a house of Earl's of Inchequeen's house; I stayed about eight months.

My dear father sent for me over to England, my son being crippled by the carelessness of his nurse, and about 14 of December broke his leg short in the hacklebone, which she kept private for near a quarter of a year till a jelly was grown between it; she keeping him in his cradle, and everybody believed he was breeding of his teeth, he having two at eighteen weeks old, and at that age could stand almost alone till this misfortune befell him. . . .

2 May, 1677

About the second of May I lay in of another son in Southampton Square in London; which, by hard labor and several frights, was dead born, and lies buried at the upper end of St. Giles (in the Fields) chancel in London, with one of my Lord Halifax's in the same grave.

32

A NARRATIVE OF GOD'S GRACIOUS DEALINGS
WITH THAT CHOICE CHRISTIAN
MRS. HANNAH ALLEN*

Soon after this my mother returned home into the country, and left me in my brother's house, who was a young man unmarried, and had only a man and a maid, and he much abroad himself about his occasions; and now my opinion of dying suddenly began to leave me, therefore I concluded that God would not suffer me to die a natural death, but that I should commit some fearful abomination, and so be put to some horrible death: One day my brother going along with me to Doctor Pridgeon, as we came back, I saw a company of men with halberds, "Look, Brother," said I, "you will see such as these (one of these days) carry me to Newgate": to prevent which I studied several ways to make away myself, and I being so much alone, and in a large solitary house, had the more liberty to endeavor it; first I thought of taking opium that I might die in my sleep, and none know but that I died naturally (which I desired that my child might not be disgraced by my untimely end) and therefore sent the maid to several apothecaries' shops for it; some said they had none, others said it was dangerous and would not sell it her. Once she had got some, and was coming away with it; the master of the shop coming in, asked what she had, and when he knew, took it from her (this the maid told me). When I had sent her up and down several days, and saw she could get none, then I got spiders and took one at a time in a pipe with tobacco, but never scarce took it out, for my heart would fail me; but once I thought I had been poisoned; in the night awaking out of my sleep, I thought I felt death upon me (for I had taken a spider when I went to bed) and called to my brother and told him so,

*London, 1683. Wing A1025, Reel 1734, pp. 30–34, 44, 64–65, 68–73.

who presently arose and went to his friend an apothecary, who came and gave me something to expel it; the next day my uncles and brother (considering the inconveniency of that lonesome house) removed me to Mr. Peter Walker's house, a hosier at the Three Crowns in Newgate Market (whose wife was my kinswoman) who received me very courteously, though I was at that time but an uncomfortable guest.

In the time I was at my brother's, I had strange apprehensions that the lights that were in neighboring houses were apparitions of devils, and that those lights were of their making; and if I heard the voice of people talk or read in other houses, I would not be persuaded but that it was devils like men, talking of me, and mocking at my former reading, because I proved such an hypocrite. . . .

Here I practiced many devices to make away myself, sometimes by spiders (as before), sometimes endeavoring to let myself blood with a pair of sharp scissors, and so bleed to death; once when the surgeon had let me blood, I went up into a chamber and bolted the door to me, and took off the plaster and tied my arm, and set the vein ableeding again; which Mrs. Walker fearing, ran upstairs and got into the chamber to me; I seeing her come in, ran into the leads, and there my arm bled upon the wall; now (said I) you may see there is the blood of a cursed reprobate . . . .

When my grandmother had told me of the depths of the mercy of God in Christ, I would answer with indignation, "What do you tell me of a Christ; it had been better for me if there had never been a savior, then I should have gone to hell at a cheaper rate."

Towards winter I grew to eat very little (much less than I did before) so that I was exceeding lean; and at last nothing but skin and bones (a neighboring gentlewoman, a very discreet person that had a great desire to see me, came in at the back door of the house unawares and found me in the kitchen, who after she had seen me, said to Mrs. Wilson, "She cannot live, she hath death in her face"). I would say still that every bit I did eat hastened my ruin; and that I had it with a dreadful curse; and what I eat increased the fire within me, which would at last burn me up; and I would now willingly live out of hell as long as I could.

. . . but as soon as I saw them, I cried out in a violent manner several times, "Ah, Aunt Wilson, hast thou served me so!" and ran into the chimney and took up the tongs. "No," said they, "Your aunt knows not of our coming." "What do you do here?" said I. "We have something to say to you," said they. "But I have nothing to say to you," said I. Mr. Shorthose took me by the hand and said, "Come, come, lay down those tongs and go with us into the parlor," which I did, and there they discoursed with me, till they had brought me to so calm and friendly a temper, that when they went, I accompanied them to the door and said, "Methinks I am loathe to part with them." Mr. Shorthose having so good encouragement, came the next day again, being Sabbath day after dinner, and prevailed with me to walk with him into an arbor in the orchard, where he had much discourse with me, and amongst the rest he entreated me to go home with him; which after long persuasions both from him and my aunt, I consented to, upon this condition, that he promised me, he would not compel me to anything of the worship of God, but what he could do by persuasion; and that week I went with them, where I spent that summer; in which time it pleased God by Mr. Shorthose's means to do me much good both in soul and body; he had some skill in physic himself, and also consulted with physicians about me; he kept me to a course of physic most part of the summer, except when the great heat of the weather prevented. I began much to leave my dreadful expressions concerning my condition, and was present with them at duty; and at last they prevailed with me . . . to walk with them to visit friends, and was much altered for the better.

A fortnight after Michaelmas my aunt fetched me home again to Snelston, where I passed that winter much better than formerly, and was pretty conformable and orderly in the family; and the next summer was much after the same manner, but grew still something better; and the next winter likewise still mending though but slowly, till the spring began, and then I changed much from my retiredness, and delighted to walk with friends abroad.

And this spring it pleased God to provide a very suitable match for me, one Mr. Charles Hatt, a widower living in Warwickshire; with whom I live very comfortably, both as to my inward and outward man, my husband being one that truly fears God.

As my melancholy came by degrees, so it wore off by degrees, and as my dark melancholy bodily distempers abated, so did my spiritual maladies also; and God convinced me by degrees that all this was from Satan, his delusions and temptations, working in those dark and black humors, and not from myself, and this God cleared up to me more and more; and accordingly my love to, and delight in religion, increased; and it is my desire that, lest this great affliction should be a stumbling block to any, it may be known, (seeing my case is published) that I evidently perceive that God did it in much mercy and faithfulness to my soul; and though for the present it was a bitter cup, yet that it was but what the only wise God saw I had need of according to that place, 1 Peter 1:6, "Tho' now for a season, if need be, ye are in heaviness through manifold temptations," which scripture did much comfort me under my former afflictions in my first husband's days.

33

LIVING TESTIMONIES CONCERNING
THE DEATH OF THE RIGHTEOUS

OR The blessed end of Joseph Featherstone and Sarah, his daughter *

Sarah Featherstone Browne
and Thomas Browne (her second husband)

There hath a weight lain upon my spirit for some time to write this testimony concerning my dear and only child. . . .

And when I married the second time, the innocency of my dear child did much appear in her tenderness and obedience to us her parents. . . . And when she went abroad to be educated, she would be very careful in improving her time, and was a good example where she went, amongst Friends [Quakers] and others, and hath left a good favor behind her, and her removal hath tendered the hearts of many that did know her; and when my dear husband was taken to prison from me and his tender family, she was a true sympathizer with me. . . . Oh, the consideration of my great loss of so dear a child now in my old age hath caused me sometimes to say in my heart, if David said of Absalom, *would God I had died for thee, O Absalom my Son!* surely I have more cause than David had, I having no more of my own to be a comfort to me (this being the last of ten, nine of them were buried before her father). . . .

In the seventh month on the ninth day, about the eleventh hour of the night, it pleased the Lord to visit my dear child with this sickness whereon she died; and when my maid came and told me my child was taken sick, my heart was much troubled, and it seized upon me very deeply, that my dear child would be taken from me; and when I came at my child, she did lie in a sweet frame of spirit, under a great weight of

*London, 1689. Wing F576B, Reel 1884, pp. 14, 17–19, 22–23.

sickness   I said, "My dear child, if the Lord should be pleased to take thee from me, where hast thou a wish to be buried, wilt thou be buried by thy dear father, in Friends Burying-place, in Crowland, where we came from?" She said, "I have thoughts formerly to have been buried by my dear father, but considering the greatness of the journey, and so many buried near him, I am satisfied, I leave it to thee and my father." I said, "My dear child, art thou willing to be buried in our burying-place, where I hope to be buried by thee?" She said, "Dear Mother, bury me where thou and my father pleaseth, I leave it to you, it's no matter how many miles distance these bodies lie, our souls shall one day rejoice together. . . ."

Some time before she departed, her speech failed her, after which a sweet harmony often ran through her, often lifting up her hands with a very cheerful countenance, and so she fell asleep in the Lord.

Sarah Browne, Her Mother

34

THE WORK OF GOD IN A DYING MAID

Being a short account of the dealings of the Lord
with one Susannah Whitrow about the age of fifteen years,
and daughter of Robert Whitrow, inhabiting in Covent Garden
in the county of Middlesex. Published for the warning
and good of others who are in the same condition
she was in before her sickness. *

Joan Whitrow

Concerning that false report that was raised by some envious persons, which she formerly kept company with, hearing of her change from that vain conversation she had formerly lived in, they reported that she was in love, and that was the cause of her distemper. When her father came home and had given me a relation of what those persons had infused into him, although I was satisfied to the contrary, I went to my dear child and examined her concerning it; and because I would be clear of whatever might happen hereafter concerning it, I said unto her, "My dear child, thy father and I will give our consent freely for thee to marry him, and we will do to the uttermost of our power for thee to make thy life comfortable with him all thy days."

Then she said, "My dear Mother, I thank you; but that man is no more to me than one I never saw with my eyes, neither will I ever [have] him, if he had all the possessions of the earth. It's true, there was something betwixt us, he being very urgent with me upon the account of marriage, proffering to settle a considerable estate on me, and my father at that time being a little harsh to me, I thought I would set myself at liberty; but upon better consideration, I told him I would do

*London, 1677. Wing W2039, Reel 1559, pp. 14–20, 38–40.

nothing without my father and my mother's advice, which he was unwilling to; in that and some other things I was dissatisfied; I considered
if I should have him I should be ruined; so, that small affection I had to
him I withdrew; and before I fell sick this last time, I did desire never to
see him more. And now, my Mother, I am clear of him and all men
living.

"Oh, my bowed-down and broken-hearted Mother! What hath been
thy sufferings in this family? Oh! how hast thou been oppressed with
our iniquities? Ah, bowed down! Ah! how often hast thou told my
father the Lord would visit him with sore and grievous judgment if he
did not repent, and turn from the evil of his ways? Ah, how often hast
thou said the Lord would plead thy righteous cause with us? Now the
day is come thou hast so long warned us of; now the Lord is risen; now
the Lord is broke in upon us. Oh how great hath been thy care and
pains which thou hast taken to bring us into the fear of the Lord? Oh,
thou blessed of the Lord! Great shall be thy reward, the Lord will give
beauty for ashes, and the garment of praise for the spirit of heaviness:
Blessed be thou my mother. . . .

"My dear Mother, send for that dear Friend (meaning R. T.) that
prayed by me the other day. . . . I love her; let her pray by me to the
Lord against the Tempter. And send for that faithful servant of the Lord
W. P. The Lord will hear the prayers of the faithful. . . .

"Oh! how have I been against a woman's speaking in a meeting?
but now, whether it comes from man, woman, or child, it is precious
indeed. . . ."

Witnessed by me,

Ann Martin

. . . After several days lying in the sweet solace and heavenly life of
the Lord (in which time she uttered many heavenly things, which were
not taken in writing), she did express these words, "O thou Beloved
of my Soul! what shall I say of thee? for thou art too wonderful for
me. . . . Ye glorious angels, you that excel in glory, sing praises to him
that sits upon the throne. . . . Ah! thou has ravished my soul. My dear
Mother, I shall be as a newborn babe; I shall be very simple; but bear
with me; for the Lord is with me.

"My dear Mother, I must lay down this body; the Lord will not trust
me longer in this wicked world; happy am I, my Savior, my soul loves

thee dearly. . . . my heart is overcome with thy sweet countenance: O how lovely art thou! . . . O come away, come away; why dost thou stay? I am ready, I am ready."

Then lying some time very still, I heard her in a heavenly harmony, in which frame of spirit she departed without either sigh or groan.

Joan Whitrow, her testimony concerning
the loving-kindness of the Lord

35

THE JOURNEYS OF CELIA FIENNES*

Death of a Queen, 5 March 1695

This Abbey [Westminster] also is the place where the solemnities of the King's interments and coronations are performed, of which I shall give a particular: at the death of a prince, which I have been a mournful spectator or hearer of two of the most renowned that ever was, King William and Queen Mary, the Queen dying before the King, he omitted no ceremony of respect to her memory and remains, which lay in state in Whitehall in a bed of purple velvet, all open, the canopy the same with rich gold fringe, the middle being the arms of England curiously painted and gilt, the headpiece embroidered richly with a crown and cipher of her name, a cushion with the sword and gauntlets, on the corpse which was rolled in lead, and over it a coffin covered with purple velvet with the crown, and gilt in moldings very curious; a pall on all of a very rich tissue of gold and silver, ruffled round about with purple velvet, which hung down on the ground, which was a half [dais] railed as the manner of the princes' beds are; this in a room hung with purple velvet; full of large wax tapers, and at the four corners of the bed stood four of the Ladies of the Bed Chamber—countesses—with veils; these were at several times relieved by others of the same.

The antechamber hung with purple cloth, and there attended four of the Maids of Honor, all in veils, and the Gentlemen of the Bed Chamber: pages [in] another room all in black, the stairs all below the same. The Queen dying while the Parliament sat, the King gave mourning to them (500) and cloaks, which attended thus: their Speaker having his train borne up, then the Lord Mayor the same, and attended by the aldermen and officers all in black, and the judges; then the officers of the household, then the guards, then the Gentleman Master of the

*Ed. Christopher Morris (London: Cresset Press, 1949), pp. 294–96.

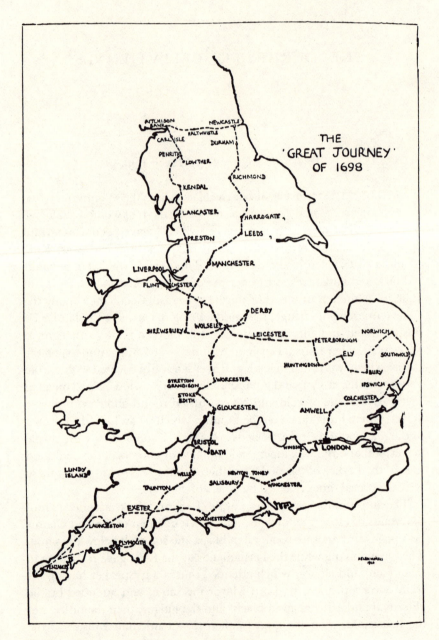

Figure 11. Illustration from *The Journeys of Celia Fiennes*.

Horse led the Queen's lead horse covered up with purple velvet, next came the open chariot made as the bed was, the canopy the same all purple velvet, a high arched teister ruffled, with the rich fringe and pall, which was supported by six of the first dukes of the realm that were not in office; this chariot was drawn by the Queen's own six horses covered up with purple velvet and at the head and feet was laid the emblems of her dignity, the crown and scepter on a cushion at the head, and glove and sword and gauntlets at the feet; after which the first duchess in England, Duchess of Somerset, as chief mourner walked, being supported by these lords, the Lord President of the Council and the Lord Privy Seal, she having a veil over face, and her train of six yards' length being borne up by the next duchess assisted by four young ladies, after which two and two the ladies followed and lords, all long trains according to their rank, the bishops likewise, all on foot on black cloth strained on boards, from Whitehall to Westminster Abbey, where was a sermon, in which time the body of the Queen was reposed in a mausoleum in form of a bed with black velvet and silver fringe round, and hanging in arches, and at the four corners was tapers, and in the middle a basin supported by cupids' or cherubims' shoulders, in which was one entire great lamp burning the whole time.

Then after the service of burial, which is done with solemn and mournful music and singing, the sound of a drum unbraced, the breaking of all the white staves of those that were the officers of the Queen, and flinging in the keys of the rest of the offices devoted by that badge into the tomb; they seal it up and so return in the same order they went. There is always a High Steward made for all solemnities of the Kings and Queens, and he is only so for that day, and he goes just before the lead horse. The pages also lead all the horses that draw the chariot, and the Yeomen of the Guard walk on each side, and the Gentlemen Pensioners, the guards on horseback being set in rank on each side all the way. This is the manner of public funerals, but if it be Kings' then the ladies attend not.

PART SEVEN

WOMEN MEDITATING
AND PRAYING

Introduction

"an harmonious apprehension of God . . ."

According to Douglas Bush in *English Literature in the Earlier Seventeenth Century,* "more than two-fifths of the books printed in England from 1480 to 1640 were religious, and for the years 1600–40 the percentage is still higher. In Jaggard's *Catalogue* of 1619 nearly three-fourths of the books are religious and moral; in William London's *Catalogue of the most Vendible Books in England* (1657–58) the space given to works of divinity equals that occupied by all other kinds together" (310). In Protestant England there was a burgeoning of the publication of meditations, prayers, and manuals on the art of meditation to replace the well-known and much-used meditations, prayers, and manuals of the Roman Catholic tradition.

Protestant modes of meditation drew on Protestant theology and developed distinctly Protestant forms. While Roman Catholic meditations focused on events in the Christian year and especially on major events in the life of Christ, with emphasis on the recapitulation of those events in the individual soul (*Spiritual Exercises* of St. Ignatius Loyola; *Introduction à la Vie Dévote* of St. François de Sales), Protestant meditation sought to redirect the focus to the written Word of God, to the engagement of the individual soul with the scriptures, and then to the individual experiences of the meditator. In engaging with the scriptures, the meditator would by divine light and spiritual conviction recognize the sinfulness of the human heart and the need for repentance, would experience through divine revelation God's forgiving and restoring grace, and would use individual experiences as a response to express gratitude to God for deliverance from sin and death and from the impact of the exigencies of human life. Anna Trapnel, for example, in *Report and Plea* (1654) drew heavily on the scriptures when she meditated and when she dialogued with God in mystical trances. Her dialogues with God were cast in the words of the saints and apostles:

277

Satan tempts me; but such is the goodness of the Lord to me, who lets not out Satan till he hath first established me; and then before I have the mercy, the sentence of death is put upon what is in order to the bringing it forth to view: so that the Lord thereby strengthens me the more, and makes me live by faith, which is the life of the just: it's a lovely life the life of faith. But further, as for Satan's temptations, they lasted but for half a day, and a little part of the night, and they were removed; for in the night in my sleep the Lord refreshed me with many scriptures, as being my refuge, stay, and defense, and strong tower, guide and succorer. And at break of day I awoke out of sleep, refreshed as one with new wine; and indeed I had that night such well-refined wine, as scripture makes mention of. And hearing the birds cherup in the morning early, about my chamber window, I had this saying given into my heart, "Thou hearest those birds in their notes and motion, which pleaseth thy ear: And doth the great creator take care of birds, still maintaining them with a supply of food suitable for them, that so they may live, and be lively in their service to man? And doth God take care of fowls, that not a sparrow shall fall to the ground without the Father's providence or ordering it to be so? Then what care and provision doth he make for rational created pieces, which the whole Trinity was in the make thereof: as for other pieces, he said, 'let it be,' and it was so; but as to man's make, the whole Trinity gave their judgment. And," said the Lord to me, "hath God honored thee with his first honor, in making thee a rational piece, and also giving thee a share and interest in the death and resurrection of his son, and hath made thee partaker of the divine nature, of that heavenly-born state, of that second creation in Christ, spoken of in Ephesians 2:19. Art thou thus provided for, to be made a possessor of two creation-works, a first and a second? and also hast thou the Spirit of adoption whereby thou canst cry, 'Abba, Father'? then having done thus much for thee, will he withhold anything that's good for thee? He will not. . . ."

 . . . all this begat such an harmonious apprehension of God in my heart, that I began to sing forth his praises, and continued while it was so late in the evening, that my friends that walked with me thought it convenient to lead me into the house . . . my spirits was so much in divine rapture, and my spirits so heat with Spirit-fire, which produced singing-melody. . . . (3–5; for Trapnel's description of life in prison, see part 2)

Both Protestant and Roman Catholic meditations were designed ultimately to awaken the passions and stir the heart with devotion and affection to God. The Protestant Edmund Calamy, in *The Art of Divine*

Meditation (1680), identifies the time-honored goal of meditation: "the very life and soul of Meditation . . . to get your affections warmed and heated by the things you meditate upon; for the work of the understanding is nothing else but to be as a Divine pair of bellows, to kindle and inflame the heart and affections" (189–90).

For Protestant women the meditative mode was a congenial mode of addressing God. Although men continued to dominate the field of meditation and prayer, women discovered that they could approach God without male mediation and through channels that redirected institutionally endorsed methods. Their meditations and prayers were, of course, private exercises and not designed for public worship. Women took to writing meditations and prayers and recording their experiences first for themselves and then for other women, since women's meditations and prayers could not, in a male-controlled religious environment, be used by men (except in the rare instances when mothers wrote meditations for their sons). Men's meditations and prayers were written for both men and women, and women were instructed in their use.

When women wrote to God and conversed with him, they made personal discoveries about who God is and who a woman is, of how God worked in the lives of women and of the role women played in the social and redemptive orders. In this specifically religious activity (although it must be remembered that women of these centuries did not dichotomize religious and secular activities), women began to recognize the power of their own words—in the life of the female writer herself and in the lives of female readers. Meditations and prayers did not, however, become self-empowering strategies but gender-based modes of discourse that expanded female consciousness and raised the level of spiritual experience.

Women's meditations and prayers gave voice to gender-specific concerns. Pregnancy, labor, childbirth, and infant and maternal mortality loom large in many of them. In these meditations and prayers, the female perception of the self found its identity in God and in other females. The meditative mode became for women writers a "freeing" mode, even though women made references in their prefaces to their passive place or abject state in society. Freedom from male intervention gave women a secure identity in a world that had made females conspicuously covert.

Women's meditations and prayers appeared in various forms: as printed books of meditations and prayers; in diaries and letters; in miscellaneous papers; and in poetry. A major contribution to the publication of women's meditations and prayers was *The Monument of Matrones* (1582), collected and edited by Thomas Bentley, a student of Gray's Inn. Bentley describes his 1,000-page compilation as "the worthy works partly of men, partly of women; compiled for the necessary use of both sexes out of the sacred Scriptures and other approved authors" (title page). He adds, however, that it is "more proper and peculiar for the private use of women than heretofore hath been set out by any." The Second Lamp in the collection contains the writing of contemporary women, including Elizabeth I (prayers), Katherine Parr *(Lamentacion of a Sinner)*, godly women martyrs, and a "godly hearted gentlewoman" (prayers adapted from the Psalms). Three prayers by Elizabeth I were published in the Second Lamp: Elizabeth's prayer when imprisoned in the Tower, when she was afraid of being murdered; and before her coronation, when she compared herself to Daniel and his rescue from the lion's den.

Katherine Parr, the last wife of Henry VIII, was the author of *The Lamentacion of a Sinner* and of *Prayers or Meditacyons*. One of the most popular of the books of meditation in the sixteenth century, *Prayers or Meditacyons* went into fifteen editions between 1545 and 1608. Heavily doctrinal, the prayers or meditations were shaped by Katherine's Protestant reading of the scriptures and perhaps served a political purpose in directing women readers to the Reformed apprehension of the faith and away from Roman Catholic readings and modes of meditation in the disturbing religious climate of the time.

Alice Thornton's *Autobiography* is prefaced by a meditation of praise:

> For as much as it is the duty of every true Christian to remember and take notice of Almighty God our Heavenly Father's gracious acts of Providence over them, and merciful dealings with them, even from the womb until the grave bury them in silence, as also to keep particular remembrances of His favors, both spiritual and temporal, together with His remarkable deliverances of their souls and bodies, with a true and unfeigned gratitude, to His glorious Majesty from them all, I therefore, his creature and unworthy handmaid, who have not tasted (only) of the droppings of His dew, but have been showered plentifully upon my head with the continued streams of goodness, do most humbly desire to furnish my heart with the deep thoughts and apprehensions and sincere meditations of a thankfulness for His free grace, love, mercies, and unconceivable goodness to me. (Preface)

Her experience of abuse (see part 1) and catalog of her deliverances (see part 6) are absorbed into the meditative mode and liberated by it. Meditation brought Thornton psychological relief and placed her experiences in a context of personal gratitude that inflamed "the heart and affections."

Included in the unpublished miscellaneous papers left by Elizabeth Egerton, countess of Bridgewater, are prayers and meditations, evidence that many women wrote meditations and prayers for their own personal edification and growth. Beginning with a lengthy formal but personal confession of faith, Elizabeth Egerton becomes introspective when she focuses on pregnancies, safe deliveries, and her fear of death in childbirth. (She did, as a matter of fact, die in childbirth.) Especially revealing are her prayers on the death of her twenty-one-month-old daughter Katherine. The mother begins one of her prayers with an allusion to the Old Testament "unwise" who regard death as "utter destruction." The relevance of the allusion is part of the hidden text; she identifies briefly with the "unwise," no matter how strong her written confession of faith. The identity is a daring one for a woman. Her prayer pierces the facade of religious equanimity supposed to assuage a grief and allows the female writer to work her way through the agony of the destructiveness of death to submission, if not quite to consolation:

> In the sight of the unwise, the righteous seem to die; and their departure is taken for misery, and their going from hence, as utter destruction, but they are in peace; and my dear Jewel to show she was going to happiness, when her eyes were set (Death having seized upon her) the last word she spoke was to me, when in passion I asked her if I should kiss her, she said yes, lengthening the word as if she was in high bliss, and lay so sweetly, desiring nothing but her Lord Jesus. Thus her life and death was nothing but sweetness, showing us what we should perform at our last day; and God found her worthy of himself; so must my sorrow submit. (BL MS. Egerton 607, 125–26)

Embodied in Aemilia Lanier's long poem *Salve Deus Rex Judaeorum* (1611) is a meditation on Christ's passion, death, and resurrection. The poem is notable for the place it assigns to women in redemptive history. With eleven dedications to prominent women of her day, Lanier supplies her female readers with a survey of biblical women and their contributions to the life of the church, giving them a female context for meditation. She deflects attention away from the Eve of contemporary male vindictive writing and to women in the life of Christ.

As also in respect it pleased our Lord and Savior Jesus Christ, without the assistance of man, being free from original and all other sins, from the time of his conception, till the hour of his death, to be begotten of a woman; and that he healed women, pardoned women, comforted women: yea, even when he was in his greatest agony and bloody sweat, going to be crucified, and also in the last hour of his death, took care to dispose of a woman: after his resurrection, appeared first to a woman, sent a woman to declare his most glorious resurrection to the rest of his disciples. . . . (*Salve Deus,* "To the Virtuous Reader")

Lanier's portrayal of the crucifixion is closer to Roman Catholic than to Protestant meditation. It directs the eyes of the reader to the sufferings of Christ:

His joints disjointed, and his legs hang down,
His alabaster breast, his bloody side,
His members torn, and on his head a crown
Of sharpest thorns, to satisfy for pride:
Anguish and pain do all his senses drown,
While they his holy garments do divide:
   His bowels dry, his heart full fraught with grief,
   Crying to him that yields him no relief.
                    (stanza 146)

The poem has many aggressive moments: it gives the counterpart to the traditional "wicked women" theme by providing a survey of "wicked men," and it demonstrates the need for women to reclaim their place in the history of redemption.

    The first document in this section is an excerpt from *Miscelanea, Meditations, Memoratives,* a collection of meditative writings by Elizabeth Grymeston, who was a recusant (an illegal adherent to Roman Catholicism) in the Protestant England of Elizabeth I. She wrote the book on her deathbed for the only surviving son of nine children, Bernye Grymeston, because she wished her son to "see the true portraiture of thy mother's mind." This "mother's mind" had been nourished by the church fathers, by the scriptures, by the poetry of Robert Southwell (her Roman Catholic relative who was executed at Tyburn for his faith), and by the poetry and prose of Richard Rowlands (also known as Verstegan). Her book is an assimilation of the rich traditional devotional literature on which she was raised. Her voice echoes not only that of the psalmist but also that of Gregory, Jerome, Ambrose, Augustine, Chrysostom, Seneca, Virgil, Terence, and Pindar.

Her book, intended only for her son's instruction in meditation, went into four posthumous editions between 1604 and 1618(?). The first edition consisted of fourteen chapters, the three subsequent editions of twenty chapters. The author intermingles Roman Catholic and Protestant traditions, borrowing freely from and adapting the traditions to her own meditative needs. Chapter 7 of the first edition follows the Catholic tradition of meditation on the sufferings of Christ. She directs Bernye to look at Christ on the cross and participate with him in his passion and death: "Behold thy Savior with his head full of thorns, his eyes full of tears, and his ears full of blasphemies, his mouth full of gall, his body full of wounds, his heart full of sorrow; and blame him not if ere thou find him he give thee a sip of the chalice whereof he drunk so full a cup. Thy love must be great, when his sorrow is more at thy ingratitude than at his own affliction, when he lost himself to win thee . . ." (D2r).

The "sixteen sobs" and the "sixteen staves of verse taken out of Peter's Complaint" (Southwell) resonate with Protestant modes and themes of meditation. She calls attention to her sins and the need for forgiveness, to Christ's deliverance of her from the miseries of sin and death, and to her gratitude for this deliverance. Interwoven in the songs and prayers is a profound sense of the tenderness of the Savior and the sweet grace of "sweet Jesu." (Her son's poetic response is also included here.)

Ruth Hughey and Philip Hereford in an article in *The Library* regard Elizabeth Grymeston's book as the reflection of a sixteenth-century female mind: "By no other means than her own book could we have had so surely this portrait of her mind. No male writer of the period, if he had chosen her as the prototype for a fictitious feminine character, or if he had taken upon himself the writing of a book of remembrance on her, or even if he had intended merely to write about her as an actual individual, could have drawn for us so real a picture of the inner life of this sixteenth-century woman—her reading, her talents, her limitations, her prepossession with the moral and religious side of things, her consuming love for her son" (91).

Elizabeth Richardson's legacy to her four daughters, her two daughters-in-law, and by personal autograph (presentation copy at Houghton Library, Harvard University) to her grandson was a book of prayers.

She did not include her sons "lest being men, they misconstrue my well-meaning; yet I presume that you my daughters will not refuse your mother's teaching" (6). Written in three books at various times in her life—1625, 1634, and 1638—the prayers were designed by a mother for private use or in families. She excused her "boldness" of going into print by saying "the matter is but devotions or prayers, which surely concerns and belongs to women as well as to the best learned men" (3).

The prayers reflect the Protestant focus on the scriptures but also the tenderness of the Catholic focus on Christ. Interwoven with the language of the scriptures are phrases addressed to "sweet Jesus" and prayers that ask Him to "shroud me under thy innocent wing . . . and stretch forth thy hand of mercy, as thou didst Peter from sinking in the sea" (44). Her concerns in the prayers are the concerns of the Protestants—male and female—of the sixteenth and seventeenth centuries: "First, the multitude and greatness of his benefits towards us, for which we ought to give him continual thanks. Secondly, the infiniteness of our grievous sins, for which we must of necessity daily ask mercy and pardon from him. Thirdly, our own manifold miseries and infirmities, for which we are constrained to seek relief and remedy" (8). In addition, however, the maternal voice can be heard, the voice that reminds the daughters of the fact that their mother "not only with great pain brought you into the world, but do now still travail in care for the new birth of your souls" (6); the voice of the widow, of one in sickness, of one who confronts "the grim and cruel sergeants of sickness and death" (147).

Lady Anne Harcourt meditates on the special mercies of God to herself and to her family. Unpublished until 1880, the meditations and prayers uncover the life of a woman who lived in perilous political times. Her first husband, Sir Simon Harcourt, was killed in Ireland, and she and her second husband, Sir William Waller, were imprisoned for a time in the Tower.

Although her meditations include prayers of gratitude for deliverance from hostile political forces, they are mainly concerned with the private domestic life of a woman. The mercies that surround Lady Anne Harcourt and for which she gives such heartfelt thanks are "female" mercies: escapes from miscarriage and death in childbirth (labor, she confesses, was accompanied by "exorbitant fear") and escapes from multiple sicknesses and diseases of all members of her family and herself, those "sad distempers and agues" that plagued so many days of their lives. The meditations chart a life whose equanimity derived from the ability of the meditator to see "remarkable mercies" rather than "remarkable disasters."

Mary Pennyman was a Quaker who later rejected Quakerism. In the preface to her *Letters and Papers*, her husband describes her as "one of the best of wives, and certainly one of the suitablest, serviceablest, and comfortablest companions for many years, especially in divine matters, to me, of anyone upon the earth." Her meditations, interspersed throughout her letters and papers, are "a short hint" of great preservations, especially from the great plague and fire of London in 1665 and 1666. The final days of her life were spent "in secret praising and magnifying the Lord my God, for his mercies to me."

Elizabeth Carey, Viscountess Mordaunt, kept a diary from 1656 until her death in 1678. Hidden for two centuries behind books in the Old Library at Dundalk House, Ireland (a house owned by her daughter and her descendants), the diary is a series of meditations that were written for her personal use. Focusing on the major events in her life—childbirth, deliverance from the plague, the great fire of London, the restoration of the king to the throne—the diary contains a lengthy narrative of her husband's escape from death on a charge of high treason against the Commonwealth and Cromwell. She reminds herself of the remarkable providential intervention of God on her husband's behalf. At the trial the judge whose vote would have condemned Lord Mordaunt to death became acutely ill and could not stay to cast his vote. By the time the judge had recovered, her husband's acquittal had been announced. He was saved by one vote. She vows to express her gratitude every subsequent June 2nd, the date of his deliverance, by meditating and praying the prayer that she had written for the occasion and by giving 5£ in gold to the poor. Obviously, her diary was a calendar for articulating commemorative gratitude but also for reminding herself to express gratitude in tangible gifts to the poor.

Viscountess Mordaunt's meditative voice is confident and firm. Her worshiping life is filled with sober reflections, resolutions to assist the needy, and exuberant responses to God's grace. On March 1, 1664, she burst into a song of praise: "O how am I filled with love and wonder when I meditate upon thy mercies to me and mine." Her meditations show that she dared to speak to God by herself and for herself. Her lists of charitable contributions reflect the financial resources available to some women.

On the surface, the meditations of Lady Elizabeth Delaval are narrative accounts of the personal trials and conflicts that could have marred the life of any young aristocratic woman in the seventeenth century. The meditation on the root canals on her teeth (performed by a female "dentist" who was accused of being a witch) is followed by lengthy meditations on the unkindness of a father, the treachery of a friend, and the forsaking of her by lovers. Hidden beneath the surface, however, is the personal anguish that the young Lady Elizabeth experienced regarding friendship, courtship, love, and marriage. Her meditations are her preoccupations with her future, a future so arbitrary and cloudy that it caused depression and even thoughts of suicide.

Lady Elizabeth's meditations are in neither the Roman Catholic nor the Protestant mode but are the chronicles of the "tormenting passions" of a young woman who had no power to resolve these conflicts. The only power available to her was the written word, and it operated as a kind of cathartic. Meditative narratives of her personal problems form the psychological and spiritual relief needed so desperately by this powerless young woman.

The prayers written in response to each meditation are intensely personal and existential. They do not show the calm that penetrates the heart of one in touch with the "God of all peace" but are the attempts of a woman to work her way to serenity through the voice of anguished prayer. The meditations are not the outpourings of a soul enamored of God but of one who calls upon God because he has power to resolve personal conflicts. She petitions him for her tormentors and deceivers, asking him to show them the errors of their ways. She calls on him to help her forgive them after they have admitted their faults. She insists that the sins of lovers, friends, parents, and guardians were perpetrated against her and not by her, although she does confess her general sins and unworthiness.

Lady Elizabeth addresses God as the friend who "will take from us all destructive grief." She breathes forth her "sad sighs" in his presence only, relates her "most dejected thoughts" to him alone, and, echoing the scriptures, urges herself to cast all her care upon him.

With the coming of maturity, after marrying Mr. Delaval, she meditates on her position as a married woman and observes that the "pleasing word of liberty being now no more to be pronounced by me as what I have a right to, I cannot but at the first putting on of shackles find their weight heavy." She vows to "make a full stop and daily allow myself one hour at least of retirement, besides my usual morning and evening devotions, lest my love to God grow not only cold but dead also, and I forget my vows" (Christmas Eve 1670). In 1671, at the end of her diary, she has final prayers in which she asks God "that our prayers may never more be hindered by unkind disputes" (prayer 5).

Sarah Davy, who died at age thirty-two, reveals much about her personal emotional and spiritual life in her meditations. Recalling her loneliness when her mother and her baby brother died and her spiritual homelessness, she writes about the struggle to alleviate loneliness and to find love. Through the efforts of another woman, Sarah Davy embraced the faith of an Independent congregation, where she found release for her previously starved emotions. Her conversion experience freed her, enabling her to meditate on life, on death, on love.

Introspective and poetic, hers was a mind that reveled in transcendence. Unlike the women who poured out their souls in spontaneous mystical rapture, Sarah Davy used strict stanzaic forms in which she warmed her soul at the "Heavenly fire." Her voice was not stilled at her death, for through her meditative poetry she did "not cease to sing / The Song of Canaan unto Israel's King."

Helen More, great-great-granddaughter of Sir Thomas More, went to Cambrai in 1623 to enter an English Benedictine congregation for women. There she took the vows of an enclosed nun and assumed the name Gertrude, after the famous medieval contemplative nun St. Gertrude. Since Henry VIII had dissolved the monasteries in England in 1536, English Catholics who wished to go into orders had to go to the Continent to pursue a religious vocation.

Her life in the monastery was filled with interior struggles that originated in the modes of meditation and prayer imposed upon this religious order. For Dame Gertrude, "Vocal prayer was insufficient. Meditate or use immediate acts she could not—or, at least to any good purpose. For though she could revolve images in her mind, and thereby discourse and draw inferences, yet this did not serve to move her will towards God, and enable her to break forth into acts of love. On the contrary, she remained as cold as if she had discoursed or preached to a stone" (*Inner Life*, 28).

Probably written over a period of eight years, the meditations can be viewed as the confessions of a lover. Through Dom Augustine Baker, a Benedictine who was assigned to Cambrai, Dame Gertrude found the true way of meditation and prayer—by learning to subject all meditation to the act of love. In the Forty-fifth Confession, she reflects the concerns of St. Augustine in his *Confessions:* she pleads for the peace that comes to a restless soul when it finally rests in God.

Her Forty-sixth Confession uses St. Mary Magdalene as an entry to meditation and prayer. Identifying with St. Mary Magdalene, Dame Gertrude charges Christ with rejecting the love of Mary by refusing to allow her to kiss his feet at the tomb after his resurrection. Her bafflement gives way to understanding when she recognizes that Christ desires to raise the level of love to spiritual conversation—which indicates progress in the spiritual life—rather than to allow love to sink into the comfort that comes from physically touching the beloved.

Dame Gertrude died of smallpox in 1633. Her meditations were published posthumously.

Suggested Readings

Bentley, Thomas. *The Monument of Matrones.* London, 1582.

Bush, Douglas, ed. *English Literature in the Earlier Seventeenth Century.* 2d. ed. Oxford: Oxford University Press, 1966.

Calamy, Edmund. *The Art of Divine Meditation.* London, 1680.

Egerton, Elizabeth. *Book of Occasional Meditations and Prayers.* C. 1648–63. BL MS. Egerton 607.

Hobby, Elaine. *Virtue of Necessity: English Women's Writing 1649–88.* Ann Arbor: University of Michigan Press, 1989.

Hughey, Ruth, and Philip Hereford. "Elizabeth Grymeston and Her *Miscellanea." The Library* 15 (June 1934): 61–91.

Lanier, Aemilia. *Salve Deus Rex Judaeorum.* London, 1611.

Lewalski, Barbara Kiefer. "Of God and Good Women: The Poems of Aemelia [sic] Lanyer." In *Silent But for the Word,* ed. Margaret Patterson Hannay. Kent, Ohio: Kent State University Press, 1985.

———. *Protestant Poetics and the Seventeenth-Century Lyric.* Princeton, N.J.: Princeton University Press, 1979.

Martz, Louis L. *The Poetry of Meditation.* New Haven: Yale University Press, 1962.

Norman, Marion. "Dame Gertrude More and the English Mystical Tradition." *Recusant History* 13 (1975): 196–211.

Parr, Katherine. *The Lamentacion of a Sinner.* London, 1547.

———. *Prayers or Meditacyons.* . . . London, 1545.

Thornton, Alice. *Autobiography.* Durham, London, Edinburgh: Surtees Society, 1875.

Trapnel, Anna. *Report and Plea*. London, 1654.

Travitsky, Betty S. "His Wife's Prayers and Meditations." In *The Renaissance Englishwoman in Print*, ed. Anne M. Haselkorn and Betty S. Travitsky, 241–60. Amherst: University of Massachusetts Press, 1990.

White, Helen C. *The Tudor Books of Private Devotions*. Madison: University of Wisconsin Press, 1951.

36

MISCELANEA, MEDITATIONS, MEMORATIVES*

Elizabeth Grymeston

To Her Loving Son, Bernye Grymeston

My dearest son, there is nothing so strong as the force of love; there is no love so forcible as the love of an affectionate mother to her natural child: there is no mother can either more affectionately show her nature, or more naturally manifest her affection, than in advising her children out of her own experience, to eschew evil, and incline them to do that which is good. Out of these resolutions, finding the liberty of this age to be such as that *quicquid libet licet,* so men keep themselves from criminal offenses; and my mother's undeserved wrath so virulent, as that I have neither power to resist it, nor patience to endure it, but must yield to this languishing consumption to which it hath brought me: I resolved to break the barren soil of my fruitless brain, to dictate something for thy direction; the rather for that as I am now a dead woman among the living, so stand I doubtful of thy father's life; which albeit God hath preserved from eight several sinister assaults, by which it hath been sought; yet for that I see that *Quem saepè transit casus, aliquando inuenit,* I leave thee this portable *veni mecum* for thy counselor, in which thou mayest see the true portraiture of thy mother's mind, and find something either to resolve thee in thy doubts, or comfort thee in thy distress; hoping, that being my last speeches, they will be better kept in the conservance of thy memory; which I desire thou wilt make a register of heavenly meditations.

For albeit, if thou provest learned (as my trust is thou wilt; for that without learning man is but as an immortal beast) thou mayest happily

---

*London, 1604. STC 12407, Reel 680. (The first edition has fourteen chapters; the subsequent editions have twenty chapters.)

think that if every philosopher fetched his sentence, these leaves would be left without lines; yet remember withal, that as it is the best coin that is of greatest value in fewest pieces, so is it not the worst book that hath most matter in least words.

> The gravest wits, that most grave works expect,
> The quality, not quantity, respect.

And the spider's web is neither the better because woven out of his own breast, nor the bee's honey the worse, for that gathered out of many flowers; neither could I ever brook to set down that haltingly in my broken style, which I found better expressed by a graver author.

> God send thee too, to be a wit's chameleon,
> That any author's color can put on.

I have prayed for thee, that thou mightest be fortunate in two hours of thy lifetime: In the hour of thy marriage, and at the hour of thy death. Marry in thine own rank, and seek especially in it thy contentment and preferment: let her neither be so beautiful, as that every liking eye shall level at her; nor yet so brown, as to bring thee to a loathed bed. Defer not thy marriage till thou comest to be saluted with a "God speed you Sir," as a man going out of the world after forty; neither yet to the time of "God keep you Sir," whilst thou art in thy best strength after thirty; but marry in the time of "You are welcome Sir," when thou art coming into the world. For seldom shalt thou see a woman out of her own love to pull a rose that is full-blown, deeming them always sweetest at the first opening of the bud. It was Phaedra her confession to Hippolytus, and it holds for truth with the most: *Thesei vultus amo illos priores quos tulit quondam iuuenis.* "Let thy life be formal, that thy death may be fortunate: for he seldom dies well that liveth ill." To this purpose, as thou hast within thee reason, as thy counselor to persuade or dissuade thee, and thy will as an absolute prince with a *Fiat vel Evitetur,* with a "Let it be done or neglected"; yet make thy conscience thy *Censor morum,* and chief commander in thy little world: let it call reason to account whether she have subjected herself against reason to sensual appetites. Let thy will be censured, whether her desires have been chaste, or as a harlot she have lusted after her own delights. Let thy thoughts be examined. If they be good, they are of the spirit (quench not the spirit), if bad, forbid them entrance; for once admitted, they straightways fortify; and are expelled with more difficulty than not admitted.

> Crush the serpent in the head,
> Break ill eggs ere they be hatched.
> Kill bad chickens in the tread,
> Fledge they hardly can be catched.
> In the rising stifle ill,
> Lest it grow against thy will.

For evil thoughts are the devil's harbingers; he never resteth, but where they provide his entertainment. These are those little ones whose brains thou must dash out against the rock of true judgment: for

> As a false lover that thick snares hath laid,
> T'entrap the honor of a fair young maid,
> When she (though little) list'ning ear affords
> To his sweet, courting, deep affected words,
> Feels some assuaging of his freezing flame,
> And soothes himself with hope to gain his game,
> And rapt with joy, upon this point persists,
> That parleying city never long resists:
> Even so the serpent that doth counterfeit
> A guileful call t'allure us to his net,
> Perceiving us his flattering gloze digest,
> He prosecutes, and jocund doth not rest,
> Till he have tried foot, hand, and head, and all,
> Upon the breach of this new battered wall.

I could be content to dwell with thee in this argument: but I must confine myself to the limits of an epistle, *Quae non debet implere sinistram manum*. To which rule I do the more willingly submit myself, for that the discourses following are motives to the same effect: which I pray thee use to peruse, even in that my affectionate love, which diffused amongst nine children which God did lend me, is now united in thee, whom God hath only left for my comfort. And because God hath indued thee with so violent a spirit, as that *quicquid vis valdè vis;* therefore by so much the more it behooveth thee to deliberate what thou undertakest: to which purpose my desire is, that thou mightest be seasoned with these precepts in thy youth, that the practice of thy age may have a taste of them.

And because that it is incident to quick spirits to commit rash attempts: as ever the love of a mother may challenge the performance of her demand of a dutiful child; be a bridle to thyself, to restrain thee from doing that which indeed thou mayest do: that thou mayest the better forbear that which in truth thou oughtest not to do; for *haud citò progreditur ad maiora peccata, qui parua reformidat;* "he seldom commits deadly sin, that makes a conscience of a venial scandal."

Thou seest my love hath carried me beyond the list I resolved on, and my aching head and trembling hand have rather a will to offer than ability to afford further discourse. Wherefore with as many good wishes to thee as good will can measure, I abruptly end, desiring God to bless thee with sorrow for thy sins, thankfulness for his benefits, fear of his judgments, love of his mercies, mindfulness of his presence; that living in his fear, thou mayest die in his favor, rest in his peace, rise in his power, remain in his glory forever and ever.

Thine assured loving mother,

Elizabeth Grymeston.

Chapter XI

*Morning Meditation, with sixteen sobs of a sorrowful spirit,
which she used for mental prayer, as also an addition of
sixteen staves of verse taken out of Peter's Complaint;
which she usually sang and played on the wind instrument.*

Happy is the man whose life is a continual prayer.

O God to whom nothing is so great as can resist, nothing so little as is contemptible: O Christ the guide of those that seek thee, the light of those that find thee: O Holy Ghost that both fillest and includest all things; I am ashamed to be seen of thee, because I am not assured to be received by thee, having neither deserved pardon for my faults, nor participation of thy glory: yet sweet Jesu, supply my defects, that by thy mercy I may obtain remission, and by thy merits deserve salvation. Let thy passion work compassion for me,

A sorry wight the object of disgrace,
The monument of fear, the map of shame,

The mirror of mishap, the stain of place,
The scorn of time, the infamy of fame,
An excrement of earth to heaven hateful,
Injurious to man, to God ungrateful.

[stanza 5][1]

Lord, I am depressed with the burden of my sins, and oppressed with the fear of the punishment belonging to them; having neither power to resist thy wrath, nor patience to endure thy indignation: wherefore I am become as it doth become me, thy humble suppliant. Lord be merciful to me a sinner. My abject countenance witnesseth my distressed mind, my words are seasoned with sighs, and bathed in tears. O let the dew of my devotion be drawn up with the beams of thy remorse: for behold, as a hunger-starved beggar do I knock at thy gate, oh honorable householder. Open, oh open the gates of thy mercies, to the greatness of my miseries.

Sad subject of my sin hath stor'd my mind,
With everlasting matter of complaint:
My throwes [threnes, a song of lament] an endless alphabet do find,
Beyond the pangs that Jeremie doth paint.
That eyes with errors may just measure keep:
Most tears I wish that have most cause to weep.

[stanza 7]

Preserve my body from eternal death, reserve my soul from everlasting damnation: let me neither ungratefully remember thy benefits, nor ungraciously forget thy severe judgments: for albeit, there be no folly which hath not had his seat in my mind, and left his footstep in my actions; yet for that thou lookest for my amendment, that I may have thy favor, grant me thy favor that I may have amendment.

Give vent unto the vapors of my breast.
That thicken in the brims of cloudy eyes,
Where sin was hatch'd let tears now wash the nest.
Where life was lost, recover life with cries

1. Stanza numbering taken from *The Poems of Robert Southwell, S.J.*, ed. James H. McDonald and Nancy Pollard Brown (Oxford: Clarendon, 1967). (First published in London, 1595.)

My trespass foul, let not my tears be few:
Baptize my spotted soul in weeping dew.
[stanza 3]

Conform my life, confirm my faith, endue my soul with thy love, subdue my flesh with thy fear: Let me not die ere I begin to live: give me time to repent, and occasion to amend: direct my reason: regenerate my will: lead my desires, that I may seek thee: illuminate my understanding, that I may find thee: let my joy be in enjoying thee, in whom desire wants no satiety, for satiety breeds discontent.

For gripes in all my parts do never fail:
Whose only league, is now in bartering pains:
What I engross, they traffic by retail:
Making each other's misery their gains:
All bound forever prentices to care,
Whilst I in shop of shame trade sorrow's ware.
[stanza 94]

Let thy majesty appear in thy mercy, cover my sins, and I am recovered of my infirmities: for my conscience accuseth me, my memory gives evidence against me, and my reason condemneth me. Convert oh Lord, convert my life, and divert my punishment.

My guilty eye still seems to see my sin:
All things characters are to spell my fall.
What eye doth read without heart rues within:
What heart doth rue to pensive thought is gall,
Which when my thought would by my tongue digest,
My ears convey it back into my breast.
[stanza 114]

Out of a maze of amazements do I cry out unto thee, oh God my Savior and Redeemer: Grant, oh Lord, that I may firmly resolve, speedily begin, constantly continue in performing thy will, let me honor thee as a Creator, love thee as a Redeemer, expect thee as a Savior: for by thy goodness I was created, by thy mercy redeemed, by thy power preserved, and by thy grace I shall be glorified. Grant, oh gracious God, that wast made man, that men might be made the sons of God, that I may live in thy fear, die in thy favor, rest in thy peace, rise in thy power, remain in thy glory forever and ever.

> For life's a maze of countless straying ways:
> Open to erring steps, and strowed with baits:
> To wind weak senses into endless strays,
> Aloof from virtue's rough unbeaten straits,
> A flower, a play, a blast, a shade, a dream,
> A living death, a never turning stream.
>
> [stanza 16]

Gracious God, whose honor is more in saving through pity, than in condemning through judgment, thou canst mitigate griefs present, and canst turn away dangers to come: pardon, I beseech thee, my sins past, aid me against all temptations to come, and I shall praise thy name forever and ever.

> Else weeping eyes resign your tears to me,
> A sea will scantly rinse my ordur'd soul.
> Huge horrors in high tides must drowned be.
> Of every tear my crime exacteth toll.
> My stains are deep: few drops take out none such,
> Even salve with sore, and most is not too much.
>
> [stanza 8]

Good Lord, make me covet those things that be pleasing to thee, let me find them easily, and search them wisely, know them truly, and exercise them effectually, to thy glory and my salvation. Dispose the course of my life, that it may accomplish that which thou requirest: Lay forth thy passions that I may feel them; satisfy me in thy mercies, that I may rejoice in them: remove from me all lets to serve thee, and give me those things that may draw me to thee: instruct my judgment, rule my affections according to thy will, in the depth of thy mercies confound the devises of my enemies against me.

> Lest shame the livery of offending mind,
> The ugly shroud that overshadoweth blame,
> The mulct at which foul faults are justly fin'd,
> The damp of sin, the common sluice of fame,
> By which impostum'd tongues their humors purge,
> Do light on me: for I deserve thy scourge.
>
> [stanza 87]

Lord thou hast delivered me out of the jaws of death and redeemed my soul out of the gates of perdition; sanctify my life, that it may be a witness of my thankfulness; let my memory be a record to show thy goodness; so shall my lips show forth thy praise, and my heart shall be possessed with the glory of thy greatness.

For fawning vipers, dumb till they had wounded,
With many mouths do now upbraid my harms:
My sight was vail'd, till I myself confounded,
But now I see the disenchanted charms,
Now can I cut th'anatomy of sin,
And search with linx's eyes what lies within.

[stanza III]

Give me, oh Lord, sorrow for my sins, thankfulness for thy benefits, fear of thy judgments, and love of thy mercies: give me an understanding heart, that I may conceive a right love of thy law, that I may desire to perform it, strength of thy spirit that I may have power to execute it: and because by thy grace I am that I am, let thy demands be no greater than thou hast given me grace to perform. Lord give what thou commandest, and then command what thou wilt: let the greatness of thy mercies supply the wants of my miseries: that my heart may rejoice in the Lord, and thy saving health may be known among all nations.

O beams of mercy beat on sorrow's cold [cloud],
Pour suppling showers on my parched ground,
Bring forth the fruit of your due service vow'd,
Let good desires with like deserts be crowned,
Water young blooming virtue's tender flower,
Sin did all grace of riper growth devour.

[stanza 80]

Have mercy upon me, oh Lord, have mercy upon me, according to the multitude of thy mercies, do away my offenses: wash me from my wickedness, and cleanse me from my secret sins: for I acknowledge my faults, and my sins have made me odious to myself. Be merciful, Lord, be merciful unto thy servant, and let not the gates of hell prevail against him: for though the stipend of his sin is death, and the merit of his transgression eternal perdition; yet is thy mercy above all thy works, and thou canst forgive more than he could offend: thou that willed not the death of a sinner, deny not the request of a repentant sinner: thou which hast given me repentance, which is the seal of forgiveness, grant me forgiveness, which is the assurance of repentance.

If David night by night did bathe his bed,
Esteeming longest days too short to moan:
Inconsolable tears if Anna shed,
Who in her son her solace had forgone:
Then I to days, to months, to weeks, to years,
Do owe the hourly rent of stintless tears.
                              [stanza 82]

Out of the depth of my soul do I cry unto thee, Lord put me not to rebuke in thine anger; let not thine hand press me, neither chasten me in thy displeasure; for I confess my wickedness, and am sorry for my sin; suffer not my name to be touched with dishonor, neither give me over to be clothed in rebuke: cleanse my heart from corrupt thoughts, and purge my mouth from all uncleanness, and impath me in that course that is best pleasing to thee.

Christ health of fever'd soul, heaven of the mind,
Force of the feeble, nurse of infant loves,
Guide to the wandering foot, light to the blind,
Whom weeping wins, repentant sorrow moves,
Father in care, mother in tender heart,
Revive and save me slain with sinful dart.
                              [stanza 126]

Praise the Lord, oh my soul, oh let all that is within me praise his holy name. Praise the Lord, oh my soul, and let not the least of his benefits be forgotten: for he hath delivered thy body from death, and thy soul hath he redeemed out of the estate of damnation: for he hath created thee after his own image, and breathed a living soul into thee, to praise his name forever and ever: for his providence hath preserved thee, his strength defended thee, his mercy comforted thee, and his grace shall glorify thee: O therefore praise his holy name; O let all that is within me sing praises to my God, my Savior and Redeemer.

Lazar at pity's gate I ulcered lie,
Craving the refuse crumbs of children's plate.
My sores I lay in view of mercy's eye:
My rags bear witness of my poor estate.
The worms of conscience that within me swarm,
Prove that my plaints are less than is my harm.

[stanza 130]

Give me, oh Lord, an understanding heart, that I may have a true feeling of the greatness of thy benefits, instruct thou my lips, and my mouth shall show forth thy praise: for my heart desireth to have her love known, and my spirit rejoiceth in God my Savior: I will magnify thy holy name, for thou hast heard my voice, and not suffered my foes to triumph over me: thou hast relieved my wants, and given me plenty when I was in necessity. I will lift up my hands unto the king of glory, even unto his mercy's seat from whence is my redemption; for I know the weakness of our flesh, and acknowledge there is no help that comes not from above.

Prone looks, crossed arms, bent knee, and contrite heart,
Deep sighs, thick sobs, dew'd eyes, and prostrate prayers,
Most humbly beg release of earned smart,
And saving shroud in mercy's sweet repairs:
If justice should my wrongs with rigor wage,
Fears would despairs, ruth breed a hopeless rage.

[stanza 129]

I give thee thanks, oh most merciful Father, for all thy benefits bestowed upon me, desiring thee long to continue them, and to make me thankful for them: direct the words of my mouth, the meditations of my heart, the actions of my body, that they may be pleasing to thee, and profitable for me: Lord hear my voice, accept this my sacrifice of thanksgiving, which thy bountiful goodness hath extorted. Let not the world, the flesh, nor the devil prevail against me, but let thy gracious spirit conquer them in all my conflicts. Lord, I have reposed my whole trust in thee, let not thy servant be put to confusion.

With mildness Jesu measure my offense,
Let true remorse thy due revenge abate,
Let tears appease when trespass doth incense,

Let pity temper thy deserved hate,
Let grace forgive, let love forget my fall:
With fear I crave, in hope I humbly call.

[stanza 131]

Lord, though I can neither praise thee as becometh me, nor pray to thee as I ought to do; yet accept I beseech thee, these my halting speeches brokenly uttered, as an oblation for my most grievous offenses: look upon me in thy mercies, and let the blood of that immaculate lamb Christ Jesus, stand betwixt me and thy judgments. Lord, into thy hands do I commend my soul, and my body into thy custody, Lord Jesu receive them: Lord bless me and all that belongs unto me from this time forth forevermore. Sweet Jesu sanctify my life, and bless me with sorrow for my sins, thankfulness for thy benefits, fear of thy judgments, love of thy mercies, mindfulness of thy presence, that living in thy fear, I may die in thy favor, rest in thy peace, rise in thy power, remain in thy glory forever and ever.

Redeem my lapse with ransom of thy love,
Traverse th'indictment, rigor's doom suspend,
Let frailty favor, sorrow succor move.
Be thou thyself, though changeling I offend,
Tender my suit, cleanse this defiled den,
Cancel my debts, sweet Jesu say Amen.

[stanza 132]

Chapter XII

A Madrigal made by Bernye Grymeston upon the conceit of his mother's play to the former ditties.

How many pipes, as many sounds
 Do still impart to your son's heart
  As many deadly wounds.
 How many strokes, as many stounds,
 Each stroke a dart, each stound a smart,
  Poor captive me confounds.
And yet how oft the strokes of sounding keys hath slain,
As oft the looks of your kind eyes restores my life again.

37

A LADIES LEGACIE TO HER DAUGHTERS

in Three Books
composed of prayers and meditations,
fitted for several times, and upon several occasions
as also several prayers for each day in the week *

Elizabeth Richardson, wife to the late Sir Thomas Richardson, Knight, Lord Chief Justice of the King's Bench

This for my dearly beloved & worthy Grandson, Sr. Ed: Dering Kt Baronet. My love-worthy, & first Grand-Child, I present (as due) this poore book unto you, which at first intended, only for all my Children & Grand-children; for their instruction in their youth, & for their use, & remembrance of me afterwardes; now you being one of mine, & this coming from me, I nothing doubt of your loving acceptance of it, for my sake, though in it selfe, unworthy to have a roome in your library, or to come into the view of any judicious eye, that may soon spye more faultes, than leaves: yet I know you would in your owne goodnes, pardon & excuse, all defectes therein, that comes from me, a weake unlearned woman, who being so neare unto you, you will gently censure, & beare it all. But indeed it is so falsely printed, as without it be corrected, you will meet with many absurdities, which by some may be imputed unto me, though not by you; therefore I have a little helped the most faulty places, desiring you to do the like by this, in the other 2

---

*London, 1645. Wing R1382, pp. 1–7, 47–48, 51–52, 87–88, 133–36, 156–57. The copy in the Houghton Library, Harvard University, is inscribed with the introductory autograph presentation to her grandson. This copy also has a handwritten emendation of the title: *A Mother's Legacie to Her Six Daughters*.

This, for my dearly beloued & worthy
Grandson, Sr Ed: Dering Kt Baronet
My sone worthy, & first Grand-Child, I psent
(as due) this poore Booke vnto you wch I at
first Intended, only for all my Children &
Grand-children; for their Instruction in
yr youth, & for their vse, & remembrance
of me afterwardes; now you being one of
mine, & this coming from me, I nothing
doubt of yor louing acceptance of it, for
my sake; though in it selfe, vnworthy to
haue a roome in yor Liberary, or to come into yt veiw of any Iudicious eye, yt may
soone spye more faultes, yn leaues; yet I
know you would in yor owne goodnes,
pdon & excuse, all defectes therein, yt
comes from me, a weake vnlearned wo=
man; who being so neare vnto you, you
will gently censure, & beare wt all. But
indeed it is so falsly printed, as wthout
it be corrected, you will meet wt many
absurdities, wch by some may be imputed
vnto me, though not by you; therefore
I haue a little helped yt most faulty
places, desiring you to do yt like by this,
in yt other 2 bookes. Now I hope of
one Comfort, wch you will vouchsafe me,
at my ernest request, yt you will not
faile, to make daily vse thereof, to Gods
seruis & glory; wch I beleeue will turne
to yor owne happines, in drawing
downe all blessings from God vpon
you, as is desired by;
            yor most affectionate
            Granmother Eliz: Cramond

Figure 12. Autograph of Elizabeth Richardson, inscribing a copy of her *A Ladies Legacie to her Daughters* to her grandson. By permission of the Houghton Library, Harvard University.

bookes. Now I hope of one Comfort which you will vouchsafe me, at my earnest request, that you will not faile, to make daily use thereof, to God's service & glory; which I believe will turn to your happiness, in drawing downe all blessings from God upon you, as is desired by,

Your most affectionate Grandmother

Elizabeth Camond

My dearly beloved daughters (of which number I account my two sons' wives, my daughters-in-law, the Countess of Marlborough, and Mrs. Francis Ashbournham, to be mine also), assuring myself of your loves and kind acceptance, I present this little book unto you all, which being mine, I hope you will carefully receive it, as coming from my love and affection towards you, and that you will please for my sake, the more to employ it to your good; to which I will (while I live) daily add my prayers and blessing for your present and future happiness: and that this my poor labor may prove a happy furtherance to all your good endeavors towards virtue and piety: Therefore let me as a mother entreat and prevail with you to esteem so well of it, as often to peruse, ponder, practice, and make use of this book according to my intention, though of itself unworthy; for you shall find your greatest happiness will be in the true fear, constant love, and faithful service of Almighty God, which never faileth of comfort and reward, he being the only and most liberal giver of all good gifts and blessings, both spiritual and temporal; to whose infinite mercy and gracious guidance, I most humbly commend you all, and daily will do the like in my prayers so long as I live. And further, most dear hearts, consider, That these petitions are presented to a most bountiful and all-sufficient Lord, that vouchsafeth in Christ to make us his adopted children, and to be our gracious Father, who gave his only Son for us, in whom he will deny us nothing: And greater benefits than here are asked, cannot be received; therefore give me leave, since I have such great interest in you, to persuade and obtain of you all, often to beg these blessings of God, by these prayers faithfully offered up unto his Majesty: Whereby you shall glorify his holy name, make yourselves eternally blessed, and bring much joy and comfort to

Your most affectionate mother,

Elizabeth Ashbournham

I had no purpose at all when I wrote these books, for the use of myself, and my children, to make them public, but have been lately overpersuaded by some that much desired to have them that I would suffer them to be printed. Therefore I have adventured to bear all censures, and desire their patience and pardon, whose exquisite judgments may find many blameworthy faults, justly to condemn my boldness; which I thus excuse, the matter is but devotions or prayers, which surely concerns and belongs to women as well as to the best learned men: And therefore I hope herein I neither wrong nor give offense to any, which I should be very loath to do.

This book was written at Chelsea in the year 1625 by E. A. at the Duke of Buckingham's house, a part whereof was lent me by the good duchess, my most honored Lady, when the great sickness was in London.

A letter to my four daughters, Elizabeth, Frances, Anne, and
Katherine Asbournham, of whom three were then unmarried,
only Anne was married to Sir Edward Deering, Knight and Baronet.

My dear children:

I have long and much grieved for your misfortunes, and want of preferments in the world: but now I have learned in what estate soever I am, therewith to be content, and to account these vile and transitory things to be but vain and loss, so I may win Christ the fountain of all bliss, wishing you with me, to condemn that which neglecteth you, and set your hearts and affections on better subjects, such as are above, more certain and permanent; and fear not but what is needful for this present life shall be supplied by him who best knows our wants: and had it not been for your sakes, whose advancements love and nature bindeth me to seek, I had prevented the spite of my enemies and retired myself from the world before it despised me: But though I am so unhappy as to be left destitute, not able to raise you portions of wealth, yet shall I joy as much to add unto the portion of grace, which I trust, and pray, that God will give to each of you, to whose mercy I daily commit you, nothing doubting but that he will receive you into the number of those fatherless he graciously taketh care of. . . . Neither hath the Lord withdrawn his favor so from us as to leave us utterly desolate to despair, but hath graciously raised us comfort by honorable friends to be careful and dear parents unto us, whom God preserve and show mercy to them and theirs, as they have done to us. And here I send you a motherly

remembrance, and commend this my labor into your loving accep
tance, that in remembering your poor mother, you may be also put in
mind to perform your humble duty and service to our heavenly Father,
who hath created us to his own glory and service. . . . Now prayer
being the winged messenger to carry our requests and wants into the
ears of the Lord (as David saith), he will praise the Lord seven times a
day, and prevent the light to give thanks unto God; and indeed, who
can awake to enjoy the light and pleasure of the day and not begin the
same with entreaty of the Lord's gracious direction in all things. . . .
Or how can we possess or hourly receive so many favors and benefits
from God, and not offer unto him an evening sacrifice of thanksgiving?
Or who dares adventure to pass the dreadful night, the time of terror,
and yield themselves to sleep, the image of death, before they are at
peace with God, by begging pardon for their sins, and craving his
protection and care over them in the night? I know you may have many
better instructors than myself, yet can you have no true mother but me,
who not only with great pain brought you into the world, but do now
still travail in care for the new birth of your souls, to bring you to eternal
life, which is my chiefest desire, and the height of my hopes. And howsoever this my endeavor may be contemptible to many (because a
woman's) which makes me not to join my sons with you, lest being men,
they misconstrue my well-meaning; yet I presume that you my daughters will not refuse your mother's teaching (which I wish may be your
ornament, and a crown of glory to you) who I hope will take in the best
part my careful industry, for your present and future happiness, towards
which I have not failed to give you the best breeding in my power,
to bring you to virtue and piety, and the God of peace sanctify you
throughout, that your whole spirits, souls and bodies, may be kept
blameless unto the coming of our Lord Jesus Christ, which shall be the
endless joy of your most loving mother,

Elizabeth Ashbournham

Book I

Here is one prayer more which I join to these, because it concerned one
of my daughters, to whom this book belonged, though it was lately
penned upon a very strange accident.

A thanksgiving to Almighty God, for his most merciful preservation of my noble kinswoman, the Lady Elizabeth Feelding, and of my own daughter, the Lady Elizabeth Cornwalleis, from drowning under the bridge, and was long under water: And one worthy gentlewoman in the company could not be recovered. This may serve upon any such fearful accident.

Most Mighty God, Creator of heaven and earth, and the only disposer of all things therein, thou art the defender and protector of all thy children and servants, and the gracious preserver of all those that depend upon thee: thy power ruleth both by sea and land, and thy all-guiding providence directeth all things in the world, according to thy own high will and good pleasure, and for the good of all them that trust in thee. Whereof thou hast given many, and me the unworthiest of thy servants, an especial testimony of thy infinite mercy towards my dear daughter and kinswoman, in that great and miraculous deliverance lately of them, in the dreadful danger of sudden death by drowning in the Thames; for thou didst mercifully provide and take care to save their lives when they were past sense to take care of themselves, or to call upon thee for help: yet beyond all hope, thou didst bring them back from the gates of death, praised forever be thy most glorious Name; and let neither us, nor any of our generation forget this thy great mercy. Now Lord, make us duly to acknowledge all thy benefits, and let us not pass them out of our minds without true thankfulness for all thy favors continually vouchsafed unto us and undeserved: for all which we poor creatures have nothing to return to thee, but devout love, faithful service, and careful obedience, with the humble sacrifice of praise and thanksgiving; which by thy assistance, I will perform towards thee with a grateful heart, so long as I live, and forever, Amen.

Book II

A weekly exercise of prayers for each day.

The Epistle.

This book I began to write at my house at Barking in Essex, where I retired myself in solitariness after the death of my worthy and dear husband, Sir Thomas Richardson, Knight, Lord Chief Justice of the King's Bench: who died at Candlemas, 1634.

Where shortly after I finished these prayers following my own private use; being the fittest employment for my time, who was then in so much heaviness.

I call this book a weekly exercise of prayer, either for a private person, or in their own family: To which there are added some other necessary prayers, very useful for those particular occasions, whereto they are directed; which I shall be very glad and joyful if my children, grandchildren, kindred, friends, or any good Christian that shall peruse them, may make a good and right use of them to God's glory: And I do most heartily and humbly pray that God will vouchsafe to hear in heaven, and to receive, accept, and grant their just requests, to his own honor, their comfort, and my great happiness, who am a well-wisher, and true lover of their souls in the Lord,

Elizabeth Richardson.

To the Reader

These prayers I composed for the instructions of my children and grandchildren, after the example of my dear parents, Sir Thomas Beaumont, and his Lady, of Stoughton in the County of Leicester, who I think were as careful and industrious to breed up their children in the instruction and information of the Lord, to serve and obey God, as any parents could possibly be, which made them take much pains with us, more than is usual, by their endeavors to bring us to know and fear God, and to keep his commandments: which Solomon saith is the whole duty of man. But when parents have done the best, and all we can, it is God's grace and blessing that must perfect the work: which I humbly pray him to add to accomplish my desire, to their eternal happiness.

The conclusion of Wednesday at night, to the blessed Trinity

Merciful God, Heavenly Father, Blessed Son, and Holy Ghost, who hast appointed the night for all mortal creatures to take rest, without which our weak natures cannot subsist: I am now in health by thy gracious providence, by thy favor, and laid down in my bed, which representeth the grave, and by thy mercy hope also to take quiet rest and sleep, that is the image of death, from which I know not whether ever I shall awake again to this world's light, for my life dependeth on thy good pleasure; therefore, I most humbly pray thee of thy infinite mercy, O God, to forgive all my sins past that I have committed against thee, this present day or heretofore, through the merits and sufferings of my Redeemer Jesus; and vouchsafe, Heavenly Father, to be reconciled unto me, thy most guilty sinful servant, in and through thy dear and innocent Son, who is my righteous Savior: And grant while I live here, that in Christ I may hereafter live to thee, and thy faithful service; and when I sleep, Lord, let me safely rest by thy blessed preservation, and by the assistance of thy holy Spirit, that I may continue in thy true faith, fear and favor with a good conscience unto my last breath; that so if thou call me away this night, or any other time in my sleep, thou wilt in Christ pardon my sins, and after death receive my soul to thy grace and mercy, to remain with thee forever, and may praise thee, my God, everlastingly. Amen, Amen.

Book III

Written 1638. This containeth divers prayers, for several occasions, very requisite [her handwritten insertion].

A sorrowful widow's prayer and petition unto the gracious protector
and defender of widows, and father of the fatherless,
which I composed shortly after the death of my dear husband:
And this may also serve any other upon the like occasion.

. . . still holding me up by thy gracious hand from sinking in the midst of a sea of sorrows; and like a most loving Father in my divers change of fortunes, hast at all times provided for me and mine beyond our deserts, or the world's expectation, having in thy merciful goodness made me see with comfort all my children, who were left destitute, now by thy provident provision and blessing, well settled for this life: All which by thy infinite favors, Lord, make me ever thankful to acknowledge, and grant that I and all mine, may serve, obey, praise, and glorify thy great and blessed Name forever and ever. And as thou, Lord, hast stretched forth thy hand of bounty to supply all my worldly wants; so, dear God, vouchsafe more especially to extend thy gracious care over my soul, to prevent and keep me from sin, and endue me with all spiritual graces, so that my whole life and ways may ever be serviceable and acceptable to thy heavenly Majesty. And now, O Lord, since it hath been thy will and pleasure to take away and call to thyself my dear husband out of the transitory life before me, and to bereave me of him who was my chief comfort in this world: I humbly beseech thee, vouchsafe to take me into thy care, and give me grace to choose with Mary that better part which may never be taken from me, chiefly to serve and follow thee, that so I may turn this freedom from the bond of marriage only the more to thy service, and may become thy bondswoman to serve and praise thee day and night like Hanna, so long as I live. . . . Now dear God, make me to change and far exceed the fervent affection and careful observance I have lived in towards my husband, into a holy fear, with devout and sincere love of thy Majesty and service, and due watchfulness over myself, that I displease not thee, My God, in anything. . . . Finally, I most humbly beg that thou wilt vouchsafe to be a loving and gracious Father in thy care and comfort to me, and all mine, and let thy mercy, blessing, and favor rest always upon me, my children and grandchildren, kindred, and friends, with all that thou hast given thy poor servant, who doth in all humility commend and commit myself, my ways, my works, wholly to thy most blessed protection and direction, to dispose according thy good pleasure; that so I may do all things to thy glory here, and by thy mercy be a happy partaker of thy eternal kingdom of glory hereafter, through Jesus Christ my Lord, Amen.

A prayer to be prepared for a happy death, and to gain a joyful resurrection.

. . . when I go from hence carry me to be where he [Christ] is, and give me grace and faith in and through him, to make my peace while I am in the way and passage of this life, and while I have breath to call upon thee, before I am laid into the dark dungeon of the earth, when the worms shall eat my corrupt flesh; yet I trust and do believe through him that hath overcome death, the grave, and hell for me, that at the blessed resurrection of thy children and servants, that my corruption shall put on incorruption, and I shall see my blessed Lord and Saviour with these my eyes, who did redeem me, and shall be my merciful judge to save me . . . Amen.

38

THE HARCOURT PAPERS*

Lady Anne Harcourt

*An account of such remarkable mercies as I can call to mind
since I married Sir William Waller.*

April the 13th, 1652.

First. I had much mercy in my marriage with him, he being the answer of my prayer, he being a religious, prudent, and a loving husband.

Secondly, in that his children prove so hopeful, and do improve daily under my care, and that they are all alive, and do enjoy their healths better than they did when they came to me, and do grow.

Thirdly. It's a great mercy my own children are alive, in health and hopeful. (One of them since dead, may the Lord stay his hand.)

Fourthly. The support I had under all that terrible pain and weakness at St. Johns.

Fifthly. Yet God gave me there a safe deliverance of a living child, which was born with all its parts and limbs—and a son—that I had such a comfortable childbed after it.

Sixthly. That I have been supported under all the pain and weakness I have had of my last child—in my labor—and in my childbed, notwithstanding the danger I was in.

Seventhly. The health my husband enjoys, notwithstanding the many diseases he is subject to—the great support he has under his pain, his patience—and his merciful deliverance from that fit of the stone, and from three more of the gout.

Eighthly. The supply we have of means from time to time, the comfort we enjoy in our constant converse one with another; the love of our

*Ed. Edward William Harcourt (Oxford: James Parker and Co., 1880), pp. 173–94.

servants, their health, the good success of our affairs, and that degree of health we have had in our family.

Ninthly. Those afflictions I have had, which the Lord has been pleased to accompany with his grace—as I trust, he did my want of health, and the fits which my last child died of—because the first has made me desirous to improve my health, for the making my calling and election sure—and, in the latter, God made me very willing God should dispose of me and mine as he pleased.

Tenthly. The great and strange deliverance I received in St. Martins Lane, when I fell down from first step to the lowest step in my Lady Clotworthy's house, with my head downward, putting out my shoulder, and yet received no prejudice either to life or limb.

Eleventhly. The great preservation I had when I miscarried at Westminster, and in the weakness that followed me to Osterly—and especially my last miscarriage at Osterly, when I lay swooning eleven hours.

Enumerations of further mercies I have received
since I married Sir William Waller.

Upon the 22nd of March, 1651, my husband being in my brother Irby's house, we having lived peaceably in town most part of the winter, there came two messengers from my Lord Protector, to search the house, to seize his papers, and to bring him in safe custody to Whitehall, whither he was carried about 9 of the clock in the morning, and there attended all day, was examined by my Lord himself of many particulars, and sent home again at night; which was a mercy quite above my hopes, and contrary to the expectation of all people, and a thing very unusual with those in power. The Lord receive the praise and glory of this his wonderful goodness, which he showed so personally to me when my heart was very much afraid, both in regard of what my husband had suffered so long together, without any declared cause, and in regard of the infirmities that his former imprisonment made him liable to; also in regard of the great charge that imprisonment was like to be to him, and the hindrance that would have followed in his estate; therefore will I strive to trust in the Lord, and say, at what time my heart is afraid, I will trust in the Lord.

Upon the 5th of August in the year 1659, being in Kent to drink the waters, for the health of myself, children, and divers of our family, Sir William was taken prisoner by Captain Barington at two of the clock in the night, and caused to rise out of bed, and to ride four miles at that time in the night, which might have been a great prejudice to his life, or health at least; but the Lord did mercifully prevent any inconvenience, and made that imprisonment an occasion of good, in that we broke up house, and did not long after continue in prison. Praise the Lord, O my soul, and all that is within me praise his holy name; praise the Lord, O my soul, and forget not all his benefits.

I have since to acknowledge the continuance of those mercies formerly mentioned; concerning my husband; concerning all his children; and concerning our support. These I desire constantly to praise God for; because from him both the mercies themselves, and the continuance of them does proceed. Likewise the Lord has added new mercies, in making me instrumental to preserve the life and restore the health of the youngest child, who fell dangerously into a high degree of the King's evil [scrofula], and, by God's blessing upon a medicine I gave her, was recovered.

Also the Lord was very gracious to me, in preserving me all the while I went with child of my daughter Katherine Waller, who was, by the merciful assistance of the great God, born the 30th day of August 1657, about a quarter after II of the clock, at night. The Lord help me, with all humble sorrowfulness, to remember my own exorbitant fear of my travail, notwithstanding the former experiences of God's goodness in helping me at the like times; and, withal, to be mindful of and joyful in the great goodness of God, who supported me under and carried me through this travail also; and gave me a child—alive—perfect in its shape, and hopeful to continue with me. I desire likewise to acknowledge the great mercy of God, in supporting me under and through the many troubles that befell me in this childbed.

Before I was brought to bed, my midwife, one that had been long very careful of me and loving to me, lay a fortnight in a dying condition in the house, and died two days before I fell in travail. Within six days after, my dear cousin Elisabeth Hamond, an ancient and faithful friend from my youth up—sickened—and about eight days after died. And, within two days after, my dear child, Fred Harcourt, sickened of the same disease, and died about eight days after that. And, some few hours after that, Doctor Baytts sent to me by Doctor Beavour, that he suspected the principal parts of my other, and now only son, to be eminently defective. And, within two days after that, the counsel at Whitehall threw out my husband's cause with scorn. Yet, I hope I can truly say, God has not only supported me under all this, but done me good by it. Praised be his name.

Special mercies. The Lord also has been pleased to give me many gracious experiences in my soul of his fatherly goodness to me, in prayer, and in hearing and in communicating at his table. I have found him always a God near at hand, and not far off, when my own wretched and deceitful heart did not wickedly and grossly fail in desiring his help. So that I may and must say these two things from my own experience; first, that if the heart be according to rule prepared for ordinances, and uprightly desirous to honor God, and receive good in the use of them; if there be a true endeavor to do this, the soul does receive the benefit. My own soul has found a reality and substance in them, beyond what is in all the world besides; there is a force in them, which I believe is the Spirit's accompanying of them, to weaken lusts, though at other times very prevalent; and to strengthen faith, to more of love to God and rejoicing in God; to encourage and comfort the heart, being never so much cast down; to support the spirit under trouble, nay, to make them welcome; and to take away immoderate fears, to which I am grievously inclined.

On the other side, when the heart is careless, and churly in the performing of them, they then prove only an aggravation of sin and trouble; and one's wretched heart, by the instigation and help of the devil, is apt to think that there is really nothing in them. Therefore, O my soul, be not too much amazed, though many in these sad times do use ordinances frequently, and find no benefit in them, but continue in scandalous sins. Consider, therefore, thine own experiences in both the forementioned respects; and, as in respect of the former, thou art obliged to praise and bless the great and glorious name of thy Heavenly Father— so, in regard of the latter, beg earnestly God's assistance, that, from that evil, thou may learn to dread such a temper in thy own soul, and to lament it in others, that, when God gives ordinances as a means of great good, they should be turned by our corrupt hearts into occasion of so much evil.

Temporal mercies. The Lord did graciously look upon me in my second choice, first in helping me to choose, upon mature consideration; second in bestowing the mercies of that condition upon me, when I was in such a condition as I needed them most (my children grown up, my estate still filled with doubt and other troubles—so that in likelihood it could not, without much scarcity, have supplied me and them too; my mind so worn with public and private troubles, that I began apparently to sink in my bodily health and strength), then did God give me a religious, wise, and faithful, loving husband, and by him a hopeful, and likely son, the bearing of which (God graciously supporting me under all my weakness, the time I went with child) was a great means of my after health. The constant comforts of my condition have been and are very great; and I relish them far more because, I hope I may say, they were from the hand of God's love; and they did therefore quiet and comfort at another rate than any comforts arising from any condition that I was ever in before. I take this for my ground of that hope—I sought to marry in God's way, I begged his blessing, and I hope I propounded his glory in what charge I undertook in that match, and therefore I think I may account what I enjoy as an answer of prayer. God did support me under much weakness while I went with child of my second boy, and especially in that dangerous childbed I had—when want of sleep, and some other distempers, frequently assaulting me, did, for divers weeks, in that childbed endanger my life.

1657, October.

The Lord has graciously preserved me while I was with child of my third child; and did bestow it a thriving and hopeful child; and, though it pleased the Lord to afflict me and keep me in heaviness all that childbed, it was because he saw great need in me; and, therefore, I do esteem the rod in that case a seasonable mercy, and do hope I may say that through God's grace I found it was good for me that I was afflicted; for it made me desirous more to prefer God's glory, it made me stir up myself to meet God, to humble myself before him and to learn by his chastising hand. A very great mercy I acknowledge to have received from God in my health; which has been such, that unless in childbeds, or miscarryings, I have been able to attend upon others constantly, though under some indispositions. This is the more to be taken notice on, because the times have been very sickly for divers years.

I praise God for the preservation of my husband in health in these sickly times; and now, this latter end of November, the Lord did visit him with a fit of the gout, which made me much afraid in regard of the bitter frosty weather; which did so hinder the operation of medicines, that though, through God's great mercy, his extreme pain was abated, and his fever, which the gout brought upon him, had left him; yet his feet swelled to a very great bigness, and began to discolor so much, that I apprehended some danger of a gangrene; but the Lord has mercifully supported him, and prevented all my fears hereto; blessed be his holy name for it.

About the beginning of November 1658, little Moll Waller had a dangerous fit of sickness, first a terrible fever, and then a pleurisy; she being but young and weak I was fearful for her, but the Lord did very graciously help; and, I bless his name, she and all the rest of them are now in good health.

About this month likewise, we heard from our children beyond the seas, of a great deliverance that Will Waller had from being mischiefed, by the going off of a piece in his arms, and breaking as it went off; blessed be the Lord, who watches to do us good, and to prevent evil, when we are not aware of it.

The Lord has likewise graciously supported Philip Harcourt under his quartern ague, and has now wholly delivered him from it; blessed forever be his holy name.

Also in January, 1658, the Lord was pleased to visit me with an ague; I had but three fits, but they were so terrible to me, that in the last I expressed great impatience; which afterwards, upon consideration, did so trouble me, as that the fear of being in the like manner distempered, did make me apprehend the coming of another fit, with such dread, as did add to my affliction; yet, notwithstanding all this failing on my part, enough to have provoked the Lord to have laid his hand more heavily upon me, he was pleased to deliver me, even by his own hand; when the doctor thought I should have one terrible fit more, I had not so much as a grudging of it. Bless the Lord, O my soul, and all that is within me bless his holy name. Bless the Lord, O my soul, and forget not all his benefits—hence learn to trust God—in the like trouble.

In February 1658, the Lord was pleased to visit my husband with many sad distempers, as with an ague, which being joined with the scurvy, and the remainder of an ill fit of the gout, did threaten much danger to his life; but the Lord was a God near at hand, and did deliver him from his ague after four fits, and did graciously at this time prevent all my fear—blessed be his holy name—after his ague, while he was very faint with fasting and sweating, he was threatened with a sore fit of the stone, of which I was greatly afraid; but the Lord has hitherto stayed his hand, so that his extremity has neither been long nor great; O my soul, labor for enlargement in praising God; be not content to do it in an ordinary manner—because of the many and great mercies which the Lord bestows upon thee continually.

About the eighth of this instant, February, coming into my chamber hastily to speak with the doctor about my husband, a heavy great folding screen being put up together fell upon me; it might have done me much hurt, but the Lord did graciously prevent that, I had none at all, blessed be his holy name for it.

February 17.

I heard from Wattford, that my sister's child had one of the feet set without great pain, and is in a hopeful way of cure; the Lord grant grace that the parents and myself may never forget so seasonable and precious a mercy.

It has pleased the Lord about the beginning of April to deliver me from any hurt, notwithstanding two great falls I had, the one in Breyntford town—the other in my chamber where I lie—when I consider the pain my mother had with such a chance, then I have cause to value it—for how little pain I have, and how much evil such a chance might bring. Concerning my husband's business, this last term in May it was like to go very ill—the judges being on a sudden strangely set against him—but they became mild and kind again without any apparent reason. Blessed be God who can turn any heart when he pleases. O my soul, remember how often the Lord has delivered me from the evil I have feared—and has spared me, notwithstanding my fears. As concerning my sister Irby, about this time, for six weeks together still I feared, and still the Lord sent comfortable tidings, blessed be his holy Name for it.

The Lord's name be praised that I have frequently heard comfortable tidings from our children beyond the seas.

February the 4th.

I had another gracious experience concerning my sister, who having been five weeks ill, and growing out of heart, and somewhat impatient, I was much perplexed with fear and grief for her; but last night she rested very much better than was looked for, and was this day again refreshed and comforted. Blessed be the Lord who is graciously pleased to stay his rough wind in the day of his east wind.

All the last winter the Lord was very gracious to my husband and self, in giving us a great measure of health, and our children, and family.

The custom taken of my husband's estate in March by the Rulers was taken off.

I account it a great mercy likewise that the Lord has kept my husband from being biased, notwithstanding all the endeavors of malignants, or all the hopes that might have been from court by his complaints.

The Lord has been very gracious to me at the waters, which I humbly and thankfully acknowledge, in preserving me from all ill accidents of which I was much afraid, and in returning me in health and safety from that place. While I was there, on the 6th of August, 1660, I was overtaken by vain and sinful thoughts, to which I did at that time give too much way.

It pleased the Lord, who is infinite in mercy, so to order it by his providence, that the heavy burden of excise was taken off by the parliament and King from my husband this day.

O that this circumstance of the time might so heighten the mercy to me, as that it might shame me out of my sin, and strengthen my resolution against it for the time to come; there also I hope I may reckon that I received an answer of prayer.

I desire likewise to acknowledge that I have been preserved in Kent, notwithstanding the doubtful condition I was in myself, which was such that I knew not what to pray for; yet to the Lord's will I did submit myself; I waited upon God and he has been wonderful gracious to me— so that neither my own indisposition—nor my overthrow in coming up—nor my fright then—nor since, when my man fell off the ladder, has hitherto brought any such weakness upon me as I have cause to apprehend; wherefore I will engage my heart to praise and serve the Lord as long as I live, for he is infinitely merciful and gracious, and his mercy endures forever and ever.

Some remarkable experiences of God's wonderful mercy.

February 11, 1659.

This day is by the whole nation to be regarded, and especially by the great city of London, who did this day receive a remarkable deliverance as ever they had before; for the remnant of the long Parliament sitting at Westminster, finding that the city would not comply with them in their wicked ways; having General Monck with his army obedient to them, and having the day before tried their trust, by employing them in the city to imprison the aldermen, to dissolve the Common Council, and to pull down and break down all their gates; did this day order him to go in the city and to disarm the citizens, and to burn their charter and records, and to hang some of the chief of them, as is confidently affirmed, and to seize all their public treasuries. No help did now appear on this side heaven. The militia was not yet settled—the Lord Mayor (Alderman Alen) was their enemy, and had obstructed them in the business of their militia and was ready to comply with those that did intend their absolute ruin. Their enemies had a powerful army at their command, and had given out their orders, and the general and soldiers were gone up into the city to perform their commands, as was generally feared.

Then was the time (thought not till then) that our gracious God appeared glorious in their deliverances, by doing that which all the power of the world could not do, namely, by inclining the general's heart to the city; so that when it was least looked for, the city was preserved from the imminent danger they were in; and not only so, but the general declared that he would join with the city for a free Parliament; which caused the greatest public rejoicing that ever was known in the memory of man. O how fully did this appear to be the work of the great God in whose hand is the heart of all men, and he turns them, as the rivers of water, which way it pleases him. Surely this work of mercy was so done that it ought to be had in remembrance. The Lord help me to be mindful of it, and thankful for it, and to have my faith much strengthened by it. To Him be glory forever.

The 19 May, 1659.

I received from God a very great mercy, which I humbly beg of him that my sinful heart may never be ungrateful for it. Namely, the return of my only son Philip Harcourt from his travel, in which complicated mercy there are these things very considerable—first he is naturally very hasty, and yet was preserved from quarrels—secondly, he went over very sickly and weak—for the recovery of his health; and I hope in the Lord that it is more confirmed than it was—thirdly, that he was no way caught by evil company—nor his judgment any way changed that I can discern—nor I trust any way taken with the vanity and pomp of the Romish religion—fourthly, his preservation in all his travels by sea and land, notwithstanding my immoderate fear for him, which might have procured me the very sorrow which I was so apprehensive of. O bless the Lord my soul and forget not all his benefits.—Surely the Lord has graciously delivered me and my child, our souls from death, our eyes from tears, and our feet from fall. Therefore I engage in the strength of

Christ, saying that I will walk before God in the land of the living Amen.

I account it a very great mercy to me that I was not overwhelmed with grief and weakness and fear, when my husband was made a prisoner by Captain Barington, the 5th of August, 1659. Being taken out of his bed at 2 o'clock at night, as if he had been a great offender—and yet the counsel laid nothing to his charge, but, after he had been prisoner a fortnight, then they made him an offender by tendering some promise to him, which, he refusing, was sent to the Tower.

I account it a very great mercy that neither Sir George Booth, who they report is very fearful, nor any of the Cavaliers have accused my husband to please those now in power; for, if they had, how false soever, it should first have been believed, and secondly, it should at least have justified his imprisonment.

This is a wonderful mercy.

The many mercies in our imprisonment and our release.

While we were prisoners in Kent, the trouble of that condition was sweetened by the great kindness of many there, and when we were in the Tower, we found great kindness from the warden; which was a great lessening of our trouble; and the more to be taken notice of, because it is a rare thing, as I perceive by the relation of what other gentlemen suffered from their keepers, to find any amongst them that were not severe, cross, and covetous, to the great prejudice of their prisoners. We found it quite contrary, although we were utter strangers, and therefore are bound wholly to attribute it to the overruling hand of God, that we should be directed at 10 of the clock at night (when we had no time to look about us, or to choose, or inquire what might have been best for us), to the only man's house in the Tower which was best for us. Blessed be the Lord.

Secondly, it was a great comfort and mercy to us that the cause of my husband's imprisonment was owned and approved by the people of God, notwithstanding the scorns and endeavors of his enemies; who first made him a prisoner without any appearing occasion, and secondly made themselves sport with his trouble; saying he chose to be at the Tower that he might retire; whereas, our charge was much greater there than it would have been at another place. The frequent and kind visits of godly people, ministers and others was another great comfort to us, the Lord be praised for it. The lessons which I hope we have in some measure learned there, I acknowledge to be the greatest mercy of all, as self-denial; a moderate use of creature comforts; compassion to other sufferers, especially prisoners; an acknowledgment of God's sovereignty; and a quiet dependence on God for deliverance in his own time, and way—though there was no likelihood of any deliverance from man.

The mercies of our deliverances are so many and great that I am not able to recount them as I ought. First, the times full of sad confusions in the nation, and at the time especially of an opposition in Monck to those in power, which made them unwilling to release any.—The manner— which was by a way clearly legal, and so the more satisfactory to my husband, but in that the more offensive to those in power; the judge was not terrified—the legal proceeding was not interrupted, although they that had forcedly broken in upon parliaments, and did take notice of the proceeding, and expressed great rage against it, by uttering many threatening speeches; yet the Lord did, by his power, so retain and overrule them that they did not put forth the force they had in this matter, nor interrupt our liberty. Blessed be the Lord forever and ever, who has stayed his rough wind, in the day of his east wind; and has, by his own outstretched arm, restrained the rage of the adversary, so that the men of might were not able to find their hands. The Lord give me grace constantly to remember this manifold mercy, and to walk suitably to it; by adoring—and loving God above all—by a quiet and confident dependence upon God for the future; by loving the world, where so much wickedness and sorrow is, the less; and by loving heaven and heavenly things, where holiness and happiness, is, the better. Amen. Amen.

From October the 7th to the 12th.

Concerning my dear sister, I do acknowledge it a great mercy, that, notwithstanding her natural temper, which is hasty, and the melancholy of her disease, both which make her unapt to bear her distemper with the patience and quietness that were to be wished; yet the Lord is wonderfully gracious to her, and not only to her, but to me—who am nearly concerned in, and affected with her condition; Lord make me forever mindful of this wonderful condescension to poor sinners—that my heart may be more drawn to thee by the cords of thy love.

October the 13th.

Hitherto the Lord has helped that my sister's pain, though it has threatened her and kept me in fear, yet it has not been so raging, nor so continual upon her, as in former fits.—Blessed be the Lord, especially for that the Lord has helped me, at what time I was afraid concerning her, to trust in him and to call upon him; and he has several times mercifully prevented my fears; therefore will I praise the Lord as long as I live, and labor to rest on him and to seek to him in all my distress.

I received a very great mercy concerning my husband, who, being ill of his eyes, had a mind to take pills for to purge his head, and made me write for them when it was late, and accordingly took them at night, which made him so ill that I greatly feared his life; but forever blessed by the Lord, who restrained the working of the pills, and brought out the erysipelas, and has supported him all this while in bed, and has prevented any ill accident hitherto, so that he is pretty well; the Lord grant that I may remember this and be thankful, that I may labor to be serviceable all my time to the Lord and his glory.

Saturday the 27th of October, 1660.

The Lord has given me a gracious answer to prayer, touching my sister's extremity; the Lord be praised forever for his wonderful mercy, who gives a poor sinful creature leave to boast of him, and is pleased to answer my hopes—Lord, according to these experiences help me to wait upon thee hereafter.

On the 29th of October the Lord has bestowed on me another gracious experience of his never-failing goodness to me; in preventing a sad fit of pain to my poor sister, when all circumstances did seem to threaten; being very ill when she went to bed, and yet she lay quiet all night: blessed forever be his holy name; the Lord increase my faith by these experiences.

39

SOME OF THE LETTERS AND PAPERS*

Mary Pennyman

On the Great Plague and Fire, 1665 and 1666

I went to visit many that had the distemper upon them, yet got not the least hurt thereby, and my house joining to the graveyard, my two children went daily to follow the dead corpses that died of it, to the grave; this they did of their own accord, the sight of which was ready to shake my faith . . . and such was his love and mercy to me, that myself, children, and family were all preserved, not having the least of that distemper, but in health all the time. . . . And in the year 1666, when that great consuming fire was in this city, then was wonders also wrought for us. The week before it began, I was much pressed in my mind to owe no man anything but love. [She paid all her debts.]

And when the fire began to come near us, my children and servants being fearful, I sent them all to Mile-End-Green, and stayed myself in the house, expecting it might be burned down; yet I believed if anything saved it, it must be by keeping the goods in it that had been so honestly got; but if they should be carried out, then the house must down. But this was hid from others, though made known to me.

Many friends and neighbors came in much love to help out with my goods, to save them for me, using many arguments to prevail with me, saying, If all I had was lost, what should they do I owed money to? I told them I owed none in the world. . . .

. . . one John Holmstead came above twenty miles with his wagon, purposely to save my goods, and (as he said) to sell them for me . . . but I durst not in the least consent thereto. . . .

The fire stayed before it came at us, and we were all preserved. All goods were sold then at a great rate, but I durst not raise the price of

*Ed. John Pennyman (London, 1690), pp. 5–7, 33, 47.

mine, but let others have the benefit of my preservation. Thus have I given a short hint of our great preservation, little in comparison of what might be written; but if I should forget these mercies, the stones in the street might rise up in judgment against me. . . .

1690

In the year 1662 I was a widow, having three children, viz., two sons and a daughter . . . for when they were young I knew no children beyond them, for sobriety, honesty, and plainheartedness, and even without guile. . . . I put my two sons out apprentices from me into the wide world, alas! they were quickly changed . . . turned aside into the broad way that brings to death and darkness. . . . But the God of wonderful compassion is, I trust, bringing them home to himself, into whose tender care I commit them. . . .

17 July 1700

The most of my time, both night and day, is spent in secret praising and magnifying the Lord my God, for his mercies to me.

40

THE PRIVATE DIARY
(1658–1678)*

Elizabeth Carey, Viscountess Mordaunt

June, the 2nd, 1658

In the year of our Lord 1658, on the first of June, my dear husband was
tried for his life by a court, called the High Court of Justice, and on the
second day of June was cleared by one voice only, 19 condemning of him
and 20 saving him, and those twenty had not prevailed, but by God's
immediate hand, by striking one of the court with an illness, which
forced him to go out, in whose absence the votes were given, and
recorded, so that his return no way prejudiced Mr. Mordaunt, though
in his thoughts he resolved it (Prid was the person), many other miraculous blessings were showed in his preservation, for which blessed be
God.

He was the first example that pleaded not guilty, that was cleared
before these courts.

Wednesday, June, the 2nd, 1658

Praise the Lord, O my Soul, and all that is within me praise His holy
name.

Praise the Lord, O my Soul, and forget not all his benefits, which
saved thee from destruction, and crowned thee with mercy and loving-
kindness.

Praised be the Lord forever, for He hath preserved the life of my dear
husband from the power and malice of his enemies, and hath blessed us
with mercies on every side. It was thy hand, and the help of thy mercy,
which relieved us, when the waters of afflictions had nigh drowned us,

*Duncairn, Scotland, 1856; pp. 16–23, 31–32, 43–45, 59–61, 67–68, 79–80, 91–92.

and our sins had justly deserved it, and our enemies earnestly desired and pursued it; for they had privily laid a net to destroy him, without a case, and false witnesses did rise up against him; they laid to his charge things that he knew not and his own familiar friends accused him, rewarding him evil for good, to the great discomfort of his soul, but thou O Lord didst revoke that angry sentence . . . by frustrating the designs and malice of his enemies . . . as thou broughtest water out of a stony rock to relieve thy servants the children of Israel, so didst thou turn that stony heart of his, that where he designed destruction, he endeavored safety; therefore we will be glad and rejoice in thy mercy, for thou hast considered our trouble and hast known our souls in adversity, for thou gavest not up my dear husband into the hands of his enemies, but hast set his feet in a large room . . . and thou hast heard my supplication, and hast considered my complaint; thou hast granted me my heart's desire, and hast not refused me the request of my lips, when I begged deliverance for my dear husband from the hands of his enemies and from those that persecuted him . . . and thou never forsakest those that love thee. Thanks be to the Lord, for he hath showed us marvelous great kindness in this strange deliverance. . . . Amen, Amen.

The Prayer

O my God, my just and merciful God, sanctify this blessing unto me, and so fill my heart with the apprehensions of thy miraculous mercies to me in this great deliverance of my dear husband's, that I may not dare to offend thee that so highly hath blessed me; but grant that both me and my dear husband may spend that life, which we have again received from thy hands, with so great strictness that we may eminently show forth thy mercy to us in the spending of our time as in the saving of our lives. Make us instruments of thy mercy, to thy Church, and to thy Chosen, and as thou hast given to my dear husband a second life, so give him a new one, in all virtue and holiness . . . make us both thine, and then in thy great mercy keep us so. . . . Amen.

A Prayer

For the 2nd of June, every year and every Wednesday in the week, since the death of my dear husband.

I must never omit to praise thee my Lord and my God, on this day, for the miraculous deliverance of my dear husband, from the power and malice of his enemies and from the jaws of Death, for though thou hast taken this blessing from me now, yet so numerous have been thy mercies to this family since the first day of his deliverance, that they must always be repeated by me, to the great glory of thy most glorious name. Thou hast given to my dear husband and to me many years of comfort since; thou hast given us the great blessing of many children, the increase of fourteen, of honor, of goods, of friends, and all this I have been so little worthy of, that thou hast justly withdrawn my greatest worldly comfort, my dear husband; but merciful Lord, do thou increase my spiritual joys, and give me grace to make so good use of thy remaining blessings in this world, that thou mayest never withdraw them in judgment from me, but grant that I may so entirely leave myself, my children, my fortune, and interest, to thy disposal, that I may neither think, nor act, but by thy directions; I have none but thee, my God, to assist me, and in having thee, I have all; do thou never forsake me, and then I shall be blest forever. Amen.

What I am to pay out of my purse, blessed be God.

10 pound a year to be given to a _____ beginning 1661.

06 pound a year to Mrs. Broune in great distress beginning 1663.

20 pound a year to the keeping Mr. Jamot's child till she shall be by the King or somebody else provided for beginning 1663. *She is now provided for.*

05 pound a year to be paid for the keeping of Maris' old father, so long as it shall please God to enable me.

01 pound a year to the breeding of Ley the cook's child being fatherless and motherless.

20 pound a year to Mrs. Cor being fourscore years old till she has something else to live on.

4 pound a year to Miss Payne, till she be in a better condition, begins Christmas 1676.

2 pound a year to a poor woman by Miss English.

10 pound a year to Mr. Owen till he be provided for, begins Christmas 1676.

4 pound a year apiece to two Jews.

4 pound a year to two women, by Miss Lloyd, ten shillings a quarter apiece.

What I promise to pay to the poor every year, so long as God shall enable me, and I humbly beg His Grace to perform them.

He that giveth to the poor lendeth to the Lord, and it shall be returned him sevenfold. The Lord loveth a cheerful giver.

1. On the 2nd of June every year, to keep a thanksgiving for the miraculous deliverance of my dear husband on that day, from the peril of death, and on the same day, to give 5 pounds in gold to the use of the poor; to acknowledge my husband's life and the comforts I receive by it, wholly from God's hands, and to praise him for it.

2. To dedicate to the use of the poor the tenth part of all the rent I shall receive from my own land of inheritance, which was my own before I was to marry.

3. To pay to my poor box sixpence every night and morning, in acknowledgment that the safety, content, and preservation of my dear husband, my children, and myself, the day and night past, came from the hand of God.

4. To dedicate to my God 5 pound sterling in gold upon the 2nd of March every year, and to receive the sacrament on the same day, so long as I shall be able to do it, in remembrance and acknowledgment of the great blessing confirmed to me on that day 1659, and an act of parliament then published, for the life, freedom, and estates of Sir George Bouthe and all those that had assisted in that business, for whose safeties I had before made this vow. . . .

A Thanksgiving for the 29th of May every year, it being the day of the King's happy restoration, and a beginning to the church's settlement

What praises can I render unto thee, my God, worthy thy acceptance at any time, though in the greatest afflictions, which still is less than my sins do daily deserve, and therefore requires my hearty and humble thanks for thy goodness, in not punishing them, according to their merit.

O what praises then can I now render upon this day, on the which thou hast showered such multitudes of mercies upon me, upon me as I partake in the public good, upon me as being a member of thy Church, upon me in the particular and personal comforts, that my dear husband and I have received by the King's most happy and miraculous restoration upon this day, a miracle past expectation. For how did they increase that troubled the peace and prosperity of this Church and nation, and many they were that rose up against the just rights of thine anointed, saying, *There is no help for him in his God,* but thou, O Lord, were his defender, and the lifter up of his head, thou didst arise thy power and in thy mercy and smotest all his enemies, and hast broken the bonds of the ungodly. . . . Amen, Amen.

1664: July the 15th

A Thanksgiving for the birth of my daughter Sophia

Thou art my God, and I will praise thee, thou art my God, and I must love thee, for all thy mercies continually vouchsafed me, and in particular for this last great deliverance from the pain and peril of childbirth, and for the great blessing of a perfect child, thy goodness is so known to me, that I have great reason patiently to attend upon thy will, in all conditions whatsoever, and to praise thee more and more, for thou hast showed me great troubles and adversities, and yet hast thou never forsaken me, but hast returned in mercy and brought me out of them all. . . .

June the 1st 1665, in the Great Plague

Ponder my words, O Lord, and consider my petitions. O hearken thou unto the voice of my calling, my King and my God. For unto thee do I make my prayer, in the behalf of the whole nation in general, and of my family in particular, that thou willst be pleased to command thy angel to cease from punishing, that this plague of pestilence, which is begun in this nation, may go no farther, but at thy command may stop, for though thy wrath be just against us, yet Lord, remember mercy.

And that in thy great mercy thou hast been pleased hitherto to keep it out of my family, Let me and mine never forget to praise thee. . . . Amen.

September the 6th 1666. Thursday.

A Thanksgiving for the stopping of the fire in London.

It is to thee, my dearest Lord, that I
For help, and safety, in distress do cry,

To thee 'tis fit I should all praise return,
That when the City great in flames did burn,
My husband, children, self, and all that's mine,
Was safely guarded by thy power divine,
Thy power I saw in that devouring fire,
Admired thy justice, and yet dared desire
That thou would'st thy destroying angel bede [command]
To stop, and hear unworthy mortals plead
For mercy, which so often I had felt,
The thoughts of it my soul in tears did melt,
And gave me courage constantly to pray,
Till at the last thou heard'st, and bede'st him stay,
Saying it is enough, I will now try
Once more whether they'll choose to live or die;
O let us never such a blessing lose,
Refusing mercy, and destruction choose,
Let the remembrance of thy power and love
Raise all our thoughts and praises high above,
That by the strictness of our lives, we may
Show our resentment [appreciation] of the love, and say
'Tis from thy hands we did this mercy take,
O let us never thy just laws forsake;
Thus ending our life here, we may be blest,
In Abraham's bosom, with eternal rest. Amen.

41

THE MEDITATIONS[*]

Lady Elizabeth Delaval

This following meditation was also written in my 17th year.

Upon the Having Worms in My Gums
and the Taking of Them Out

Pain seldom seizes us but physicians can tell what evil is the cause of it, from whence our distempers proceed, and what are the most proper remedies (or at least they make us believe so), and by those remedies one may be cured, perhaps suddenly too; but if not me, who it may be God will punish longer making me smart under his rod, even till I humbly kiss it, by suffering willingly, yet some other person in pain might find ease by the physician's skill.

But what I now endure, as it can scarcely be described, so neither can it be cured by any of those who are most learned in diseases that afflict us.

My head, my eye, my teeth, and my neck are most miserably tormented with raging pain, all which a poor unlearned woman (with God's blessing) promises to ease me of. She tells me that what I suffer is caused by the gnawing of little worms that run along with the blood in my veins. I know, tell this now to any learned doctor of physic and he will rather smile at my simplicity, for expecting to be eased by this woman's skill, then not believe her more likely to cheat than cure me. I

[*]Ed. Douglas G. Greene for the Surtees Society (Gateshead: Northumberland Press, 1978), pp. 77–79, 161–79. (Written between 1662 and 1671; MS. Rawlinson D.78, Bodleian Library.)

must have patience till tomorrow before I can know the truth, for her art cannot be showed till there is daylight for her to work in.

Meditations the Next Day after
the Worms Were Taken Out

Most strangely has this woman surprised me and many more here present, for behold here is no less than 200 worms in this basin which she has taken out of my gums where (though I was willing to try her skill) I did not believe there had been any.

But though I wonder much to see a plain demonstration of what very few will believe, yet at the same time I consider we are far from understanding all the secrets of nature; nor can I give credit to any man's judgment before my own eyes.

Nor because this woman's art in taking these little creatures of my gums (where they have so many days and nights bitterly tormented me) is unusual, must I therefore conclude it impossible to be done but either by witchcraft or cozenage [deception].

As for the first of these, God forbid I should ascribe such power to a wicked creature, as is only due to our glorious creator.

'Tis at his word that the stormy winds arise and not at the command of a witch (as some people do foolishly imagine), and 'tis God alone that can still the raging of the sea.

We were certainly in a most miserable condition if a professed servant of the devil's could at her pleasure cause sorrow, pain, or sickness to seize us. But blessed be our merciful God who preserves us from such sad evils and himself corrects us, but with judgment not in his anger lest we should be consumed and brought to nothing.

Correction (saith Solomon) is grievous unto him that forsaketh the way, and he that hateth reproof shall die.

Most welcome then be all my afflictions. Oh may I ever submit like old Eli, saying it is the Lord, let him do what seemeth him good.

Most convincing arguments there are to me this woman deserves not the hated name of a witch, which many people give her amongst the giddy multitude, whilst the more sober sort reckon her to be a cheat; and that she cannot be neither, for 'tis impossible she can have cunning enough (as it has been reported) to put worms into my mouth through the quill with which she takes them out.

I am sure she neither brought the quill with her, nor did so much as make it, for it was made by one of my own servants, and I plainly enough (as well as others) saw the worms stir (after she left me) in the water where she washed the quill that she opened my gums withal.

Nay more, some curious people that were here took some of those little worms out of the water to try if they had life, and when they were cut in pieces we saw blood, which was a certain proof that they were not little pieces of lutestring which some incredulous people used to say she might slip into my mouth with the quill with which she opened my gums, and so washing it [in] the basin she might make those pieces of strings move in the water, as if there were life in them; but these arguments were not made use of by any of those persons who were eyewitnesses of the sudden cure that was wrought upon me.

In fine, after all critical arguments I dare affirm it for a truth that worms have caused those torturing pains my God has punished me withal and in his good time mercifully removed.

The Prayers Belonging to These Meditations

1. I adore thee, O glorious majesty the great God of heaven and earth; I acknowledge thy power and tremble at thy judgments, humbly desiring ever to submit to thy holy will without the least murmur.

2. I praise thee with my whole heart for all thy mercies and amongst them for thy gentle corrections.

Oh my God, be thou pleased still to deal graciously with thy unworthy servant. Now, I beseech thee, incline my ear and hear me; I call, thou God of my salvation. . . .

Meditations upon the Unkindness of My Father and the Treachery of a Friend

There is nothing in this world that I could not with greater ease part withal than the kindness of a friend, which great misfortune I now feel.

After nine years' experience (which goes far in the short time I have yet lived), I find myself unexpectedly deprived of what I most valued. Under the sacred name of friendship, a friendship that I believed firmly established, treachery is hid, so uncertain are all things here below. Oh good God, what can make me any longer delight to be in this valley of

tears, how many have I vainly shed, and how many has this last affliction cost me, which yet I acknowledge to be just.

For I find myself more grieved for the loss of those daily comforts I
received from the conversation of my friend than for her faults.

There is only two sorts of evils which can wound my heart, and the
last of them touches it too nearly. The one is when I discover my own
grievous offenses against God or the iniquities of those who are dear to
me; the other is when I meet with unkindness from those I love.

This last cause of sorrow which I feel (so frail is our weak nature) to
be the most piercing, I must endeavor to moderate and by degrees
wholly to overcome.

Oh that I were so free from placing my heart upon things below that I
could lament nothing but what displeases my God. . . .

But what I grieve for is so little truly worth my sorrow that as a
reward of my sin and folly I have brought sickness and an unquiet
mind to be my companions; whereas sorrow rightly placed only takes of
the vain jollity of our sinful lives and fits us for the grave.

I shall easily part with riches or beauty (which I never doted on)
when I can once (without unspeakable grief) bring myself to part with a
friend that I have patiently loved with great truth and far above all
worldly advantages, being ever ready to sacrifice any interest of my
own for her sake.

And as for honors (which I must confess I too long looked upon as
they appeared, the best side outward), I have now a good while discovered the dear expense at which they are purchased, and the vanity
of being fond of possessing what a hundred accidents may make me
swiftly lose: the breath of a giddy multitude constantly attending the
wheel of fortune, and if that turns ill for me, farewell to all the applause I
have and to all the court that is made me now.

God grant that I may always keep my innocence, and as for prosperity, when it comes I will thankfully receive it. When it vanishes I will
not ungratefully murmur.

But what is yet more sad than the falseness of my friend, even my
own father endeavors to ruin me by designing to tear me from my aunt
(who has taken me as her own child and resolved to provide for me),
and this I cannot find out is a punishment that I deserve, for I have
always obeyed him diligently and loved him with a true affection; yet
perhaps I have erred and cannot find it out, and what I call cruelty to
me 'tis possible may be justice, and then I am in the wrong, not he.

I believe also a third person did tempt my friend to be false to me by telling of her lies, but, alas, I can make no excuse for her forsaking me, without examining the truth of what she heard.

I must still love and pity her; my heart can do no otherwise.

But I will trust none hereafter (when I can possibly avoid it) who are not truly pious and can moderate their passions by the grace of God beyond the rules of morality.

As for my dear father, I mourn for all his sins in general, and if amongst them his unkindness to me be one (alas) it will cut my heart the more, but yet not make me lose my duty.

When I should receive kindness from him or a mark of friendship from her, I will accustom myself to think they are both dead, because my sins has, as a punishment, made them so to me in kindness; but when I am to pay to either of them what I owe, I will remember they are alive to receive duties from me.

Prayers

1. Blessed be thy holy name, Oh Lord God, for all thy mercies and particularly for my afflictions, which are good monitors of my duty. Oh give me grace to consider wisely the uncertainty of all delights here below (which I have too great a part of my life looked upon as inestimable happiness).

2. Oh my God, I adore thee for thy wisdom in all things, and for thy justice in afflicting me by the unfaithfulness of a friend whom I chose and doted on for the charms of her conversation and the sharpness of her wit, and not as thy servant David chose his friends, for their leading a godly life; (woe is me) to please this false friend I have often neglected my duty to thee and to my parents.

3. Oh Lord, in much mercy graciously pardon her treachery to me and all other evils of her life; turn her heart to thee, and then I am sure she will become faithful to me. Oh grant I may now take warning by her, and nevermore choose a friend so much to delight as to instruct me.

4. Oh dear God, forgive, I beseech thee, my father's unkindness to me (if he displeases thee by it). Oh let me be no occasion of increasing his sins, which are I much fear (though a burden too heavy for him to bear) what he feels not enough the load of. Oh for Christ Jesus' sake, the

son of thy love, have mercy on him, and give him true repentance, that the devil may not rejoice at his ruin, but good angels at his conversion.

5. Enable me I humbly pray thee to make the best use of all the crosses I meet withal here below. Oh let me no longer grieve at what happens only displeasing to myself, but turn my sorrow aright, and then shall I (as a true Christian) only mourn for what offends thee.

6. Oh let me be no longer disturbed because I have lost the comforts of a friend, nor because I find unkindness in a parent; for even these afflictions are not evil to me except I make them so by my resentment.

Oh give me an indifference for all earthly joys; then I shall hunger and thirst after righteousness and at last be filled.

7. Having once quit all tender concern for things here below, how willingly shall I depart from hence. The beauties of this visible world, all thy glorious works cannot once tempt me to think 'tis good for me to continue here, who have lived to see a father unkind and a friend unfaithful.

Oh grant I may so overcome my frail nature by the power of thy grace, that I may no more shed tears for my own misfortunes but for their faults, and so looking upon things in this world, I shall surely never be troubled to leave it, but even now remove from hence in preparation of mind.

8. Let, O Lord, the sorrow for my sins and the consideration of my friend's trangressions, together with the iniquities of the whole world, take of the vain gaiety of my sinful life. Oh give me a sober spirit, and thy grace to live holily all my days, redeeming the time for the days are evil.

God be merciful to me the chief of sinners, for Christ Jesus' sake. Amen.

Here ends the prayers and meditations written from my 14th year to my 20th.

Thus far the thoughts which I had in the springtime of my life are set down. Now follows what I wrote in the summer of it, which passed away more full of cares, and with less of innocence in it, than the former.

But blessed be God (who never forsakes them that put their trust in him), I was delivered by his grace out of those many snares the devil had cunningly laid in my way, to make me fall into such shameful heinous crimes as would not only have ruined me forever, but also have disgraced my family and most justly have made me be hated and scorned in this world, as well as eternally miserable in the next.

After the Comte Dona was obliged with the ambassador his uncle to return into his own country, not being able to persuade me to marry him without the consent of my parents, and not being in a condition at that time (his eldest brother being alive) to make any proposals that might be suitable to my fortune, I soon in his absence overcame the growing inclination I had for him, though he continually wrote me letters full of passion and respect, which did not hinder me from receiving very favorably the addresses of my Lord Anesley, which I had reason to believe would have been most agreeable both to his parents and mine, nothing being more suitable than both our birth and fortunes were, and our age also. For he was just then four years older than I. I was not mistaken in my guess, for his father and mother and my father also were extremely well pleased with Lord Anesley's having declared to them, he never could be happy without me. Only my aunt opposed it for the secret reason I have already told you, and carried me out of town, intending to keep me for her friend and neighbor, the Earl of Rutland, till he had obtained an act of Parliament for his divorce, which business then advanced very fast.

The Earl of Rutland (who at that time was only Lord Roos, his father being yet living) presently after my coming into the country left Bellvoire Castle, and took a hunting house about six miles from Nocton, and brought two of his sisters with him who were young ladies that had been my playfellows when I was ten years old. We were fond of one another's company, and therefore 'twas easy for him to make parties for us to be frequently together. Sometimes we hunted together and sometimes danced. He lived in great splendor and had always fine music; so had my aunt, who was of an extraordinary cheerful good humor and promoted the mirth of young people always in the most agreeable manner imaginable. As for my part, I was very desirous to have my aunt go back to London, for though my Lord Anglesy was much offended at my aunt's cold answer when he offered her his son for me, yet my Lord Anesley could not be brought to think of any other marriage, though several were proposed to him; and I imagined that if I could get my aunt to London again, perhaps I might get some friends of mine to work upon her so far as to get her consent to what I thought it was so very unreasonable for her to refuse. My place at court not allowing me to be very long absent, I had a very fair pretense to press her going with me to London, which after being about eight months in the country she agreed to. I was no sooner come to town, but in the court, at my father's house, and in all other places my Lord Anesley was continually at my elbow, and not content with that, no day passed in which he did not write to me, and generally more than once a day, which made me do all that I could possibly imagine to change my aunt's mind; but the more she found my kindness to him increase, the more her aversion to him did also, and she privately gave my Lord Rutland an account of all that she knew, when she first told him she found my heart was engaged, [he] fell into a most violent passion, for his heart had been for some years mightily bent upon having me for his wife. My aunt renewed her promises to him, and his passion being not one of anger but of grief, the knowing that I loved another did not in the least make him change his design. He did not blame me at all for being favorable to his rival (who he could not say was a person unfit to pretend to me), since he had never yet presumed to speak to me of love, which he always told my aunt he had too much respect for me to do till he was divorced, and he found more difficulty to get that act of Parliament than he expected (though at last it was obtained). In the meantime my aunt and he consulted how they might keep me till that time unmarried, for they extremely dreaded I should dispose of myself; and as all men are apt enough to flatter themselves that a woman's heart is to be gained whenever the attempt is made in good earnest, so my Lord Rutland did not doubt but that when he was in proper circumstances to speak to me of love he should prevail; and therefore the first thing he did was to go out of town to my Lady Rutland his mother, whom he had all along trusted with the secret of his passion for me, to beg that she would employ a friend of hers (who had interest with the Earl of Anesley) to make a marriage betwixt one of her daughters and Lord Anesley. My Lord Rutland begged that they would make it up with all haste and stick at no terms that my Lord Anglesy could desire, and that till all was concluded it might be kept very private and not so much as spoken of to the young lord, for he dreaded that if he and I had foreseen such an opposition to our inclinations was coming on, it might have made us take the resolution of marrying privately; but my Lord Rutland little knew my heart, for I was not capable of doing it, having a niceness in my conscience which hindered me from marrying anybody contrary to the consent of their parents. Since I have known the world better, I have been satisfied that I might have done it without any crime or dishonor, but even my own father could not persuade me to think so at that time of my life, who gave me counsel not to refuse a marriage so advantageous to me and so agreeable to my own heart.

My Lord Anesley, being almost out of his wits that my aunt continued so obstinately bent against him, pressed me to steal a marriage, and with a thousand passionate expressions, and said I could not possibly know what love was, since I refused to share his fortune whatever it might be. I endeavored to appease his anger with all the obliging things I could say to him, but still continued firm in the resolutions I had made never to marry without the consent of his parents and mine, and I told him we were young enough to wait for a change in their minds, and that if his love was as true as he had so often endeavored to persuade me it was, he had reason to be satisfied, since nothing upon earth could ever happen to make me give myself to another if he continued constant. He seemed most extremely afflicted that I could possibly have a doubt of him, and with many extravagant words endeavored to persuade me it was impossible he could ever change. My aunt did all she could at that time to get me to go with her again for a little time into the country, where she knew my Lord Rutland might see me often and have the pleasure to know his rival was at a great distance, who he hoped would soon give me reason to hate him, for by this time my Lord Anglesy had received the proposition the Countess of Rutland made him, which was the choice of her daughters and ten thousand pounds to be paid upon the wedding day for his son, who knew nothing of this matter no more than I did, it being resolved amongst them that till my aunt could get me out of town nothing should be said to Lord Anesley of his father's intentions to dispose of him. His passion for me and my way of receiving it was no secret; all the court and town rang of it, it being not a thing any way disgraceful either to him or me. So one day the king took me aside in the queen's lodgings and spoke to me of it, and what I have since wondered at in myself, I was not at all out of countenance, but presently owned the truth, and told the king at the same time that I would not marry without his [Lord Anesley's] father's consent. The king smiled at my being so positive in that, but at the same time said, well, Lady Betty, I will take care of you, trust this affair to me, and in a little time I will bring my Lord Privy Seal to consent that his son shall be so happy as to have you. I was mightily pleased with what the king had said, and presently took the resolution to please my aunt by going with her into the country for some months. My Lord Anesley, who was in the Privy Chamber when the king spoke to me, as soon as I went out of the room came to me with great impatience to know what had passed, which he was overjoyed at, but when I told him I would presently tell my aunt I would wait upon her into the country as soon as she pleased, he was extremely mortified at that resolution and opposed it all he could but to no purpose, for I thought it might fit to keep some measures with my aunt, and therefore resolved to please her in what I could. So within two days she carried me away. Betwixt her house and London my cousin Essex Griffin lived, who was my companion and bosom friend in the court. Out of complacence to me, my aunt consented to make her a visit in our journey, and to stay with her three or four days. She received us extremely well and was transported with joy to see me. With much importunity when my aunt would stay there no longer, she prevailed with her to leave me with her for one week, and promised after that she would take care to send me to Nocton in her coach. I was very glad to stay with her awhile, having a very true kindness for her and much esteem for her husband, he having always had very much for me.

My aunt was no sooner gone but I opened my heart to them, and told them all things that had happened to me, and how my Lord Anesley and I parted. My cousin Essex Griffin very much condemned my refusing to marry him when he desired to have married me privately. Her husband and she used many arguments to persuade me 'twas a very great folly, and laid before me their own example, for though their marriage was treated of betwixt their parents, as Lord Anesley's and mine had been, yet theirs was broken off by my uncle Suffolk about settlements, which having not at the same time broke off the kindness betwixt them too, they stole a marriage and were very soon after pardoned both by her parents and his. They bid me consider that my father approved of my choice and had himself encouraged me to steal a marriage when my Lord Anesley pressed me to it, at the time that the Earl of Anglesy and my aunt broke off the treaty. In short they used so many arguments to persuade me to what I wished that they prevailed, and I consented to write to my Lord Anesley to let him know where I had got leave to stay by the way, my aunt being gone home, and that he might come thither where I was resolved no longer to refuse the making myself his forever. This letter was sent by a servant of my Lord Griffin's, who had the indiscretion to give it into the Earl of Anglesy's hands instead of his son's, which strangely alarmed all the house, both his father and his mother were out of their wits, having made an end of the treaty of marriage betwixt their son and the Countess of Rutland's daughter, and just upon the point of declaring it to Lord Anesley, they showed him my letter, and the Earl of Anglesy (who was one of the most passionate men upon earth) swore, if he presumed to disobey his will, that he might beg with me if he pleased, but that he would not give him a sixpence of his estate, which should all be settled upon his second son and married to my Lady Betty Manners, if my Lady Rutland would accept of him; for she should see that he showed himself as much a man of honor to her, as much as 'twas in his power to be. My Lord Anesley (being as I imagine) covetous in his nature, frighted with these threats, yielded to his father's will, and instead of coming to my cousin Essex Griffin's house sent me a letter in which he said that he had done all that was possible to have the happiness of being ever mine, without absolute ruin to us both; and therefore he begged I would release the promise that had passed betwixt us. 'Tis impossible for me to express the surprise I was in upon the reading of this letter, nor the rage I felt. I did not balance one moment but immediately wrote him word, since he was capable to write me such a letter, I freed him with great willingness and scorn; and the next day I resolved to go on my journey to my aunt's house, where I wrote what follows. . . .

December the 3rd, 1669, written at Nocton, my aunt Stanhope's house,
upon the news of my Lord Anesley being married to my
Lady Elizabeth Manners, in the 21st year of my age.

Though at my cousin Essex Griffin's house I released all my Lord Anesley's vows to me, yet I was still fool enough to think 'twas impossible he could be prevailed withal to break them.

But now sure the extrem'st ill fate of my whole life is past, since the man who wholly possessed my heart has proved himself false and unworthy of it, and I have lived to see him that I loved above all things in this world (excepting my conscience and my honor) guilty of such crimes that I tremble to think what rewards he will one day receive for them.

Never could any man more earnestly profess to love than he, nor I believe scarcely did ever any real passion appear more moving than his dissembled one did; for what can I call it else, how can I conclude that he ever truly loved me, who had so little value for my good name in the world as to hazard the loss of it by his sudden change, for had not God in much mercy even miraculously preserved my reputation; for one (almost) in this censorious world that would have had charity enough not to suspect my virtue when they saw that four or five days' time of absence had banished me from my lover's heart, hundreds would have condemned me for his sake. I will never trust sighs, tears, nor vows anymore, nor believe that 'tis possible by any obligations in the world to make a man that does not truly fear God faithful or just; my Lord Anesley's last actions have plainly declared that he is neither.

For his sake, I did not scruple to displease my best friends. For his satisfaction I offered to avoid forever the conversation of one of them who he believed to be his enemy.

Rather than break the promises solemnly made betwixt us, which (if I know myself at all) I would have lost my life rather than have broken, I refused to be married to a man of great merit whose rank in the world is equal to his, and his fortune far greater. In fine, I gave him all the innocent marks of a most tender affection that he could reasonably wish for. 'Tis true he never could persuade me to steal a marriage with him, which he said could proceed from no cause but want of love, which he much mistook; I had other principles than his, and never could be prevailed withal by him not to think it a crime ever to marry without the consent of his parents and mine. All I could do for him was to promise (if he continued constant) I never would give myself to any other. We were both young enough, I told him, to wait till that consent could be gained. He seemed out of his wits almost for my saying that word (if he continued constant), and by a hundred extravagant expressions endeavored to make me repent the having had one minute's doubt of him. Among other things I remember well that he begged of God (if ever he could be capable of breaking his vows to me) that the church in which he was to be married to another might fall upon his head and crush him to pieces, and if that judgment failed that he might never live a happy day with his wife, that their discord might be known to all the world, that at last he might not die a common death but some remarkable way, by which God's heavy judgment might be visible upon him, and that as for his race, if he left any behind him he wished they might all be miserable as well as himself. After all these wicked curses upon himself, he swore he loved me beyond expression, and that he could not bear with my manner of temper, my having a doubt of his truth; for he was sure there was nothing (except the murder of his father) which he would not do to be ever mine. His extravagant expression made my blood chill, and I blamed him very much for them. At the same time I cannot but own I was guilty of tasting a secret pleasure when I thought of all his flights of passion, which made me foolishly believe he never could have changed.

And yet when the time was come that my cousin Essex Griffin and her lord (encouraged by their example) had persuaded me to break my resolutions and resolve upon a private marriage, Lord Anesley was no more the same man; and now I have lost him forever, and that, too, in so short a time after the repeating of his vows that this is a blow which would go near to breaking a harder heart than mine.

I was not at all impatient for a change in his father's resolutions, not at all doubting but, if the king's power had not, time and perseverance in our love would most certainly have done it, and that much sooner, too, than he hoped; and therefore most rash as well as unjust was he to break his vows rather than for a short while to endure the threats of an incensed father, which had they been put in execution, would certainly have proved sorrows much lighter for him to groan under than those he will (if not in this world to be sure in the next) for having broken his faith.

How often has he wished himself eternally damned if ever he were guilty of such a crime, and I now do as earnestly wish him true repentance here, which may prevent his torments in another world, for revenge is a mistaken sweet that never shall have place in my heart.

I am sometimes strangely amazed when I consider how immediately after I left him Lord Anesley proved false. Had he seen and loved the lady he has married before I lost his heart, he would have had some little (though but an ill) excuse, for some beauties are so dazzling that they conquer young men by surprise, but that was not his case. Had he been naturally of a covetous temper, and so far dreaded the effects of his father's anger that he resolved to sacrifice both his love and his honor rather than risk the loss of his estate for my sake, I might have expected to be forsaken when an estate came once to be put into the balance with me; but by those offers he made at the time our marriage was treated of to accept of a far less maintenance during his father's lifetime with me than he would have done when other marriages were proposed to him, and by his pressing me when my aunt Stanhope had broken off that treaty to venture the marrying of him privately without any settlement at all, I had reason to believe covetousness was not his vice, which indeed is more likely to be an attendant of old age than youth.

The very day that Lord Anesley and I parted, he had so much grief in his face, and spoke to me with so much reason and generosity of all his father's threatenings, that I left him without the least suspicion or uneasiness of mind.

After loving me passionately for three years together without knowing whether ever he should be able to touch my heart or no, he was well assured that he had gained it, and might well believe that a kindness which was not got with ease would always last, and therefore 'twas natural enough for him to have resisted his father's will with an unshaken resolution, when he proposed to give him to another; and 'tis incredible that in the short space of only four days' absence he should become thus perjured and ungrateful.

Such changes are so little ordinary and so very surprising that I could never cease wondering at these things, did I not consider that nothing can happen without the permission of a just God whom I have offended, and who has taught me by the sorrows which I feel how unworthy I have been to desire with such unreasonable earnestness anything in this world which I was not sure God had allotted for me, and to place my heart, which God alone has right to, upon a frail, deceitful creature, by whom I am punished for that sin and folly. . . .

Prayers

3. Oh Lord, I confess that I willingly yielded my heart to love even almost to a degree of madness that ungrateful youth who has so cruelly deceived me. Alas, I did not in the least oppose my inclinations to love a man that my best friends with earnestness advised me to avoid, but in spite of all the reasons before my eyes to fly the danger of his conversation, I sought for nothing more and so lost my precious hours, which were many of them without regret dedicated to the charms of his cheating discourses.

4. Oh sweet Savior, have mercy upon me and destroy me not, who have been so lost in a vain impertinent amour that my memory has been so filled with what concerned my love, that it forsook me as to sober remembrances; for in those days I never once thought of those secret vows I made when my father forbid me to receive any longer the courtship of Comte Dona, never any more to listen to any man's addresses unless we were chosen for one another by our parents, nor how

much I repented the having done it that once. Thus my passion for Lord Anesley drew me into the great guilt of being perjured.

5. I repent bitterly, O my God, I repent this crime, which though not committed willfully since I remembered not till now how I had tied myself up from such follies, yet heedlessly have I thus grievously offended thee for Lord Anesley's sake, being blinded by my passion and believing the false words he swore to me so oft, that his love could never end but with his life. . . .

7. Had I earnestly pressed him the duty that he owed his father, before I suffered him to vow himself my husband before thee, though we had not passed the ceremony of the church, 'tis very possible he might have taken my advice in that as well as he did in many other things.

But, alas, with too much joy I readily accepted a heart he ought not to have given me, or at least if he could not have resisted its being mine, he ought never to have removed it.

O forgive his unworthiness towards me, and pardon both our offenses against thee, who without due consideration bound ourselves in bonds which he without scruple has rashly broken, and which misfortune I never should have felt, had I not trusted to his words more than all my friends could say, and too well loved that man whom thou has justly suffered to cause me those sorrows my sin and folly has deserved. . . .

Candlemas Eve, 1669: upon a continual melancholy for several weeks,
Mr. Delaval being then at Nocton,
my father having promised that I should be his wife.

'Tis not to be questioned but that the sorrow which now oppresses my spirit is as certainly criminal as 'tis afflictive.

'Tis caused by a mixture of all the unpleasant thoughts I have ever entertained of what has happened to me in my whole life, and it does not only rob me of my natural cheerful temper, which used to divert those friends I conversed withal, but it also destroys my health, in the room of which a heavy drowsiness has seized me and rendered me unfit even to perform those holy duties which alone have power to charm an immortal soul; for after all the experience I have gained I must conclude that, if there were but this world only to be thought of, the pleasures of piety are the only true joys to be valued—

Whence comes it then, oh my wretched heart, that against all prudent considerations, against the clearest reason in the world, thou hast chosen unquiet sorrows for thy portion rather than those joys which thou canst not but prefer before all others, even in this sad time that thou art insensible of them.

It is but too plain that I am thus afflicted because I sought for ease in the beginning of my sorrows (which have since increased) rather in company than in retirement, for now already do I begin to feel those mists disperse which have for so many weeks clouded my understanding.

Fool that I was to be so far deluded by my mortal enemy the devil (who is perpetually finding out new cheats to ruin me) as to think that I might, with innocence enough, spend much of my time in discoursing the causes of my sorrows with a friend whose compassion can no way cure, but may increase, my trouble. Fool that I was to pass delights, when I believed the heart I doted on and prized so much could never be mine, till at the length, with vain unnecessary conversations, I have again made those sorrows which are past become present to me; for I could not talk of what is past without a mixture of bitter things which I have tasted. I will no more thus employ my thoughts and entertain sorrow as a welcome guest, unless she is guided by reason, which without doubt she often is (though not at this time in my case).

'Tis God alone that can remove all unreasonable sorrows from my heart, by giving me a content of mind with an indifference for all those things that I have unquietly mourned for.

If we make our addresses to God himself as to our friend, if we do not only fear but also love him with our whole hearts, then shall we retire from all the world and breathe forth our sad sighs in his presence only. To him alone shall we relate our most dejected thoughts, and all our cares in our deepest distresses shall we cast upon him, who to be sure has both power and will to comfort us.

If we make our approaches to him as we ought, no doubt but God will give us wisdom to shed our tears upon such occasions only as that we may not repent them. He will take from us all destructive grief, and leave us only such a portion of sorrow as may serve to allay the vain gaieties of our sinful lives, such a sorrow as may make us sensible how full of miseries this world is, and how unreasonable we should be to leave it unwillingly if we deserve the glorious name of Christians, since all those who in naming the name of the Lord Jesus depart from iniquity are assured of eternal happiness in heaven such as has not yet entered into the heart of man to conceive, and since those glories which appeared even to God's own people behind a cloud are revealed to us in our blessed Savior. Oh my soul, faint no more under any tribulation or anguish here below, bear all thy crosses most willingly which are light (if weighed in just balance) in comparison of thy sins.

Fret and grieve thyself no longer at displeasing accidents in this life, for thou hast merited a fortune much more miserable than God has hitherto allotted thee. My time shall no more be spent foolishly in discontented complaints, but by the grace of God I will improve the talents he has given me, and since Christ Jesus is risen from the dead, I will set my affection upon things that are above.

Prayers

1. Oh my God, pity and pardon me, I beseech thee, and remove from my heart all remains of a tormenting passion which has so long destroyed the quiet of my nights and days.

2. Oh take from me, I humbly pray thee, that height of spirit which makes me impatiently remember how cruelly I have been deceived, and give unto me true charity to bewail his crimes who has deceived me. . . .

42

HEAVEN REALIZED*

Sarah Davy

My Further Meditations on Death

Death is a jailer who unlocks the prison doors of a gracious soul, and ushers it into the presence of his heavenly father, who is a gracious and a merciful God, there to be embraced in the arms of a loving Savior and to enjoy a fullness of eternal glory, by hearing the voice, "Come ye blessed of my father, receive the Kingdom prepared for you." But the wicked, Death arrests and brings bound before the tribunal seat of God, where he shall behold alone the frowns of an angry God before whose anger who is able to stand? There shall he see Divine Justice eternally satisfying on him, and never satisfied. Satan on one side and his own conscience on the other accusing of him, and Jesus Christ, who would have him his Savior, now his judge, pronouncing the dreadful sentence of that eternal damnation, "Go ye cursed of my father into everlasting destruction prepared for the Devil and his Angels. . . ." Then in Christ I shall be through grace more than a conqueror; then, Death, I will bid thee welcome, blessed messenger, when thou art sent to break my chains and unlock my fetters, locks, bolts, which keeps me from the presence of my Lord. . . . O Lord, my soul desires to do thy will. . . . I could desire to live if by my living I might glorify thy name, yet also wish to be dissolved to be with Christ, to be disrobed of sin, and clothed upon with his eternal righteousness, to be freed from imperfection, to be complete in Christ, in all perfection so to enjoy a free communion with my Lord in glory to all eternity. . . .

*London, 1670. Wing D444, Reel 1227, pp. 131-34, 144-46.

Sparks of Divine Love

Love is a heavenly fire fetched from above,
Irradiant beams shot from the God of Love,
Under those blessed shines my soul abide,
Let all thy paces there be multiplied,
In strength and beauty there to rest secure
Through love divine which ever shall endure.

* * *

Lord, shall a heaven-born soul forget to sing
Eternal praises to her Lord and King,
Shall she be one that seemeth not to know
The hand from which her mercies still do flow.
O quicken, Lord, thy servant, O that she,
May have her life all praises unto thee.

O 'tis a life of praises thou wouldst have,
Thy poor redeemed ones return to thee,
Give Lord what thou art pleased from them to crave
Of thy own store, what thou acceptest must be,
Then, my dear Lord, I shall not cease to sing
The Song of Canaan unto Israel's King.

Though in a land so far and strange I be,
As destitute of what I would enjoy,
Let me by faith my native country see,
And not forsake my treasure for a toy,
O blessed be thy name which still doth keep
My drowsy soul which else would ever sleep.

And lose its glorious comforts, sweet delights,
Which in the presence of its Lord is found,
Those heavenly glories and transcendent sights
In which to empty souls Grace doth abound.
O glorious Grace, let my soul still admire,
And warm itself at this blest Heavenly fire.

O shall I grieve that glorious spirit which
Is pleased to bow and condescend so low,
Thus to a poor unworthy sinful wretch.
How is it, Lord, that I thy Grace should know,
And that thou shouldst be pleased to look on me
So as redeem me from such misery.

43

CONFESSIONES AMANTIS*

Dame Gertrude More

The Forty-fifth Confession

O Lord my God, to Whom on all occasions I (most unworthy), with Thy leave, presume to speak and ask questions in my simple manner, open the eyes of my soul, that I may know and understand Thy will and law, and have grace to perform them to Thine honor. Thou, my God, Who art more mine than I am mine own, do not reject me speaking and writing to Thee. For do I desire or wish aught but Thee? Or what are all things to me without Thee? Surely, nothing; for Thou hast showed me through Thy sweet mercy and grace, without any desert of mine own, that all things are vanity but to love and please Thee. May I do this, I beseech Thee, with all the forces of my heart and soul, for truly there is no true peace nor comfort out of Thee. Let me, therefore, know myself and know Thee, that in all I may praise and please Thee. Amen.

The Forty-sixth Confession

Lord, it is read today [The Gospel of Thursday in Easter Week, John 20] of Thee that, St. Mary Magdalene approaching to kiss Thy feet, it was not permitted her by Thee. If it may please Thee, I will humbly ask of Thee the meaning of this, for I am somewhat amazed at it. For when she came to Thy feet laden with many grievous sins, Thou admittest her most easily; but when she had a long time been trained up in Thy happy school of perfection, and had accompanied Thee in Thy Passion, and

* *The Inner Life and the Writings of Dame Gertrude More,* ed. Dom Benedict Weld-Blundell, 2 vols. (London, 1910), pp. 118–20. (First published in Paris, 1658.)

mourned for Thee at Thy tomb, taking no rest till Thou, her Beloved, returned to her again, offering besides to take Thee away from all the world if they would but tell her where they had laid Thee, yet dost Thou now deny her to touch and kiss Thy blessed feet. What! shall we think she loves Thee less now than when she first desired to love Thee? Or shall we think that as her love grew more and more to Thee, Thine grew less and less to her? No; God forbid I should ever admit of such a thought. But, O my Lord, Thou, being Wisdom itself, intendest to bring this great and ardent lover to a love more spiritual than that with which she loved Thee when Thou conversedest with her before Thy Death and Passion. For it is Thy custom to receive sinners with great mildness, and when they grow more strong in love Thou seemest to treat them with more severity. And this Thou dost that they at first may hope in Thee and go forward in Thy love and service, and that, after being a little strengthened with light and comfort from Thee, Thou mayst try them in many ways, lest they should attribute that which they have done to their own powers, and that favor which they have received to their own labors and deserts. This Thou knowest we are very apt to do if Thou dost not, by permitting us to fall into temptation, show us our own frailty. But this blessed saint (whose intercession I most humbly implore for Thy sake, of Whom none now can deprive her) did not think that by forbidding her to touch Thy feet she received a wrong; for her humble soul thought itself unworthy of such a favor, when Thou didst put her in mind that she was to converse with Thee in a more spiritual manner than before. Neither did she reflect on the labor, pain, and grief she had sustained; for, as Thou knowest, love feeleth no labor nor complaineth of any burden. For only to have seen Thee alive again, was sufficient to make her forget all former afflictions. For her sake and for all their sakes that love Thee, be merciful to my sins, and bring me by true love to be united to Thee with them, where forever, without ceasing, I may praise Thee, my only Beloved. Amen.

PART EIGHT

WOMEN DEFENDING THEIR RIGHT TO PREACH

Introduction

"Directed unto Christ by the declaration or preaching of a woman . . ."

Although women frequently outnumbered men in the church in the sixteenth and seventeenth centuries, women were barred from preaching and from holding office in the church. Two passages from the Epistles of St. Paul were adduced to support the argument that women should be excluded from preaching and from governance:

> Let your women keep silence in the churches: for it is not permitted unto them to speak; but they are commanded to be under obedience, as also saith the law. And if they will learn anything let them ask their husbands at home: for it is a shame for women to speak in the church. (1 Corinthians 14:34–35)

> Let the woman learn in silence with all subjection. But I suffer not a woman to teach, nor to usurp authority over the man, but to be in silence. (1 Timothy 2:1–12)

Under the assumption that the prohibition of St. Paul to the Corinthians and to Timothy had universal application and was binding for the English church of the sixteenth and seventeenth centuries, the ruling males in the church adopted these two scriptural passages for the contemporary church. Refusing to acknowledge that the prohibition was probably applicable only to the specific historical situations that St. Paul faced in those particular churches, males in ecclesiastical authority appropriated these passages as scriptural guards for protecting male rights to preach and govern. Roman Catholics, Anglicans, and members of churches in the Reformed tradition did emphasize the ancillary role of females in the church and provided opportunities for service, but they insisted that women "keep silence" and avoid any semblance of authority over males.

To bolster the Pauline injunction, the church searched the scriptures

353

for evidence to show that the Pauline prohibition was not arbitrary or temporary but had its roots in the metaphysics of creation. They chose the second creation account found in Genesis 2:22 ("And the rib, which the Lord God had taken from man, made he a woman, and brought her unto the man") to establish the creational order of precedence—male before female, male over female. This passage was regarded as definitive: the male was created first and hence was superior to the female; the female was created second, out of the body of the male, and hence was inferior to the male. The ancillary but silent position of the female in the church was supported first by the Pauline prohibition and second and perhaps more fundamentally, by the inferior metaphysical position of the female.

The first account of the creation of human beings found in Genesis 1:27 ("So God created man in his own image, in the image of God created he him; male and female created he them") was not disregarded but was interpreted as a general statement whose elaboration and definition occurred in Genesis 2. The hermeneutic principles applied in interpreting the two Genesis accounts may have sprung from the psychological need of males to dominate and subdue females in the church, although the need remained unacknowledged and subversive.

The unadmitted ambiguity of the Genesis 1 and 2 accounts of the creation of the two sexes was further reinforced by the constant reference by the church to the fall of Eve and her seduction of Adam in Genesis 3. The sixteenth and seventeenth centuries joined the long ecclesiastical tradition that assigned blame for the fall of the human race (and all subsequent evil) to Eve and to all women who came after her. "Fallen," seductive woman, males argued, could not be trusted with authority in church, home, or state; she, like Eve, would cause the male to fall. The literature of the day, including even horticultural manuals, frequently contains derogatory references to "our Grandmother Eve."

With the rise of the sects and Independent congregations, however, women began to preach and to share in the authority and governance of the church. Women challenged the interpretations of the Pauline prohibition by suggesting that Paul was writing to congregations troubled with specific problems and that the specificity of these problems precluded universal applications. In addition, although women in the sects recognized the power of the Pauline prohibition, they insisted that males look at the Pauline Epistles again and that they not only reassess the prohibition but reread Galatians 3:28: "There is neither Jew nor Greek, there is neither bond nor free, there is neither male nor female: for ye are all one in Christ Jesus." Women went further and suggested that when St. Paul urged "every woman that prayeth or prophesieth" (1 Corinthians 11:5) to cover her head, he was speaking to women who actually prayed and preached in public meetings. The formal Pauline ban, then, had to be contextualized.

Women argued further that the Holy Spirit at Pentecost had made no gender distinctions—the Spirit's power had fallen on women as well as on men; women too were equipped with "the sword of the spirit" as their spiritual weapon and were expected by God to participate fully and unrestrictedly in the life of the church.

As for the fall of Eve and her temptation of Adam, women in the sects refused to be identified with the "evil women" whose lineage was traced to Eve in the misogynistic literature. Instead, women emphasized the fact that the Genesis 3:15 prophecy of Eve's redemptive act and its triumph over evil was the most significant prophecy in the history of human life: the seed of the woman, God said in Paradise to Adam and Eve after the fall, would be the seed that would redeem the whole human race. This prophecy, women pointed out, was fulfilled when a woman gave birth, without the "seed" of a man, to the Redeemer of the world.

It is difficult to obtain accurate figures on the number of women who were members of the sects, since historical records focus on male rather than female participation. Richard L. Greaves's researches lead him to conclude:

> Numerically, women were significant in strengthening the Nonconformist churches, especially those of a Separatist persuasion. Edmund Grindal, Bishop of London, asserted in 1568 that most Separatists in one London church were females from the lower social orders, an observation that is indeed true with respect to some other congregations. Of the thirty-two members of John Smyth's Baptist church who initially applied for admission to the Waterlander Mennonites in the Netherlands, seventeen were women. The signatories of "A Short Confession of Fayth" prepared by those who refused to join the Mennonites in 1610 included twenty-four women and seventeen men. In 1645 the Independent church in Norwich, Norfolk, had eighty-three women but only thirty-one men; and of the twenty-eight Separatists living in Great Yarmouth, Norfolk, in 1630, twenty or twenty-one were women. . . .
>
> In some cases women actually helped found new churches. Women as well as men were present for the organizational meeting which

established Francis Johnson's Separatist church at Southwark in September 1592. Accompanied by four men, Mrs. Dorothy Hazzard seceded from her husband's parish church in 1640 to establish the Separatist congregation later known as Broadmead Bristol. (76, 78)

According to Claire Cross, the Broadmead Bristol church established by Dorothy Hazzard "grew quickly to a membership of one hundred and sixty" (197). Other women who founded churches were Katherine Chidley, who wrote *The Justification of the Independent Churches of Christ* (1641), and the eight women who, assisted by four men, began the church at Bedford, which later became the church of John Bunyan.

In some instances female worshipers separated themselves from male worshipers and held their own meetings attended by women only. In 1645 the Tuesday women's meetings of Thomas Lamb's General Baptist congregation, for example, attracted as many as 1,000 women. Quaker women organized women's meetings, autonomous gatherings which were free from male attendance, supervision, and intervention. Even the finances, including management of property and legacies, were controlled by females. The Quaker movement itself attracted so many people that by 1690 it was estimated there were 60,000 Quakers in England. If more than half were women, the full participation of 30,000 women in Quaker meetings is not unlikely.

Very few women preachers left written sermons or defenses of the right of women to preach and participate in congregational life. Of those who preached and wrote, Elizabeth Bathurst was prominent. She was imprisoned in the Marshalsea Prison in Southwark for her activities as a preacher. She traveled to Bristol in a time of persecution; she preached at Windsor, Reading, Newberry, Marlborough, Oxford, and other places. In a book published posthumously in 1691, titled *Truth Vindicated,* she gives a clear defense of the rights of women in the church. Included in *Truth Vindicated* is a section called "The Sayings of Women," whose purpose is "to show how the Lord poured out his Spirit upon the whole House of Israel; not only on the male, but also on the female" (title page). Elizabeth Bathurst (201–24 passim) cites numerous examples of women in the church of both the Old and New Testaments: Sarah, Rebecca, Rachel and Leah, Miriam, Deborah, Jephtha's daughter, Manoah's wife, Naomi, Ruth, Hannah, women who danced and sang for Saul and David's victory, Abigail, women speaking to David (2 Samuel 14:4), wise woman to Joab, poor widow to Elijah, Shunamite woman, maid to Naaman, Huldah (2 Kings 22:12ff.), Esther, Zeresh (Haman's wife), Solomon's mother, woman of Canaan (Matthew 15:22), woman with alabaster, Pilate's wife, woman that was twelve years diseased, Virgin Mary, Elizabeth, Anna, Mary and Martha, Mary Magdalene, Joanna, Mary the mother of James, woman at the well, women at the tomb, Lydia, woman who cried after Paul (Acts 16:17–18), Dorcas, Priscilla, Philip's four daughters, Phoebe, John to the elect Lady (Epistles). She concludes: "Male and female are made one in Christ Jesus. . . . Women receive an office in the truth as well as men. . . . They have a stewardship to their Lord" (225). In a postscript she adds that although woman was the first to transgress, woman gave birth to the Redeemer (226).

In 1679 Isabel Yeamans's *An Invitation of Love* was published for "all who hunger and thirst after righteousness." Allying the persecutors of women preachers with "Haman, an informer against Mordecai," she traces their lineage to Haman: "This corrupt seed and birth of the flesh, whose offspring as well as himself has been persecuting the members of the true church and seed of God for these many hundred years . . . so that our persecutors, who have been rending and tearing (like dogs and bears) and persecuting people for their Nonconformity and different persuasions about religion, may see their offspring, and who was their captain and general in this wicked work" (40). She allies herself and women preachers with the woman of Samaria who, after talking with Christ, preached to the people of her city: "Now these men were directed unto Christ by the declaration or preaching of a woman, who was not despised by them because of her sex" (33).

Gaining in strength as the Spirit of God inspired them, women tackled the academic world and preached at Oxford and Cambridge. In 1653 Mary Fisher and Elizabeth Williams preached at the gate of Sidney College, Cambridge. The mayor of Cambridge ordered them to be scourged in public at Market Cross. In 1654 two young women, Elizabeth Fletcher and Elizabeth Leavens, preached at Oxford. The response of Oxford to the preaching of two females is recorded in *First Publishers of Truth*: ". . . they suffered by the black tribe of scholars—for they dragged them first through a dirty pool, afterwards had them to a pump, and holding their mouths to the pump, endeavored to pump water thereinto with other shameful abuses; after threw the said Elizabeth Fletcher down upon a gravestone . . . and bruised her so sore that she never recovered it" (Penney, 258–59).

In *A Testimony Concerning the Life and Death of Jane Whitehead* (1676), Theophila Townsend published defenses of the preaching career of Jane Waugh Whitehead. John and Jane Anderdon described her as being "called to the work and service of the Lord. We never found her forward to speak in Meetings, or to seek the preeminence, but to clear her conscience before the Lord, which was well" (19). Jane and Jasper Butt testified: "I have known her for near twenty years past, about the time when Truth first broke forth in the southern parts of this nation; she was one on whom God fulfilled his promise . . . he having committed a dispensation of the everlasting Gospel to her" (20).

Confronted by female preachers and the arguments adduced by females, males in the mainstream churches counterattacked. Persecution and imprisonment were not enough; women preachers were also vilified in print. Males turned to derision of the female as interpreter of the scriptures, as preacher, and as governor, instead of expanding, clarifying, or reevaluating their own arguments for the exclusion of women from offices in the church. In 1641 a tract titled *Discovery of Six Women Preachers* was published, which attacked women preachers in Middlesex, Kent, Cambridge, and Salisbury. Women preachers were described as "ambitious . . . they would have superiority" (5). Ridiculed as "tub preachers," women were maligned in a rash of pamphlets that were both scurrilous and savage. A few representative titles indicate the tone of the male argument: *Lucifer's Lackey: Or, The Devils New Creation* (1641); *Hopes Deferred and Dashed* (1645); *The Schismatick Sifted: Or, A Picture of Independents Freshly and Fairly Washt over Again* (1646); *Tub Preachers Overturned: Or, Independency to be Abandoned and Abhorred* (1647); *Gangraena* (1646). One of the male attackers, John Vicars, described women preachers as "bold, impudent housewives, without all womanly modesty, to take upon themselves (in natural volubility of their tongues, and quick wits, or strong memories only) to prate (not preach or prophesy) after a narrative or discoursing manner, an hour or more, and that most directly contrary to the Apostle's inhibition (*Schismatick Sifted,* 34).

In addition to the attacks in the pamphlet literature, an appeal was made to Parliament to halt the practice of women preaching. In 1646 the House of Commons voted 105 to 57 that only officially ordained males would be allowed to preach (*Journals of the House of Commons,* vols. 22–23, 34). The decision was based on the fear that women preaching and in authority would introduce anarchy into civil and religious life. This law, however, could not prevent the rise of women preachers in the sects, where in most cases neither male nor female preacher was or dained. Lay preachers of both sexes exhorted and preached. (For documents by women persecuted for their religious activities, see part 2.)

Margaret Fell's pamphlet *Womens Speaking Justified,* the first document in this section, was not the first defense by a woman of a woman's right to preach. In 1655 Priscilla Cotton and Mary Cole had coauthored a pamphlet titled *To the Priests and People of England.* By invoking a new hermeneutic, these two women devastated the opposition to women preachers. They argued that the word *woman* in the scriptures was not to be taken literally as a gender-specific word but to be interpreted metaphorically as a non-gender-specific condition: Woman = weakness. All the weak—including males—were denied the right to preach and govern. The *strong* were those who operated on a spiritual level with inspiration from God; the *weak* were those who operated on a human level apart from divine inspiration. This was obviously a radical stance: it challenged even ordained male ministers in the established church whom the authors regarded as "weak."

Margaret Fell's "justification" ten years later probably benefited from the work of her female predecessors. Hers was a lucid and more measured rebuttal of the standard arguments. *Womens Speaking Justified* was written in prison, where Margaret Fell was confined for several years because she held Quaker meetings in her home, refused to take an oath, and protested the payment of tithes.

Although Margaret Fell herself never preached, she presented a strong biblically based case for the right of females to preach. The contours of her argument are as follows:

1. The seed of the woman will crush the seed of the serpent (Satan = evil).

2. The church of Christ is addressed in both Testaments as a woman; the seed of the woman is Christ, who is the head of the church.

3. Christ preached to women and freely associated with them.

4. Christ showed himself at his resurrection first to women, who went out and proclaimed that he had risen.

5. The apostle Paul's injunction that women refrain from preaching is still under the burden of the Law; women in Christ are free from the Law and live under grace.

6. The spirit of God was poured out at Pentecost on women, who were among the 5,000 assembled; they, as well men, were commissioned to preach the Gospel.

7. In Christ there is neither male nor female.
8. There are scriptural precedents for female preaching.

Margaret Fell came to Quakerism by the preaching of George Fox (whom she later married). His preaching so inspired her and her daughters that they made lasting contributions to the Quaker movement. Her daughter Sarah Fell became a spellbinding preacher (who learned Hebrew to refute her male opponents); her daughter Isabel Fell Yeamans was the author of two books, *A Lively Testimony* (1676) and *An Invitation of Love* (1679).

Mary Waite's epistles were written as sermons to be read aloud in Quaker meetings. The "Epistle from the Women's Yearly Meeting," a collaborative effort of eight women, deals with the governance and conduct of the meetings. Beginning with an affirmation of the presence of God's spirit in women's meetings, Mary Waite and her collaborators praise God for releasing members from prison and for establishing harmony in the body of Christ. They warn against the "separating and quarreling spirit which leads unto strife," and they pray for the preservation of the "rest and safety" of the flock. They speak to young women about appropriate dress and conduct. And finally they urge women to keep records (on a monthly as well as on a yearly basis) of the blessings that God had showered upon them.

Mary Waite's "Warning" is a conversion narrative used as a model for Quakers. Describing her own spiritual barrenness and her physical illness, she tells them that God appeared to her and healed her, both spiritually and physically. Then in a vision God showed her the sins of the day and commanded her to preach against the "fashions, customs and friendships of this world." She urges Friends to love God and enjoy his nourishments, to be faithful in their witness to the faith, and to be zealous for the Lord and his truth. Addressing parents, young people, masters and mistresses, children, servants, and apprentices, she enjoins them to live godly lives.

The writing of this "Warning" sermon enabled Mary Waite to discharge a burden on her conscience. She signs the sermon with a salute, reminiscent of St. Paul's letters, "in the endless unchangeable love of God."

By 1680 women in the Quaker movement were noticing changes in the practices and emphases of their sect. Social, political, and religious change in England in the latter part of the seventeenth century affected

Quaker forms of worship and piety. External opposition, including imprisonment, had served to strengthen the movement; internal dissension could only weaken the movement and erode its values, commitment, and beliefs. Even the continuation of the women's meetings was threatened.

Anne Whitehead and Mary Elson, who praise the Lord for blessing the women's meetings for twenty-three or twenty-four years, felt the need to write an epistle-sermon that pleaded for restoration of unity in the church. When the survival of a pattern of worship is at stake, bitterness, rancor, and discord can make inroads into the fellowship of believers.

Whitehead and Elson defend the women's meetings by recalling the origin of these meetings. George Fox, the founder of the Quakers, believed it essential to establish women's meetings for conducting the works of benevolence in the community. The women's meetings supervised charitable endeavors, dispensed help and care to those in need, and carried on a vital mission of the church.

Whitehead and Elson express optimism for the future, observing that the young women are "heirs of the grace of God with us." The young "sisters" recognize the need to carry on the social programs established by women so early in the history of Quakerism.

Suggested Readings

Bathurst, Elizabeth. *Truth vindicated.* London, 1691.

Cotton, Priscilla, and Mary Cole. *To the Priests and People of England.* London, 1655.

Cross, Claire. " 'He-goats before the Flocks.' " *Studies in Church History* 8 (1972): 195–202.

Discovery of Six Women Preachers. London, 1641.

Greaves, Richard L. "Foundation Builders: The Role of Women in Early English Nonconformity." In *Triumph over Silence,* ed. Richard L. Greaves. Westport, Conn.: Greenwood Press, 1985.

Hobby, Elaine. *Virtue of Necessity.* Ann Arbor: University of Michigan Press, 1989.

Huber, Elaine C. " 'A Woman Must Not Speak': Quaker Women in the English Left Wing." In *Women of Spirit,* ed. Rosemary Ruether and Eleanor McLaughlin. New York: Simon and Schuster, 1979.

Ludlow, Dorothy P. "Shaking Patriarchy's Foundations: Sectarian

Women in England, 1641–1700." In *Triumph over Silence,* ed. Richard L. Greaves. Westport, Conn.: Greenwood Press, 1985.

Mack, Phyllis. "Women as Prophets during the English Civil War." *Feminist Studies* 8 (Spring 1982): 19–45.

Morgan, Ethyn Williams. "Women Preachers in the Civil War," *Journal of Modern History* (1929): 561–569.

Peuney, Norman, ed. *First Publishers of Truth.* London: Headley Brothers, 1907.

Ross, Isabel. *Margaret Fell Mother of Quakerism.* London: Longmans, Green, 1949.

Ruether, Rosemary, and Eleanor McLaughlin. *Women of Spirit.* New York: Simon and Schuster, 1979.

Schofield, Mary Anne. " 'Women's Speaking Justified': The Feminine Quaker Voice, 1662–1797." *Tulsa Studies in Women's Literature* 6 (Spring 1987): 61–77.

Thomas, Keith. "Women and the Civil War Sects." *Past and Present* 13 (April 1958): 42–62.

Townsend, Theophila. *A Testimony Concerning the Life and Death of Jane Whitehead.* London, 1676.

Vicars, John. *Schismatick Sifted.* London, 1646.

Yeamans, Isabel. *An Invitation of Love.* London, 1679.

———. *A Lively Testimony.* London, 1676.

44

WOMENS SPEAKING JUSTIFIED, PROVED
AND ALLOWED OF BY THE SCRIPTURES*

Margaret Fell

Whereas it hath been an objection in the minds of many, and several times hath been objected by the clergy, or ministers, and others, against women's speaking in the church; and so consequently may be taken, that they are condemned for meddling in the things of God, the ground of which objection is taken from the Apostle's words, which he wrote in his first Epistle to the Corinthians, chap. 14, vers. 34, 35. And also what he wrote to Timothy in the first Epistle, chap. 2, vers. 11, 12. But how far they wrong the Apostle's intentions in these scriptures, we shall show clearly when we come to them in their course and order. But first let me lay down how God himself hath manifested his will and mind concerning women, and unto women.

And first, when God created man in his own image, in the image of God created he them, male and female, and God blessed them, and God said unto them, "Be fruitful, and multiply." And God said, "Behold, I have given you of every herb," etc. (Gen. 1). Here God joins them together in his own image and makes no such distinctions and differences as men do; for though they be weak, he is strong; and as he said to the Apostle, his grace is sufficient, and his strength is made manifest in weakness (2 Cor. 12:9). And such hath the Lord chosen, even the weak things of the world to confound the things which are mighty; and things which are despised hath God chosen, to bring to naught things that are (1 Cor. 1). And God hath put no such difference between the male and female as men would make.

It is true, the serpent that was more subtle than any other beast of the

*London, 1666. Wing F642, Reel 1010, pp. 3-10, 12-19.

VVomens Speaking

Justified, Proved and Allowed of by the

SCRIPTURES,

All such as speak by the Spirit and Power of the

LORD IESUS,

And how WOMEN were the first that preached
the Tidings of the Resurrection of JESuS,
and were sent by CHRIST·S Own
Command, before He ascended
to the Father, *John*
20. 17.

---

*And it shall come to pass, in the last dayes, saith the Lord, I
will pour out of my Spirit upon all Flesh; your Sons and Daughters shall Prophesie,* Acts 2. 27. Joel 2. 28.

*It is written in the Prophets, They shall be all taught of God,
saith Christ,* John 6. 45.

*And all thy Children shall be taught of the Lord, and great shall
be the Peace of thy Children,* Isa. 54. 13.

*And they shall teach no more every man his Neighbour, and every
man his Brother, saying, Know the Lord; for they shall all
know me, from the least to the greatest of them, saith the Lord.*
J:r. 31. 34.

London, Printed in the Year, 1667.

Figure 13. Title page from *Womens Speaking Justified*, by Margaret Fell.

field came unto the woman with his temptations, and with a lie, his subtilty discerning her to be more inclinable to hearken to him, when he said, "If ye eat, your eyes shall be opened." And the woman saw that the fruit was good to make one wise; there the temptation got into her, and she did eat, and gave to her husband, and he did eat also, and so they were both tempted into the transgression and disobedience; and therefore God said unto Adam, when that he hid himself when he heard his voice, "Hast thou eaten of the tree which I commanded thee that thou shouldest not eat?" And Adam said, "The woman which thou gavest me, she gave me of the tree, and I did eat." And the Lord said unto the woman, "What is this that thou hast done?" And the woman said, "The serpent beguiled me, and I did eat." Here the woman spoke the truth unto the Lord. See what the Lord said, verse 15, after he had pronounced sentence on the serpent: "I will put enmity between thee and the woman, and between thy seed and her seed; it shall bruise thy head, and thou shalt bruise his heel" (Gen. 3).

Let this Word of the Lord, which was from the beginning, stop the mouths of all that oppose women's speaking in the power of the Lord; for he hath put enmity between the woman and the serpent; and if the seed of the woman speak not, the seed of the serpent speaks, for God hath put enmity between the two seeds, and it is manifest, that those that speak against the woman and her seeds speaking, speak out of the enmity of the old serpent's seeds; and God hath fulfilled his word and his promise, "When the fullness of time was come, he hath sent forth his Son, made of a woman, made under the law, that we might receive the adoption of sons" (Gal. 4:4, 5).

Moreover, the Lord is pleased, when he mentions his church, to call her by the name of woman, by his prophets, saying, "I have called thee as a woman forsaken, and grieved in spirit, and as a wife of youth" (Isaiah 54). Again, "How long wilt thou go about, thou backsliding daughter? For the Lord hath created a new thing in the earth, a woman shall compass a man" (Jer. 31:22). And David, when he was speaking of Christ and his church, said, "The king's daughter is all glorious within, her clothing is of wrought gold; she shall be brought unto the king; with gladness and rejoicing shall they be brought; they shall enter into the king's palace" (Psalm 45). And also King Solomon in his Song, where it speaks of Christ and his church, where she is complaining and calling for Christ, says, "If thou knowest not, O thou fairest among women, go thy way by the footsteps of the flock" (Cant. [Song of Sol.] 1:8; 5:9). And

John, when he saw the wonder that was in heaven, he saw "a woman clothed with the sun, and the moon under her feet, and upon her head a crown of twelve stars; and there appeared another wonder in heaven, a great red dragon stood ready to devour her child." Here the enmity appears that God put between the woman and the dragon (Rev. 12).

Thus much may prove that the church of Christ is a woman, and those that speak against the woman's speaking, speak against the church of Christ, and the Seed of the woman, which Seed is Christ; that is to say, those that speak against the power of the Lord and the spirit of the Lord speaking in a woman, simply by reason of her sex, or because she is a woman, not regarding the Seed, and Spirit, and Power that speaks in her, such speak against Christ and his church and are of the seed of the serpent, wherein lodgeth the enmity. And as God the Father made no such difference in the first creation, nor never since between the male and the female, but always out of his mercy and loving-kindness had regard unto the weak, so also, his Son, Christ Jesus, confirms the same thing. When the Pharisees came to him and asked him if it were lawful for a man to put away his wife, he answered and said unto them, "Have you not read, that he that made them in the beginning made them male and female," and said, "For this cause shall a man leave father and mother and shall cleave unto his wife, and they twain shall be one flesh, wherefore they are no more twain but one flesh. What therefore God hath joined together, let no man put asunder" (Matt. 19).

Again, Christ Jesus, when he came to the city of Samaria, where Jacob's well was, where the woman of Samaria was, you may read in John 4 how he was pleased to preach the everlasting gospel to her; and when the woman said unto him, "I know that when the Messiah cometh (which is called Christ) when he cometh, he will tell us all things," Jesus saith unto her, "I that speak unto thee am he." This is more than ever he said in plain words to man or woman (that we read of) before he suffered. Also, he said unto Martha, when she said she knew that her brother should rise again in the last day, "I am the Resurrection and the Life; he that believeth in me, though he were dead, yet shall he live; and whosoever liveth and believeth shall never die. Believest thou this?" She answered, "Yea, Lord, I believe thou art the Christ, the Son of God." Here she manifested her true and saving faith which few at that day believed so on him (John 11:25, 26).

Also that woman that came unto Jesus with an alabaster box of very precious ointment and poured it on his head as he sat at meat; it's manifested that this woman knew more of the secret power and wisdom of God than his disciples did, who were filled with indignation against her. And therefore Jesus said, "Why do you trouble the woman? for she hath wrought a good work upon me. Verily, I say unto you, 'Wheresoever this Gospel shall be preached in the whole world, there shall also this that this woman hath done be told for a memorial of her'" (Matt. 26; Mark 14:3). Luke saith further, "She was a sinner," and that "she stood at his feet behind him weeping, and began to wash his feet with her tears and did wipe them with the hair of her head, and kissed his feet and anointed them with ointment." And when Jesus saw the heart of the Pharisee that had bidden him to his house, he took occasion to speak unto Simon, as you may read in Luke 7, and he turned to the woman and said, "Simon, seest thou this woman? Thou gavest me no water for my feet, but she hath washed my feet with tears, and wiped them with the hair of her head. Thou gavest me no kiss, but this woman, since I came in, hath not ceased to kiss my feet. My head with oil thou didst not anoint, but the woman hath anointed my feet with ointment. Wherefore I say unto thee, her sins, which are many, are forgiven her, for she hath loved much" (Luke 7:37 to the end).

Also, there were many women which followed Jesus from Galilee, ministering unto him, and stood afar off when he was crucified (Matt. 27:55; Mark 15). Yes, even the women of Jerusalem wept for him insomuch that he said unto them, "Weep not for me, ye Daughters of Jerusalem, but weep for yourselves and for your children" (Luke 23:28).

"And certain women which had been healed of evil spirits and infirmities, Mary Magdalene and Joanna the wife of Chuza, Herod's steward's wife, and many others which ministered unto him of their substance" (Luke 8:2, 3).

Thus we see that Jesus owned the love and grace that appeared [in] women, and did not despise it, and by what is recorded in the Scriptures, he received as much love, kindness, compassion, and [tender] dealing towards him from women as he did from any others, both [in] his lifetime and also after they had exercised their cruelty upon him, for Mary Magdalene, and Mary the mother of James beheld where he was laid: "And when the Sabbath was past, Mary Magdalene, and Mary the Mother of James and Salome, had brought sweet spices that they might anoint him. And very early in the morning, the first day of the week, they came unto the sepulcher at the rising of the sun. And they said among themselves, 'Who shall roll us away the stone from the door of the sepulcher?' And when they looked, the stone was rolled away for it was very great" (Mark 16:1–4; Luke 24:1, 2). "And they went down into the sepulcher," and as Matthew said, "The angel rolled away the stone, and said unto the women, 'Fear not, I know whom ye seek, Jesus which was crucified; he is not here, he is risen'" (Matt. 28). Now Luke said thus, "That there stood two men by them in shining apparel, and as they were perplexed and afraid, the men said unto them, 'He is not here; remember how he said unto you when he was in Galilee, that the Son of Man must be delivered into the hands of sinful men, and be crucified, and the third day rise again,' and they remembered his words, and returned from the sepulcher, and told all these things to the eleven, and to all the rest."

It was Mary Magdalene and Joanna, and Mary the mother of James, and the other women that were with them which told these things to the apostles, "And their words seemed unto them as idle tales, and they believed them not." Mark this, you despisers of the weakness of women, and look upon yourselves to be so wise; but Christ Jesus does not so, for he makes use of the weak. For when he met the women after he was risen, he said unto them, "All Hail," and they came and held him by the feet, and worshiped him. Then Jesus said unto them, "Be not afraid, go tell my brethren that they go into Galilee, and there they shall find me" (Matt. 28:10; Mark 16:9). And John said, when Mary was weeping at the sepulcher, that Jesus said unto her, "'Woman, why weepest thou? What seekest thou?' And when she supposed him to be the gardener, Jesus said unto her, 'Mary.' She turned herself and said unto him, 'Rabboni,' which is to say 'Master.' Jesus said unto her, 'Touch me not, for I am not yet ascended to my Father, but go to my brethren, and say unto them I ascend unto my Father, and your Father, and to my God, and your God'" (John 20:16, 17).

Mark this, you that despise and oppose the message of the Lord God that he sends by women, what had become of the redemption of the whole body of mankind, if they had not believed the message that the Lord Jesus sent by these women, of and concerning his resurrection? And if these women had not thus, out of their tenderness and bowels of love, who had received mercy, and grace, and forgiveness of sins, and virtue, and healing from him, which many men also had received the like, if their hearts had not been so united and knit into him in love, that they could not depart as the men did, but sat watching, and waiting, and weeping about the sepulcher until the time of his resurrection, and so were ready to carry his message as is manifested, else how should his disciples have known, who were not there?

Oh! blessed and glorified be the glorious Lord, for this may all the whole body of mankind say, though the wisdom of men, that never knew God, is always ready to except against the weak; but the weakness of God is stronger than men, and the foolishness of God is wiser than men.

And in Acts 18 you may read how Aquila and Priscilla took unto them Apollos and expounded unto him the way of God more perfectly; who was an eloquent man, and mighty in scriptures. Yet we do not read that he despised what Priscilla said, because she was a woman, as many now do.

And now to the Apostle's words, which is the ground of the great objection against women's speaking. And first, 1 Cor. 14, let the reader seriously read that chapter and see the end and drift of the Apostle in speaking these words, for the Apostle is there exhorting the Corinthians unto charity, and to desire spiritual gifts, and not to speak in an unknown tongue, and not to be children in understanding, but to be children in malice, but in understanding to be men; and that the spirits of the prophets should be subject to the prophets, for God is not the author of confusion, but of peace. And then he saith, "Let your women keep silence in the Church, etc."

Where it doth plainly appear that the women, as well as others that were among them, were in confusion, for he said, "How is it brethren, when ye come together, every one of you hath a Psalm, hath a doctrine, hath a tongue, hath a revelation, hath an interpretation? Let all things be done to edifying." Here was no edifying, but all was in confusion speaking together. Therefore he said, "If any man speak in an unknown tongue let it be by two, or at most by three, and that by course, and let one interpret, but if there be no interpreter, let him keep silence in the church." Here the man is commanded to keep silence as well as the woman, when they are in confusion and out of order.

But the Apostle said further, "They are commanded to be in obedience," as also saith the Law, and "if they will learn anything, let them ask their husbands at home, for it is a shame for a woman to speak in the church."

Here the Apostle clearly manifests his intent, for he speaks of women that were under the Law, and in that transgression as Eve was, and such as were to learn, and not to speak publicly, but they must first ask their husbands at home, and it was a shame for such to speak in the church. And it appears, clearly, that such women were speaking among the Corinthians, by the Apostle's exhorting them from malice and strife, and confusion, and he preached the Law unto them, and he said, in the Law it is written, "With men of other tongues, and other lips, will I speak unto this people" (verse 21).

And what is all this to women's speaking, that have the everlasting gospel to preach, and upon whom the promise of the Lord is fulfilled, and his spirit poured upon them according to his word? (Acts 2:16–18). And if the Apostle would have stopped such as had the spirit of the Lord poured upon them, why did he say just before, "If anything be revealed to another that sitteth by, let the first hold his peace and you may all prophesy one by one"? Here he did not say that such women should not prophesy as had the revelation and spirit of God poured upon them, but their women that were under the Law, and in the transgression, and were in strife, confusion and malice in their speaking, for if he had stopped women's praying or prophesying, why doth he say, "Every man praying or prophesying having his head covered dishonoreth his head, but every woman that prayeth or prophesieth with her head uncovered dishonoreth her head? Judge in yourselves, is it comely that a woman pray or prophesy uncovered? For the woman is not without the man, neither is the man without the woman, in the Lord" (1 Cor. 11:3, 4, 13)?

Also that other scripture in 1 Tim. 2 where he is exhorting that prayer and supplication be made everywhere, lifting up holy hands without wrath and doubting, he said in the like manner also that "Women must adorn themselves in modest apparel, with shamefastness and sobriety, not with broidered hair, or gold, or pearl, or costly array." He saith, "Let women learn in silence with all subjection, but I suffer not a woman to teach, nor to usurp authority over the man, but to be in silence; for Adam was first formed, then Eve, and Adam was not deceived, but the woman being deceived was in the transgression."

Here the Apostle speaks particularly to a woman in relation to her husband, to be in subjection to him, and not to teach, nor usurp authority over him, and therefore he mentions Adam and Eve. But let it be strained to the utmost, as the opposers of women's speaking would have it, that is, that they should not preach nor speak in the church, of which there is nothing here. Yet the Apostle is speaking to such as he is teaching to wear their apparel, what to wear and what not to wear, such as were not come to wear modest apparel, and such as were not to come to shamefastness and sobriety, but he was exhorting them from broidered hair, gold, and pearls, and costly array; and such are not to usurp authority over the man but to learn in silence with all subjection, as it becomes women professing godliness with good works.

And what is all this to such as have the power and the spirit of the Lord Jesus poured upon them, and have the message of the Lord Jesus given unto them? Must not they speak the word of the Lord because of these undecent and unreverent women that the Apostle speaks of, and to, in these two scriptures? And how are the men of the generation blinded that bring these scriptures, and pervert the Apostle's words, and corrupt his intent in speaking of them, and by these scriptures endeavor to stop the message and word of the Lord God in women, by condemning and despising of them? If the Apostle would have had women's speaking stopped and did not allow of them, why did he entreat his true yokefellow to help those women who labored with him in the gospel (Phil. 4:3)? And why did the apostles join together in prayer and supplication with the women, and Mary the mother of Jesus, and with his brethren (Acts 1:14) if they had not allowed, and had union and fellowship with the spirit of God, wherever it was revealed in women as well as others? But all this opposing and gainsaying of women's speaking hath risen out of the bottomless pit, and spirit of darkness that hath spoken for these many hundred years together in this night of apostasy, since the revelations have ceased and been bid, and so that spirit hath limited and bound all up within its bond and compass, and so would suffer none to speak but such as that spirit of darkness approved of, man or woman. . . .

And so let this serve to stop that opposing spirit that would limit the power and the spirit of the Lord Jesus, whose spirit is poured upon all flesh, both sons and daughters, now in his resurrection, and since that the Lord God in the creation, when he made man in his own image, he made them *male* and *female;* and since that Christ Jesus, as the Apostle said, was made of a woman, and the power of the Highest overshadowed her, and the Holy Ghost came upon her, and the holy thing that was born of her was called "the Son of God," and when he was upon the earth, he manifested his *love,* and his *will,* and his *mind,* both to the woman of Samaria, and Martha, and Mary her sister, and several others, as has been shown; and after his resurrection also manifested himself unto them first of all, even before he ascended unto his Father. "Now when Jesus was risen, the first day of the week, he appeared first unto Mary Magdalene" (Mark 16:9). And thus the Lord Jesus has manifested himself and his power, without respect of persons; and so let all mouths be stopped that would limit him, whose power and spirit is infinite, that is pouring it upon all flesh.

And thus much in answer to these two scriptures, which have been such a stumbling block, that the ministers of darkness have made such a mountain of; but the Lord is removing all this, and taking it out of the way.

M. F.

A further addition in answer to the objection concerning women keeping silent in the church, for it is not permitted for them to speak but to be under obedience, as also says the Law, "If they will learn anything, let them ask their husbands at home, for it is a shame for a woman to speak in the church." Now this as Paul writes in 1. Cor. 14:34 is one with that of 1 Tim. 2:11, "Let women learn in silence with all subjection."

To which I say, if you tie this to all outward women, then there were many women that were widows which had no husbands to learn of, and many were virgins which had no husbands; and Philip had four daughters that were prophets; such would be despised, which the Apostle did not forbid. And if it were to all women, that no woman might speak, then Paul would have contradicted himself, but they were such women that the Apostle mentions in Timothy that "grew wanton, and were busybodies, and tattlers, and kicked against Christ." For Christ in the male and in the female is one, and he is the husband, and his wife is the church, and God has said that his daughters should prophesy as well as his sons. And where he has poured forth his spirit upon them, they must prophesy, though blind priests say to the contrary and will not permit holy women to speak.

And whereas it is said, "I permit not a woman to speak, as saith the Law," but where women are led by the spirit of God, they are not under the Law, for Christ in the male and in the female is one; and where he is made manifest in male and female, he may speak, for "he is the end of the Law for righteousness to all them that believe." So here you ought to make a distinction what sort of women are forbidden to speak, such as were under the Law, who were not come to Christ, nor to the spirit of prophecy. For Hulda, Miriam, and Hannah were prophets, who were not forbidden in the time of the Law, for they all prophesied in the time of the Law, as you may read in 2 Kings 22 what Hulda said unto the priest and to the ambassadors that were sent to her from the king, "Go," said she, "and tell the man that sent you to me, Thus saith the Lord God of Israel, 'Behold, I will bring evil upon this place, and on the inhabitants thereof, even all the words of the book which the King of Judah hath read, because they have forsaken me, and have burnt incense to other gods to anger me with all the works of their hands. Therefore my wrath shall be kindled against this place and shall not be quenched.' But to the King of Judah, that sent you to me to ask counsel of the Lord, so shall you say to him, Thus saith the Lord God of Israel, 'Because my heart did melt, and thou humblest thyself before the Lord, when thou heardest what I spake against this place, and against the inhabitants of the same, how they should be destroyed, behold I will receive thee to thy Father, and thou shalt be put into thy grave in peace, and thine eyes shall not see all the evil which I will bring upon this place.'" Now let us see if any of you blind priests can speak after this manner, and see if it be not a better sermon than any you can make, who are against women's speaking? And Isaiah, that went to the prophetess, did not forbid her speaking of prophesying (Isaiah 8). And was it not prophesied in Joel 2 that "handmaids should prophesy"? And are not handmaids women? Consider this, ye that are against women's speaking, how in the Acts the spirit of the Lord was poured forth upon daughters as well as sons. In the time of the gospel, when Mary came to salute Elizabeth in the hill country in Judea, "and when Elizabeth heard the salutation of Mary, the babe leaped in her womb, and she was filled with the Holy Spirit; and Elizabeth spoke with a loud voice, 'Blessed art thou among women, blessed is the fruit of thy womb; whence is this to me, that the mother of my Lord should come to me? for lo, as soon as thy salutation came to my ear, the babe leaped in my womb for joy, for blessed is she that believes, for there shall be a performance of those things which were told her from the Lord.'" And this was Elizabeth's sermon concerning Christ, which at this day stands upon record. And then Mary said, "My soul doth magnify the Lord, and my spirit rejoiceth in God my Savior, for he hath regarded the low estate of his handmaid; for behold, from henceforth all generations shall call me blessed, for he that is mighty hath done to me great things, and holy is his name; and his mercy is on them that fear him, from generation to generation; he hath showed strength with his arm, he hath scattered the proud in the imaginations of their own hearts; he hath put down the mighty from their seats, and exalted them of low degree; he hath filled the hungry with good things, and the rich he hath sent empty away. He hath helped his servant Israel, in remembrance of his mercy, as he spake to his father, to Abraham, and to his seed forever." Are you not here beholding to the woman for her sermon, to use her words to put into your common prayer? And yet you forbid women's speaking. Now here you may see how these two women prophesied of Christ and preached better than all the blind priests did in that age, and better than this age also, who are beholding to women to make use of their words. And see in the Book of Ruth, how the women blessed her in the gate of the city, of whose stock came Christ. "The Lord make the woman that is come into thy house like Rachel and Leah which built the house of Israel; and that thou mayest do worthily in Ephrata and be famous in Bethlehem, let thy house be like the house of Pharez, whom Tamar bare unto Judah, of the seed which the Lord shall give thee of this young woman. And blessed be the Lord, which hath not left thee this day without a kinsman, and his name shall be continued in Israel." And also see in the first chapter of Samuel, how Hannah prayed and spoke in the temple of the Lord, "Oh Lord of Hosts, if thou wilt look on the trouble of thy handmaid, and remember me, and not forget thy handmaid." And read in the second chapter of Samuel, how she rejoiced in God and said, "My heart rejoiceth in the Lord; my horn is exalted in the Lord and my mouth is enlarged over my enemies, because I rejoice in thy salvation, there is none holy as the Lord, yea, there is none besides thee; and there is no God like our God. Speak no more presumptuously, let not arrogancy come out of your mouths, for the Lord is a God of knowledge, and by him enterprises are established; the bow, and the mighty men are broken, and the weak hath girded to themselves strength; they that were full are hired forth for bread, and the hungry are no more hired, so that the barren hath born seven, and she that had many children is feeble; the Lord killeth, and maketh alive; bringeth down to the grave, and raiseth up; the Lord maketh poor, and maketh rich, bringeth low and exalteth; he raiseth up the poor out of the dust, and lifteth up the beggar from the dunghill to set them among princes, to make them inherit the seat of glory; for the pillars of the earth are the Lord's, and he hath set the world upon them. He will keep the feet of his saints, and the wicked shall keep silence in darkness, for in his own might shall no man be strong. The Lord's adversaries shall be destroyed, and out of heaven shall he thunder upon them; the Lord shall judge the ends of the world, and shall give power to his king, and exalt the horn of his anointed." Thus you may see what a woman hath said, when old Eli the priest thought she had been drunk, and see if any of you blind priests that speak against women's speaking can preach after this manner, who cannot make such a sermon as this woman did, and yet will make a trade of this woman and other women's words. And did not the Queen of Sheba speak, that came to Solomon, and received the Law of God, and preached it in her own kingdom, and said, "Blessed the Lord God that loved Solomon, and set him on the throne of Israel, because the Lord loved Israel forever, and made the king to do equity and righteousness"? And this was the language of the Queen of Sheba. And see what glorious expressions Queen Esther used to comfort the people of God, which was the Church of God, as you may read in the Book of Esther, which caused joy and gladness of heart among all the Jews, who prayed and worshiped the Lord in all places, who jeopardized her life contrary to the King's command, went and spoke to the King, in the wisdom and fear of the Lord, by which means she saved the lives of the people of God. And righteous Mordecai did not forbid her speaking, but said, "If she held her peace, her and her father's house should be destroyed"; and herein you blind priests are contrary to righteous Mordecai.

Likewise you may read how Judith spoke, and what noble acts she did, and how she spoke to the elders of Israel and said, "Dear Brethren, see ye are the honorable and elders of the people of God, all to remembrance how our fathers in time past were tempted, that they might be proved if they would worship God aright; they ought also to remember how our father Abraham, being tried through manifold tribulations, was found a friend of God; so was Isaac, Jacob, and Moses, and all they pleased God, and were steadfast in faith through manifold troubles." And read also her prayer in the Book of Judith and how the elders commended her and said, "All that thou speakest is true, and no man can reprove thy words; pray therefore for me, for thou art an holy woman, and fearest God." So these elders of Israel did not forbid her speaking, as you blind priests do; yet you will make a trade of women's words to get money by, and take texts, and preach sermons upon women's words and still cry out, "Women must not speak, women must be silent." So you are far from the minds of the elders of Israel, who praised God for a woman's speaking. But the Jezebel, and the woman, the false church, the great whore, and tattling women, and busybodies, which are forbidden to preach, which have a long time spoken and tattled, which are forbidden to speak by the true church, which Christ is the head of, such women as were in transgression under the Law, which are called a woman in the Revelations. And see further how the wise woman cried to Joab over the wall, and saved the city of Abel, as you may read in 2 Samuel 20, how in her wisdom she spoke to Joab, saying, "I am one of them that are peaceable and faithful in Israel, and thou goest about to destroy a city and mother in Israel. Why wilt thou destroy the inheritance of the Lord? Then went the woman to the people in her wisdom, and smote off the head of Sheba, that rose up against David, the Lord's anointed. Then Joab blew the trumpet, and all the people departed in peace." And this deliverance was by the means of a woman's speaking, but tattlers and busybodies are forbidden to preach by the true woman, whom Christ is the husband, to the woman as well as the man, all being comprehended to be the church; and so in this true church, sons and daughters do prophesy, women labor in the gospel, but the apostle permits not tattlers, busybodies; and such as usurp authority over the man would not have Christ reign, nor speak neither in the male nor female. Such the Law permits not to speak, such must learn of their husbands. But what husbands have widows to learn of, but Christ? And was not Christ the husband of Philip's four daughters? And may not they that learn of their husbands speak then? But Jezebel, and tattlers, and the whore that denies revelation and prophesy are not permitted, which will not learn of Christ; and they that be out of the spirit and power of Christ, that the prophets were in, who are in the transgression, are ignorant of the scriptures; and such are against women's speaking, and men's too, who preach that which they have received of the Lord God; but that which they have preached, and do preach, will come over all your heads, yea, over the head of the false church, the Pope; for the Pope is the head of the false church, and the false church is the Pope's wife, and so he and they that be of him, and come from him, are against women's speaking in the true church, when both he and the false church are called "Woman," in Revelation 17, and so are in the transgression that would usurp authority over the man Christ Jesus, and his wife too, and would not have him to reign, but the judgment of the great whore is come. But Christ, who is the Head of the church, the true woman which is his wife, in it do daughters prophesy, who are above the Pope and his wife and atop of them. And here Christ is the Head of the male and female, who may speak; and the church is called "a Royal Priesthood"; so the woman must offer as well as the man (Rev. 22:17). "The Spirit saith, Come, and the Bride saith, Come." And so is not the bride the church? And doth the church only consist of men? You that deny women's speaking, answer. Does it not consist of women as well as men? Is not the bride compared to the whole church? And doth not the bride say, "Come"? Does not the woman speak then, the husband, Christ Jesus, the "Amen," and does not the false church go about to stop the bride's mouth? But it is not possible, for the bridegroom is with his bride, and he opens her mouth. Christ Jesus, who goes on conquering and to conquer, who kills and slays with the sword, which is the words of his mouth. The Lamb and the saints shall have the victory, the true speakers of men and women over the false speaker.

Postscript

And you dark priests, that are so mad against women's speaking and it's so grievous to you, did not God say to Abraham, let it not be grievous in thy sight, because of the lad, and because of thy bondwoman? In all that Sarah hath said to thee, hearken to her voice (mark here) the husband must learn of the woman, and Abraham did so, and this was concerning the things of God, for he saith, in Isaac shall thy seed be called, and so Abraham [did] obey the voice of Sarah, as you may read in Genesis 21, and so he did not squench the good that was in his wife for that which he spoke to Abraham was concerning the church.

And you may read Deborah and Barak, and so how a woman preached and sang in Judges 5, what glorious triumphing expressions there were from a woman, beyond all the priest's servants, whom Barak did not bid be silent, for she sang and praised God, and declared to the church of Israel, which now the hungry priest that denies women's speaking makes a trade of her words for a livelihood.

And in Judges 13, there you may see, how the angel appeared to a woman, and how the woman came to her husband and told him, saying, "A man of God came to me, whose countenance was like the countenance of a man of God," and said that she should conceive and bear a son, and again the angel of the Lord appeared to the woman, she made haste and ran, and showed her husband and said unto him, "Behold he hath appeared unto me that came unto me the other day," and when the angel of the Lord was gone, the woman's husband said, "We should surely die because we have seen God," and then you may read how the woman comforted her husband again, and said, "If the Lord were pleased to kill us he would not have showed us all these things, nor would this time have told us such things as these," and this was a woman that taught.

45

EPISTLE FROM THE WOMEN'S
YEARLY MEETING AT YORK (1688)
AND AN EPISTLE
FROM MARY WAITE (1679)*

A testimony for the Lord and his Truth, given forth by the women Friends, at their yearly meeting, at York, being a tender salutation of love, to their Friends, and sisters, in their several monthly meetings, in this county, and elsewhere, greeting.

Dear Friends and sisters,

We, being met together in the fear of the Lord, to wait upon him for his ancient power, to order us, and, in his wisdom and counsel, to guide us in our exercise relating to church affairs: It hath pleased him to break in among us in a glorious manner, to our great satisfaction, and he hath filled our meeting with his living presence, and crowned our assembly with his heavenly power, and opened the fountain of life unto us, and caused the streams of his love freely to flow among us, and run from vessel to vessel, to the gladdening of our hearts, which causeth living praise, and hearty thanksgiving to be rendered unto him, who alone is worthy. And, Friends, we hereby signify to you, that there hath been many living testimonies delivered among us from the divine openings of the spirit of life, in many brethren and sisters, whereby we are fully satisfied that the Lord is well pleased with this our service, and doth accept our sacrifices and freewill offerings, and returns an answer of peace unto our bosoms, which is greatly our reward. Here hath also been brought several testimonies in writing from divers of our monthly meetings, to our great satisfaction, touching the care of Friends for the

*Wing W224, Reel 402.

honor of God, and prosperity of truth in one another. And, dear Friends, in that unchangeable love and precious truth of our God, we dearly salute you, wherein our relation and acquaintance with him, and one with another, in spirit, is daily renewed, and our care and concern for his honor, and one another's good, is still continued; and therein we see there is as great need as ever to watch over one another for good; though it hath pleased God, in his infinite mercy and love, to give us a day of ease and liberty, as to the outward, and hath broken the bonds of many captives, and hath set the oppressed free, and hath opened the prison doors in a great measure: living praises be given him forever! And now, Friends, it is our desire that we all may make a right use of it, and answer the end of the Lord in it, and neither take nor give liberty to that part in any which may give the Lord occasion to suffer our bonds to be renewed, but in his fear and holy awe walk humbly before him, in a holy and self-denying life, under the cross of Christ Jesus, which daily crucifies us to the world, and the world to us, and teacheth us to deny ungodliness and worldly lusts, and to live righteously and soberly in this present world, that by our holy lives and righteous conversation, others, seeing our good works, may glorify our heavenly Father, and that, by our truthlike and Christian behavior, and upright dealing in all our affairs among the children of men, we may walk as become the truth. And, dear Friends, join not with any sort of people further than will stand with truth's honor, and reach God's witness in every conscience, but as much as in you lieth live peaceably with all men, and do good unto all, especially unto the household of faith, and so daily fulfill the royal law of love, in showing to all men that you are Christ's disciples, by loving him and one another. And, Friends, we cannot but warn you of the separating and quarreling spirit which leads unto strife, contention, and jangling, and would thereby lay waste your concern for God's honor, and one another's good; this is that old adversary and enemy of mankind, who, in all ages, "went about like a roaring lion, seeking whom he might devour," and as a ravenous wolf, sometimes gets the sheep's clothing, and never wants specious pretenses to accomplish his design, and bring about his end, which is to divide, rend, tear, destroy and separate from God and one another; and would lay waste the heritage of God, and make spoil of his plantation, and leave his tender plants without care, in the briars and thorns, and every hurtful weed to wrap about them to hinder their growth, and draw them out of their order, by reason of which, as in the days of old, the way of truth might be evil spoken of. The Lord disappoint him of his purpose, and frustrate him of his end, is our prayer, and keep him livingly sensible, that the end of the Lord, in all his fatherly corrections, gentle chastisements, and kind reproofs, hath been to preserve us from the snares of the enemy. Therefore, dear Friends, be concerned for the preservation of one another in every of your respective monthly meetings, and be faithful in performing your service and duty to God, and to one another, as he opens it in you, and lays it upon you, in exhortation, admonition, and reproof, in tender love, for so it will be as the balm of Gilead unto those who are wounded by the wiles of the enemy; for, dear Friends, it is the very end of our travel and labor of love, "that the hungry may be fed, the naked clothed, the weak strengthened, the feeble comforted, and the wounded healed." So that the very weakest and hindermost of the flock may be gathered into the fold of rest and safety, where no destroyer can come, where the ransomed and redeemed by the Lord have the songs of deliverance and high praise in their mouths, giving him the honor, who alone is worthy forever. And, Friends, let us ever remember the tender dealing and mercies of the Lord to us, and that it was not for our deserts, nor any worthiness in us, but his own good will, and for his seed's sake, in which he heard our many cries, and had regard to our tears, and helped us through many exercises and trials inwardly and outwardly, and hath been our rock and refuge, and our sure hiding place, in many storms and exercises; and yet preserves in perfect peace all those that trust in him, who keep his new creation full of joy; and the voice of thanksgiving and melody is heard in our land, and the Lord becomes unto us the place of broad rivers, and makes us before him as well-watered gardens, and affects our hearts with his divine love to praise his name. And now to you young women, whom our souls love, and whom the Lord delighteth to do good unto, and hath visited with the tastes of his love, be you ordered by him in all things, that, in your modest and chaste behavior, your comely and decent dresses in your apparel, and in all other things you may be good examples to others, not only those that are without, but to some professing of the faith, that in the line of life, and language of truth, we may speak one to another and say, "Arise, ye daughters of Zion, shake yourselves from the dust of the earth," put on beautiful garments, even the robes of righteousness, the saints' clothing, the ornament of a meek and quiet spirit. And be not too careful for preferment or riches in this world, but be careful to know the Lord to be your portion and the lot of your inheritance. Then testimonies will arise as in the days of old; our lot is fallen in a good ground, we have large possessions. And, Friends, be not concerned in reference to marriage out of God's fear, but first wait to know your Maker to become your husband and the bridegroom of your souls, then you will come to know that you are not your own, but that he must have the ordering and disposing of you, in soul, body and spirit, which are all his; for he, being the only one unto you, and the chiefest of ten thousand among you, will be your beloved and your friend. Oh! Friends, this state is happy, and blessed are they that attain it, and live in it; the Lord is not unmindful of them, but in his own time, if he see it good for them, can provide meet helps for them; then will your marriage be honorable, being orderly accomplished with the assent of parents, and the unity of friends, and an honor to God, and comfort to your own souls: Then husbands and children are a blessing in the hands of the Lord, and you will arise in your day, age, and generation, as mothers in Israel, as those holy ancients whose living testimonies reacheth unto us, and blessed memories liveth with us according to our measures; as Lydia openhearted to God and one to another, as Dorcas careful to do one another good, as Deborah concerned in the commonwealth of Israel, and as Jael zealous for the truth, who was praised above women. And you, Friends, who are under the present concern, and in your day's work, do it not negligently, not with careless minds, but be you diligent in every of your women's meetings, and order two faithful women in every meeting to take the care upon them, and so far as may answer truth, do you endeavor that nothing be practiced among you, but what tends to God's honor and one another's comfort; let nothing be indulged or connived at in any, whereby truth is dishonored, and let that be cherished and encouraged in all wherewith truth is honored; and these our testimonies cast not carelessly into a corner, but sometime peruse them, and mark well the wholesome advice therein; that our travail may be answered, the Lord honored, and you reap the benefit; and let a record be kept from month to month, and from year to year, of the Lord's dealing with us, and mercy to us, to future ages; that from age to age, and one generation to another, his own works may praise him, to whom all praises do belong, and be ascribed both now and forever.

From our yearly meeting at York, the 28th of the 4th month, 1688

Signed on the behalf of the meeting by

Catharine Whitton	Mary Waite
Judith Boulby	Deborah Winn
Elizabeth Sedman	Elizabeth Beckwith
Frances Taylor	Mary Lindley

*A Warning to all Friends, who profess the everlasting truth of
God, which he hath revealed and made manifest in this his
blessed day, whether on this side, or beyond the seas.*

Dear Friends,

In tender bowels of love do I feel, from the Lord, a warning spring up
in my heart to you, that you all may be kept low in his humble self-
denying life, where safety is to be found; for, assuredly, the great and
notable day of the Lord is at hand, in which he will arise in the greatness
of his strength, to plead the cause of his suffering seed with all its
enemies, whether within or without.

So all dear Friends, be faithful under your several dispensations; for
in our Father's house are many mansions. Keep in the low valleys, for
there will be your safety, there will the green pastures of God's love be
partaken of, and with such will he delight to dwell. So, all Friends, keep
to your watch, that the day of the Lord come not in an hour you look not
for it, and so you receive the unfaithful servant's reward; for indeed,
Friends, my soul is in great travail for the prosperity of Zion, that her
walls may be built, her breaches repaired and made up; for, for many
months, yea some years, hath my spirit been bowed down, and groaned
under the sense of an easeful, selfish, lukewarm spirit, that hath crept
in upon many for want of watchfulness, and keeping to the daily cross of
Christ Jesus, and in the narrow way and savory life, that only will bring
honor and praise to the name of the Lord. And how to be eased of these
weights and burdens I did not know: my cry was to the Lord, that he
would give me wisdom and strength to do his will. And it pleased him
to lay his hand upon me, and bring me near to the gates of death, so far
as I saw; and was pleased to hide himself from me, and my soul was in a
languishing condition, and my cries were great unto the Lord, that he
would not hide his face from me, but let me feel of his wonted goodness
and mercy, by which I had received daily comfort and satisfaction from

him in his unerring path, in which he had been pleased to lead me. And, at length, the Lord appeared, and said he would be my physician, and cure my disease, and came in and comforted my spirit with his overcoming love, which greatly revived me. And in the openings of the bowels of his endless love, he showed me a terrible day drew near, even as one may say, at the door, and laid it upon me, to go warn his people in this city, and elsewhere, to depart from all filthiness both of flesh and spirit, from all lukewarmness, from the fashions, customs and friend-ships of this world; from pride, covetousness, and every sin that sepa-rateth from the Lord, and brings dryness, barrenness, and deadness upon many, and makes as unsavory salt, that is good for nothing, but to be cast forth and trodden upon.

And to warn them not to delay time, but come into the true humility, lowliness of spirit, and self-denying life, that the Lord might be a hiding place to them, for terrible will that day be to all the unfaithful and disobedient. All the sinners in Zion shall be afraid, fearfulness shall take hold of the hypocrite, dread and horror shall surprise them. O whither will you unfaithful fly! Would you not be glad that either rocks or mountains could hide you from the presence of the Lord, and the wrath of the Lamb? O this will be a terrible day indeed unto all those that have had a form of godliness, but denied the power that would have saved them out of all defilements and pollutions of this world.

For long hath the spirit of the Lord been grieved with these, who have long come and sat among God's people, as if they had been of them, but never came to sink down to the heart-searching light of Christ Jesus in them, that by it they might be cleansed from all secret and open sins, from every Delilah that lodgeth in the bosom, as pride and covetous-ness, which often the one attends the other; covetousness, saith the servant of the Lord, is the root of all evil, and advised them to fly from it; but who abide not in the spirit of judgment, and of burning, which God hath prepared to purge away the filth of the daughter of Zion, their filth hath not been purged or done away, which causeth many miscar-riages, blots, and stains, and great reflections have such brought upon the blessed truth, and much dirt hath been thrown on the pure, holy, and undefiled way of the Lord, which he hath cast up for the ransomed to walk in, and so through the unfaithfulness and uneven walking of such, the name of the Lord hath been greatly dishonored, his spirit grieved, and the hearts of the righteous made sad. And many a wounded soul there is among the Lord's people, who are bowed under these weights and pressures; but assuredly the day hastens that everyone must bear their own burden, and the Lord will ease his innocent ones, who have been bowed down before him, and have mourned and groaned under these things; yea the day hastens, that the unfaithful and disobedient shall bear their own burdens. And the Lord will arise for his own name and glory sake, and will ease him of his enemies, and avenge him of his adversaries, and take to himself his great power, that he may reign and rule in the hearts of his, that faithfully labor in his work, and order their conversations aright before him. His glory shall rest upon them, for he will not give it to another seed or birth, but to Christ Jesus, the seed of the woman, who was given to bruise the serpent's head; he hath born the iniquities of all, and been pressed under them as a cart with sheaves; his face hath been more marred than any man's, and his voice not heard in the streets, no beauty nor comeliness seen in him; and, because he hath been a man of sorrows, and acquainted with grief, therefore hath he been passed by, and not regarded, but the Lord will make him the joy of many generations, and his Zion the praise of the whole earth.

Therefore, dear Friends, love him with all your souls, and be you delighted in him above all enjoyments whatever, that you may lie down in the bosom of his love, and be nourished by his side, as children of our heavenly Father, begotten by the immortal word of life, to live and reign here in it, and, when time shall be no more, enter into that blessed rest prepared for all those that have obeyed his glorious gospel; and though as yet we be but as the gleaning of the vintage, yet the Lord hath many to gather, yea the numberless number shall be gathered, and great will be the work of our God, which he is bringing to pass in this his blessed day; it cannot be declared as it is seen and felt in the spirit.

So, Friends, be faithful in the work of your day, be valiant for the Lord and his blessed truth; come up in the nobility of his life, and stand faithful witnesses for him; for we are the city set upon a hill, yea battle-axes in God's hand, though our weapons are not carnal, but spiritual and mighty, through the power of God, to the pulling down the strong-holds of sin and Satan. Friends, we are they whom the Lord hath raised to hold forth Christ Jesus, whom he hath given for an ensign to the nations, unto whom all the ends of the earth must come for salvation.

So, dear Friends, let your light shine forth before men, that they may see your good works, and glorify your heavenly Father, so that by your godly life and holy conversation many may inquire the way to Zion.

All Friends be faithful, and keep your meetings in the fear of the Lord; be diligent in his work, for the woe and curse belongs to them that do the Lord's work negligently, or with careless minds, and it is come on some already, and will come more upon others, if by speedy repentance they return not unto the Lord. So be zealous for the Lord and his truth, and, as much as in you lies, gather orderly together as near the time as possible that the meeting is appointed at; for disorderly coming hath been a hurt, and burdened the faithful, who dare not be negligent in the Lord's work, and often they have waited a considerable season, and God's power hath been felt, and the manifold grace of God been dispensed among us, and then others come in and miss of the counsels, admonitions, and refreshments, which the Lord, by the operation of his blessed spirit, hands forth to his people, and so, for want of zeal in coming duly to meeting, especially on the weekdays, truth hath not grown in them, but such have long traveled in the wilderness, and many carcasses fallen there, and so, for want of zeal and faithfulness, the enemy hath crept in and darkened many minds, where once there was tender good desires raised after God. So all have need to be faithful, and wait diligently every opportunity the Lord gives you to feel your strength renewed; for in the world are many encumbrances and entanglements, some on one hand, and some on another, to draw the mind from God, and but one to draw it to him; so there is great need of holy zeal and diligence, in observing the time to wait upon the Lord to feel your strength renewed, to help through the many things, and his power to strengthen and support, that in your families, and all your undertakings, you may be a good favor to the Lord, being guided by his wisdom to rule and order your children and servants, and he will give authority to stand over everything that is contrary to his witness. And in the fear of the Lord I warn and exhort all parents not to wink or connive at any sin in your children, as you tender their everlasting well-being; let no sin go unreproved or uncorrected, but take the wise man's counsel, who saith, "Folly is bound up in the heart of a child, but the rod of correction must drive it out, and he that corrects his child shall deliver his soul from death." So, Friends, train up your children in the blessed truth and fear of the Lord, so may you have hope they will not depart from it when they are old. And take heed of giving way or suffering them to get into pride, and the vain and foolish fashions, which are a shame to sober people, and a great inlet to many evils, for they are prone to that by nature, and it may soon be set up, but hard to get it down. So, Friends, keep the yoke upon that nature that is proud, stubborn, or disobedient to parents, break that will in them betimes which comes from the evil one, and bend them while they are young, lest when they grow up you cannot. And then you may sorrow greatly when it is too late; for by your overlooking their folly or pride, the wrong nature grows in them to a strong head, whereby you have helped them forwards in the broad way which leads to destruction, and their blood may come to be required at your hands. Ah, Friends! Friends! as much as in you lies keep down the evil, and the good will arise, then there will be room for the tender seed to grow up in them, and they will bless the Lord on your behalfs, for your love and care of their immortal souls.

And all masters and mistresses of families, keep in the dominion of truth, that in it you may rule over every unclean thing and wrong spirit that is contrary to the Lord, that you abiding in him who is the highest power, and higher than the powers of darkness, may in it keep your authority in your families; and look that all be kept sweet and clean out of the condemnable state, first in yourselves, and then in your families, to see that all wildness, wantonness, and rudeness be kept under by the power, yea everything that would blot or stain the precious truth. And then if the Lord requires any service or testimony of any of you, for his name and blessed truth, that all may be clear in yourselves, and justified by God's witness, that you have stood in his counsel and authority in your families, and been good examples in life and conversation, by keeping your own houses in order, and ruling there for God; then may you openly with boldness appear for the Lord, and thresh down sin and every evil way, in the power and authority of his life, that none may have anything to accuse any of you on the accounts above mentioned. And, dear Friends, all keep in the savory life; but more especially you who are drawn forth to bear public testimony for the Lord and his blessed truth, keep you to the watch, that at all times, places, and on all occasions, your lives may preach for God, by a clean unspotted conversation, which is the crown of all the faithful, who labor in the work of the Lord, and are upright before him; his glory shall rest upon them, and their reward is sure.

Now unto all you young people, sons and daughters, apprentices, men- or maidservants, all that are convinced of God's truth, and the way that leads to everlasting life and happiness, be you all faithful to God's witness in you, and mind the motions and operations of it, that thereby you may be changed, and all judge out what's contrary to his pure witness; let not your minds wander, neither look at the vanities in this world, for Christ's kingdom is not of it, nor to be found in pride, wantonness, and lust of the flesh, the fashions, customs, and friendships of this world, for the devil is the king of pride, and all its antecedents, that lead to the gates of hell and everlasting destruction, where there is woe and misery, and that forevermore, where the worm never dies, the fire never goes out; so all you young and tender ones, where desires are begotten after God, keep you low in his fear, and to the daily cross, that all the contrary may be crucified, and all the enmity slain upon it. For everyone that will be a disciple of Christ Jesus must come into the self-denying life. You cannot have two kingdoms; so my advice to you all is, stoop to Christ's appearance in you, he who invites all to come and learn of him, who is meek and lowly, and you shall find rest to your souls. So all be faithful in your several places and the exercises you may be under, that you may grow in grace, and in the fear and wisdom of God. Let not your eyes look out at others, but mind your own conditions; for, if you do, it will spy many faults in others, and maybe overlook more at home. This hinders the growth of many, so all wait low within to feel your growth in the blessed truth, and know how the work goes on, and whether thou feel God's love, mercy, and goodness, renewed to thee day by day, or not; for your accounts will be for the deeds done in your bodies, and not for others, so everyone is to labor to know your calling and election made sure.

And you that are apprentices, keep in the truth, love and obey it, for it will keep you faithful in your places, and out of every deceitful way, performing them not with eye service, but with singleness of heart, as unto the Lord, from whom you must receive a reward. And if the enemy entice, consent not, though he come in with never so fair pretenses, that thou mayest deceive thy master, and it will never be known, etc., or purloin or waste his goods: believe him not, he is a liar, and the father of lies; for there is an eye that sees in secret, which will bring all the hidden deeds of darkness to light, and every work to judgment. So as thy work is, shall be thy reward. But fear the Lord and obey his voice in thee, and he will deliver thee out of every unclean way and polluted path, by his dear son Christ Jesus, whom he hath given for a highway of holiness, and a restorer of paths to dwell in. Glory to his name forever saith the redeemed, who are now returning unto Zion with songs of deliverance in their mouths, and everlasting high praises are founded unto him, by those whose garments are made white in the blood of the

Lamb, for Zion's redeemer is come, the taker away of sin and iniquity is made manifest, the mourners in Zion comforted, the weary travelers are refreshed, the feeble knees are strengthened, the broken spirit bound up, and the wounded soul hath oil poured in: who can but rejoice and be exceeding glad? for he hath put a new song in our mouths, he hath given his people beauty for ashes, and, instead of heaviness, the spirit of praise. All that know him will speak well of his name, for all the noble acts he hath brought to pass for his children. My soul is greatly affected in the remembrance of the Lord's numberless mercies (to me) and a little remnant whom he hath plucked as brands out of the fire, to show forth his praises and declare of his goodness in the land of the living, to hold forth Christ, the way to the Father, to the nations, that his scattered seed may be gathered from all the ends of the earth.

So I have cleared my spirit of what hath long lain upon me, and discharged my conscience, in delivering the Lord's message faithfully, according to the ability he hath given me. And so am clear in my spirit: The Lord set it home upon every heart whom it may concern, and that it may be received in the same bowels of love it was given forth. Then shall I have my reward, and the Lord his glory. And so shall return to my tent, and enter into the hole of the rock, where safety is to be found, till the indignation be overpast; and in the endless unchangeable love of God do I salute you, and bid you farewell in the Lord.

Mary Waite

York, the 10th of the 2nd month, 1679.

Let this be read in Friends' meetings, when they are gathered together, in the fear of the Lord, and in his weighty savory life.

46

AN EPISTLE FOR TRUE LOVE,

UNITY, AND ORDER IN

THE CHURCH OF CHRIST

Against the spirit of discord, disorder, and confusion, etc.
by two servants of the church, according to our measures *

Anne Whitehead and Mary Elson

A true information of our blessed Women's Meeting (for we are blessed,
and the Lord hath blessed us, praised be that Everlasting Arm of Power
that gathered us in the beginning to be a Meeting) betwixt three or four
and twenty years ago.

Thus it was, after the Word of eternal life and salvation, and Light of
Christ Jesus in the conscience had been preached in this city for some
time, many there were that received the report, and was convinced of it,
many poor as well as rich; and ofttimes sickness and weakness came
upon many poor ones, and many distressed and troubled in mind . . .
and they would oftentimes desire the servants of the Lord to come unto
them, such that had a word in season to speak to them. And our dear
Friend George Fox, that man of God, for so he is, the Lord has made
him a blessing in his hand to many, praised be the Lord forever. He was
many times sent for to many that were sick and weak in this city, and
when he came to behold their want of things needful for them, some
scarcely clothes to cover them, or food to eat, or anyone to look to them
in their distresses and wants. The consideration of it was weighty upon
him, and he was moved of the Lord to advise to a woman's meeting; and
in order thereunto, he sent for such women as he knew in this city, of

*London, 1680. Wing W1882, Reel 1559, pp. 10–14.

which there are many living to this day that can testify to the same, who keep the meeting in the faith of that power that gathered us together. . . . And when dear G. Fox declared unto us what the Lord made known unto him by his power, that there should be a woman's meeting, that so all the sick, the weak, the widows, and the fatherless should be minded and looked after in their distresses, that so there should be no want amongst the Lord's people, but that all distressed ones should be minded and looked after: I can truly say we had an answer of God in our hearts to his testimony, and my soul was refreshed at that time and my heart tendered, with many more of my sisters, in the sensible feeling of that everlasting life and the power of the Lord and his universal love that had moved in his dear servant to call us to this work: and we joined with him in the power of God in it: and so we appointed a meeting, and after we had met for some time, we considered which way we should answer the necessities. . . . And there were found among us some that were unworthy that we could not relieve out of that which was provided for the faithful; and yet they were such that frequented our public meetings and looked unto us for charity; and we could not send them empty away. So we considered and had a weekly gathering for them, that it might be fulfilled, as it is written, "Do good unto all, but especially to the household of faith."

And after some time of our meeting together, there came two of the brethren from the men's meeting to us, when we were met together, expressing their unity with us, and also did declare the mind of the men's meeting, (viz.) that they would be ready to help and assist us in anything we should desire of them for truth's service. And so in some time it was agreed upon, in the unity of the truth, that the men Friends should pay the poor Friends' rents, and find them coals . . . and put out such poor Friends' children as we should offer to them. And this has been done almost from the beginning of our Meeting to this day. . . .

And now, my dear Friends and sisters, in the blessed truth of our God, you that have kept this our Meeting for many years, and some of you from the first day the Lord gathered us together and made us a Meeting, I do believe that you with me can truly say, that we have felt the drawings of the Father's love from time to time to this our meeting, and his blessing is amongst us; insomuch as we dared not to suffer any of our own occasions to hinder us from this our service to which the Lord hath called us, but many times have pressed through the crowd of much business; and many things that would have hindered, but we dared not to give way unto it, but in faithfulness answer the Lord's requirings. The Lord hath been with us of a truth from time to time, his living powerful presence has been truly witnessed amongst us, to the refreshing of our immortal souls, which is a true confirmation to us that the Lord owns us in this our service. And I can truly say, I had true breathings to the Lord in the behalf of our younger women, as they come to be settled in the world amongst us, that they may be affected with the work and service of our Meeting as truly as we have been, and are to this day, and that they may be heirs of the grace of God with us. . . . and a true sense hath been upon me of our dear Friends up and down the nation, of their great trial and exercise that hath been upon them because of this wicked dividing spirit, and especially in my native country (viz.) Wiltshire. . . . And this I can say, the more opposition we have had against our women's meeting, the more we have increased in the power of the Lord and he hath blessed our endeavors and services; and therefore, Friends, be not discouraged, but go on in the work and service of the Lord in his power, to his glory, who hath honored his daughters of Abraham and Zion in his heavenly work; and therefore we cannot but serve the Lord in our generation and be valiant for his truth upon earth, and our desires are that all our fellow sisters in the Lord's truth may do the same everywhere throughout the whole earth, where the Lord hath gathered them, so that all may live to the praise and glory of God, Amen.

BIBLIOGRAPHY OF
WOMEN WRITERS, 1540-1700

Bibliographical information about the documents reprinted in this volume appears in a source note on the opening page of each document.

References in the bibliography are to the following catalogs: A. F. Pollard and F. W. Redgrave, comps., *A Short-Title Catalogue of Books Printed in England, Scotland, and Ireland . . . 1475–1640* (London, 1926); A. F. Pollard and F. W. Redgrave, *A Short-Title Catalogue . . . 1475–1640*, rev. W. A. Jackson, F. S. Ferguson, and Katherine F. Pantzer, 2nd ed., 2 vols. (London, 1976, 1986); Donald Wing, comp., *Short-Title Catalogue of Books Printed in England, Scotland, Ireland, Wales, and British America and of English Books Printed in Other Countries 1641–1700*, 3 vols. (New York, 1945–51); Donald Wing, comp., *Short-Title Catalogue . . . 1641–1700*, 2nd ed., vols. 1 and 2 only, vol. 2 rev. and ed. Timothy J. Crist (New York, 1972–82).

Note that all catalog references before 1641 pertain to Pollard and Redgrave; all 1641 and after, to Wing.

Abbott, Margaret. *A testimony against the false teachers.* 1650, A70B.

Adams, Mary. *A warning to the inhabitants of England.* 1676, A489.

———. *A warning to the inhabitants of England.* 1678, not in Wing.

Alexander, Mary. *The state of the case.* See Levingston, Anne, L1824 and S5685.

———. *To the right honourable, the Parliament.* 1654, T1705A.

———. *To the supream authority of the nation.* 1654, T1730A.

Alleine, Theodosia. *The life and death of . . . Mr Joseph Alleine.* 1671, A1011; anr ed, 1672, A1012; anr ed, 1672, A1013; anr ed, 1672, A1013A; anr edn 1673, A1014; anr ed, 1677, A1015; anr ed, 1693, A1016.

Allen, Hannah. *A narrative of God's gracious dealings . . . Satan his methods and malice baffled.* 1683, A1025.

Anderdon, Mary. *A word to the world.* 1662, A3084A.

Anne, Queen of England. *The Princess Anne of Denmark's letter.* 1688, A3224.

Anonymous. *Advice to the women and maidens of London by one of that sex.* 1678, A664; anr edn in Stephen Monteage, *Debtor and creditor . . . made easie.* 1682, M2488.

_____. *An essay in defence of the female-sex.* 1696, A4058; anr edn, 1696, A4059; anr edn, 1697, A4060.

_____. *The gentlewoman's cabinet unlocked.* 1673, G523bA; anr edn, 1675, G523A; anr edn, 1686-88, G523cA.

_____. *The gentlewoman's delight in cookery.* 1690?, G523eA.

_____. *The humble petition of many hundreds of distressed women.* 1642, H3470.

_____. *The ladies of London's petition.* 1684–8, L157.

_____. *Letters of love and gallantry.* 1693, L1784. Vol. 2. 1694, L1785.

_____. *The mother's blessing.* 1685, M2937.

_____. *Severall petitions presented to the honourable houses of Parliament. I. The humble petition of many thousands of courtiers, citizens, gentlemen, and tradesmens wives . . . concerning the staying of the Queenes intended voyage.* 1641, B124.

_____. *Spirituall experiences of sundry believers. Held forth by them at several solemne meetings, and conferences.* Ed. Vavasor Powell. 1653, P3095.

_____. *To the Parliament. The humble petition of divers afflicted women, in behalf of M. John Lilburne.* 29 July 1653, T1585.

_____. *To the right honourable the house of Peers . . . the humble petition of many thousands of courtiers, citizens, gentlemens and tradesmens wives.* 1641, T1628; reprinted, B124.

_____. *To the supreme authority of England the Commons . . . the humble petition of divers well-affected women.* 24 April 1649, T1724.

_____. *To the supreme authority of the nation, the Commons . . . the humble petition of divers well-affected persons of . . . London.* 1649, T1730.

_____. *To the supreme authority of the Commonwealth.* August 1650, T1734.

_____. *Triumphs of female wit, in some Pindaric odes.* 1683, T2295.

_____. *A true copy of the petition of the gentlewomen and tradesmens wives, in and about the city of London.* 4 February 1642, T2656; anr edn, 1642, T2657; anr edn, 1642, T2657A; anr edn, Edinburgh, 1642, T2657B.

_____. *Unto every individual member of Parliament, the humble representation.* 29 July 1653, U99.

_____. *The womens petition to . . . General Cromwell.* 30 October 1651, W3332.

Arden, Alice. *The complaint and lamentation of.* 1633?, 732.

Askew, Anne. *The first examinacyon of Anne Askewe . . . with the elucydacyon of Johan Bale.* Wesel, 1546.

_____. *The lattre examinacyon . . . .* Wesel, 1547.

Astell, Mary. *A farther essay relating to the female sex.* 1696, A4061.

_____. *A serious proposal to the ladies.* 1694, A4062; anr edn, 1695, A4063; anr edn, 1696, A4064; anr edn, 1697, A4065; part 2, 1697, A4065A.

_____. *Six familiar essays upon marriage.* 1696, A4066.

_____. *Some reflections upon marriage.* 1700, A4067.

Atkinson, Elizabeth. *A breif and plain discovery.* 1669, A4129A.

————— *The weapons of the people.* 1669, A4199B.

Audland, Anne. "Letter" and "Testimony." Part of John Camm, *The memory.* 1689, C390.

Audland, Anne, et al. *The saints testimony.* 1655, S365.

Audland, Anne, and Jane Waugh. *A true declaration.* 1655, A4195.

Austill, Bridget. "Her testimony." Part of Anne Whitehead, *Piety promoted.* 1686, W1885.

Avery, Elizabeth. *Scripture-prophecies opened.* 1647, A4272.

—————. *Spiritual autobiography.* In John Rogers, *Ohel or Beth-Shemesh.* 1653, R1813.

Barker, Jane. *Poetical recreations.* 1688, B770.

Barwick, Grace. *To all present rulers.* 1659, B1007A.

Bastwick, Susannah. *To the High Court of Parliament.* 1654, B1073.

Bateman, Susanna. *I matter not how I appear to man.* 1657, B1097.

Bathurst, Anne. *An expostulatory appeal.* See Bathurst, Elizabeth, and Anne Bathurst.

Bathurst, Elizabeth. *The sayings of women.* 1683, B1135B.

—————. *Truth vindicated.* 1691, B1135C; anr edn, 1695, B1136.

—————. *Truth's vindication.* 1679, B1137; anr edn, 1683, B1138; anr edn, 1683, B1139.

Bathurst, Elizabeth, and Anne Bathurst. *An expostulatory appeal.* 1679?, B1135A.

Bathurst, Grace. "Her testimony." Part of Elizabeth Bathurst, *Truth vindicated.* 1691, 1695, B1135C, B1136.

—————. "Her testimony." Part of Anne Whitehead, *Piety promoted.* 1686, W1885.

Baxter, Margaret. "Diary." Part of Richard Baxter, *Breviate.* 1681, B1194.

Beck, Margaret. *The reward of oppression.* 1655, B1648; anr edn, 1656, B1649.

Beckwith, Elizabeth, and Marmaduke Beckwith. *A true relation of the life & death of Sarah Beckwith.* 1692, B1655B.

Behn, Aphra. *The histories and novels.* 1696, B1711.

—————. *Histories, novels, and translations.* 1700, B1711A.

—————. *All the histories and novels.* 1698, B1712; anr edn, 1699, B1713.

—————. *The histories and novels.* 1700, B1714.

—————. *Abdelazer.* 1677, B1715.

—————. *Abdelazer.* 1693, B1716.

—————. *Agnes de Castro.* 1688, B4693A.

—————. *The amorous prince.* 1671, B1717.

—————. *The amours of Philander and Silvia.* 1687, B1718.

—————. *The city-heiress.* 1682, B1719; anr edn, 1698, B1719A; anr edn, 1698, B1720.

—————, ed. *A collection of poems.* 1672, C5177.

_____, ed. *A collection of poems.* 1693, C5178.

_____. *A congratulatory poem to her most sacred.* 1688, B1721.

_____. *A congratulatory poem to her most sacred.* 1688, B1722.

_____. *A congratulatory poem to . . . Queen Mary.* 1689, B1723.

_____. *A congratulatory poem to the king's.* 1688, B1724.

_____. *The Dutch lover.* 1673, B1726.

_____. *Emperor of the moon.* 1687, B1727.

_____. *The emperor of the moon.* 1688, B1728.

_____. *The fair jilt.* 1688, B1729.

_____. *The false count.* 1682, B1730.

_____. *The false count.* 1687, B1731.

_____. *A farce call'd the false count.* 1682, B1732.

_____. *The feign'd curtizans.* 1679, B1733.

_____. *The forc'd marriage.* 1671, B1734; anr edn, 1688, B1735; anr edn, 1690, B1736.

_____. *The history of the nun.* 1689, B1737.

_____. *The lady's looking-glass.* 1697, B1738.

_____. *The lives of sundry notorious villains.* 1678, B1739.

_____. *Love letters between a noble-man and his sister.* 1684, B1740; anr edn, 1694, B1742.

_____. *Love letters between Polydorus and.* 1689, B1743.

_____. *Love letters from a noble man . . . second part.* 1685, not in Wing.

_____. *Love letters from a nobleman . . . second part.* 1693, B1743A.

_____. *The luckey chance.* 1687, B1744.

_____. *The lucky mistake.* 1689, B1745.

_____. "Memoirs on the court." 1697, B1746. Part of her *All the histories and novels.* 1698, B1712.

_____, ed. *Miscellany, being a collection of poems.* 1685, M2230.

_____. *A new song sung in Abdelazer.* 1695, B1747.

_____. *Oroonoko.* 1688, B1749.

_____. *A Pindarick on the death of our late sovereign.* 1685, B1750.

_____. *A Pindarick on the death of our late sovereign.* 1685, B1751.

_____. *A Pindarick on the death of our late sovereign.* 1685?, B1752; anr edn, 1685, B1753.

_____. *A Pindaric poem to the reverend doctor.* 1689, B1754.

_____. *A poem humbly dedicated.* 1685, B1755.

_____. *A poem to Sir Roger L'Estrange.* 1688, B1756.

_____. *Poems upon several occasions.* 1684, B1757.

_____. *Poems upon several occasions.* 1697, B1758.

_____. *A prologue by . . . to her new play.* 1682, B1759.

_____. *Prologue spoken by Mrs Cook.* 1685, B1759A.

_____. *Prologue to Romulus.* 1682, B1760.

————. *The roundheads*. 1682, B1761.

————. *The roundheads*. 1698, B1762.

————. *The rover*. 1677, B1763; anr edn, 1697, B1764.

————. *The second part of the rover*. 1681, B1765.

————. *Sir Patient Fancy*. 1678, B1766.

————. *Three histories*. 1688, B1766A.

————. *To poet Bavius*. 1688, B1767.

————. *To the most illustrious Prince Christopher*. 1687, B1768.

————. *The town-fopp*. 1677, B1769.

————. *The town-fopp*. 1699, B1770.

————. *The town raves*. 1696, B1770A.

————. *Two congratulatory poems*. 1688, B1771.

————. *The unfortunate bride*. 1698, B1772; anr edn, 1700, B1773.

————. *The wandering beauty*. 1698, B1773A; anr edn, 1700, B1773B.

————. *The widdow Ranter*. 1690, B1774.

————. *Young Jemmy*. c. 1681, B1775.

————. *The young king*. 1683, B1776; anr edn, 1698, B1777.

————. *The younger brother*. 1696, B1778.

————. "Poems." Part of Charles Gildon, ed., *Miscellany poems*. 1692, G733A.

Bell, Susanna. *The legacy of a dying mother*. 1673, B1802.

Benson, Mabel. "Testimony." Part of John Camm, *The memory*. 1689, C390.

Bettris, Jeane. *A lamentation*. 1657, B2085.

————. *Spiritual discoveries*. 1657, B2086.

Biddle, Hester. *Oh! wo, wo, from the Lord*. 1659, B2864C.

————. *To the inhabitants of the town of Dartmouth*. 1659, B2864D.

————. *The trumpet of the Lord God*. 1662, B2864E.

————. *The trumpet of the Lord soundeth forth*. 1662, B2865.

————. *A warning from the Lord God*. 1660, B2866.

————. *Wo to thee town of Cambridge*. 1655, B2866A.

————. *Wo to thee city of Oxford*. 1655, B2867.

————. "Something in short." Part of Thomas Woodrow, *A brief*. 1659, W3474.

Blackborow, Sarah. *Herein is held forth the gift*. 1659, B3063.

————. *The just and equal balance discovered*. 1660, B3064.

————. *The oppressed prisoners complaint*. 1662, B3064A.

————. *A visit to the spirit in prison*. 1658, B3065.

————. "Dear friends." Part of Richard Hubberthorne, *A collection*. 1663, H3216.

Blaithwaite, Mary. *The complaint of*. 1654, B3129.

Blandford, Susannah. *A small account given forth*. 1698, B3163A.

_____. *A small treatise writ by one of the true Christian faith.* 1700. B3163B.

Blaugdone, Barbara. *An account of the travels.* 1691, A410.

Bleming, Jone. *The new prayers for K. William and Q. Mary.* 1693, B3187A.

Blount, Lady Amy. To the honourable assembly of the Commons house. The humble complaint of. 1621?, STC3134.5.

Boerman, Mary, and John Pennyman. *The ark is begun to be opened.* 1671, P1403.

Booth, Mary. "Preface." Part of James Nayler, *Milk for babes.* 1661, 1665, 1668, N299, N300, N301.

Boothby, Frances. *Marcelia.* 1670, B3742.

Boulbie, Judith. *A few words to the rulers of this nation.* 1673, B3827A.

_____. *A testimony for truth.* 1665, B3828.

_____. *To all justices of peace.* 1688, B3828A.

_____. *A warning and lamentation.* 1679, B3828B.

Bradmor, Sarah. *Prophecy of the wonders.* 1686, B4139.

Braidley, Margret, et al. *Certain papers which is the word.* 1655, T260.

Braytwhaite, Elizabeth. Part of C.T., *A brief relation of the life and death of.* 1684, C128.

Brooksop, Joan. *An invitation of love.* 1662, B4983.

Browne, Sarah Featherstone. *Living testimonies.* 1689, F576B.

Burch, Dorothy. *A catechisme of the several heads of Christian religion.* 1646, B5612.

Caldwell, Elizabeth. Letter by her in Gilbert Dugdale, *A true discourse of the practises of Elizabeth Caldwell on the parson of T. Caldwell.* 1604, STC7293.

Camfield, Elizabeth. "Many are the testimonies." Part of Anne Whitehead, *Piety promoted.* 1686, W1885.

Carey, Mary. "Upon the sight of my abortive birth. . . ." In Germaine Greer et al., eds., *Kissing the Rod: An Anthology of Seventeenth-Century Women's Verse.* London: Virago Press, 1988.

Carleton, Mary. *The case of.* 1663, C586A.

_____. *An historicall narrative.* 1663, H2106.

_____. *A true account of the tryal.* 1663, not in Wing.

_____. *The memoires of.* 1673, C587.

Cartwright, Joanna. *The petition of the Jewes.* 1649, C695.

Cartwright, Ursula. *The case of.* 1680?, C1191.

Cary, Lady Elizabeth. *The tragedie of Mariam, the faire queene of Jewry.* 1613, STC4613.

Cary, Mary. *The little horns doom and downfall.* 1651, C736.

_____. *The resurrection of the witnesses.* 1648, C737A; anr edn, 1653, C738.

_____. *Twelve humble proposals.* 1653, R51.

_____. *A word in season.* 1647, C739.

Cavendish, Margaret, Duchess of Newcastle. *De vita et rebus gestis.* 1668, N848.

_____. *The description of a new world.* 1666, N849; anr edn, 1668, N850.

_____. *Grounds of natural philosophy.* 1668, N851.

_____. *The life of the thrice noble . . . duke.* 1667, N853; anr edn, 1675, N854.

_____. *Natures pictures.* 1656, N855; anr edn, 1671, N856.

_____. *Observations.* 1666, N857; anr edn, 1668, N858.

_____. *Orations.* 1662, N859; anr edn, 1662, N860; anr edn, 1663, N861; anr edn, 1668, N862.

_____. *The philosophical and physical opinions.* 1655, N863; anr edn, 1663, N864.

_____. *Philosophicall fancies.* 1653, N865.

_____. *Philosophical letters.* 1664, N866.

_____. *Plays, never before printed.* 1668, N867.

_____. *Playes.* 1662, N868.

_____. *Poems, and fancies.* 1653, N869; anr edn, 1664, N870; anr edn, 1668, N871.

_____. *CCXI sociable letters.* 1664, N872.

_____. *The worlds olio.* 1655, N873; anr edn, 1671, N874.

Cellier, Elizabeth. *The ladies answer.* 1670, C1660.

_____. *Madam Celliers answer.* 1680, C1659.

_____. *Malice defeated.* 1680, C1661.

_____. *The matchless rogue.* 1680, C1662.

_____. *Mistress Celliers lamentation.* 1681, C1660A.

_____. *To Dr. ____ an answer.* 1688, C1663.

_____. *A true copy.* 1681, C1663A.

Channel, Elinor, and Arise Evans. *A message from God.* 1654, C1936.

Chevers, Sarah. "To all people." Part of Katherine Evans and Sarah Chevers, *A true account.* 1663 (listed in Wing as separate, C3776A).

Chidley, Katherine. *Good counsel, to the petitioners for Presbyterian government.* 1645, C3831.

_____. *The justification of the independant [sic] churches of Christ.* 1641, C3832.

_____. *A New-Yeares-gift, or a brief exhortation to Mr. Thomas Edwards.* 1645, C3833.

Cholmley, Elisabeth, and Sarah Cholmley. *The case of.* 1673, C911.

Chudleigh, Lady Mary. *The female advocate.* 1700, C3984.

Clark, Mary. *The great and wonderful success.* 1685, C4483A.

Clarke, Frances. *A briefe reply to the narration.* 1653, C4439.

Clayton, Anne. *A letter to the king.* 1660, C4609.

Cleveland, Barbara (Barbara Palmer, Countess of Cleveland). *The gracious answer of.* 1668, C4653.

Clifford, Anne. *The diary.* Introduction by Vita Sackville-West. 1923.

_____. *Lives of Lady Anne Clifford and of her parents summarized by herself.* Ed. J. P. Gibson. The Roxburghe Club, 1916.

Clinton, Elizabeth, Countess of Lincoln. *The countess of Lincoln's nursery.* 1622, STC5432.

Clipsham, Margery. See Ellwood, Mary, and Margery Clipsham.

Cobb, Alice. "Testimony." Part of Alice Curwen et al., *A relation.* 1680, M857.

Cockburn, Mrs. Catherine. *Agnes de Castro.* 1696, C4801.

_____. *Fatal friendship; a tragedy.* 1698, C4802.

Cole, Mary. See Cotton, Priscilla, and Mary Cole.

Coleman, Elizabeth. See Travers, Ann, and Elizabeth Coleman.

Collins, An. *Divine songs and meditacions.* 1653, C5355.

Conway, Anne. See Finch, Anne, Lady Conway.

Cook, Lucretia. "A short testimony." Part of Anne Whitehead, *Piety promoted.* 1686, W1885.

Cooke, Frances. *Mris Cooke's meditations.* 1650, C6008.

Cottington, Angela. *The case of.* 1680, C882.

Cotton, Priscilla. *A briefe description.* 1659, C6473B.

_____. *As I was in the prison-house.* 1656, not in Wing (Friends' Library, London).

_____. *A visitation of love.* 1661, C6475.

_____, and Mary Cole. *To the priests.* 1655, C6474.

Crashawe, Elizabeth. *The honour of vertue.* 1620, STC6030.

Crouch, Ruth. "Her tsetimony" [*sic*]. Part of Anne Whitehead, *Piety promoted.* 1686, W1885.

Culpeper, Alice. "Preface." Part of Nicholas Culpeper, *Last legacy.* 1657, C7519.

_____. "Preface." Part of Nicholas Culpeper, *Treatise.* 1656, C7549.

Cuninghame, Lady Margaret. *A part of the life of.* Edinburgh, 1827.

Curwen, Alice, et al. *A relation of the labour.* 1680, M857.

Dale, Lady Elizabeth. *A briefe of the Lady Dales petition to the Parliament.* 1624, STC6191.5.

D'Anvers, Alicia. *Academia; or, the humours of the University of Oxford.* 1691, D220.

_____. *A poem upon his sacred majesty, his voyage for Holland.* 1691, D221.

Darcie, Lady Grace. *To the honourable assembly of the Commons house in Parliament. The humble petition of.* 1624. STC6273.7.

Davies, Eleanor. See Douglas, Eleanor.

Davy, Sarah. *Heaven realized.* 1670, D444.

Delaval, Lady Elizabeth. *The meditations of.* Ed. Douglas Greene, for the Surtees Society. 1978.

Dew, Susanna. "A testimony." Part of Anne Whitehead, *Piety promoted.* 1686, W1885.

Docwra, Anne. *An apostate conscience exposed.* 1699, D1777

――――. *A brief discovery.* 1683, D1777A.

――――. *An epistle of love.* 1683, D1778.

――――. *A looking-glass for the recorder.* 1682, D1779.

――――. *The second part.* 1700, D1780.

――――. *Spiritual community, vindicated.* 1687, D1781.

――――. *True intelligence to be read.* 1683, not in Wing (Friends' Library, London).

Dole, Dorcas. *Once more a warning.* 1683, D1834; anr edn, 1684, D1834A.

――――. *A salutation and seasonable exhortation.* 1683, D1835; anr edn, 1700, D1835A; anr edn, 1685, D1836; anr edn, 1687, D1836A.

――――. "To you." Part of Elizabeth Stirredge et al., *A salutation.* 1683, S5685A.

Douglas, Eleanor. *Amend, amend.* 1643, D1967.

――――. *And without proving what we say.* 1648?, D1968.

――――. *Apocalyps.* Chap. 2. 164–?, D1969.

――――. *Apocalypsis Jesu Christi.* 1644, D1970.

――――. *The Lady Eleanor, her appeale.* 1641, D1971.

――――. *The Lady Eleanor her appeal.* 1646, D1972.

――――. *The appearance.* 1650, D1972A.

――――. *The arraignment.* 1650, D1972B.

――――. *As not unknowne, this petition.* 1645, D1973.

――――. *Before the Lords second coming.* 1650, D1974.

――――. *The benediction . . . I have an errand.* 1651, D1975.

――――. *The benidiction* [sic] *. . . I have an errand.* 1651, D1976.

――――. *The benediction . . . I have an errand.* 1651, D1977.

――――. *Bethlehem signifying the house of bread.* 1652, D1978.

――――. *The bill of excommunication.* 1649, D1979.

――――. *The blasphemous charge against her.* 1649, D1980; anr edn, 1649, D1981.

――――. *The brides preparation.* 1645, D1982.

――――. *The crying charge.* 1649, D1982A.

――――. *The day of judgements modell.* 1646, D1983.

――――. *The dragons blasphemous charge.* 1651, D1984; 1651, D1993.

――――. *Elijah the Tishbite's supplication.* 1650, D1985.

――――. *The everlasting gospel.* 1649, D1986.

――――. *The excommunication out of paradice.* 1647, D1987.

――――. *Ezekiel, cap. 2.* 164–?, D1988.

――――. *Ezekiel the prophet explained.* 1649, D1988A.

――――. *For the blessed feast of Easter.* 1646, D1989.

――――. *For the most honorable states.* 1649, D1989A.

――――. *For the right noble, Sir Balthazar Gerbier.* 1649, D1989B.

――――. *For Whitsontyds last feast.* 1645, D1990.

_____. *From the Lady Eleanor, her blessing.* 1644, D1991.

_____. *The gatehouse salutation from.* 1647, D1991A.

_____. *Given to the elector Prince Charles.* 1648, D1992; anr edn, 1651, D1993.

_____. *Great Brittains visitation.* 1645, D1994.

_____. *Hells destruction.* 1651, D1995.

_____. *I am the first, and the last.* 1645, D1996.

_____. *Je le tien.* 1646, D1996A.

_____. *The Lady Eleanor Douglas, dowager.* 1650, D1996B.

_____. *The mystery of general redemption.* 1647, D1996C.

_____. *The new Jerusalem at hand.* 1649, D1997.

_____. *The new proclamation.* 1649, D1998.

_____. *Of errors loyned with Gods word.* 1645, D1999.

_____. *Of the general great days approach.* 1648, D1999A.

_____. *Of times and seasons their mystery.* 1651, D2000.

_____. *A prayer or petition for peace.* 1644, D2001; anr edn, 1645, D2002; anr edn, 1647, D2003.

_____. *A prophesie of the last day.* 1645, D2004.

_____. *Prophetia de die.* 1644, D2005.

_____. *Reader, the heavy hour.* 1648, D2005A.

_____. *The Lady Eleanor her remonstrance.* 1648, D2006.

_____. *The restitution of prophecy.* 1651, D2007.

_____. *The restitution of reprobates.* 1644, D2008.

_____. *The revelation interpreted.* 1646, D2009.

_____. *Samsons fall.* 1649, D2010.

_____. *Samsons legacie.* 1642, D2011.

_____. *The [second] co[ming].* 1645, D2012.

_____. *The serpents excommunication.* 1651, D2012A.

_____. *A sign given them.* 1649, D2012AA.

_____. *Sions lamentation.* 1649, D2012B.

_____. *The star to the wise.* 1643, D2013.

_____. *Strange and wonderfull prophesies.* 1649, D2014.

_____. *To the most honourable.* 1643, D2015.

_____. *Tobits book.* 1652, D2016.

_____. *Wherefore to prove the thing.* 1648, D2017.

_____. *The word of God.* 1644, D2018.

_____. *The writ of restitution.* 1648, D2019.

_____. *Zach. 12. And they shall look.* 1649, D2020.

Dyer, Mary. Part of Marmaduke Stephenson, *A call.* 1660, S5466.

Ebbs, Joyce. *The last speech, confession & prayer.* 1662, E126A.

Eeds, Judith. *A warning to all the inhabitants.* 1659, E241A.

Egerton, Elizabeth. *Book of occasional meditations and prayers.* C. 1648–63. BL MS. Egerton 607.

Egerton, Sarah. See Fige, Sarah, F251A and F251B.

Elestone, Sarah. *The last speech and confession.* 1678, L504F.

Elizabeth, Queen of England. *Her majesties most princelie answere, delivered at Whitehall.* 1601, STC7578; anr version, c. 1628, STC7579.

———. *The golden speech of.* 1659, E528; anr edn, 1698, E528A.

———. *Injunctions given by the queenes majestie.* 1641, E529.

———. *The last speech and thanks of.* 1671, E530.

———. *A most excellent and remarkabl [sic] speech.* 1643, E531.

———. *Queen Elizabeth's opinion concerning transubstantiation.* 1688, E532.

———. *A speech made by.* 1688, E533.

———. *Queene Elizabeths last speech to her last Parliament.* 1642, E534; anr edn, 1648, E535.

Ellis, Sarah. "Testimony." Part of Joan Whitrow, *The work.* 1677, W2039.

Ellwood, Mary, and Margery Clipsham. *The spirit that works.* 1685, C4716A.

———. *The spirit that works.* 1685, C4716B and S4994.

Elson, Mary. *A tender and Christian testimony.* 1685, E642.

———. "A testimony." Part of Anne Whitehead, *Piety promoted.* 1686, W1885.

———. "A true information." Part of Anne Whitehead, *An epistle.* 1680, W1882.

Evans, Katherine. *A brief discovery.* 1663, E3453.

Evans, Katherine, and Sarah Chevers. *This is a short relation.* 1662, B487.

———. *A true account.* 1663, not in Wing (Friends' Library, London).

Evelyn, Mary. *The picture of the princesse.* 1660, E3523A.

Everhard, Margaret. *An epistle of.* 1699, E3535.

Fage, Mary. *Fames roule.* 1637, 10667.

Fairman, Lydia, *A few lines given forth.* 1659. F257.

Fanshawe, Lady Ann. *The memoirs of Anne, Lady Halkett and Ann, Lady Fanshawe.* Ed. John Loftis. 1979.

Fearon, Mrs Jane. *Universal redemption.* 1698, F576A.

Fell, Lydia. *A testimony and warning.* 1676, F625.

Fell, Margaret. *A call to the universall seed of God.* 1665, F625A.

———. *A call unto the seed of Israel.* 1668, F626.

———. *The citie of London reprov'd.* 1660, F626A.

———. *Concerning ministers.* 1659, F626B.

———. *The daughter of Sion awakened.* 1677, F627.

———. *A declaration and an information.* 1660, F628.

———. *An evident demonstration to Gods elect.* 1660, F629; anr edn, 1660, F630.

———. *The examination and tryall.* 1664, E3710.

———. *False prophets, Anticrists [sic].* 1655, F631.

_____. *For Manasseth Ben Israel.* 1656, F632.

_____. *A letter sent to the king.* 1666, F633.

_____. *A loving salutation, to the seed.* 1656, F634; anr edn, 1660, F634aA.

_____. *A paper concerning such as are made ministers.* 1659, F634A.

_____. *The standard of the Lord revealed.* 1667, F635.

_____. *A testimonie of the touch-stone.* 1656, F636.

_____. *This is to the clergy.* 1660, F637.

_____. *This was given to Major Generall Harrison.* 1660, F638.

_____. *To the generall councill of officers.* 1659, F638A.

_____. *To the general councel.* 1659, F638C.

_____. *To the magistrates and people of England.* 1664, F638D.

_____. *A touch-stone, or, a perfect tryal.* 1667, F639.

_____. *A true testimony.* 1660, F640.

_____. *Two general epistles to the flock of God.* 1664, F641.

_____. *Womens speaking justified.* 1666, F642; anr edn, 1667, F643.

Fiennes, Celia. *The journeys of.* Ed. Christopher Morris. 1949.

Fige, Sarah. *Female advocate.* 1686, E251A; anr edn, 1687, E251B.

Finch, Anne, Lady Conway. *The principles of . . . philosophy.* 1692, C5989.

_____. *Conway Letters.* Ed. M. H. Nicholson. 1930.

Fisher, Abigail. "Testimony." Part of Anne Whitehead, *Piety promoted.* 1686, W1885.

Fletcher, Elizabeth. *A few words in season to all.* 1660, F1328.

Ford, Bridget. "Testimony." Part of Anne Whitehead, *Piety promoted.* 1686, W1885.

Forster, Mary. *A declaration of the bountifull.* 1669, F1603; anr edn, 1693, F1603A.

_____. *Some seasonable considerations.* 1684, F1604.

_____. *These several papers.* 1659, F1605.

_____. *A living testimony.* 1685, L2598A.

_____. "Testimony." Part of Anne Whitehead, *Piety promoted.* 1686, W1885.

_____. *These several papers was sent to the Parliament.* 1659, F1605.

Freeman, Ann-Mary. "Testimony." Part of Anne Whitehead, *Piety promoted.* 1686, W1885.

Freke, Mrs. Elizabeth. *Her diary.* Ed. Mary Carbery. 1913.

Furly, Anna, et al. *A testimony to the true light.* 1670, F2541A.

Gainsborough, Katherine, Countess of. *Baptist, earl of Gainsborough . . . appellants. Katherine countess dowager of Gainsborough, respondent. The respondents case.* 1693, G131A.

Gargill, Ann. *A brief discovery.* 1656, G258.

_____. *A warning to all the world.* 1656, G259.

Gaunt, Elizabeth. *Mrs Elizabeth Gaunt's last speech.* 1685, G381A.

Gethin, Grace Norton, Lady. *Misery's virtues whetstone. Reliquiae Gethinianae.* 1699, G625; anr edn, 1700, G626.

Gilman, Anne. *An epistle to friends.* 1662, G768.

———. *To the inhabitants of the earth.* 1669, G768A.

Goodenough, Mary. Letter by her in *An account of the trial, condemnation of.* 1692, not in Wing.

Gotherson, Dorothea. *To all that are unregenerated.* 1661, G1352.

Gould, Ann, et al. *An epistle to all Christian magistrates.* 1659, G1414.

Greenway, Margret. *A lamentation against the professing.* 1657, G1861.

Grey, Elizabeth, Countess of Kent. *A choice manuall, or rare and select secrets.* 1653, K310; anr edn, 1653, K310A; anr edn, 1653, K310B; anr edn, 1653, K311; anr edn, 1654, K312; anr edn, 1655, K312A; anr edn, 1656, K312B; anr edn, 1659, K313; anr edn, 1659, K313A; anr edn, 1661, K313B; anr edn, 1663, K314; anr edn, 1664, K315; anr edn, 1667, K315A; anr edn, 1671, K315B; anr edn, 1682, K316; anr edn, 1687, K317.

———. *A true gentlewomans delight.* 1653, K317A; anr edn, 1653, K317B; anr edn, 1671, K317C; anr edn, 1687, K317D.

Grey, Lady Jane Dudley. *An epistle.* 1570, STC7279; anr version, STC 7279.5.

———. *The lamentacion.* 1563, STC7280.

———. *The life, death, and actions of.* 1615, STC7281; anr edn, 1629, STC7281.5; anr edn, 1636, STC7282.

Grymeston, Elizabeth. *Miscelanea, meditations, memoratives.* 1604, STC12407; anr edn, 1608, STC12407.5; anr edn, 1606?, 12408; anr edn, 1618?, STC12410.

Halkett, Lady Anne. *Autobiography.* Camden Society, 1875.

Hamilton, Elizabeth. *To the Parliament.* 1651, H477A.

Hamilton, Margaret, Baroness. *Unto his grace, his majesty's high commissioner . . . the humble petition of.* 1695, H485A.

Harcourt, Lady Anne. *The Harcourt papers.* Ed. Edward William Harcourt. 1880.

Hastings, Lucy, Countess of Huntingdon. *The new proclamation.* 1649, D1998.

Hatt, Martha. *To the right honourable, the Commons.* 1660, H1141A.

———. *To the right honourable, the Lords.* 1669, H1141B.

Hatton, Lady Elizabeth. *A true copy of a letter from.* 1642, H1149.

Haynes, Elizabeth. "Testimony." Part of Anne Whitehead, *Piety promoted.* 1686, W1885.

Hayward, Amey. *The females legacy.* 1699, H1227.

Henrietta Maria, Queen of England. *De Boodtschap ende brief van de.* 1642, H1455.

———. *A copie of the queen's letter.* 1642, H1456.

————. *The queens majesties declaration and desires to the states of Holland.* 1642, H1457.

————. *The queens majesties gracious answer to the Lord Digbies letter.* 1642, H1458.

————. *The queens letter from Holland.* 1643, H1459.

————. *The queens majesties letter to the Parliament.* 1649, H1461.

————. *The queens majesties message and declaration.* 1649, H1462.

————. *The queens majesties message and letter.* 1642, H1463.

————. *The queenes majesties propositions to the states of Holland.* 1642, H1465.

————. *The protestation of.* 1643, H1466.

————. *The queens speech.* 1641, H1467; anr end, 1641, H1467A.

Henshaw, Anne. *To the Parliament of . . . England.* 1654, H1477.

Herring, Anne. *The case of.* 1678, H1600A.

Heusde, Sarah Cornelius de. *Loving reader . . . secret arts.* 1670?, G1672A.

Hewytt, Mary. *To the honorable knights, citizens, and burgesses of the Commons House. . . .* 1660, H1640.

Higges, Susan. *A true relation of one S. Higges.* 1635?, STC13441.

Hincks, Elizabeth. *The poor widows mite.* 1671, H2050.

Hoby, Lady Margaret. *Diary of.* Ed. Dorothy M. Meads. 1930.

Holden, Mary. *The womans almanack . . . 1688.* 1688, A1827; anr edn, 1689, A1827A.

Homel, Anne. *French cruelty.* 1689, H2536B.

Hooton, Elizabeth. *False prophets and false teachers.* 1652, A894BA.

————. "Testimony." Part of William Simpson, *The life.* 1671, L2042.

————. *To the king.* 1670, H2710A.

————. *In pursuit of the king.* In *Elizabeth Hooton, First Quaker Woman Preacher 1600–1672.* Ed. Emily Manners. 1914.

Hopton, Susannah. *Daily devotions.* 1673, H2761.

Howard, Arabella. *The case of Mrs Arabella Thompson.* 1680, C960.

Howgill, Mary. *A remarkable letter.* 1657, H3191.

————. *The vision of the lord of hosts.* 1662, H3192.

Huntingdon, Countess of. See Hastings, Lucy, Countess of Huntingdon.

Hyde, Anne. *A copy of a paper.* 1682, Y46.

————. *Reasons of her leaving the communion.* 1670, Y47.

Ivy, Lady. [Claim to lands]. 1696, L166C.

James, Elinor. *Mrs James's advice.* 1688, J415.

————. *Mrs. James's apology.* 1694, J415A.

————. *Mrs. James's application.* 1695, J415B.

————. *The case between a father and his children.* 1682, J416.

————. *Dear soveraign.* 1687, J416A.

————. *Mrs. James's defence.* 1687, J417.

————. *Mrs. James's humble letter.* 1699, J417aA.

————, *I can assure your honours.* 1699?, J417bA.

————. *An injur'd prince vindicated.* 1688, J417A.

————. *May it please your honours.* 1699?, J417AB.

————. *May it please your majesty.* 1689, J417AC.

————. *May it please your most sacred majesty.* 1685, J417B.

————. *Most dear soveraign.* 1689, J417C.

————. *My lord.* 1687, J418.

————. *My lords, I can assure.* 1688, J419.

————. *My lords, I did not think.* 1690, J419A.

————. *My lords, you can't but be sensible.* 1688, J419B.

————. *Mrs. James her new answer.* 1681, J420.

————. *Sir, my lord mayor.* 1690?, J421.

————. *This being your majesty's birth-day.* 1690, J421aA.

————. *To the honourable convention.* 1688, J421A.

————. *To the honourable House of Commons.* 1685, J421B.

————. *To the honourable House of Commons.* 1699, J421C.

————. *To the honourable the House of Commons.* 1696, J422.

————. *To the kings most excellent majesty.* 1685, J422aA.

————. *To the right honourable convention.* 1688, J422bA.

————. *To the right honourable the House of Lords.* 1688, J422A.

————. *To the right honourable, the lord mayor.* 1683, J422B.

————. *Mrs. James's vindication.* 1687, J423.

Jeffries, Joyce. "Account-book." Ed. John Webb. In *Archaeologia* 37. 1857.

Jermyn, Rebecca. *A true state of the right and claime of.* 1655, J681bA.

Jesserson, Susanna. *A bargain for bachelors.* 1675, J686.

Jinner, Sarah. *An almanack or prognostication . . . 1658.* 1658, A1844.

————. *An almanack or prognostication . . . 1659.* 1659, A1845.

————. *An almanack or prognostication . . . 1660.* 1660, A1846.

————. *An almanack for . . . 1664.* 1664, A1847.

————. *The womans almanack.* 1659, A1848.

Joceline, Elizabeth. *The mothers legacie to her unborne childe.* 1624, STC14624; anr imp., 1624, STC14624.5; anr imp., 1625, STC14625; anr imp., 1632, STC14625.5; anr imp., 1635, STC14625.7; anr edn, 1684, J756.

————. *Uyterste wille van een moeder ann haar toekomende kind.* Amsterdam, 1699; anr edn, 1748.

J[ones], Mrs. S[arah]. "A diars wife." *To Sions lovers.* 1644, J990.

————. *This is the light's appearance.* 1650, J989.

Kent, Countess of. See Grey, Elizabeth, Countess of Kent.

Killigrew, Anne. *Poems.* 1686, K442.

Killin, Margaret, and Barbara Patison. *A warning.* 1655. K473.

Knight, Mary. "To the most honoured." Part of Henry Lawes, *Second book.* 1655, L641.

Lamb, Catherine. *A full discovery.* 1688, L205C.

Lanier, Mrs Aemilia. *Salve deus rex judaeorum. Containing, the passion of Christ.* 1611, STC15227; anr issue, STC15227.5.

Lead, Jane. *The ascent to the mount of vision.* 1699, L782.

――――. *The Enochian walks with God.* 1694, L783.

――――. *A fountain of gardens.* 1696, L783aA; anr edn, 1697, L783bA; anr edn, 1697, L783A.

――――. *A fountain of gardens.* Vol. 2. 1697, L783B.

――――. *A fountain of gardens.* Vol 3, pt. i. 1700, L784.

――――. *The heavenly cloud.* 1681, L785.

――――. *The laws of paradise.* 1695, L786.

――――. *A message to the Philadelphian Society.* 1696, L787.

――――. *A messenger of an universal peace.* 1698, L788.

――――. *The revelation of revelations.* 1683, L789.

――――. *A revelation of the everlasting gospel-message.* 1697, L789A.

――――. *The signs of the times.* 1699, L790.

――――. *The tree of faith.* 1696, L791.

――――. *The wars of David.* 1700, L791A.

――――. *The wonders of God's creation manifested.* 1695?, L792.

Leigh, Dorothy. *The mothers blessing. Or the godly counsaile of a gentle woman.* 1616, STC15402; anr edn, 1607, STC15402.5; anr edn, 1618, STC15403; anr edn, 1618, STC15403a; anr edn, 1621, STC15404; anr edn, 1627, STC15405; anr edn, 1629, STC15405.5; anr edn, 1630, STC15406; anr edn, 1633, STC15407; anr edn, 1634, STC15407.3; anr edn, 1636, STC15407.5; anr edn 1640, STC15408; anr edn, 1656, L980; anr edn, 1663, L981; anr edn, 1667, L981A; anr edn, 1674, L982.

Levingston, Anne. *Some considerations.* 1654, L1825A.

――――. *The state of the case.* 1654, L1824 and S5685.

――――. *A true narrative of the case.* 1655, L1825.

Lilburne, Elizabeth. *To the chosen and betrusted knights, . . . the humble petition of.* 1646, L2077.

Lilburne, Elizabeth (fl. 1696). *Elizabeth Lilburne . . . against William Carr . . . the case.* 1696, L2077A.

Love, Mary. *Love's name lives.* 1651, L3141; anr edn, 1663, L3142.

――――. *Love's name lives.* 1660, not in Wing (Bodleian Library).

Lynam, Margaret. *The controversie of the Lord.* 1676, L3564.

――――. *For the Parliament.* 1659, L3564aA.

――――. *A warning from the Lord.* 1680?, not in Wing (Friends' Library, London).

M., A. *Queen Elizabeths closet of physical secrets.* 1652, M5A; anr edn, 1656, M5B.

――――. *A rich closet of physical secrets.* 1652, M7; anr edn, 1653, M7A; anr edn, 1653, M7B.

M., M. *The womens advocate*. 1603, M013EA, anr edn, 1687, M813EB; anr edn, M813F. (Wing attributes this work by M. M. to M. Marsin. If this is correct, then several other works may be by this same woman.)

M., W. *The queens closet opened*. 1665, M96; anr edn, 1656, M97; anr edn, 1658, M98; anr edn, 1659, M99; anr edn, 1661, M99A; anr edn, 1662, M100; anr edn, 1662, M100A; anr edn, 1664, M100B; anr edn, 1668, M100C; anr edn, 1671, M101; anr edn, 1674, M102; anr edn, 1679, M103; anr edn, 1683, M104; anr edn, 1684, M104A; anr edn, 1696, M105; anr edn, 1696, M105A; anr edn, 1698, M106.

Mackett, Ann. "Testimony." Part of Anne Whitehead, *Piety promoted*. 1686, W1885.

Major, Elizabeth. *Honey on the rod*. 1656, M305.

Makin, Bathsua. *An essay to revive the antient education of gentlewomen*. 1673, M309.

———. *The malady and remedy*. 1646, L310.

Markham, Jane. *An account of the life and death of . . . Thomas Markham*. 1695, not in Wing.

Martel, Margaret. *A true copy of the paper delivered by*. 1697, M817A.

———. *A true translation of a paper . . . delivered by*. 1697, M817B.

Martin, Ann. "Concerning that false report." Part of Joan Whitrow, *The work*. 1677, W2039.

Martindall, Anne. "A relation." Part of Alice Curwen, *A relation*. 1680, M857.

Masham, Damaris, Lady. *A discourse concerning the love of God*. 1696, M905; anr edn, 1697, M905A.

Meekings, Margaret. "Testimony." Part of Anne Whitehead, *Piety promoted*. 1686, W1885.

Melville, Elizabeth. *Ane godlie dreame*. 1603, STC17811; anr edn, 1604?, STC17812; anr edn, 1606, STC17813; anr edn, 1620, STC17814; anr edn, 1644, M1649; anr edn 1686, M1649A; anr edn, 1698, M1650.

Moore, Elizabeth. "Evidences for heaven." Part of Edmund Calamy, *Godly man's ark*. 1669, C247.

Mordaunt, Elizabeth, Viscountess. *The private diary*. Duncairn, 1856.

More, Gertrude. *Confessiones amantis*. Ed. Dom Benedict Weld-Blundell. 1910.

———. *The holy practices*. 1657, M2631A.

———. *The spiritual exercises*. 1658, M2632.

Morey, Dewans. *A true and faithful warning*. 1665, M2726A.

Morton, Anne Douglas, Countess of. *The countess of Mortons daily exercise*. 1666, M2817; anr edn, 1679, M2817A; anr edn, 1689, M2818; anr edn, 1692, M2818A; anr edn, 1696, M2819.

Mudd, Ann. *A cry, a cry: a sensible cry*. 1678, M3037.

Newcastle, Margaret, Duchess of. See Cavendish, Margaret.

Northumberland, Elizabeth. *Meditations.* 1682, M1308.

_____. *Meditations.* 1687, M1308A; anr edn, 1693, M1309; anr edn, 1700, M1309A.

Osborne, Alice, *The case of the Lady Wandesford.* 1660, C1102A.

Osborne, Dorothy. *Letters from Dorothy Osborne to Sir William Temple.* Ed. E. A. Parry. 1914(?).

Overton, Mary. *To the right honourable, the knights . . . the humble appeale.* 1647, O617.

Owen, Jane. *An antidote against purgatory.* 1634, STC18984.

Oxlie, Mary. [Poem]. Part of William Drummond, *Poems.* 1656, D2201.

P., Mrs. T. Letter by her in Abiezer Coppe, *Some sweet sips of spirituall wine.* 1649, C6093.

_____. Letter by her in Elizabeth Poole, *A prophecie.* 1649, P2809A.

Paget, Briget. Preface to John Paget, *Meditations of death.* 1639, STC19099.

Parr, Katherine. *The lamentacion of a sinner.* London, 1547. In Thomas Bentley, ed., *The monument of matrones.* 1582, STC1892.

_____. *Prayers or meditacyons.* . . . London, 1545. In Thomas Bentley, ed., *The monument of matrones.* 1582, STC1892.

Parr, Susanna. *Susanna's apologie against the elders.* 1659, P551.

Partridge, Dorothy. *The woman's almanack for . . . 1694, adapted to the capacity of the female sex.* 1694, A2016.

Patison, Barbara. See Killin, Margaret, and Barbara Patison.

Pembroke, Mary Sidney, Countess of. Poems in Francis Davison, *A poetical rapsody.* 1602, STC6373.

Pendarves, Theodosia. "A letter." Part of Elizabeth Poole, *An alarum.* 1649, P2809.

Pennyman, Mary. *Something formerly writ.* 1676, P1429.

_____. *Some of the letters and papers.* Ed. John Pennyman. 1690, 1696, 1700, not in Wing.

Perrot, Lucy. *An account of several observable speeches.* 1679, P1643.

Pettus, Katherine. *Katherine Pettus, plaintiffe.* 1654, P1913.

Philips, Mrs Joan. *Advice to his grace.* c. 1681/2, P2029.

_____. *Female poems on several occasions. Written by Ephelia.* 1679, P2030; anr edn, 1682, P2031.

Philips, Katherine. *Poems.* 1664, P2032.

_____. *Poems.* 1667, P2033; anr edn, P2034; anr edn, P2035.

_____. [Poem]. Part of William Cartwright, *Comedies.* 1651, C709.

_____. [Poem]. Part of Henry Lawes, *Second book.* 1655, L641.

_____. "Letters to Berenice." Part of John Wilmot, *Familiar letters.* 1697, R1743.

Phoenix, Anne. *The saints legacies.* 1631, STC10635; anr edn, 1633, STC10635.3; anr edn, 1640, STC10636.

Pinder, Bridget, and Elizabeth Hopper. *A lively testimony.* 1676, J514.

Pix, Mary. *Alass! When charming Sylvia's son.* 1697, P2325.

_____. *The beau defeated.* 1700, P2326.

_____. *The deceiver deceived.* 1698, P2327.

_____. *The false friend.* 1699, P2328.

_____. *Ibrahim.* 1696, P2329.

_____. *The innocent mistress.* 1697, P2330.

_____. *Queen Catherine.* 1698, P2331.

_____. *The Spanish wives.* 1696, P2332.

_____. *To the right honourable the earl of Kent,* . . . *this poem.* 1700?, P2332A.

_____. *When I languish'd* . . . *song in the innocent Mrs.* 1697?, P2333.

Plumely, S. "Testimony." Part of Anne Whitehead, *Piety promoted.* 1686, W1885.

Plumsted, Mary. "Testimony." Part of Anne Whitehead, *Piety promoted.* 1686, W1885.

Poole, Elizabeth. *An alarum of war.* 1649, P2808; anr edn, 1649, P2809.

_____. *A prophecie touching the death of king.* 1649, P2809A.

_____. *A vision.* 1649, P2810.

Pope, Mary. *Behold, here is a word.* 1649, P2903.

_____. *A treatise of magistracy.* 1647, P2904.

Price, Elizabeth. *The countess of Banburies case.* 1696, not in Wing.

Primrose, Diana. *A chaine of pearle. Or a memoriall of Queene Elizabeth.* 1630, STC20388.

Quaker women. *From our half-years meeting in Dublin.* 1691, F2239A.

_____. *From our women's meeting held at York.* 1692, F2239B.

_____. *From our womens yearly meeting held at York.* 1698, F2239C.

_____. *From our womens yearly meeting held at York.* 1700, F2240.

_____. *From our yearly meeting at York.* 1690, F2240A.

Redford, Elizabeth. *The love of God is to gather the seasons.* 1690, R660A.

_____. *A warning, a warning from the Lord.* 1696, R661.

_____. *The widow's mite.* 1690?, R662.

Rich, Mary Boyle. See Warwick, M., Countess of.

Richardson, Mrs. Elizabeth. *A ladies legacie.* 1645, R1382.

Rolph, Alice. *To the chosen and betrusted knights* . . . *the humble petition of.* 1648, R1889.

Rone, Elizabeth. *A reproof to those church-men.* 1688, R1914A.

Rowe, Mrs Elizabeth Singer. *Poems on several occasions.* 1696, R2062.

Rowlandson, Mrs Mary. *The soveraignty & goodness of God.* 1682, R2093.

_____. *A true history of the captivity & restoration of.* 1682, R2094.

Sandilands, Mary. *A tender salutation of endeared love.* 1696, S654.

Scaife, Barbara, et al. *A short relation.* 1686, S806.

Sharp, Jane. *The midwives book.* 1671, not in Wing.

Shaw, Hester. *Mrs Shaw's innocency restored.* 1653, S3018.

_____. *A plaine relation of my sufferings.* 1653, S3019.

Simmonds, Martha. *A lamentation for the lost sheep.* 1655, S3791; anr edn, 1656, S3792.

_____. *O England; thy time is come.* 1656-65, S3793.

_____. *When the Lord Jesus came.* 1655, S3794.

Simpson, Mary, et al. *Faith and experience.* 1649, S3818.

Smith, Mary. *These few lines are to all.* 1667, S4130.

Smyth, Anne. *The case of.* 1650, S4358.

Somerset, Margaret. *To the Parliament of the Commonwealth.* 1654, W3537.

Sowle, Jane. "Testimony," Part of Anne Whitehead, *Piety promoted.* 1686, W1885.

Stirling, Mary, Countess of. *The state of the case in brief.* 1654, S5685.

Stirredge, Elizabeth, et al. *A salutation.* 1683, S5685A.

Stone, Katherine. *To the High Court of Parliament.* 1654, S5731.

Stout, Mary. "Ah William Haworth." Part of John Crook, *Rebellion.* 1673, C7212.

_____. "Testimony." Part of Anne Whitehead, *Piety promoted.* 1686, W1885.

Stranger, Hannah. "Consider I beseech you." Part of Martha Simmonds, *O England.* 1656–65, S3793.

Strong, Damaris. *Having seen a paper printed.* 1655, S5988.

Sutcliffe, Alice. *Meditation of man's mortalitie. Or, a way to true blessednesse.* 1634, STC23447.

Sutton, Katherine. *A Christian woman's experience.* 1668, S6212.

Swinnerton, Mabel. *A brief description.* 1628, STC15177.

Taylor, Mrs. [Three songs]. Part of Aphra Behn, *Miscellany.* 1685, M2230.

Thornton, Mrs. Alice. *The autobiography of.* Surtees Society, 1875.

Tickell, Dorothy. Part by her in *Some testimonies concerning the life and death of Hugh Tickell.* 1690, S4622.

Tillinghast, Mary. *Rare and excellent receipts.* 1678, T1182; anr edn, 1690, T1183.

Tipper, Elizabeth. *The pilgrim's viaticum.* 1698, not in Wing; anr edn, 1698, T1305.

Townsend, Theophila. *An epistle of love.* 1686?, T1987A.

_____. *An epistle of tender love.* 1690, T1988.

_____. *A testimony.* 1676, T1989.

_____. *A word of counsel.* 1687, T1990.

Trapnel, Anna. *The cry of a stone.* 1654, T2031.

_____. *A legacy for saints.* 1654, T2032.

_____. *Anna Trapnel's report and plea.* 1654, T2033.

_____. *Strange and wonderful newes.* 1654, T2034.

———, *A voice for the king of saints* 1658, T2035.

Travers, Ann. "Testimony." Part of Anne Whitehead, *Piety promoted*. 1686, W1885.

Travers, Ann, and Elizabeth Coleman. "Unto which." Part of Stephen Crisp, *A backslider*. 1669, C6925.

Travers, Rebeckah. *For those that meet to worship*. 1695, T2059.

———. *Of that eternal breath*. 1659, T2060.

———. *A testimony concerning the light*. 1663, T2061.

———. *A testimony for God's everlasting truth*. 1669, T2062.

———. *This is for all or any*. 1664, T2063.

———. *This is for any of that generation*. 1660, T2064.

———. "Testimony." Part of Anne Whitehead, *Piety promoted*. 1686, W1885.

Trye, Mary. *Medicatrix, or the woman physician*. 1675, T3174.

Turner, Jane. *Choice experiences*. 1653, T3294.

Venn, Anne. *A wise virgins lamp burning*. 1658, V190.

Vokins, Joan. *God's mighty power magnified*. 1691, V685.

———. *A loving advertisement*. 1671, V686.

———. *A tender invitation*. 1687, V687.

W., Ez. *The answere of a mother unto hir seduced sonnes letter*. 1627, STC24903; anr edn, 1627, STC24903.5.

Wails, Isabel. *A warning to the inhabitants of Leeds*. 1685, W221.

Waite, Mary. *A warning to all friends who professeth*. 1679, W224.

———. *Epistle from the women's yearly meeting*. 1688, W224.

Walker, Mrs Elizabeth. Letters and an autobiography by her in Anthony Walker, *The holy life of Mrs Elizabeth Walker*. 1690, W305.

Walker, Mary. *The case of*. 1650, W395.

Warren, Elizabeth. *The old and good way vindicated*. 1646, W958; anr edn, 1646, W959.

———. *Spiritual thrift*. 1647, W960.

———. *A warning-peece from heaven*. 1649, W961.

Warwick, Mary Boyle Rich, Countess of. *Some specialities in the life of*. Percy Society, 1848.

Waters, Margaret. *A Warning from the Lord*. 1670, W1058.

Waugh, Dorothy. "A relation." Part of *The lambs defence*. 1656, L249.

Waugh, Jane, and Anne Audland. *A true declaration*. 1655, A4195.

Weamys, Anna. *A continuation of . . . Arcadia*. 1651, W1189.

Webb, Mary. *I being moved of the Lord*. 1659, W1205.

Wells, Mary. *A divine poem*. 1684, W1296.

———. *A divine poem*. 1690, not in Wing.

Wentworth, Anne. *A true account of*. 1676, not in Wing.

———. *The revelation of Jesus Christ*. 1679, W1355.

_____. *A vindication of.* 1677, W1356.

Wentworth, Henrietta Maria. *The case of.* 1677, C1102.

Wharton, Anne. "Copies of verses." Part of Edward Young, *The idea of Christian love.* 1688, Y61.

Wharton, Mrs. Poems by her in *The temple of death, a poem.* 1695, T663.

White, Dorothy. *An alarum sounded forth.* 1662, W1744.

_____. *An alarm sounded to Englands inhabitants.* 1661, W1745.

_____. *A call from God.* 1662, W1746.

_____. *The day dawned.* 1684, W1747.

_____. *A diligent search.* 1659, W1747A.

_____. *An epistle of love.* 1661, W1748.

_____. *Friends.* 1662, W1749.

_____. *Greetings of pure peace.* 1662, W1750.

_____. *A lamentation.* 1661, W1751.

_____. *A salutation.* 1684, W1752.

_____. *This to be delivered.* 1659, W1753.

_____. *To all those that worship.* 1664, W1754.

_____. *A trumpet.* 1662, W1755.

_____. *Universal love.* 1684, W1756.

_____. *Unto all Gods host* 1660, W1757.

_____. *Upon the 22nd day.* 1659, W1758.

_____. *A visitation of heavenly love.* 1660, W1759.

_____. *A visitation of love.* 1684, W1760.

_____. *The voice of the Lord.* 1662, W1761.

White, Elizabeth. *The experiences.* 1696, W1762; anr edn, 1698, W1763.

Whitehead, Anne. *An epistle for true love.* 1680, W1882; anr edn, 1680?, W1883.

Whitehead, Anne, et al. *For the king and both houses.* 1670, W1884.

_____. *Piety promoted.* 1686, W1885.

Whitrow, Joan. *Faithful warnings.* 1697, W2032A.

_____. *The humble address of.* 1689, W2033.

_____. *The humble salutation.* 1690, W2034.

_____. *The widow Whitrows humble thanksgiving.* 1694, W2035.

_____. *To King William and Queen Mary.* 1692, W2036.

_____. *To Queen Mary.* 1690, W2037.

_____. *To the king and both houses of Parliament.* 1696, W2038.

_____. *The work of God in a dying maid.* 1677, W2039.

Whitton, Katherine. *An epistle to friends.* 1681, W2050.

Whitton, Katherine, et al. *A testimony for the Lord.* 1688, W2051.

Wight, Sara. *The exceeding riches of grace advanced by the spirit of grace in an empty nothing creature.* 1647, J687; anr edn, 1647, J688; anr edn, 1648, J689; anr edn, 1648, J690; anr edn, 1652, J691; anr edn, 1658, J692; anr edn, 1658, J692A; anr edn, 1666, J692B.

————. *A wonderful pleasant and profitable letter.* 1656, W2106

Wigington, Leticia. *The confession.* 1681, W2110.

Wilks, Judith. *The confession of.* 1689, W2257.

Wilmot, Elizabeth. [Poem]. Part of John Wilmot, *Poems.* 1680, R1753.

Winchilsea, Anne Finch, Countess of. *The prerogatives of love.* 1695, W2966.

Wolley, Hannah. *The ladies delight.* 1672, W3279.

————. *The ladies directory.* 1661, W3280; anr edn, 1662, W3281.

————. *The queen-like closet.* 1670, W3282; anr edn, 1672, W3283; anr edn, 1675, W3284; anr edn, 1681, W3285; anr edn, 1684, W3286.

————. *A supplement to the queen-like closet.* 1674, W3287; anr edn, 1684, W3288.

Woolley, Mary. "Testimony." Part of Anne Whitehead, *Piety promoted.* 1686, W1885.

Worcester, Margaret Somerset, Countess of. *To the Parliament of the Commonwealth . . . the humble petition of.* 1654, W3537.

Wriothesley, Rachel, Lady Russell. *Letters* of Rachel Lady Russell. 2 vols. London: Longman, 1819.

Wroth, Lady Mary. *The countesse of Mountgomeries Urania.* 1621, STC26051.

Yeamans, Isabel. *An invitation of love.* 1679, Y20.

Yeamans, Isabel, et al. *A lively testimony.* 1676, J514.

York. Anne Hyde, Duchess of. *A copy of a paper written by the late duchess of York.* 1670, Y46.

————. *Reasons of her leaving the communion.* 1670, Y47.

York, Anne Hyde, Duchess of, and Charles II. *Copies of two papers.* 1686, C2943; anr edn, 1686, C2944; anr edn, 1686, C2945; anr edn, 1686, C2946; anr edn, 1687, C2946A.

INDEX